PRAISE FOR *A VILLAGE IN THE THIRD REICH*

"Penetrating beneath the clichés about Nazi Germany, here are ordinary people trying to cope with extraordinary times. Their vivid, moving stories leave us asking 'What would I have done?'"

—**Professor David Reynolds, author of**
Island Stories: An Unconventional History of Britain

"Laying bare the tragedies, the compromises, the suffering and the disillusionment. Exemplary microhistory."

—**Roger Moorhouse, author of** *First To Fight: The Polish War 1939*

"Brilliantly researched and expertly told, this is a truly fascinating exploration of how a small village community responded to the rise and fall of the Nazis in Germany."

—**Keith Lowe, author of** *Savage Continent* **and** *Prisoners of History*

"A fascinating glimpse into one little corner of a vast nightmare."

—**James Hawes, author of** *The Shortest History of Germany*

"Masterly . . . [an] important and gripping book . . . [Boyd is] a leading historian of human responses in political extremis."

—*The Oldie*

PRAISE FOR THE *SUNDAY TIMES* BESTSELLER *TRAVELERS IN THE THIRD REICH* BY JULIA BOYD

"A compelling historical narrative . . . both flatters and challenges our hindsight. [Boyd] lets her voices, skillfully orchestrated, speak for themselves, which they do with great eloquence."

—*The Daily Telegraph*

"Fascinating . . . surreal scenes pepper Boyd's deep trawl of travelers' tales from the scores of visitors who were drawn to the 'new Germany' in the 1930s."

—*The Spectator*

"Contains many amazing anecdotes . . . It warns us that we, with our all-seeing hindsight, might ourselves have been fooled or beguiled or inclined to make excuses, had we been there at the time. I can thoroughly recommend it as a contribution to knowledge and an absorbing and stimulating book in itself."

—**Peter Hitchens,** *Mail on Sunday*

"Meticulously researched . . . Julia Boyd's research has been exhaustive. She has visited archives all over the world and assembled a vast and entertaining cast of travelers . . . makes for thought-provoking reading."

—**Caroline Moorehead,** *Literary Review*

"A fascinating book."

—**Robert Elms, BBC Radio London**

"To a younger generation it seems incomprehensible that after the tragic Great War people and political leaders allowed themselves to march into the abyss again. Julia Boyd's book, drawing on wide experience and forensic research, seeks to answer some of these questions."

—**Randolph Churchill**

"With an almost novelistic touch, [Boyd] presents a range of stories of human interest . . . The uncomfortable moral of *Travelers in the Third Reich* is that people see and hear only what they already want to see and hear."

—**David Pryce-Jones,** *Standpoint*

"Fascinating . . . This absorbing and beautifully organized book is full of small encounters that jolt the reader into a historical past that seems still very near."

—**Lucy Lethbridge,** *The Tablet*

"In the 1930s the most cultured and technologically advanced country in Europe tumbled into the abyss. In this deeply researched book Julia Boyd lets us view Germany's astonishing fall through foreign eyes. Her vivid tapestry of human stories is a delightful, often moving read. It also offers sobering lessons for our own day when strong leaders are again all the rage."

—**Professor David Reynolds,** author of *The Long Shadow: The Great War and the 20th Century*

A VILLAGE
IN THE
THIRD REICH

HOW ORDINARY LIVES WERE
TRANSFORMED BY THE RISE OF FASCISM

Julia Boyd

& Angelika Patel

PEGASUS BOOKS
NEW YORK LONDON

A VILLAGE IN THE THIRD REICH

Pegasus Books, Ltd.
148 West 37th Street, 13th Floor
New York, NY 10018

ISBN: 978-1-63936-641-5

www.pegasusbooks.com

For my mother Joan Raynsford
JB

*For Max Maile, Thea Stempfle and all their friends
and contemporaries who shared their memories
with me; and as a reminder that peace, freedom
and justice cannot be taken for granted*
AP

Contents

Maps

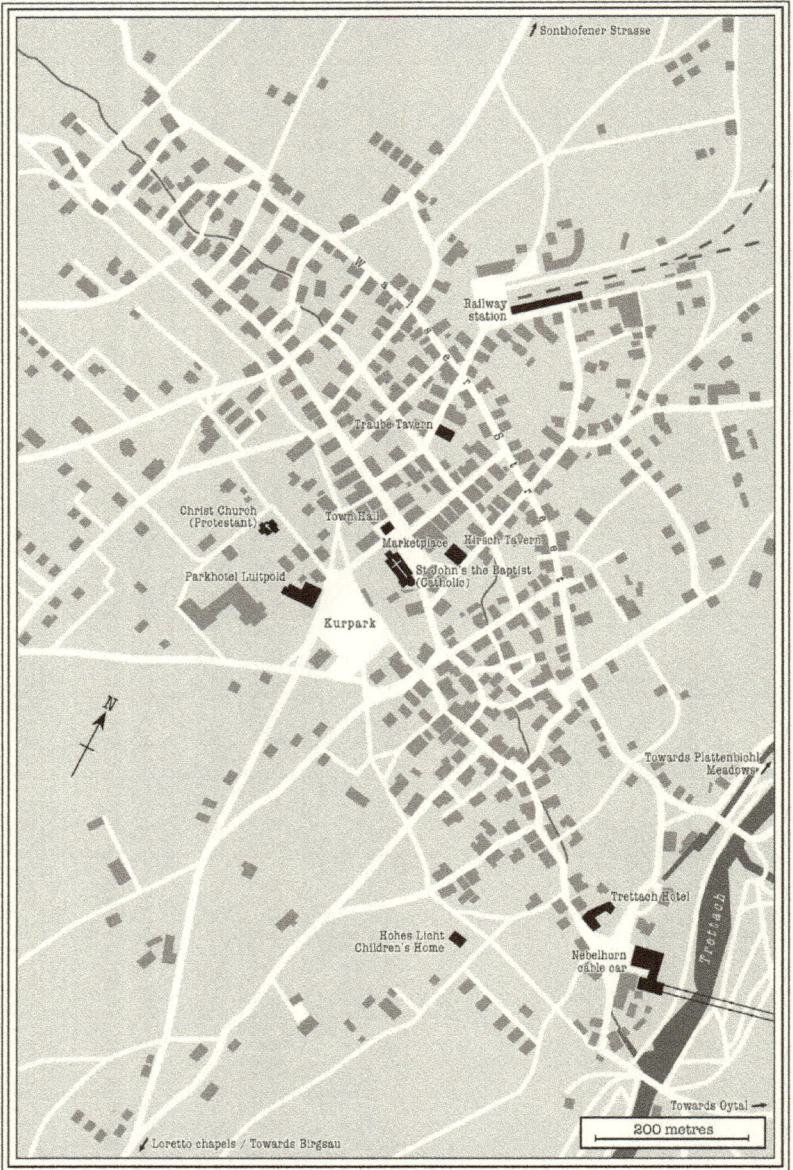

Sonthofener Strasse

Railway
station

Traube Tavern

Christ Church
(Protestant)

Town Hall

Marketplace

Hirsch Tavern

St John's the Baptist
(Catholic)

Parkhotel Luitpold

Kurpark

N

Towards Plattenbichl
Meadows

Trettach Hotel

Hohes Licht
Children's Home

Nebelhorn
cable car

Trettach

Towards Oytal ➞

200 metres

Loretto chapels / Towards Birgsau

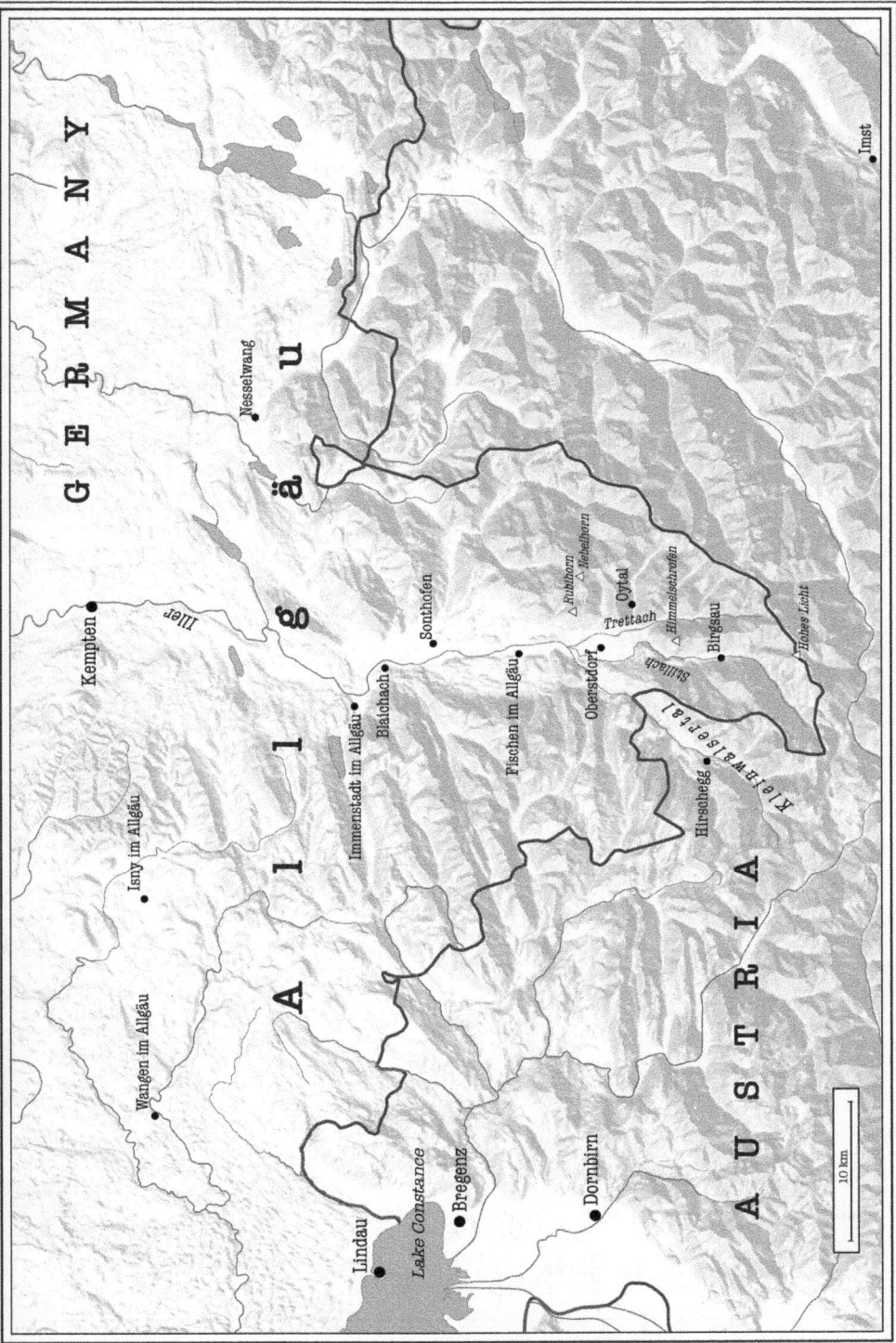

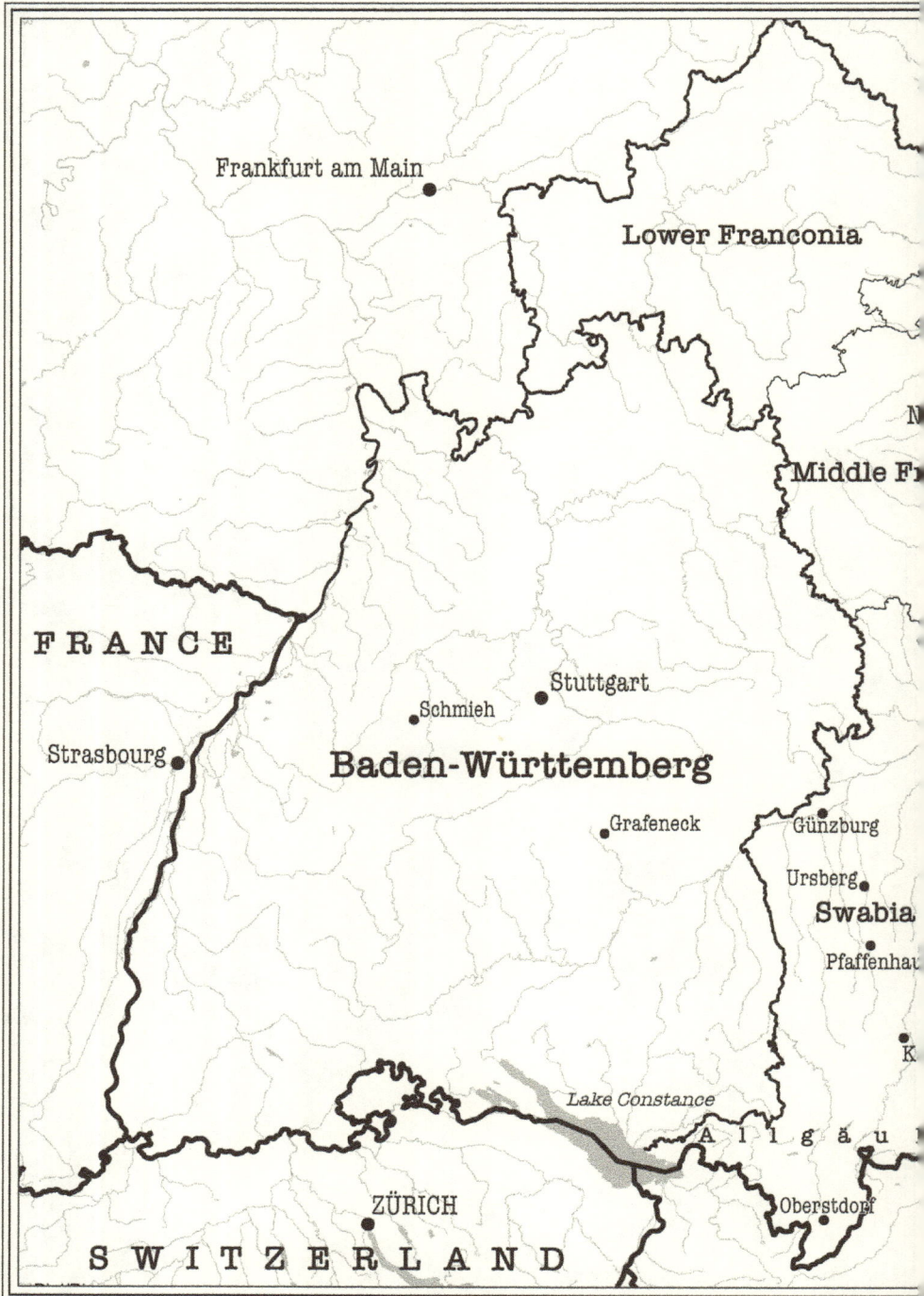

Frankfurt am Main

Lower Franconia

Middle F

FRANCE

Strasbourg

Schmieh

Stuttgart

Baden-Württemberg

Grafeneck

Günzburg

Ursberg

Swabia

Pfaffenha

K

Lake Constance

Allgäu

ZÜRICH

Oberstdorf

SWITZERLAND

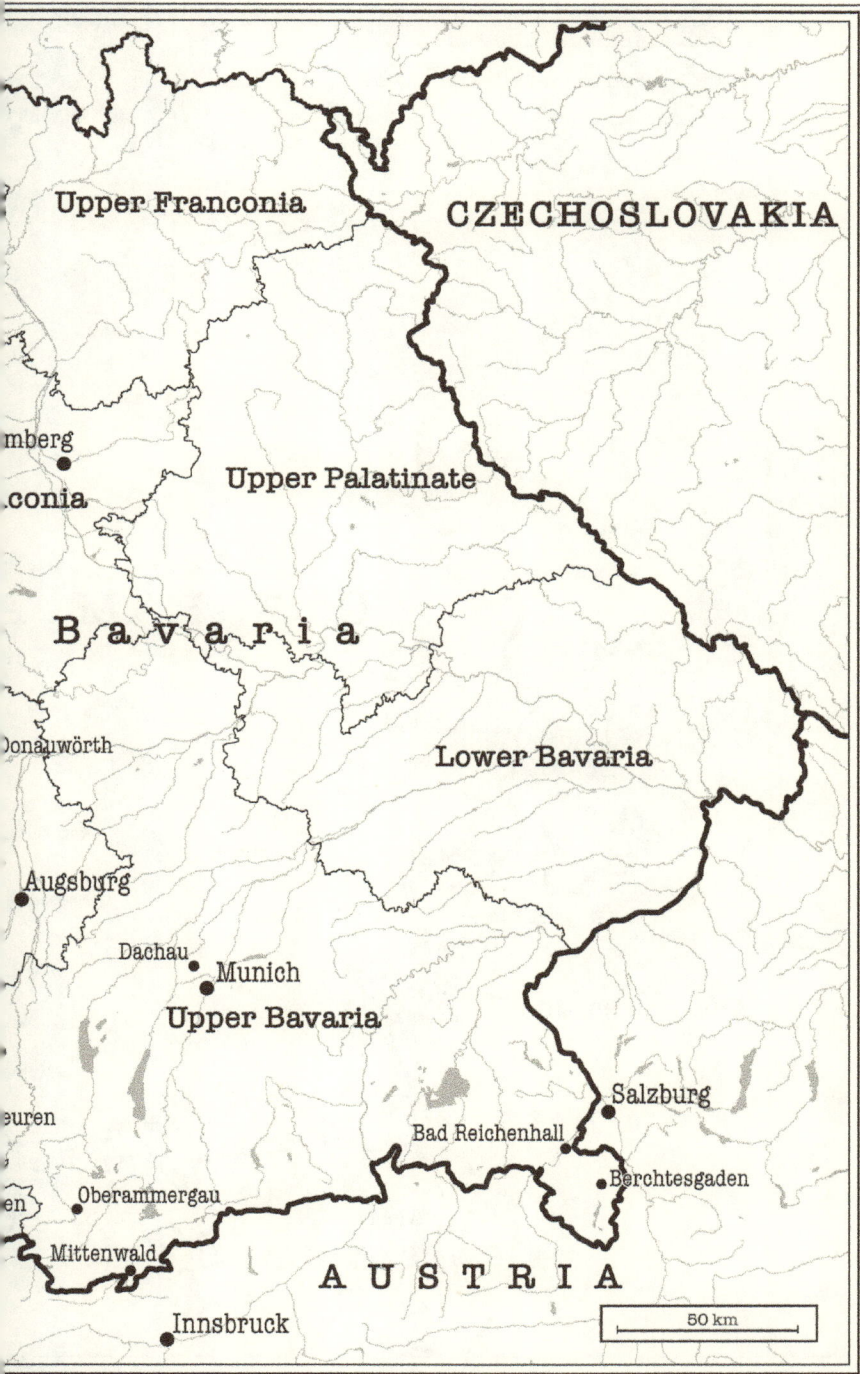

Upper Franconia

CZECHOSLOVAKIA

mberg

.conia

Upper Palatinate

B a v a r i a

Donauwörth

Lower Bavaria

Augsburg

Dachau

Munich

Upper Bavaria

euren

Salzburg

Bad Reichenhall

en

Oberammergau

Berchtesgaden

Mittenwald

A U S T R I A

Innsbruck

50 km

Territory lost by Germany by the Treaty of Versailles
German border 1919
Other country border
Maginot Line

COPENHAGEN

DENMARK

NORTH SEA

Lübeck

Hamburg

Bremen

NETHERLANDS

Amsterdam

THE HAGUE

Osnabrück
Bückeburg
Hanover
Hamelin
Magdel

GERMA

Dunkirk

Essen Ruhr
Düsseldorf

Weser Göttingen

Harz

Le

BELGIUM

BRUSSELS

Aachen Cologne
Bonn

Weimar Jena

Kamsdor

Rhine

Koblenz

Ardennes

Frankfurt

Main

Bayreuth

LUXEMBOURG

Darmstadt

Reims

SAAR
French 1919 to 1935

Heidelberg

Nuremberg

Hesselberg

PARIS

Alsace-Lorraine Strasbourg

Rhine

Gien

FRANCE

Dachau
Munic

Oberammergau

Oberstdorf

Garmisch-
Partenkirche
Innsbruc

Loire

BERN

SWITZERLAND

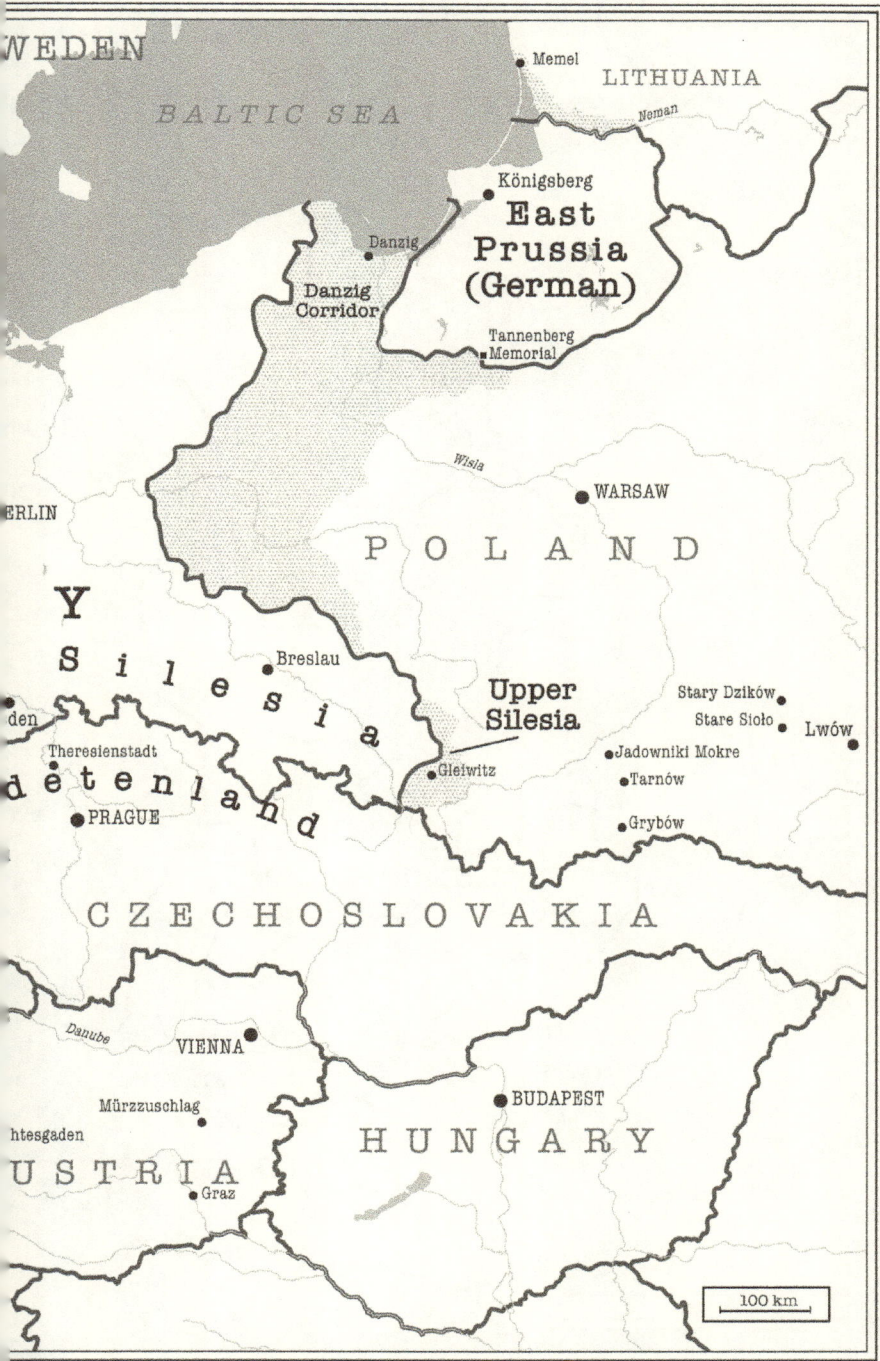

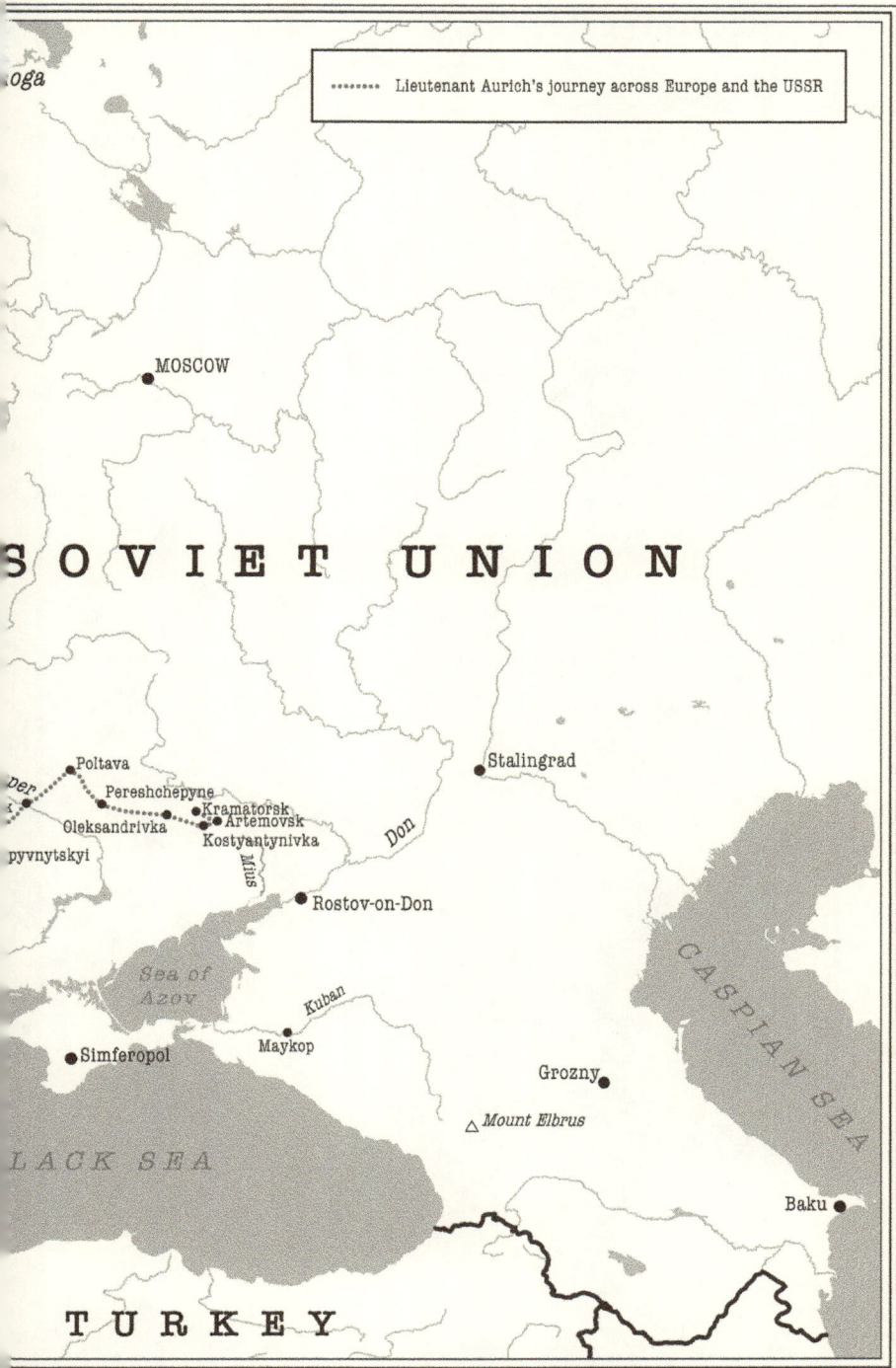

oga

MOSCOW

S O V I E T   U N I O N

Poltava
Pereshchepyne
Kramatorsk
Oleksandrivka ● Artemovsk
Kostyantynivka

pyvnytskyi

Stalingrad

Don

Mius

● Rostov-on-Don

Sea of Azov

Kuban

● Simferopol   Maykop

Grozny ●

△ *Mount Elbrus*

C A S P I A N   S E A

LACK SEA

Baku ●

T U R K E Y

Introduction

On the evening of 5 March 1933, the inhabitants of the Bavarian village of Oberstdorf began making their way to the marketplace, eager to hear what the mayor had to say about the federal election held earlier that day. Mingling with the native residents of this pretty resort, with its wooden houses and taverns, were large numbers of holidaymakers from north Germany drawn to the village by the winter sports it had to offer. The surrounding snow-clad peaks, silhouetted against a sky brilliant with stars, provided a natural grandeur to the scene. Among the crowd there was a palpable sense of anticipation as everyone, warmly wrapped against the cold night air, waited for events to unfold. Many of those present no doubt chatted to their friends about the extraordinary sight they had witnessed the night before when, as a prelude to the election, numerous bonfires had been lit in the mountains. Most spectacular of all had been the huge swastika formed of flickering flares, set high up on the Himmelschrofen mountain.

It was not quite five weeks since 30 January, when Adolf Hitler had been sworn in as Germany's new chancellor, but it was clear to everybody – even in this far-off Alpine village – that the political landscape had already changed radically. What Oberstdorfers could not have known that evening was that they had just voted in the last multi-party election to be held in the country until 1946.

Shortly after eight o'clock, the faint sound of beating drums grew louder as a unit of paramilitary storm troopers marched into the marketplace carrying flaming torches and shouting out party slogans. The villagers had long since become accustomed to the presence of these noisy brownshirts on their streets, even if they did not necessarily approve. But if the trappings of the *Nationalsozialistische Deutsche Arbeiterpartei* (National Socialist German Workers' Party, NSDAP or Nazi Party) were not to everyone's taste, Hitler's message and style of leadership had caught the imagination of enough of the electorate, including the visiting skiers, to result in Oberstdorf casting more votes for the Nazis on 5 March than for any other party.[1]

The marketplace where they had all gathered lay at the core of this devoutly Catholic village. Dominated by the church of St John the Baptist, its spire visible for miles around, it was also where Oberstdorfers came to remember their fallen soldiers at memorials to the Franco–Prussian War (1870–71) and to the First World War (1914–18), the latter housed in a small chapel next to the church. In the middle of the square stood two flagpoles, one flying the black-white-red flag of the old German empire, the other – a swastika. The crowd fell silent as a gun salute marked the official start of the rally. Then, an 'outsider', a relative newcomer to Oberstdorf, stepped on to the podium, causing surprise among the villagers who had been expecting their mayor to speak. For those not already in the know, it was soon apparent that this man was the village's new National Socialist leader. His speech was short but his authoritative manner left little doubt in anyone's mind that he intended to take control over much more than the local Nazi Party.

Later, as the crowd dispersed and they returned to the warmth and security of their homes, even those villagers who had voted for Hitler must have wondered what exactly the future held in store.

～

Hitler's consolidation of power following the 5 March election was to have consequences that would change the world forever. The death and destruction, the misery, torment and horror endured by so many millions of people during the twelve years of the Third Reich were on such a vast scale that it is impossible to absorb fully the extent of global suffering. This book tells that story from the perspective of one village in southern Germany.

Oberstdorf lies in Swabia (part of Bavaria) in a region known as the Allgäu, long recognised for the beauty of its mountains and the toughness of its people. It is uniquely defined by its geographical position as the most southern village in Germany. Once there, the traveller has quite literally reached the end of the road since only footpaths lead south across the mountains. Thus, in contrast with its Alpine neighbours such as Bad Tölz, Garmisch-Partenkirchen or Bad Reichenhall, Oberstdorf never enjoyed the benefits of lying on a trade route; it did not, like Berchtesgaden, possess extensive salt mines, nor did it develop any specialised craft or industry, as did the famous violin-producing village of Mittenwald. Before tourism arrived at the end of the nineteenth century it survived chiefly on subsistence farming, cheese production and small deposits of iron ore.

The village has always cared deeply about its history and as a result possesses a particularly well-maintained archive. It contains a wealth of detail on almost every feature of village life under the Nazis – data that in the post-war longing to forget everything to do with the Third Reich might so easily have been 'lost' or abandoned. Other important sources include local newspapers, unpublished memoirs and interviews given by the villagers themselves. This book has also been enriched with diaries and letters from private collections and documents preserved in various national, state and church archives. Drawing on all these sources, it has been possible to create a remarkably intimate portrait of Oberstdorf during the momentous period between the end of the First World War in 1918 and the granting of full sovereign rights to the Federal Republic of Germany in 1955.

Of course, Oberstdorf's experience of the Third Reich was not replicated all over Germany; each town or village's response was unique. But by closely following these people as they coped with the day-to-day challenges of life under the Nazis, there emerges a real sense of how ordinary Germans supported, adapted to and survived a regime that, after promising them so much, in the end delivered only anguish and devastation.

We encounter foresters, priests, farmers and nuns; innkeepers, Nazi officials, veterans and party members; village councillors, mountaineers, socialists, slave labourers, schoolchildren, Jews, entrepreneurs, tourists and aristocrats. We also meet a blind boy condemned to die in a gas chamber because he was living 'a life unworthy of life'. Then, of course, there are the soldiers, many of them eager to fight for a dictatorship they had been brainwashed never to question, while others were opposed to the war from the start. All of life is here: brutality and love; courage and weakness; action, apathy and grief; hope, pain, joy and despair – in other words, the shades of grey that make up real life as we know it, rather than some stereotyped narrative of heroes and villains. And as we get to know the villagers better, it comes as no surprise to learn that their response to these cataclysmic events was driven as much by practical everyday concerns, the instinct to safeguard their families and personal loyalties and enmities, as by the great political and social issues of the time. Oberstdorf's story also drives home the point that statistical numbers, however overwhelming, cannot lessen the impact of each and every individual tragedy.

This village saga begins at the end of the First World War, when Germans were trying to recover from a defeat so traumatic that the very foundations of their world had been shaken. From the wretchedness caused by the Treaty of Versailles through the madness of hyperinflation, Oberstdorf had nevertheless by the late 1920s been transformed into a flourishing holiday resort. But despite the constant influx of people from the north bringing with them new ideas and a fresh outlook on the world, the village's rural roots and traditional values remained at the heart of its identity.

Focused on economic recovery, Oberstdorf initially ignored the noise generated by Hitler and his new party 100 miles away in Munich. When in 1927 a postman tried to establish a branch of the NSDAP in the village's staunchly Catholic community, it was, as he later complained to Joseph Goebbels, an uphill struggle.[2] But, in tune with so many of their fellow countrymen, the villagers were exasperated with the political chaos of the Weimar Republic and yearned for strong government. By 1930 it became clear that they had changed their minds about National Socialism when more of them voted for Hitler in the September federal election than for anyone else.

But when the reality of Nazi rule hit the village two and a half years later, it came as a shock. National Socialism, everyone now discovered, was not just a system of government but aimed to control every aspect of their lives and to reshape their centuries-old traditions in the Nazi image. So while the villagers stood firm in their loyalty to Hitler, they did not take kindly to their first Nazi mayor, who ruthlessly stripped them of all autonomy over their own affairs. Even those who actively supported National Socialism were forced to make unwelcome adjustments. At the same time, it became frighteningly clear that anyone who stepped out of line or criticised the regime risked 'protective custody' in the newly established camp for political prisoners at Dachau. As the months went by, some villagers found Nazi methods increasingly disturbing but others, dismissing the more unpleasant rumours as foreign propaganda, were to remain committed to the regime through thick and thin.

After the outbreak of the Second World War, the villagers' initial anxiety largely faded, as Germany's military successes appeared to underpin Hitler's promise of a quick and total victory. But their morale plummeted in the months following the invasion of the Soviet Union, when, apart from depressing reversals on the battlefield, they also lived in daily dread of receiving a letter informing them that a loved one had been killed or wounded, or was missing. Through the unpublished diaries of a lieutenant and a sergeant who served alongside Oberstdorf's soldiers in the 99th Regiment of the 1st Mountain Division, we can follow the young men as they fought in Poland, France, the Soviet Union and the Balkans right up to the desperate final months of retreat and defeat.

While its men were away fighting, Oberstdorf, despite its remote geographical position, was by no means isolated from the war. Not only did the villagers receive first-hand news of conditions – and atrocities – on the various battlefronts from their soldiers returning home on leave, but in addition Dachau sub-camps and foreign labour camps were located close by.

These supplied much of the workforce for the various BMW and Messerschmitt manufactories that sprang up in and around the village in the later stages of the war. A *Waffen*-SS* training camp operated six miles south of the village, while a Nazi stronghold visited regularly by such leading figures as Heinrich Himmler lay only ten miles to the north. On top of all that, evacuees from bombed cities, and, later, refugees fleeing the Russians, more than doubled the village's pre-war population.

There are numerous aspects of Oberstdorf's Third Reich history that make it an absorbing study, but one is particularly surprising. After the first Nazi mayor had been dispatched, his successor turned out to be a man who was both a committed Nazi and a decent human being – a statement that would strike many people as a contradiction in terms. The evidence, however, is clear. Not only did this mayor (well known for his robust pro-Nazi speeches) treat people with respect and consideration, he also protected a number of Jews living in the village and supported other inhabitants who found themselves on the wrong side of the Nazi legal system.

We are so used to thinking of the Third Reich in terms of black and white that the idea of any high-ranking Nazi behaving honourably is hard to accept. But Oberstdorf's 'good' Nazi mayor is not the village's only anomaly. A surviving list of NSDAP members includes the names of men well known for their opposition or indifference to the regime but who in the end had joined the party for any number of reasons, especially the need to protect their jobs and families but also, sometimes, simply to make their lives a little easier. This is not to imply that there was any lack of dedicated Nazis in the village, many

* The military branch of the SS.

of whom remained passionately loyal to Hitler to the end. But a system that forced everyone to conform or risk imprisonment, torture or death makes it difficult to assess accurately why so many Germans – including Oberstdorfers – appear to have been complicit in the Reich's crimes against humanity.

After it all finally came to an end in May 1945, the villagers learned to live with the occupying forces, picked themselves up and started again. For many of them, the issue of confronting the nation's guilt and culpability in relation to Nazi atrocities was left on hold while they set about rebuilding their lives.

By putting one village under the microscope, this book aims to contribute in some small way to our understanding of why Germans responded to Hitler in the manner that they did, of how their attitudes to the regime evolved and, when all hope of a reinvigorated, powerful state under the Nazis had fallen apart and their country lay in ruins, of how they worked their way through to a new beginning. If Oberstdorf's story has much to tell us, it also leaves many questions unanswered – questions that will forever remain part of the legacy of the Third Reich.

1

Going Home

Wilhelm Steiner was lucky. He had survived the First World War. Given that he had been in the thick of the fighting from the moment he enlisted in February 1915, this was something of a miracle. He had seen action at Verdun, the Somme, Arras, Lys – in fact right up until the Armistice. When at last the guns fell silent at 11 a.m. on 11 November 1918, Wilhelm's regiment was in Flanders not far from Antwerp. This placed him roughly 500 miles north of Oberstdorf – the picture-book village in the southernmost tip of Bavaria that was his home.

In later years, Wilhelm was to look back on the war with some nostalgia, remembering especially the intense bonding with his fellow soldiers. There were other reasons, too, why his war memories were not all bad. For a lad of twenty who had seen little of the world beyond his own village, soldiering had brought with it the excitement of travel, new people and new skills. During the First World War teams of horses were still used to pull heavy artillery and Wilhelm had been trained to ride the lead horse – a responsible task requiring not only courage and strength but also a deep understanding of the animals. Such positive recollections, however, were overwhelmed by images of utter devastation, of hated officers shot in the back by their own men, and of comrades hideously maimed or dying in agony.[1]

In December 1918, Wilhelm, now bearer of the Military Merit Cross with Swords and the Iron Cross (second class), was finally given leave to begin his long journey home. A photograph of Oberstdorf, taken about the time of Wilhelm's return, shows a substantial village of several hundred houses standing in a wide, green valley set against the glorious backdrop of the Bavarian Alps. It is easy to imagine Wilhelm's heart missing a beat when, for the first time in nearly four years, he was confronted by the grandeur of the snow-covered peaks he had known all his life. In summer, the meadows surrounding the village were full of cows, the air fragrant with wild flowers, but now, in the depths of winter, the snow lay heavy in the valley and on the forested mountain slopes. A couple of miles north of the village, Wilhelm would have caught his first glimpse of Oberstdorf's church spire rising high above the cluster of village roofs. Then, after walking past all the familiar timber houses, pubs and shops with their grey or green painted window-boxes, he would have finally reached home – 117 Hintere obere Gasse (Upper Back Alley). Immediately opposite the Steiner house stood a smithy (one of nineteen in the village) where his father made a living forging nails.

We can only guess how Wilhelm felt when at last he stood before his own front door. Were his family expecting him, or was his sudden appearance a surprise? Did they even know that he was still alive? His father had been able to afford just one apprenticeship and that had gone to his other son Friedrich, 'the good one'. But now Wilhelm – survivor of a supremely testing war – returned home knowing that he had more than redressed the balance.

Over the next weeks and months he would have learned how physical distance and natural beauty had not been enough to protect the village from the miseries of the war. As soon as it began, the army had commandeered all the horses – and much else. Even such basic essentials as nails and flour were committed to the war effort. Food became so scarce that the few elderly guests still living in the nearby Trettach Hotel would go foraging for stinging nettles along the riverbanks or walk deep into the forest in search of nuts. Pinecones were prised open for their meagre seeds. At mealtimes the old people huddled around the only table still standing in the dining room 'like cattle in a storm'.[2]

In the early months of the war, the village women had felt satisfaction at the way they were coping, pleased that when their men returned they would find clean houses and healthy cattle. But by 1917, as the number of families receiving death notices increased, village morale sank to a new low. It was the grim duty of the mayor, Fritz Gschwender, to deliver to the families the dreaded piece of paper that would change their lives forever. His great-granddaughter has written movingly of one such visit:

> My husband did not 'fall', the young woman responded angrily. 'He never fell. He was a good mountaineer. He climbed the Trettach and even the Höfats. He was a fine, strong man. He was murdered. The crazy Prussian Kaiser forced him to invade another country. It was not the fault of the one who shot him, the one who only defended his country.' Her children looked up to her. The youngest held on to her apron. She held on to it tightly with a small round fist.[3]

The lack of a proper Catholic burial with its comforting rituals only intensified the villagers' grief. In this context, the funeral of Gschwender's stepmother in February 1917 had special significance for the entire village:

> She was eighty. Everyone was at the funeral. At last there was a body, a coffin and a grave where people could stand and listen to what the priest said. At last a funeral, an appreciation of a life. They cried and sobbed for the young lads, whose bodies lay somewhere far away, where no one had put a flower, or shed a tear; where neither family nor friend had been present to remind the world of how good, strong and loving they had been. Half frozen the people tore themselves away from the grave of the old Oberstdorf woman whose death had at last allowed them to mourn.[4]

Of the 604 village men who fought in the war, 114 were either killed or died later of their wounds. To each returning veteran, Oberstdorf gave a traditional welcome fit for a hero. The ceremony attended by Wilhelm took place on 28 January 1919. The village newspaper *Oberstdorfer Gemeinde- und Fremdenblatt* (OGF, *Oberstdorf Village and Tourist News*) outlined the programme:

> The veterans' welcome will proceed as follows: A ceremonial Mass attended by the veterans' association will begin at 9 a.m. Following the Mass receptions will be held in the Trettach and Löwen Hotels . . . There will be an informal gathering in the same hotels that evening. The cost of the reception, a simple lunch with beer, will be covered by the communal purse. In line with the decision made on 26 November 1918, each former soldier will receive 50 Marks as a gift.[5]

Wilhelm was among the first soldiers to arrive back, but those who came later were not neglected. The newspaper welcomed each man by name and with this message: 'To those who have returned after the long days of suffering, we would like to say a heartfelt "Welcome Home". For all the hardship endured in battle and imprisonment, may they find compensation in the gratitude of their fellow citizens, and in a sunny future.'[6]

No detailed description of Wilhelm's journey to Oberstdorf survives, but it is likely that he had entered Germany near Aachen and then travelled up the Rhine. We know he went to Alsace, from where, if on foot, it would have taken him several weeks to cover the 200-odd miles to Oberstdorf. Perhaps Wilhelm, still a strapping young man despite the privations of war, had journeyed home in step with his fellow veterans, thousands of whom were walking or limping their way back to their towns, villages and farms. In the zones occupied by the British and Americans, a few soldiers in threadbare grey uniforms could already be seen in the fields, helping to harvest the turnips that for much of the population continued to be their chief source of food.

If at any stage on his journey home Wilhelm had boarded a train, he would have found the experience deeply frustrating. Shortage of coal resulted in the grossly overcrowded trains crawling along at snail's pace, often halting for hours in the middle of nowhere. There was nothing to eat, no sanitation, and any material covering the seats had long since been stripped away for clothing. Freezing temperatures, compounded by broken windows, only added to the passengers' woes. Those who still had enough energy for conversation debated the popular conviction that Germany's defeat had been caused not by any

weakness on the part of its brave warriors but by civilian trai-
tors in Berlin who had stabbed the Imperial Army in the back.

Anarchy and violence were rampant in many German
cities during the immediate aftermath of the war. When on
11 November representatives of the two-day-old republic
signed the Armistice, Germany's new leaders were faced with
national collapse on all fronts. On 9 November the Kaiser
had left Germany for the Netherlands, never to return. Even
before the war ended, revolution triggered by a naval mutiny in
Kiel had spread rapidly across the country, prompting strikes,
desertions and civil war. On the one side were the Spartacists
(their name deriving from the rebel gladiator Spartacus), who
soon formed themselves into the German Communist Party,
and on the other the *Freikorps* – right-wing militias intent on
destroying every trace of Bolshevism. Wilhelm was himself
on the receiving end of this new and uncharacteristic lawless-
ness afflicting Germany when on his journey home his kitbag,
containing all his worldly possessions, was stolen.

Even those not directly caught up in the strife faced a
miserably uncertain future. They had lost faith in their leaders,
many dreaded communism and, with the Allied wartime block-
ade still firmly in place, millions were on the verge of starvation.

Despite its own hardships, Oberstdorf must have seemed
far away from the chaos engulfing the big cities. It had for
centuries existed as a poor peasant community, counting as
many cows among its inhabitants as humans. Indeed, the most
important measure of an Oberstdorf farmer's wealth was the
number of cows he could feed in winter. An 1866 guidebook
sums up the villagers' simple lifestyle:

Most of them live off the produce of their small farms;
even the craftsmen (of whom there are very few) have

their own little piece of land. They are very hard-working and thoroughly domestic; their food is rustic and ample: cabbage, potatoes, beans, peas, rough homemade bread, milk, onions etc. are the main ingredients; meat is only on the table at important festivals such as *Kirchweih* [consecration of the church day]. The Allgäuer man is not averse to *Gerstensaft* [barley juice, beer] but knows when he has had enough.[7]

By the turn of the twentieth century the majority of villagers were still poor, but the coming of the railway in 1888, and then six years later the opening of a nearby textile factory, had heralded profound changes. In 1897 the marketplace was lit by electricity, while in support of the growing tourist trade, new villas and hotels began springing up to the south of the village where there was ample land for development. Many of these were built by outside entrepreneurs, a number of whom stayed on to marry local girls. Adding to this increasingly diverse social mix were members of the Wittelsbach (Bavarian) royal family and aristocracy who had discovered in the village's immediate vicinity the perfect place to build their hunting lodges.

Despite all these new developments, Oberstdorf's original 353 houses were a reminder that agriculture remained at the heart of village life since their owners, known as the 'commoners', possessed much of the surrounding land – the forests, pastures and byways – and controlled its usage. Through their own council, the commoners administered their mutual inheritance, as they had done for generations, for the good of the whole community. Fiercely independent, these yeoman farmers, workers and tradesmen were determined that no feudal lord was going to tell them what to do, or dictate who should inherit their land and historic rights.

Parallel to the essentially medieval structure of the commons council ran the more modern municipal council that looked after public safety, schools and the village's self-generated electricity supply. Given Oberstdorf's strong conservative and royalist sympathies, it is not surprising that only a few of its councillors elected in 1919 were Social Democrats. Nationally the response to the first Weimar Republic federal election (in which women were allowed to vote for the first time) was a moderate, centrist one. Like so many of their fellow countrymen, many of the traditional villagers not only blamed the aristocracy for leading Germany into the war, but had also developed a profound mistrust of the officer class and elites in general. In addition they were anti-French and anti-communist, but above all they hated the Prussians, deeply resenting the dominant role played by Protestant Prussia in Bismarck's united Germany, which they believed had robbed them of their autonomy. Oberstdorf's post-war councillors were, however, far from being rebels, believing that during this turbulent period it was their role to protect and sustain existing systems rather than overthrow them.

So, unlike Munich, the capital of Bavaria 100 miles to the north-east, Oberstdorf did not look to revolution to solve its problems. The villagers did not rejoice when King Ludwig III of Bavaria fled Munich a few days before the Armistice, bringing to an end 700 years of Wittelsbach rule. Nor did they regard the People's State of Bavaria, created on 7/8 November 1918 by the Jewish journalist Kurt Eisner, with anything other than deep suspicion – nor indeed the Bavarian Soviet Republic formed by the Spartacists in April 1919, two months after Eisner's assassination. In early May the *Freikorps* marched into Munich, killing the Spartacist leaders and hundreds of their followers. But Oberstdorf men must have been so anti-war or so politically moderate by this stage that only eleven joined the *Freikorps*.[8]

Apart from the fact that its young men were no longer being killed or mutilated, peace brought little immediate solace to Oberstdorf. The war years had been terrible, but the actual fighting had taken place a long way away. Now, paradoxically, the recent violence in Munich made the village feel physically more vulnerable than at any time during the war.

The mood across Germany became yet more desperate when on 28 June 1919 the Treaty of Versailles was signed. The shock and disbelief among ordinary Germans when the terms became known are hard to exaggerate. They believed they had been honourably defeated, and had put their trust in President Wilson to see that they were treated fairly. Most people were therefore quite unprepared for the humiliation the Treaty imposed on them. Their country was to lose all its colonies (the most significant were in Africa), its chief industrial areas were to be under foreign control for at least fifteen years and it would have to pay a vast sum in compensation. Its army and its navy were to be reduced to a fraction of their former size. In the east, the 'Polish corridor' was to be created, thus dividing the bulk of Germany from the province of East Prussia. Furthermore, Germany had to sign the 'guilt clause' accepting responsibility for starting the war. But perhaps most painful of all for such a proud people was the realisation that their country was now a global outcast.

In June 1919 forty-four-year-old Ludwig Hochfeichter, the son of a blacksmith, replaced Fritz Gschwender as mayor. He was a good choice. Unusually for an Oberstdorfer, he had been educated at the *Gymnasium* (secondary school) at Kempten, the largest town in the region, and after marrying into wealth and property had become a prosperous farmer. His human- ity, cool judgement and sense of humour were exactly the qualities the village needed at a time of such high tension and national despair. Having only been mayor for three days when the Treaty of Versailles was signed, Hochfeichter faced formi- dable difficulties. In his inaugural speech, he jokingly thanked those who had *not* voted for him since they had clearly wished to spare him the sleepless nights that lay ahead.

The most urgent of Hochfeichter's problems was to provide enough food for the village. Rations were not only as stringent as they had been during the war, but, due to Oberstdorf's expanding population, had also to stretch fur- ther. Theoretically, each inhabitant received 62.5 grams of fat a week, one egg every two weeks, 200 grams of flour per day and one litre of petrol (for lighting) a month. But there was no guarantee that even these thin rations would be regularly supplied. Nor were the farmers much better off, since the slaughtering of animals without a special permit was strictly forbidden and all their produce had to be handed over to the government. After food, fuel was the most contentious prob- lem – especially as winter approached, when temperatures at night could drop as low as minus 20 degrees Celsius.

There was, however, one growing source of income for the village – tourism. In a war-weary world, Oberstdorf appeared to outsiders a haven of beauty and peace so that, unsurpris- ingly, large numbers flocked there. Each one had to register, and records show that in 1919 over 9,000 people stayed in the village for a lengthy period, and over 3,000 for a short break – a great many visitors for a village with a population of only 4,000. Politicians, aristocrats, celebrities and of course

Jews arrived from all over Germany. Some even chose to remain permanently.

But while the additional revenue was certainly welcome, this influx of 'strangers' brought with it major problems. Between November 1918 and July 1920, the number of people entitled to rations jumped from 2,852 to 4,290. As Hochfeichter remarked, feeding everyone was 'a task rich in thorns'.[9] Nevertheless, those with ready cash had ample opportunity to cheat the system, even though they knew that if caught they faced a hefty fine or imprisonment. The *OGF*, which had a circulation in the village of roughly 1,000, had plenty to say on the subject of Oberstdorf's controversial visitors:

> Some villagers welcome outsiders but others find them a provocation. Despite bringing gold – or rather paper money – not everything that 'shines' is genuine, let alone gold. Shady conduct and war profiteering go hand in hand with bad manners, gross ostentation and the callous forcing up of prices. All this we see on the streets and in the hotels of Oberstdorf. Worst of all, we see it in the daily battle for provisions.[10]

It was not just the big issues that the mayor was expected to resolve: 'We hereby request Mayor Hochfeichter to impose a fine of 50 Marks on those brazen women wearing trousers seen walking around our beautiful Oberstdorf,' posted one furious reader, adding, 'the money should be donated to the relief fund for the village poor.'[11]

However much the villagers disapproved of the newcomers, the latter did at least introduce a note of long-lost gaiety into Oberstdorf. Every Wednesday, a large group of them dressed in their best evening clothes would go dancing at the Parkhotel Luitpold, which still retained something of its pre-war glamour. That is until the police suddenly appeared one night at 11 p.m. and ordered them all to go home. 'Does anyone really think', the OGF asked indignantly a few days later, 'that this patronising behaviour – so damaging to a resort village – will drag the cart out of the rut or make our citizens any more content with the times in which we live?'[12] Fortunately, with the introduction of the more acceptable 'tea dance', a solution to the problem of late-night carousing was quickly found. If, however, traditional dancing was cautiously welcomed, the foxtrot was universally condemned – a shameless American import that even the OGF could not condone.

The visitors, enjoying all that Oberstdorf had to offer, often appeared to flaunt their relative wealth in the faces of the hard-pressed locals. The many personal advertisements printed by the OGF in the early post-war years demonstrate the sombre reality of the villagers' daily life. Although the sadness and dislocation caused by the war is poignantly captured in these brief notices, they also underline people's eagerness to put the war behind them:

Widow sells underwear and shirts of fallen sons

Who can give goat's milk to a seriously ill man?

Which generous family in Oberstdorf will take in free of charge, but in exchange for work such as sewing, piano lessons, looking after children, for several weeks two impoverished aristocratic ladies; sisters, 36 and 40 years old, urgently in need of recuperation?

Which self-sacrificing woman will take care of a poor four months' old child for payment?

Who will give a needy woman daily a litre of decent
broth and small portion of meat in exchange for a daily
litre of milk?

There were entrepreneurs eager to exploit new opportunities:
'old teeth and dentures, bones are bought, and hair of loved
ones (living or dead) is made into watch chains'; and no village is without its gossip, slander or its reprobate young men:

> The undersigned revokes the insulting statement she made
> about Josef Wechs in connection with the dispute over
> 'only the scoundrels get help'.

> Karl Richter [brewery and hotel owner] distances
> himself from the behaviour of his sons who are accused
> of gross misdemeanour.

> A mother apologises for her underage daughter Hedwig,
> who spread around the untrue statement heard from
> the farmer's son Melchior Besler in Oberstdorf Lower
> Market that Herr Johann Schmid gave rancid butter to
> the Saathoff Sanatorium. She and two others have paid
> 30 Marks to the relief fund.

With so much desperate need in the community, thieving was
inevitable; but in a village where everyone knew everyone
there was always someone watching:

> On 23 June last year a black woollen cardigan was lost
> on the way to Loretto. This cardigan has been spotted
> on a woman who was in A. Hofmann's bookstore last
> Thursday. The woman is asked to hand in the cardigan to
> the bookstore or she will otherwise be charged.

> The thief who stole laundry off Herr Lutz's washing line
> during the night is warned that he has been recognised
> by a neighbour.

In September 1919, in response to the worsening economic situation and the continuing threat of violence in the cities, the village councillors (in common with their counterparts across the region) gathered to discuss the possibility of raising a local militia. Considering the draconian terms of the Treaty of Versailles governing Germany's demilitarisation, this was a highly sensitive issue and probably the reason why the meeting was not held at the town hall as usual but in the Hirsch tavern, which, with its low ceilings, wooden furniture, painted ornaments and antlers hanging on the walls, could hardly have been more typically Bavarian.

In the smoke-filled room, reeking of beer, a socialist textile worker was the first to address his colleagues. He started by saying how sad it was that so soon after the war civilians should have to consider taking up arms. But he went on to warn, 'We don't know what madness will strike next to shatter our peace – even in a backwater like Oberstdorf.' General Count von Brand, one of the village's new residents, originally from the north and a Protestant, was keen to have his say. Only a few months earlier he had himself fought in Munich with the *Freikorps* against the Spartacists and he gave the meeting a lurid account of the fate awaiting them should the village ever come under Bolshevist attack. But, as Hochfeichter was quick to observe, no one could actually be sure that the next threat would be from the communists, emphasising that it might just as well come from the Right. In the end, it was reluctantly agreed that a village militia was justified, but that it must never ever be used for political purposes.[13]

After making this momentous decision, the council was slow to implement it. Eventually notices were posted around the village asking for volunteers, but making it clear that the militia's sole purpose was 'to defend our valley from revolutionary elements'. By the time enough men came forward, General von Brand had taken command. His immediate task was to remind his men that their rifles were the property of the state and must *not* be used for poaching. Nor, he added, should the 'immature elements' that had recently come to his notice fire off their weapons in the air at weddings. Indeed, Oberstdorf's militia was to prove a grave disappointment to the general. He lamented the men's lack of soldierly qualities, particularly their 'sloppy attitude and poor attendance'.[14]

If to some the general was little more than a caricature soldier, he nevertheless had a point. When, on 13 March 1920, the Kapp Putsch* in Berlin triggered yet another national wave of violence and political unrest, three-quarters of the militia failed to turn up for roll call even though it had been carefully timed not to interfere with Mass or milking. The final showdown came when the general returned from inspecting the militia in the nearby town of Kempten, where he had found a fine body of 300 men. Not only were they orderly and disciplined, reported the general, 'but they don't argue'. Why, he demanded, could Oberstdorfers not be more like them?[15] It was unfortunate that he chose to voice these views in public. At the next parade only eight men bothered to turn up. One of them, a farmer (who also played the tuba in the brass band),

---

* This was the failed attempt by the right-wing extremist and former member of the Reichstag Wolfgang Kapp to overthrow Friedrich Ebert's democratic government in March 1920 with the help of the *Freikorps*.

created a scene – 'shouting and making wild gesticulations'. It
was the final straw. The general resigned.

~~

In April 1920, Oberstdorf welcomed back the last of its veterans. It was, as noted by the *OGF*, a grand occasion: 'In glorious
sunshine and accompanied by the brass band, the Associations
marched with their flags to the [Franco–Prussian] war memorial on the market square. Afterwards, festivities took place in
the Löwen Hotel. Each veteran received 120 Marks donated
by the town council and an anonymous donor. The war is
finally over,' proclaimed the *OGF*, adding, 'We leave the illus-
trious veterans with a final wish: that in future, they may be
happily surrounded by their loved ones and can pursue their
working lives unhindered.'[16]

Some months later, since all threats of bloody revolution
seemed to have melted away, the village militia was disbanded.
Its last hurrah took place on another lovely sunny day. Again
accompanied by the brass band, Oberstdorf's finest marched
through the village to the shooting range. Here they spent a
merry afternoon competing for prizes and, as the official record
puts it, 'bearing witness to the beautiful spirit which unites all
hearts'.[17] For now, it seemed that Oberstdorf could at last look
forward to a period of peace and prosperity.

2

Political Chaos

While, by 1920, Germany's civil unrest appeared to be largely over, national politics remained as volatile as ever. In fact, as the new decade gathered pace, the Weimar Republic's prospects looked grim. Hamstrung by the reparations imposed by the Treaty of Versailles, the new government also had to cope with separatists in the Rhineland, a plebiscite in Upper Silesia, communist insurrection in Saxony, and a crippled economy.

Even in Oberstdorf, tucked away right at the bottom of Germany, there was no escape from politics. But it was the newcomers, many of them upper-class Protestants from the north, who were the driving force in bringing new concepts and a wider vision to the village. The more traditional, and mostly Catholic, villagers preferred to keep political discussion within the cosy confines of the *Stammtisch* ('regular table'). And regular it certainly was. These clubs, of which a great many existed in the village, would meet every few days and discuss whatever was on the agenda in the same place, at the same time, around the same table, with each man sitting on the same chair. The *Stammtisch* was the traditional way for the men to socialise and as such fulfilled an important role in village life.

But no Oberstdorfer, however disillusioned with politics, could remain unaware that in Munich political passions were still running high – not least because of a thirty-one-year-old former corporal called Adolf Hitler. One effect of Munich's socialist revolution led by Eisner in 1918 and the three post-war attempts to establish a Bavarian Soviet Republic had been to convince Hitler that a Jewish/Bolshevist conspiracy lay at the root of all Germany's problems. So while Oberstdorf's better-heeled inhabitants swirled around the hotel dance floors, Mayor Hochfeichter struggled to find food for his villagers and the farmers feed for their cattle, the teetotal Hitler was working the Munich beer halls with his hate-filled rhetoric targeted on the Treaty of Versailles, the Weimar government, Marxists and, above all, the Jews.

If the native villagers were less politically motivated than the newcomers, they nevertheless held firm convictions. Resolutely independent, theirs was a conservative community, although not especially anti-Semitic. Latent anti-Semitism had existed in Germany before the First World War, but it was the need for people to find a scapegoat for defeat, combined with the conviction that the Jews were in league with Russia's communist revolutionaries, that led to its sharp escalation after the war. Oberstdorf, however, in the interests of its tourist trade, had a long record of accepting its Jewish visitors on exactly the same terms as it did any others. So when anti-Semitic posters and graffiti suddenly appeared on the village streets blaming Jewish profiteers for current hardships and proclaiming messages such as 'Germany for the Germans! Down with Jewry', the OGF reacted indignantly, condemning 'these outsiders who have nothing better to do but damage other people's property'.[1] The article also made it clear that neither the police nor the town hall had ever received any complaints against the Jews.

The NSDAP was founded on 24 February 1920 in Munich. A few months later its virulently anti-Semitic newspaper *Völkischer Beobachter* (*People's Observer*) was launched and by August already had the village and its Jewish visitors in its sights:

> We have a report from Oberstdorf expressing outrage at the shameless conduct of its summer holidaymakers who are almost exclusively Jews. This filth feasts and carouses while the rest of the country is in desperate need and fearing for its future. Don't these impudent Jews, these ridiculous Hebrews with crooked legs in short leather trousers, these foul-smelling women in dirndls,* understand how unspeakably disgusting their behaviour seems to all decent people? It is sad to see that the local authorities do nothing but just quietly look on. Yes, and there are even councillors who cannot thank the Jews enough, because they bring so much 'culture' to Oberstdorf and to our mountains. However, there are also increasing signs of resistance . . . Our mountain people are right not to let their beautiful country be spoiled by these Palestinian immigrants.[2]

Again the OGF responded robustly, pointing out that neither Mayor Hochfeichter nor Oberstdorf's most senior civil servant, Georg Bisle, had supported a recent anti-Semitic petition, adding firmly, 'Everyone has a right to their opinion but no one can deny Jews their right to holiday wherever they want.'[3]

---

* A traditional dress worn in Bavaria.

It wasn't only with regards to anti-Semitism that most Oberstdorfers were relatively moderate. A year after the village's militia was dissolved the Bavarian government disbanded the whole network of civil defence militias in the region. In Munich, however, a number were soon to regroup back into the *Freikorps*. Indeed, many such paramilitary outfits emerged as a result of deep discontent among the veterans. Nearly one and a half million were disabled, and those fit to work faced widespread unemployment. Eager to take on the communists and socialists, thousands of angry former soldiers now joined these paramilitary organisations, which soon became rich breeding grounds for right-wing extremism.

In Oberstdorf, it was the *Stahlhelm, Bund der Frontsoldaten* (Steel Helmet League of Frontline Soldiers) that gained most prominence. Deeply conservative, anti-republic and anti-democratic, it denied membership to Jewish veterans, supported the 'stab-in-the-back' theory* and condemned the German signatories of the Treaty of Versailles as the 'November criminals'. By the end of the decade the *Stahlhelm* had evolved into an extreme right-wing political body, eventually merging with the *Sturmabteilung* (SA, Storm Troopers), a paramilitary group set up by Hitler in 1921 to provide protection at Nazi rallies and attack political rivals. The most sinister of the paramilitary groups was the *Schutzstaffel* (SS, Protection Squads) which, having started as a small unit of volunteers whose job it was to guard Nazi meetings in Munich, grew into the powerful and brutal organisation headed by Heinrich

---

* This claimed that the only reason Germany's brave soldiers were overcome in the First World War was because of their betrayal by treacherous civilians in Berlin, particularly Jews and left-wing revolutionaries.

Himmler. These groups, joined by other fascist tributaries, all contributed to Hitler's rise to power. But during the early 1920s, the *Stahlhelm* in Oberstdorf was still composed chiefly of local dignitaries and the village's more cosmopolitan residents from the north, thus forming a relatively unthreatening association, as this newspaper account of a meeting in Oberstdorf makes clear:

> On Tuesday, the *Stahlhelm* gathered for an intimate evening at the Café Holder. Herr Major Wänninger [chairman of the Bavarian section] gave a moving speech on the objectives and principles of the *Stahlhelm* and was warmly applauded by the comrades, guests and members of the Veteran Association present. Following this, five *Stahlhelm* comrades were decorated with the Memorial Medal of the World War. The emotional occasion drew to a close in a spirit of true comradeship and togetherness.[4]

The *Stahlhelm* took itself very seriously, whereas the village's own veterans' association, of which Wilhelm Steiner was a member, did not, preferring to concentrate on the welfare of war widows and their families. In any case, as the quality of postwar life gradually improved, its members' interest in it correspondingly waned. Steiner, although he was exactly the kind of veteran that the *Stahlhelm* would have liked to recruit, was having none of it. A true man of the mountains and always at odds with authority, he had no time for paramilitary patriotism. Indeed, he had every reason to be grateful to the Weimar government that after the war had made it possible for unqualified veterans to undertake an apprenticeship – in his case to a carpenter. For the likes of Wilhelm Steiner, it was more appealing to be out skiing, mountaineering or playing football than morbidly dwelling on the war, or following the fortunes of Hitler and his new political party, the NSDAP.

On 11 January 1923, 60,000 French and Belgian troops marched into the Ruhr – Germany's industrial heartland – intent on extracting the coal that their countries had been promised in reparations but which Germany was failing to deliver. The occupation was to have profound economic consequences, felt as keenly in Oberstdorf, 400 miles to the south, as anywhere else in the country. Many Germans living in the Ruhr chose to defy the French with passive resistance, an action initially supported by the Weimar government. In retaliation, the French authorities expelled thousands of strikers and their families so that, as the London *Spectator* put it,

> People of every social class . . . are wandering about, penniless, and dependent for their daily needs on dole or charity . . . What is their crime? Some of them have refused to work for the French, some of them are the dependants of those who have refused, and so their money, their houses, and their property have been seized, and they themselves have been expelled.[5]

Twenty-two of the evicted families were allocated to Oberstdorf. On 12 September 1923, the municipal council met to discuss how best to cope with this new crisis. Hochfeichter was in no doubt that the village must do everything possible for the families even though it had no available rooms. The hotel owners protested, anticipating that they would be expected to provide the refugees with free accommodation. Undaunted, the mayor appealed to the villagers' better nature and was not disappointed. When the first three families (twenty-three people) arrived, they were housed in bed-and-breakfast *Pensionen*, supplied with bedding and each given thirty pounds of flour.

Passive resistance may have eased the nation's humiliation, but because the government had to print money to pay the strikers, it also fuelled hyperinflation. Oberstdorf soon felt the consequences. Building works, including the new war memorial, were put on hold; electricity consumption dropped 40 per cent and the cost of a funeral soared. Protestants faced the prospect of celebrating Easter without Holy Communion because their church had no wine, while the compulsory beer (*Bierzwang*) which each veteran was required to buy at their association meetings to support the pub was suspended. That autumn two factory workers, Fridolin and Eugenie Thomma, noted that their simple wedding had, at 380 billion Marks, cost more than the current Shah of Persia's three weddings put together. The council even considered closing the village reading room as the heating bill had by October risen to 14 billion Marks a day. And, although the commons council undertook to provide free wood, the cost of paying workers to chop it made their offer too expensive to accept.

For much of the hyperinflation period, the council paid its bills in a new currency – milk. The sexton's wage, for instance, was raised from three to five litres, whereas the daily rate in the hospital was fixed at eleven litres. Electricity, generated by the village, was paid per kilowatt with either milk or seven bread rolls.

Hatred of the French reached a new intensity. Every few days the *OGF*'s successor, the *Oberstdorfer Heimat- und Fremdenblatt* (*OHF, Oberstdorf Local and Tourist News*), catalogued France's latest so-called crimes, such as the 'trillion Marks stolen from an office in Essen' or the '700 billion from the Düsseldorf town hall'.[6] With each new issue the list grew longer. That October the paper announced that it would be raising its subscription from a mere 450,000 Marks (with which it was possible to buy two litres of milk, a sixth of a pound of butter or one litre of beer), to 3 million.

It is hard to overestimate the social, political and psychological effects of inflation on ordinary Germans. Not only had their traditional virtues of industry, thrift and diligence been swept away, but they were also forced to witness profiteers and debtors making fortunes out of their wretchedness. It was not just their savings and income that suffered; their whole moral world had been turned on its head.

Relief finally came when the new chancellor, Gustav Stresemann, brought the Ruhr strike to an end in September 1923, thereby taking the first step in stabilising the Mark. Then, with his introduction of a new currency, the Rentenmark, solidly backed by land and infrastructure, the hyperinflation that had so devastated the country was finally brought under control. Soon one Rentenmark was worth a trillion of its predecessor. The *OHF* first mentioned the currency reform on 27 October 1923. Six weeks later, Wilhelm Steiner could once more go to the pub and buy a stein of beer for thirty-eight Pfennigs.

Germany's troubles did not end with the introduction of the new currency, however. Throughout the autumn and winter of 1923–4, as reported by the *OHF*, still the villagers' chief source of information, there were uprisings of one sort or another taking place all over the country:

Lörrach, Freiburg inflation riots (22 September)

Saxony 'cleared' of proletarian gangs (17 October)

Wiesbaden inflation riots and lootings (17 October)

Mannheim inflation riots, Thüringen red government
(20 October)

Short term Rheinische Republik, Berlin inflation riots,
casualties (27 October)

Red terror in Thüringen (10 November)

Fighting between Rheinischen Sonderbündlern
(Rhenish separatists) and self-defence units 120 dead
(28 November)

Looting and riots in Ruhr (1 December)

Separatists in Pfalz terror (16 January)

Seen in this context, it is easy to understand why, compared with the nightmare of hyperinflation that would scar their collective memory for generations, the villagers did not take any special interest in the *OHF*'s dramatic announcement on 10 November:

> We have been informed of the following telegram: To the President and all administrative bodies. The constitutional government has been declared as deposed by a Ludendorff-Hitler putsch. The constitutional government continues to exist. All administrative bodies, civil servants, police and military have to deny obedience to the revolutionaries. Acting against this is high treason. The population has to be informed.[7]

That same day, the main regional newspaper, the *Allgäuer Anzeigeblatt (AA)*,* splashed over its front page a detailed account of the extraordinary events that had taken place in Munich during the previous two days when Hitler, General Ludendorff, a number of leading Nazis (including Hermann Göring) and about 2,000 of their followers marched to the centre of the city intent on overthrowing the Bavarian government. The *AA* claimed that, although the putsch had started in Munich, Hitler's real aim was to march on Berlin and topple the Weimar government – 'just like Mussolini's march on Rome'.[8] In fact, the putsch came to a grinding halt when police confronted the Nazis, opened fire and killed fourteen party members and four policemen. Two days later Hitler, Ludendorff and eight others were arrested and charged with treason.

Although Hitler's attempt at revolution had ended in failure, his subsequent trial attracted huge publicity, providing him with a perfect opportunity to present his views to the nation. From the start, it was clear that the judge's sympathy lay with the men in the dock. As the *OHF* reported, 'The accused, the public prosecutors and the defence lawyers are seen chatting cheerfully with one another . . . a sentence – or no sentence – may be expected soon.'[9] Indeed, when it came to the summing up, it is hard to believe that the prosecutor was not acting for the defence:

> A man of humble background, Hitler has shown himself to be a true German and a brave soldier. Driven by his

---

* Other newspapers available in Oberstdorf included the *Berliner Tageblatt*, the *Frankfurter Zeitung* and the *Münchner Neueste Nachrichten*.

burning faith in the noble German Fatherland, he has created from nothing a great party – the National Socialist
Workers' Party, which aims to fight international Marxism
and Jewry, to reckon with the November criminals of
1918 ... and to spread patriotic German thinking at all
levels of society.

While it is not my job to judge his party politics, I recognise that his honest striving to reawaken in an oppressed
and disarmed people a belief in the German cause is greatly
to his credit. Aided by his extraordinary gift for oratory,
his achievements are remarkable ... His sincerity and
selfless devotion to his cause make it wrong to label him
a demagogue. Furthermore, his private life is pure and
unblemished – a particularly commendable fact given
the temptations to which he is exposed as a celebrated
party leader.[10]

Given such a glowing accolade from the prosecution, it was
not surprising that on 1 April 1924, despite the gravity of
the crime, the judge handed down the absurdly lenient sentence of five years. In the event, Hitler was to serve only nine
months. While in prison he was comfortably lodged, allowed
visitors and provided with plenty of paper to write his book
– *Mein Kampf*.

After the misery of the immediate post-war period, the prosperous and relatively stable years between 1924 and 1929
brought much-needed respite to the country and led to a
marked decrease in civil unrest. But while the world remembers Weimar Germany for the Bauhaus and Expressionism,
for its innovative theatre, music and the new opportunities

given women, many Germans, who, like the Oberstdorfers, were far removed from such intellectual adventures, saw only political chaos (there were some forty political parties represented in the Reichstag) and the nation's declining morals. As a result, during the mid-1920s Oberstdorf remained politically staunchly loyal to centrist/right parties and particularly to the *Bayerische Volkspartei* (BVP, Bavarian People's Party), a lay Catholic, conservative party with monarchist leanings.

It was during these years that Oberstdorf developed into a substantial holiday resort. It could boast a sanatorium, Catholic and Protestant churches, a cinema, a secondary school and several hotels each with a ballroom and its own orchestra, in addition to some impressive sporting facilities. The village might even have possessed an airport had the commons council not refused to release the necessary land on the grounds that it was too valuable as pasture.

Skiing had begun to develop in Oberstdorf before the First World War. The importance of the sport in rebuilding morale and confidence among the young was a theme heavily exploited by the chairman of the local ski association at a prizegiving in January 1920. Life may be difficult, he told his youthful audience, but skiing would teach them modesty, frugality and a love of nature. 'Better a sprained ankle', he preached, 'than heart and kidneys soaked in alcohol.'[11] But it was Hermann Schallhammer, appointed as Oberstdorf's director of tourism in 1922, who rapidly developed the skiing industry, thus contributing to the village's growing status as a major holiday resort. Born in Munich, Schallhammer first came to Oberstdorf during the war to train with mountain troops, before falling in love with and marrying a local girl. Ambitious, charismatic and energetic, he was to play a key role in the life of the village.

While winter sports would always be central to Oberstdorf, they were not the only source of entertainment. The commons council was persuaded to donate land for a football pitch in 1924 – the year that, thanks to Schallhammer, an ice rink was also added to the village's amenities. Gymnastics had also long been popular, although the gymnasts had a hard time finding a venue. They moved successively from Mayor Hochfeichter's barn, to the village hall, to the fire brigade headquarters, to a hotel ballroom, until at last a proper gym was built in 1933. A few years earlier the Protestant priest Pastor Friedrich Westermayer caused a scandal when he participated in a gymnastic event wearing sports clothes. This so shocked the villagers that complaints were sent to Munich, where senior churchmen discussed taking disciplinary action against the unfortunate pastor. 'I personally have nothing against gymnastics,' wrote the regional dean to Westermayer, 'but you should not have taken part, especially dressed as you were. Although it is not a sin against the Holy Spirit, there are those in Oberstdorf who believe that it is.'[12]

In 1924 the village also acquired its own secondary school, thanks to some determined lobbying by several village officials. Until then, Oberstdorf had been forced to make do with a primary school in which the girls were taught by Franciscan nuns. The girls' lessons were sometimes interrupted by the Sisters' need to monitor, day and night and in all conditions, the weather station they operated in the playground. Attendance was often patchy, especially in summer, when so many of the children were needed to tend cattle on the summer pastures high in the mountains. Yet countless newspaper advertisements seeking private tuition illustrate the general desire to provide Oberstdorf's children with a more advanced education.

The school opened in September 1924 with thirty-one

boys and ten girls all aged between ten and twelve. The head-master's daughter remembered children going barefoot to school in the summer but always wearing their school hats adorned with colourful ribbons. Despite such a promising start, the number of pupils soon began to drop, as the monthly fee was too much for many families. And, while there was a market for sickly pupils from the cities, many of them suf-fering from tuberculosis, most of these children were sent to Garmisch or Berchtesgaden, where, unlike in Oberstdorf, Latin was on the curriculum.

In December 1924, after he had so successfully guided the village through the difficult post-war years, Hochfeichter's five-year term of office came to an end. He decided not to stand again as mayor. No doubt he felt that he had earned a rest, but there was also another reason. Times were chang-ing and the village's progressive director of tourism, Hermann Schallhammer, having decided to throw his own hat in the ring, asked Oberstdorfers a pertinent question: 'What kind of mayor do we need for the future – a professional or an ama-teur?'[13] This was, of course, a thinly disguised reference to Hochfeichter, whose own skills for the job had been honed not at law school but on a farm.

At the mayoral election, the villagers could choose candi-dates from three lists. In the event they picked eight councillors from 'Farming and Trade', one from 'Workers, Civil Servants and Employees' and five from 'Tourism'. The deputy mayor, Magnus Haas, received the most votes and so was duly pro-moted to the top job. Meanwhile, everyone was expecting Schallhammer to be elected his deputy. But at the last moment 'Farming and Trade' put forward a surprise candidate – Ludwig Hochfeichter – who, winning fourteen out of fifteen votes, was duly elected the new deputy mayor.

So, despite the efforts of Schallhammer's modernising tourism faction, Oberstdorf approached the second half of the decade led by the old guard but in reverse order. With Hitler in prison, inflation under control and the stirrings of renewed national confidence, the incoming mayor might have thought that he could look to the future with optimism. But, as the *OHF* reported on 17 December, it was nevertheless with 'a heavy heart' that he accepted the 'dignity and burden' of his office.

Although women were enjoying new opportunities in many parts of Germany, in Oberstdorf it was still very much a man's world. So when in November 1925 thirty-year-old Charlotte Stirius arrived in the village as editor of the newly revived *Oberstdorfer Gemeinde- und Fremdenblatt* (OGF), it was something of a shock. The fact that she was able to wield genuine influence in the community did not help her cause. Snide comments on her substantial bust and spindly legs were typical of the derogatory remarks that to begin with followed her everywhere. Oberstdorf, it seems, was still unwilling to accept a woman who not only held strong opinions but had also the means to express them.

The daughter of a journalist, Stirius was born in Augsburg in 1895 and, like so many others, was drawn to Oberstdorf by her love of the mountains. Despite her initial unpopularity, she was to remain in the village until her death in 1971. While her editorials generally reflect the conservatism of the village (she continued to ski in a pleated skirt long after other women had converted to trousers), she did not hesitate to express more controversial views. In her very first editorial, for instance, she compared French suffering with that of the Germans – 'What is going on in France at the moment', she wrote, 'reminds one of Germany during the worst times of inflation. People are living hand to mouth.'[14] Sympathy for the French was hardly a theme likely to endear her to her readers, but when, the following month, she railed against democracy and the Weimar government, she was on much safer ground:

> Who is running our country? A dozen ministers who have no time to govern because they are always talking and travelling; who get bogged down in pointless detail so that they have no time for reflection. And the pack of political parties drag on their feet like a ton of bricks . . . this game has been played out in every possible variation since 1918. We have had thirteen cabinets in less than ten years.[15]

Stirius's readers may have regarded her with deep suspicion, but she surely struck a chord in their hearts when she dismissed 'freedom' (by which she meant weak democracies and the avant-garde) as a false god, calling for a return to 'our traditional pillars of Church, sovereign and Fatherland'.[16]

It was, of course, tempting to look across the Alps to Italy and to Mussolini. 'We need a dictator like Mussolini,' Stirius wrote that summer, 'blessed with his ruthlessness, energy and recklessness, but without his theatrical posing.' Such a man, she added, should not hold a sceptre in his hand, but an 'iron broom' which he should use vigorously.[17] As the decade progressed, it was a view with which more and more Germans would come to agree.

If the mid-1920s were a comparatively good time for most Germans despite the political chaos, the same cannot be said for the Nazis. With Hitler (now firmly established as 'the Führer') banned from public speaking until 1927, and with no seats in the Reichstag until the following year, the NSDAP was forced to remain on the fringes of national politics. Peaceful

cities and economic prosperity did not provide the right conditions needed for Hitler's message of hate to succeed. That
required crisis and financial misery. Then, on 29 October
1929, Wall Street crashed and Germany's loans were called
in. Hitler's time had come.

3

Nazi Stirrings

Arguably, Nazi history in Oberstdorf begins with the arrival of assistant postman Karl Weinlein in 1927. He had been transferred from Nuremberg to the village in the hope that the mountain air would improve his health. At first sight there would seem little to distinguish Weinlein from the millions of other veterans working in similarly modest jobs all over Germany. However, the number '4,003' would set him apart from his contemporaries for the rest of his life. On joining the NSDAP two years earlier, he had officially become its 4,003rd member. In the eyes of a dedicated Nazi, such a low party number conferred on its bearer a hallowed status. Hitler's number was 55, Goebbels' 8,762.

Once settled in the village, Weinlein wasted no time in trying to establish an NSDAP branch. But, as he made clear in a letter to Joseph Goebbels written years later, it was an uphill struggle:

> I soon discovered how difficult it was to spread Adolf Hitler's message in a tourist resort. Apart from the Bavarian

People's Party, which seemed to give some satisfaction, the
villagers had only one god – money. The Mayor [Magnus
Haas] objected to our placards on which I had printed 'No
admittance for Jews'. 'We are a tourist resort,' he said, 'and
we don't mind who comes – Christian, Negro or Jew – as
long as they bring their money.' I tried to explain our objectives to him but without success. The only option open to
me, therefore, was to speak personally to individuals, and
to supply them with flyers and newspapers. By this means,
I managed to win twenty-two votes in the 1928 Bavarian
elections. No need here to narrate the details, because every
old campaigner knows how hard it was, doubly so in an
area where there is no real poverty. After a difficult three
years, a small handful of us succeeded in forming a local
group. Party Member Dietrich [the village chimney sweep]
became our leader as my job prevented me from doing so.[1]

Some villagers, however, were prepared to listen, certainly
among the veterans, but also businessmen and professionals.
An undated newspaper obituary of Wilhelm Dietrich, the first
Nazi Party leader in Oberstdorf, found in the 1933/34 minutes
of the Ice Sport Club, suggests a man who was a much-loved
and respected pillar of the community:

An idealist in word and deed, [Wilhelm Dietrich] devoted
himself at a very early stage to supporting Adolf Hitler. In
1930, when Oberstdorf was declared a separate chimney-
sweeping district, Dietrich moved from Sonthofen to
Oberstdorf, where his open, sincere and friendly manner
soon earned him local respect, and won followers for the
NSDAP. He was founder and leader of Storm Troop 23/20
of the SA-Reserve.[2]

Of the small group of founder members, none was more devoted to the Nazi cause than the artist Rudolf Scheller. Born in 1889, he had come to the village at the age of seventeen when his father took up a teaching post at the school. Seven years later Scheller went to Paris to study at the Académie des Beaux-Arts. For a young artist, there was no more intoxicating place to be on the eve of the First World War than Paris. Cubism, Symbolism, Fauvism and Expressionism all offered thrilling new ways of looking at the world – but not for Scheller. The sole effect of modernism on him was to convince him that traditional German art, with its emphasis on realism and nature, was the only true style worth pursuing – a view shared by Hitler, who in later years was to buy one of his paintings.*

We know nothing of Scheller's wartime experiences except that he was wounded and nursed in a field hospital by Lili – the woman who was to become his wife. Shortly after the Armistice he was again in Munich, again studying art. Inevitably he was caught up in the city's post-war anarchy and it was at this stage that his right-wing views became entrenched. His claim to have joined the NSDAP as early as 1920, and worked with one of its most prominent founders, Dietrich Eckart, is unproven but is not implausible. What is certain is that in that same year he became a member of the newly formed German Art Society – an organisation providing refuge for traditionalist artists from, as they saw it, the nightmare of Weimar's avant-garde and the corrupt usurpers who sought not only to poison the nation's visual sensibilities

---

* Hitler bought Scheller's *Alpauftrieb* (*Cattle Drive in the Alps*) after it was exhibited in the *Haus Der Deutschen Kunst* (*House of German Art*) Exhibition of 1937.

but, even more dangerously, to sever the fundamental ties that bound Germans together. Several prominent artists within this group were, like Scheller, conspicuously anti-Semitic.

Soon after returning to Oberstdorf, Scheller was walking around the village sporting a swastika on his arm – one of the very first Oberstdorfers to do so – while his wife Lili in 1930 became the first woman in the village to join the party. At this stage, however, their overt support for the Nazis won them few friends.

It was not until 1930 that the NSDAP began to take real root in Oberstdorf. Until then the Nazis' aggressive behaviour and crude propaganda had put off most villagers. But the Depression triggered by the 1929 Wall Street Crash produced exactly the fertile conditions needed for the Nazis' propaganda to flourish. Their animosity targeted on the French, the communists, the 'November criminals' (signatories of the Treaty of Versailles) and particularly the Jews, balanced by a powerful promise of national renewal, catapulted the party from political obscurity to centre-stage. After his failed putsch, Hitler had decided that the Nazis' route to power lay not in revolution but in the ballot box. If, however, the NSDAP was to secure enough seats in the Reichstag, he also realised that it was vital to reach beyond his core following of disgruntled violent veterans and the unemployed to the wider electorate. With this in view, he had by 1930 adapted his image enough to win support from the likes of the industrialist Fritz Thyssen and socialites such as Helene Bechstein, of the famous piano-manufacturing family.

Despite the Depression, and compared with most of the country, economically Oberstdorf did rather well in 1930. Because Germans could no longer afford to travel abroad, visitor numbers even slightly increased, with the result that the village's retailers enjoyed a surprisingly successful summer. But if most villagers were themselves reasonably well off, they were acutely aware of the desperate state of the wider economy and of the many hardships endured by ordinary people. As unemployment and the cost of food kept rising, national morale sank to a new low. Above all, Germans remained haunted by the spectre of hyperinflation. Every day the local and national newspapers fanned the villagers' fears with grim news and tales of widespread suffering. The OGF recorded how six local jobless men, in a desperate attempt to make some money, were caught coming down the Höfats Mountain carrying between them 500 Edelweiss. One of them had concealed 200 of the protected plants so ingeniously that the policeman had to conduct an 'energetic body search to uncover them'.[3]

As the Nazis' intimidating tactics became more difficult to ignore, Oberstdorf's hoteliers and pub owners grew increasingly concerned about the numbers of SA men in brown shirts to be seen in the village. Aggressive and noisy, such groups did nothing to encourage the all-important tourist trade. As for the so-called 'Jewish question', while individuals may have held differing views, the village authorities spoke with one voice. Anti-Semitism was bad for business and should therefore be discouraged. A high proportion of Oberstdorf's wealthiest and most distinguished visitors were Jewish. Judge Neuberger, for instance, from Munich had taken the first floor of the Beslerhaus every summer for as long as anyone could remember. Then there was Maestro Ringelmann, who always rented a floor of the Rechberg house, bringing his piano with him. From 1930, however, the meetings and marches organised by the local SA branch became more frequent and were often reinforced with visiting groups from the nearby towns of Sonthofen, Immenstadt and Kempten, or from even further afield.

Village activists, many of them, no doubt, post office employees recruited by Weinlein (in later years the post office was
to become a major centre of Nazi support), put up posters and
delivered propaganda pamphlets and the *Völkischer Beobachter*
in the village and to outlying farms.

Even when they were not actually marching through the
streets, clusters of 'Hitlars' (as the committed Nazis were
called in the local dialect) shouting anti-Semitic slogans or
singing their favourite 'Horst Wessel' song, were clearly at odds
with visitors who had come to Oberstdorf to enjoy the peace
and quiet of the mountains. Many villagers were therefore
delighted when on 1 June 1930 the Bavarian government (pro-
voked by a National Socialist demonstration in a working-class
district of Munich) imposed a ban on the wearing of uniforms
at outdoor rallies and marches.

Even though in Oberstdorf the NSDAP had begun to
make headway, the *OGF* continued to ignore it. In fact, the
newspaper made no mention of Nazi activities, either locally
or nationally, until 5 April 1930 when it advertised a forth-
coming talk by a Nazi councillor from Munich on the topic of
'National Socialism and Tourism'. Unusually, however, there
was no follow-up report. The paper's refusal to engage with
the Nazis was partly because its publisher, Andreas Hofmann,
was Catholic and Catholics were much less keen on Hitler than
Protestants, and also, perhaps, because they already answered
to a strongly authoritarian organisation. In addition, its editor,
Charlotte Stirius, although implacably right-wing, remained
unconvinced that Hitler really was Germany's answer to
Mussolini.

It was not until 9 September 1930, just five days before
the federal election prompted by the government's ineffec-
tive response to the economic crisis, that the first substantial

article on the Nazis appeared in the *OGF*. It reported a speech given several days earlier by Theo Benesch (an engineer from Erlangen in Franconia) at the Hirsch tavern. As well as covering the familiar themes, Benesch, one of the party's star speakers, emphasised another major Nazi grievance – the Young Plan, whereby the Allies had eased Germany's reparations burden after the Wall Street Crash. During the prosperous mid-1920s, the shock of Germany's 1918 defeat had gradually begun to fade. But now the Young Plan brought all the shame and bitterness associated with the Treaty of Versailles sharply back into focus. As Hitler utterly rejected the whole concept of reparations, the Nazis were able to turn this latest tinkering with the war debt into a hot election topic.

On 10 September, a couple of days after Benesch's speech, the *Völkischer Beobachter* published a tirade against the Young Plan highlighting two issues that were much on Germans' minds – job security and the future of agriculture. The paper asserted that not only would 'signing the Young Plan lead to a drastic rise in unemployment', but that the 'German farmer would be ground down . . . forced to export at any price'. At the same time the country would be flooded with foreign foodstuffs.[4]

Nor did a startling statistic printed in the *OGF* do anything to soothe local nerves. During the first year of the new plan, so the newspaper claimed, Oberstdorf would be required to pay 120,000 Reichsmark (RM), which, set against the current village income of 445,000 RM, was a devastating revelation. Furthermore, the newspaper maintained that the village would thereafter be forced to contribute almost 140,000 RM annually until 1987. In other words, Oberstdorf was to be bled dry for generations with the sole purpose, as villagers saw it, of making 'the already fat French even fatter'.[5] The village veterans, with their own particular memories of the French, were not the only Oberstdorfers to find such a notion intolerable. Whether or not the OGF's figures were accurate is irrelevant, since in the months leading up to the September election the villagers believed them implicitly.

For a number of those present at the Hirsch that September evening, Benesch's speech would have been their first exposure to the full force of Nazi propaganda. And to many of them it must have seemed exciting, different – even inspiring. Here, at last, was a political party with a clear manifesto, the determination to fight for ordinary Germans – and to take on the French and the communists. And when it came to manipulating an audience, Benesch knew all the tricks. Having first given the villagers a glimpse of the hell they could expect if they continued to exist under the thumb of Jews and the Young Plan, or succumbed to the Bolshevists, he then promised them a life of 'beauty, freedom and dignity' if they would only put their trust in the Führer. Benesch made them another promise that Faustian night, one that for many Germans, wherever they stood on the political spectrum, meant even more to them than their personal welfare: the recovery of Germany's prestige.

The day after Benesch's meeting, it was the turn of the Mayor of Augsburg, Otto Bohl, to address Oberstdorfers at the Hirsch. The mayor belonged to the Bavarian People's Party, which had long been first choice for the traditionally minded villagers, especially the farmers. In drab contrast with the speech given by his Nazi rival the previous night, Bohl argued that easy solutions to Germany's current problems were not on the table since they were caused – not by the Young Plan, nor by the Jews – but by global Depression and the legacy of war.[6] Just days before the election, the mayor could offer no bright vision for the future, no quick fix.

The disparity between the two speakers goes some way to explaining how Benesch's inflammatory rhetoric could have resonated so strongly with a community whose leaders had hitherto shown such contempt for the Nazis. Textile factory workers Fridolin and Eugenie Thomma (whose wedding, at the height of hyperinflation in 1923, had allegedly cost more than the Shah of Persia's) are a good case study. Born in 1898, Fridolin was one of eleven children, his wife one of eight. He was brought up in a household dominated by an authoritarian grandfather and sent to work on a farm aged six. An older brother was killed in 1916, the year before his youngest brother was born. Fridolin and Eugenie had been married six years at the time of the Depression, which in turn led to a reduction of their working hours. They joined their factory comrades by going on strike but received only part of the strike money promised them. The last straw came when, after returning to work, they discovered their pay had actually been cut by two Pfennigs an hour. Never again, they swore to each other, would they ever trust the unions. They might have chosen, as did many others, to protest by joining the Communist Party, but because as a young man Fridolin had seen veterans attacked by communists, for him this was unthinkable. Of all the politicians vying for office in 1930, only one seemed to understand the couple's fears and needs. From then on Adolf Hitler always had their vote.[7]

On 14 September 1930, just a few days after these two contrasting speeches, the villagers went to the polls. For any Oberstdorfer who had relied solely on the *OGF* for their news, or who had underestimated the appeal of Hitler's vision, the election result must have come as a shock. Nationally the NSDAP had surpassed even its own hopes. A gain of 95 seats now gave the party a total of 107, thus making it the second-largest party in the Reichstag. This at last was the breakthrough that Hitler had so long sought. The local result in Oberstdorf was no less remarkable. On a village turnout of 70 per cent, the NSDAP had won 628 votes – more than any other party and 3 per cent higher than the vote cast for the Nazis nationwide.[8] One reason, as the still-sceptical *OGF* was quick to observe, was that almost as many holiday visitors from the north had voted as villagers. As Protestants were twice as likely to vote for Hitler as were Catholics, the newspaper had a valid point. But it is also clear that Hitler had succeeded in extending his appeal to a wider public – to women, the middle classes and, most important in the context of Oberstdorf, to farmers.

In light of the Nazi success reverberating throughout Germany, the Bavarian government's continued ban on the wearing of uniforms at outdoor rallies and marches was a bold stance. But since the Nazis had decided to seek power legally, they therefore obeyed the ban to the letter of the law, if not in the spirit. A few days after the September election, a prominent SA man from Düsseldorf died in Oberstdorf, providing the perfect excuse for the kind of showy parade so beloved by the Nazis. Large numbers of their supporters gathered to escort the coffin from the cemetery to the railway station. They did not, however, infringe the new law. Thumbing their noses, as it were, to the watching police, they abandoned their brown shirts and marched through the village bared to the waist shouting Nazi slogans, singing the Horst Wessel song and waving swastikas under the disapproving eyes of the villagers. The latter may have just voted for Hitler, but that did not mean they condoned such rowdy behaviour.

The noticeable surge in party membership that took place across Germany after the election was not reflected in Oberstdorf. This can perhaps be explained by the fact that, although the villagers were increasingly drawn to Hitler, their admiration did not necessarily extend to the high-ranking Nazis around him, nor, as we have seen, to the noisy, disruptive conduct of his most loyal supporters. Nevertheless, the 1930 election was a turning point there as in the rest of the country, and no villager was more committed to the party than the artist Hermann Otto Hoyer. A tall, good-looking man, with striking reddish-blond hair and no right arm, Hoyer's unswerving loyalty to the Nazis is best understood through his experiences in the First World War, which are minutely documented in his unpublished memoir – 'Feldgrau auf Flucht' ('Soldier in Flight').[9] It is a gripping tale worth looking at in some detail as it does much to explain why Hoyer – and by implication so many like him – turned to Hitler.

Wounded and captured in the First Battle of the Marne only five weeks after the outbreak of war, Hoyer and his fellow prisoners were loaded into cattle trucks and transported to Saint-Brieuc in Brittany. The journey lasted two days and nights. There was no ventilation, nothing to eat or drink – only 'the manic screaming of the severely wounded'. As they limped through the town, 'covered in dust and blood', crowds lining the streets flung stones and spat at them. 'The French showed no pity,' Hoyer wrote, 'deafening us with their yells of "Allemagne Kaputt" ("Germany kaput").' All this was bad enough but, as Hoyer makes clear, for a young German (he was twenty-one) 'who loves his Fatherland', it was the shame of being unable to fight when 'every healthy arm and eye was so urgently needed at home' that caused him most grief. And the fact that, at the time of their capture, Hoyer and his fellow POWs had assumed that they would soon be marching triumphantly through the streets of Paris made this shocking reversal of fortune all the harder to bear.

Following a failed escape attempt, he was sent to Tunisia, where, after yet another escape, he and his companion were recaptured and sentenced to thirty days in the *tombeau* (tomb), a tent so small that it was impossible to sit or to stretch out. Roasted by day and frozen at night, they survived on minimal rations of bread and water and half an hour's exercise each day. Some months later, Hoyer and his comrades were transferred to a mountain camp in Algeria. When their water supply became contaminated typhus broke out, killing about half their number. They made a formal request to erect a memorial to the dead POWs. It was refused. 'We were allowed only to lay a wreath for our comrades,' Hoyer noted, 'victims of this so-called Great Nation's "culture", "civilisation" and "chivalry". How we all longed for revenge!'

After being shipped back to France, Hoyer made his third escape, this time with Hubert Richter, the son of Oberstdorf's richest inhabitant, but they were soon caught.* His fourth and final bid for freedom not only ended in the death of his fellow escapee, but also in the loss of his right arm. At Saint-Étienne railway station, 150 miles from Geneva, he fell on the track in front of a moving train. 'A blow hit me and I heard the wheels grinding my bones. My right arm was gone.' The shattered arm was amputated at a field hospital, where for many days Hoyer lay beside 'German workers, princes, servants, and officers, each a living proof of duty to the Fatherland'.

His war finally ended when he was put on a Red Cross train to Switzerland. 'The train thundered into Geneva station,' he wrote. 'Women and girls dressed in white robes came on board welcoming us with songs, flowers and gifts.' For men

---

* Richter later made a successful escape.

who had come to believe that their ordeal would never end, the experience was overwhelming. 'Our transformation from tormented beast to cherished human being was too much for us and we unashamedly broke down in tears,' recorded Hoyer. 'At noon we reached the German border. We were home.'

Shortly after the war Hoyer moved to Oberstdorf, where he built a house on a plot of land given him by the Richter family. Here, having taught himself to paint with his left hand, he set up his studio and raised his family. But for a patriot like Hoyer, personal recovery could never be complete until Germany's wounds were also healed and national honour restored.

By 1930, it seemed to him – as it did to millions of other Germans – that the only political leader capable of achieving this was Adolf Hitler. On 1 January 1931 he became a member of the party.

Oberstdorf's first post-election exposure to hardcore Nazism came one bitterly cold night in January 1931 at the Trettach Hotel. Despite the freezing weather, several hundred villagers crunched their way through the snow to the elegant hotel built by Mayor Fritz Gschwender before the First World War. Located at the eastern end of the village, it stood close to the river after which it was named. It is easy to imagine the villagers stamping the snow off their boots before settling down to hear exactly what this newly elected Nazi member of the Reichstag had to say for himself. Afterwards, many may have questioned the wisdom of their decision to vote for the Nazis four months earlier.

The speaker was Ludwig Münchmeyer. Before entering politics he had been a Lutheran pastor. From 1920 to 1928 he worked on the North Sea island of Borkum, preaching an anti-Semitic message so fanatical that even by Nazi stand- ards it was considered extreme. After he joined the NSDAP in 1925 (party membership number 80,984), he began attacking Catholics as well as Jews. His clerical career came to an end four years later, when as a result of being found guilty of sexual misconduct, extortion and fraudulently passing himself off as a medical doctor, he was finally defrocked. Banned from any pastoral function, he was now free to devote himself fully to the party and to spreading its propaganda across the nation.

Since there were visitors present in the village for win- ter sports, Hermann Schallhammer, director of tourism and chairman of the Trettach Hotel board, had tried to prevent the meeting by invoking a regulation discouraging politi- cal meetings during the tourist season, but to no avail. The event, as described by Karl Weinlein to Goebbels, was 'a sensation'.[10] Charlotte Stirius, however, was not impressed, reporting the following day that Münchmeyer had immedi- ately upset everyone by attacking Schallhammer, one of the most respected members of the community. 'The audience', she wrote, 'made it clear that they did not share the views of the speaker, who showed himself to be completely ignorant of local circumstances.'[11]

Even more shocking to the villagers than Münchmeyer's fanatical speech, reported Stirius, were the thirty uniformed SA men guarding the meeting who raucously cheered and loudly clapped their approval every few seconds.[12] It was not the first time Oberstdorfers had witnessed the Nazis' strident presence in their village, but this renewed and intense expo- sure was for many of them a disturbing experience.

Those involved with the tourist business were espe- cially horrified, and with good reason. It was therefore hardly surprising that after this traumatic event Schallhammer led the hoteliers in lobbying for a complete ban on political meetings during the impending summer season. At all costs, they wanted to avoid what had happened in the spa village of Bad Reichenhall (fifteen miles from Berchtesgaden), where business had fallen so drastically that the village was in the process of suing the NSDAP.[13]

Citing the weak economy and the tense political situation, the new mayor, Thomas Neidhart (a master baker who had been elected mayor in 1930), asked all political parties represented in the village to sign a document agreeing to refrain from demonstrations between 15 June and 30 September. Everyone complied – even the NSDAP leader, Wilhelm Dietrich. It was a decision, however, that led rapidly to the chimney sweep's downfall since his fellow Nazis immediately concluded that he was not radical enough to be truly one of them. Even more damning, he had been spotted in Jewish shops in a nearby town. Rudolf Scheller succeeded Dietrich as leader in the spring of 1931.

Such power struggles were not uncommon across Germany as the Nazi Party started to coalesce and weed out dissent. In Oberstdorf, after the Münchmeyer meeting a fierce argument broke out between Karl Weinlein and Hermann Hoyer. In response to the speaker's anti-Semitic rant, Hoyer announced that he was not prepared 'to eat a Jew for breakfast' since he had known some very decent ones. He cited his wartime comrade Löwenthal, who had escaped several times from prison camp and had shown great courage. Weinlein retaliated by accusing Hoyer of spreading 'fairy tales' and lacking true anti-Semitic zeal. Moreover, so the postman claimed, Hoyer had on one occasion even passed off a blonde, blue-eyed Jewish woman as his wife.[14]

This seemingly trivial but deeply acrimonious spat was really about who owned the party. Was it the *Alte Kämpfer* (Old Fighters) like Weinlein, who had joined the NSDAP right at the beginning when its future had looked hopeless? Or was it men like Hoyer, the Johnny-come-latelies, the so-called *Septemberlinge* (Septemberlings), whose allegiance had been won only after electoral success? It was not that the contribution to the party of men like Weinlein or Scheller went unrecognised. On the contrary, they were hailed as heroes – visionaries who, against impossible odds, had fought for the Führer from the start. Nevertheless, after the 1930 election it became clear that the power once held so firmly in their hands had now passed to the newcomers, or as Scheller and Weinlein would have described them – brash opportunists. They did all, however, have one thing in common and that was their fierce loyalty to the Führer.

In the wake of the September election there was a palpable sense of change in Oberstdorf. And, as villagers grew more accustomed to the rhetoric, the jackboots, swastikas and noise so inseparable from the Nazis, many of them began to feel a new energy and purpose. Here, as in so much of the country, there was now a growing belief that even if many Nazis were, like Münchmeyer, unsavoury characters, Hitler himself might really be the great leader Germans had been waiting for, the saviour who would guide them to a bright new future in which all the shame and struggle of recent years would dissolve, and they would at last see their country restored to the top table of nations.

4

Elections, Elections

Ordinary life went on in Oberstdorf during the early 1930s much as it did all over Germany. The gymnastics club was still looking for a permanent home; the Bauerntheater (folk theatre) proved a big hit with the holiday visitors and the fire brigade proudly reported on its improved response time. Villagers were surprised that the brand-new roof of the ultra-modern Loritz garage had collapsed under heavy snow, but amused to learn that, although artist Maximilian Schels' car had survived undamaged, he had then crashed it a week later.

As for planning the village's long-term future, Oberstdorf's leaders – Mayor Thomas Neidhart, commons council chairman Ludwig Brutscher, former mayor Ludwig Hochfeichter and tourist office director Hermann Schallhammer – were united in their determination to develop tourism and provide Oberstdorf with a modern infrastructure. A spectacular example was the Nebelhorn cable car (a scheme first mooted before the First World War), which when it opened in June 1930 was the world's longest passenger cable car ride. Even for people who had spent their lives surrounded by Alpine beauty, this was a breathtaking experience. From the cable car,

Oberstdorfers could admire their village – perfectly framed by meadows and mountains – as never before. As it swung silently upwards and the village grew smaller, the stunning range of mountains normally hidden by the Himmelschrofen came into view. Then, after twenty minutes or so, the cable car reached the top, allowing non-mountaineers for the first time to wonder at the Allgäu spread beneath them. This imaginative venture was not, however, cheap. The final cost was 2.8 million RM, a substantial part of which was raised by subscription from within the village. It nearly brought former mayor Ludwig Hochfeichter to financial ruin when a number of subscribers for whom he had stood guarantor failed to pay up.

The formal opening of the cable car was greeted with great excitement. It was, after all, a technical triumph of no mean order. Just transporting the pulleys from the railway via unpaved roads to the Nebelhorn station had been a sensational event. What is more, this record-breaking piece of engineering had been built in the teeth of a global economic crisis. The day of the inaugural ceremony, one of the most significant in the village's long history, was further enriched by the presence of the Apostolic Nuncio Alberto Vassallo di Torregrossa. The villagers were charmed by the way he blessed both them and the cable car in his delightful broken German, and how he sat benignly through the ceremony, plump hands resting comfortably on his ample belly.[1]

More cause for optimism came with the long-awaited opening of Oberstdorf's war memorial on 11 October 1931, an event around which all the villagers could unite whatever their politics. The municipal councillors, dressed in frock coats and top hats, took part in a festive procession that, after winding its way through village streets especially decorated for the occasion, ended in the marketplace, where the new war memorial was housed in a small chapel standing next to the church. The two days set aside for this great moment in Oberstdorf's history were filled with speeches, reminiscences and nostalgia. The *OGF* even commented on 'that glorious time that nobody can rob us of'[2] – a curious statement given the hideous loss and misery inflicted by the First World War of which Oberstdorf had certainly suffered its share.

Prominent among those present at the memorial ceremony was a local farmer, Hans Dorn. He had fought for four years on the Western Front, rising to the rank of sergeant, and been decorated several times. After inheriting one of Oberstdorf's original 353 houses (number 278), he had become a leading member of the commons council. And, as chairman of the association for veterans and warriors, he had worked tirelessly to ensure that the village took proper care of its veterans, widows and orphans during the affluent mid-1920s, when most people were doing their best to forget the war and everything associated with it. Dorn's efforts to persuade Oberstdorfers to commemorate the anniversaries of major battles had also been a hard struggle. But now, with the heated debate over the Young Plan, and the opening of the memorial chapel, the mood had changed. Bookshops were suddenly stocked with war diaries and novels. The 1930 film *The Somme: Tomb of Millions* (*Die Somme: Das Grab der Millionen*), told from the perspective of a mother who had lost three sons, proved surprisingly popular with the young. Uniforms were also back in fashion. They were not, however, the First World War uniforms that Hans Dorn would have preferred to see on the streets, but rather the brown shirts, swastikas and jackboots that had become such powerful symbols of the emerging Germany – a country whose future Dorn now contemplated with deep misgiving.

Dorn was not, of course, the only Oberstdorfer to have doubts about the Nazis. In March 1931 a branch of the *Reichsbanner Schwarz-Rot-Gold* (Black-Red-Gold Banner of the Reich) was launched at the Hirsch tavern. This organisation had been founded nationally in 1923 by members of the *Sozialdemokratische Partei Deutschlands* (SPD, Social Democratic Party of Germany) and other liberal-minded politicians anxious to protect the Weimar Republic's fragile democracy against the immediate threats of civil unrest and hyperinflation. Long-term, their aim was to defend parliamentary democracy against extremist parties, whether from left or right. Inspiration for the name came from the Weimar Republican flag that, although only adopted in 1919, bore colours – black, red and gold – long associated with republican and democratic values.

It is likely that the prominent SPD politician Erhard Auer played a part in the founding of Oberstdorf's Black-Red-Gold group. Born in 1874, the illegitimate son of a seamstress, he was appointed Bavaria's Minister of the Interior three days before the Armistice. In the Munich riots following Kurt Eisner's assassination, Auer had been shot and badly wounded. He had chosen to convalesce in Oberstdorf, so knew the village well. Since then he had chaired Bavaria's SPD, was a Munich city councillor, editor of the *Münchener Post* and, above all, a fearless critic of the Nazis. It was perhaps his example that encouraged Wilhelm Steiner to join the SPD. Certainly, Wilhelm's family, together with his brother-in-law Xaver Noichl (a forester) and friend Hans Klopfer (a builder), were to remain staunch socialists through thick and thin. However, apart from a brief blossoming after the war, the SPD did not flourish in Oberstdorf, and the party became almost invisible. But with the Nazis continuing to make progress following their electoral success in 1930, violence and bloodshed increased throughout Bavaria as the two sides clashed.

Against this backdrop of growing political tension, 1932 in Oberstdorf got off to a particularly bad start. The local carnival, with its traditions stretching back beyond the Middle Ages, was an intrinsic part of village life and a highlight of the year. On 7 January, however, the OGF announced that it would not be covering any of the lavish balls held during the carnival. Even more shocking, the newspaper went on to urge villagers to abstain from all carnival activities given the widespread hardship and need for every local town and village to make drastic savings. This stern message underlined for villagers the seriousness of the current economic and social welfare situation like nothing else.

The cloud hanging over the carnival was not the only reason Oberstdorfers felt Germany was sliding backwards. A number of local tragedies, along with evidence of spreading poverty throughout the Allgäu, contributed to the general sense of unease as the year progressed. The fate of a popular young gardener (and the village football club's star defender), who fell to his death on the Mädelegabel mountain, depressed everyone. Unable to find work, the lad had for many months led a primitive existence in a barn on the edge of the village.[3] A week later a young hiker was discovered unconscious on a mountain path. His collapse was soon explained. He had not eaten for four days.[4] The plight of the destitute young was of such concern to the two village councils that they sent out a plea to Oberstdorfers to take in starving students for a couple of weeks in order to feed them up.[5] They also discussed deploying some old railway carriages for emergency housing.[6]

Anxiety in the village had become so endemic that Wendelin Witsch (who lived in number 270 of the original 353 houses) was recruited as a second night-watchman.[7] His services were required not least because so many beggars had turned up in Oberstdorf – drawn there by the village's relative prosperity.

The municipal council tackled the problem with its usual mix of benevolence and pragmatism. A system was set up whereby villagers could buy vouchers from the town hall, which they gave to the destitute who were then able to redeem them for food, shelter or small amounts of cash. It so happened that one day a particularly wealthy visitor was looking for a master cooper in the Lower Market. Two ladies, locked in animated conversation, were blocking his path so he waited patiently for them to finish. Sensing his lingering presence, and assuming therefore that he must be a beggar, they automatically reached into their handbags for vouchers, which – without drawing breath or giving him a glance – they held out to him.[8]

If the regional press continued to harp on about the deteriorating domestic scene, its coverage of international affairs was no less depressing. Always portrayed as the victim, Germany, so the argument ran, was encircled by enemies whose prime aim was to destroy its economy. When France's former prime minister, Aristide Briand, died on 7 March 1932, the OGF made no mention of his tireless efforts to reach a better understanding with Germany, nor the fact that in 1926 he had shared with Gustav Stresemann (then Foreign Minister) the Nobel Peace Prize. But while on the one hand Germans liked to wallow in this image of themselves as victims, on the other they began to feel a growing self-confidence. Apart from the village's successful launch of the cable car, there were also new reasons to feel proud as a nation. The

Nürburgring racetrack, for instance, demonstrated German brilliance both in building cars and racing them. In 1932 Max Schmeling became world heavyweight boxing champion for the second time, while on 2 July the *Graf Zeppelin* airship toured Britain escorted by the latest model of Junkers aircraft, to great acclaim. Arguably, it was their very real sense of foreign persecution – vigorously fanned by Nazi rhetoric – coupled with this renewed pride in Germany's achievements that convinced many in Oberstdorf, whether villager or visitor, that Hitler was their man.

Along with their fellow countrymen, Oberstdorfers went to the polls in 1932 no fewer than five times – twice for the president, once for the state parliament and twice for the federal government. And, although the last of the elections on 6 November saw a drop in Nazi support across the nation, it seemed increasingly likely that Hitler might soon be in power.

In April, after a second poll, President von Hindenburg claimed victory over Hitler and resumed the presidency for a further seven-year term. Not that he wanted the job. At the age of eighty-four, he had had quite enough of public life and wished only to retire. But the possibility that 'that Bohemian corporal', whom he loathed and mistrusted, might be elected as his successor had persuaded him to stand again. Hindenburg's role as president was an extraordinarily powerful one. Under the Weimar constitution he could, for instance, dissolve the Reichstag, sign emergency bills into law and, as it transpired, most crucially of all, appoint the chancellor. For those Germans who foresaw the dangers of Hitler inheriting such powers, the elderly field marshal's victory came as a profound relief. As for Oberstdorf, although so many villagers had turned to the NSDAP in the 1930 election, when it came to the presidency they voted overwhelmingly for Hindenburg, whose popularity and impregnable stature made him a deeply reassuring figure in such turbulent times.

Only two weeks after Hindenburg's victory, Oberstdorfers went out in appalling weather to vote yet again. This time it was to elect the Bavarian state parliament. Four years earlier the result had been the usual comfortable BVP win, with the SPD as runners-up. On that occasion, the NSDAP had won only nine seats with a mere 6 per cent of the vote. But in 1932 it was a very different story. The BVP still remained the largest party but only by a whisker, winning just two more seats than the Nazis.[9]

Then, in the federal election held on 31 July, the Nazis consolidated their already strong position and for the first time became the largest party in the Reichstag. Despite this the *OGF* continued to ignore them. During the July campaign the newspaper printed stories about building works on Walserstrasse, the unseasonal weather and the recruitment of more teachers for the secondary school. The fishing society's spring meeting and the silver anniversary of the Eagle Pharmacist were fully covered, as were Dr Philipsborn's lectures on the dowsing rod, pendulum research and the international importance of Oberstdorf's Institute for Climate Research. But of the NSDAP campaign or the widespread clashes between the SA and the *Reichsbanner Schwarz-Rot-Gold* not one word appeared. Most surprising of all was the lack of reporting on the bloodshed in Immenstadt, only fifteen miles to the north, caused by fighting between the Nazis and their left-wing opponents.

Two days after the July election, the *OGF* finally addressed the subject:

Here in Oberstdorf there was little outward evidence of the passions and fever generated by the election campaign. However, in private homes, in the pubs and coffee houses, people discussed it avidly. But while all shades of political views may be found in the village, they never led to violence or excess. Election day itself, although eagerly anticipated, was quiet and the electoral process was conducted as calmly as usual. Because regulations forbid political demonstrations during the tourist season there were no posters, leaflets or propaganda on the streets. Of the 4,000 visitors, most of them exercised their right to vote.[10]

Certainly, these visitors were statistically more likely to vote for Hitler than the Catholic villagers. Nevertheless, it is clear that a fair proportion of native Oberstdorfers had also opted for Hitler.

Despite the Nazis' strong showing in the summer election they still did not command an overall majority, and since neither they nor any other party was able to form a coalition a second election took place three months later. With the loss of some 2 million votes, the 6 November poll – the last free and fair federal election in Germany until 1949 – proved a crushing disappointment for the Nazis. But if across Germany their advance appeared to have stalled, in Oberstdorf the opposite was true. The village gave them nearly 40 per cent of its vote – well above the national average.[11]

Even though he had lost thirty-four seats in the Reichstag, Hitler was still set to take power. It is one of history's unfortunate ironies that Hindenburg, who had only run for a second term as president in order to thwart Hitler, should have been the one to appoint him chancellor. In the political machinations following the November election, Hindenburg was persuaded against his better judgement that the best way to contain Hitler was to give him the top job as part of a coalition government. So, shortly after noon on 30 January 1933, Hitler stood before the old man and solemnly swore to uphold the constitution, to respect the rights of the president and to maintain parliamentary rule. Later, thousands of brownshirts, their flaming torches crackling in the frosty air, marched through the streets of Berlin shouting 'Juden raus' ('Out with the Jews'). 'No one present that night', wrote one British observer, 'would ever forget the tramping boots and beating drums; the Nazi marching songs . . . or the triumph rampant on every face.'[12]

Although Hitler had realised his ambition to become chancellor, he still did not have a strong enough mandate to impose dictatorship on Germany. In order to achieve this, he called another election for 5 March 1933. The campaign was brutal. Thousands of storm troopers let loose across the country went on an orgy of violence, beating up communists, trade unionists, SPD supporters and anyone else suspected of not backing Hitler. Along with the terrifying violence, the Nazis used every other means of intimidation or fraud at their disposal in what was to be the last contested election until 1946.

Then on 27 February, six days before the election, the Reichstag was burned down. Hitler naturally seized the opportunity to blame the Bolshevists. The wholesale arrest of communists and other left-wing politicians swiftly followed. Although many suspected the Nazis of trapping the communists by starting the fire themselves (a popular joke at the time has one SA man saying to another, 'The Reichstag is burning', to which comes back the reply, 'No, that's not until tomorrow'), the event nevertheless shook the whole nation to its core.*

It seems that it was the destruction of the Reichstag that finally persuaded the *OGF* to embrace Hitler. Its Catholic publisher Andreas Hofmann and right-wing editor Charlotte Stirius may still have harboured doubts about the Nazis, but the fire focused fears on what they judged to be an even greater danger to Germany – the Bolshevists. It was a fear shared by millions of Germans who dreaded the communists more than the Nazis because, apart from anything else, they openly swore allegiance to a foreign power. Coming on top of Hitler's endlessly repeated warnings concerning the wave of Bolshevism about to sweep across Europe and the Communist Party's strong showing in the post-war federal elections, the Reichstag fire was enough to convince even former sceptics that the Red threat was all too real. Nevertheless, bearing in mind the newspaper's hitherto consistent opposition to Hitler, the article it published two days after the March election marks an astonishing shift in attitude:

> The burning of the Reichstag has taught the sceptical and gullible an urgent lesson regarding the communist threat to Germany. In the big cities, especially Berlin, popular fury has been targeted on the perpetrators of this terrible fire, which aimed to destroy the infrastructure of public and economic life. Like the head of the Gorgon, the Bolshevists' destructive frenzy is erupting all over Germany. However, Adolf Hitler has convincingly won

---

* The current consensus is that Marinus van der Lubbe, the Dutch communist executed for setting the fire, was indeed responsible.

the election with 92 seats and, together with the DNVP, achieved a majority in the Reichstag. This means that the current government is backed by just over 50 per cent of the electorate and can therefore rely on just enough popular support for its future actions. The extent to which the newly elected Reichstag will be given the opportunity to exercise its powers will soon become apparent. Regardless of whether the government makes use of this instrument, or whether it asserts its will, one longing of the people may now be realised: that after all these elections, political life will calm down and the economy be given the opportunity to develop and consolidate.[13]

The optimistic tone of this editorial resonated with Oberstdorfers, 52 per cent of whom (including a large number of tourists visiting the village for winter sports) voted NSDAP on 5 March. The rest of the vote was split between six farming and conservative parties, while forty-seven courageous individuals voted communist. The newspaper report of the results makes no mention of the SPD.[14] Many villagers, who like Hofmann and Stirius cared little for democracy, were frankly relieved to see the centre-left in the Reichstag replaced by such a clear majority of German nationalists. As for Hitler, now that he was so emphatically in charge, despite winning only 43.9 per cent of the vote, the general feeling was that he would calm down, and in any case the centre-right would be sure to keep him under control. Like so many of their fellow countrymen, Oberstdorfers longed for a strong government that would deal with reparations, reduce unemployment and, above all, lead with conviction.

The ramifications of the Reichstag fire were soon felt across the Allgäu. On 17 March a hay barn burned down near

Sonthofen – hardly an unusual event in a farming community. But in the febrile atmosphere generated by the Reichstag disaster, everyone assumed that communists were responsible. 'The investigation leaves no doubt that this was politically motivated arson,' reported the OGF a few days later.[15] An emergency police force, made up of men from the SS, SA and *Stahlhelm* was hastily assembled. Their task was to patrol isolated parts of the countryside and check remote mountain huts for communist fugitives. 'With multiple arrests taking place in the cities,' the OGF commented, 'communists are fleeing to the countryside. It is in the interest of everyone to report suspicious strangers to the nearest gendarmerie or police station in order to prevent communists from hiding in the district.'[16]

To stop the 'communists' escaping to Austria, police blocks were set up on all roads leading to the frontier including on Oberstdorf's Walserstrasse.[17] By the beginning of April, fifty-four communist leaders and *Reichsbanner* men had been arrested, mostly in the more industrial towns neighbouring Oberstdorf such as Sonthofen, Blaichach and Immenstadt. In the weeks following the Reichstag fire, the district prison at Sonthofen became so overcrowded that many prisoners were transferred fifty miles away to Lindau, on the eastern shore of Lake Constance, where Ludwig Siebert (soon to become Nazi Prime Minister of Bavaria) presided as mayor. On 22 March, just seventeen days after the election, Dachau, the first of the Nazi concentration camps, situated a few miles north of Munich, opened with the arrival of 200 political prisoners.

~

On that ill-fated election day, 5 March 1933, the 92 per cent turnout kept Oberstdorf's polling stations busy from the moment they opened. The previous night bonfires lit by the Nazis could be seen blazing in the surrounding mountains and high on the Himmelschrofen a huge swastika. Shortly after 8 p.m., the SA marched into the marketplace. Always at the heart of village life, this had taken on even greater significance recently since the completion of the new war memorial. Now two flagpoles stood side by side in the centre of the square. On one flew the old German black-white-red flag, on the other a swastika. Villagers who had gathered there expecting to hear their mayor, Thomas Neidhart, speak were surprised, and some a little uneasy, to see instead the newly appointed leader of the village Nazis step on to the podium, especially as he had so recently arrived in the village. After a gun salute, this 'outsider' made a short speech. Then everyone sang 'Deutschland, Deutschland *über alles*' and went home.

Two SA men were left behind to guard the flagpoles. They did so with good reason, since not everyone in the village was overjoyed to see the swastika flying alongside Germany's old Imperial flag. Hans Dorn, to whom the council had long ago entrusted the task of deciding which flags were flown and when, was one such sceptic. Early on the morning of 6 March, he returned to the marketplace to find the guards gone. No one had asked his permission to fly the swastika so he pulled it down, leaving it neatly folded at the foot of the flagpole.[18] On a morning when swastikas were flying all over Germany, above houses, shops, schools and every public building, it was a futile but moving gesture of defiance.

5

Opening Pandora's Box

As the villagers were about to discover, the transition from Weimar's political chaos to Nazi totalitarianism was swift and ruthless. If a majority awoke on Monday, 6 March 1933 thankful that at last a new, focused government was in charge, few could have had any real inkling of what lay in store. Hopes that, once in power, the Nazis' more extreme behaviour would settle down were soon to fade. With little option but to accept the new reality, Oberstdorfers then had to decide how best to live with it. Many now faced a stark choice: adapt – or end up in Dachau.

To begin with, everything seemed perfectly normal. When, on 10 March, the municipal council met for the first time since the election, the agenda consisted of reassuringly familiar items such as the state of Station Square's sewage pipes, whether or not policeman Wilhelm Baur's hours should be extended and a clutch of building applications. Mayor Neidhart and six councillors signed the minutes. Everything was as it should be.

Or was it? In the context of that tumultuous month, Hans Dorn's resignation as chairman of the veterans' association a week later was scarcely a major event. Yet, in terms of

Oberstdorf's governance it marked the beginning of a revolution. Dorn retired because, although still nominally in charge
of the flags on the marketplace, his authority was now totally
ignored. He was yesterday's man, the first of Oberstdorf's old
guard to be cast aside by the new regime.

On 21 March, four days after Dorn retreated into obscurity,
Oberstdorfers, along with the rest of Germany, celebrated the
official opening of the new parliament – the Day of Potsdam.
Because the Reichstag was a burnt-out ruin, the ceremony
had to be conducted elsewhere. Where and when it took place
was a matter of profound importance to the Nazis, since it was
on this day that the world would witness Hitler 'inherit' the
mantle of Imperial Germany. The Garnisonkirche (Garrison
Church) in Potsdam, where Frederick the Great was buried,
was an obvious choice as Potsdam had been the residence
of the Prussian kings and of the Kaiser until 1918. The date
was equally significant. Falling conveniently close to the election, it marked the sixty-second anniversary of the opening of
Imperial Germany's first parliament under Chancellor Otto
von Bismarck.

That morning, a public holiday, all was quiet in Oberstdorf
as most villagers (like the rest of the country) were at home
listening to the wireless. Goebbels had been quick to realise
the potential of radio as a propaganda tool, so that soon after
the Nazis came to power, cheap wireless sets were made available to everyone. As they listened to the Führer addressing
the nation, even those opposed to him were encouraged to
hear him promise in uncharacteristically moderate tones, 'to
maintain the great traditions of our nation', to deliver firm
government and to give 'full consideration to all individual
and human experience which has contributed to mankind's
welfare over thousands of years'.[1]

But just two days later, on 23 March, the *Ermächtigungsgesetz* (Enabling Act) was passed giving Hitler full powers to rule Germany without the Reichstag and lock up anyone he wanted, for as long as he wanted. Totalitarianism was now enshrined in law, and the Weimar constitution was officially dead. Only one check on Hitler's dictatorship theoretically remained in place – the rapidly failing eighty-five-year-old President von Hindenburg. The Enabling Act gave the Nazis the legal means to eliminate their political opponents swiftly and brutally, thus spreading terror across the country. In April Erhard Auer was taken into 'protective custody' at Munich's Stadelheim Prison, and on 21 June the SPD was banned. By the end of the month thousands of party members, along with Gypsies, Jews, homosexuals and anyone else the Nazis didn't like, had been tortured, jailed or sent to the new detention camps springing up all over Germany.

As Oberstdorf's leaders had never shown much sympathy for left-wing politics they had little reason to fear persecution. The *Gleichschaltungsgesetz* (Equalisation Act, sometimes translated as the Coordination Act), however, passed in two parts on 31 March and 7 April 1933, was a different matter. The Act stipulated that by 30 April 1933 all existing state and local authorities, as well as all the associations and societies that were such a fundamental feature of German social life, must have been dissolved and re-formed in the Nazi image. Oberstdorf's were of course no exception.

While the Enabling Act proved a terrifying piece of legislation for so many individual Germans, it was the Equalisation Act that was to have the most immediate effect on towns and villages throughout the country. Put in a nutshell, this act set out to ensure that every aspect of German life – social, political and cultural – conformed to Nazi ideology and policy. It was the means by which Nazi tentacles would reach into every last corner of society. No organisation was to be exempt, no matter how trivial or unimportant. For a village like Oberstdorf it was a devastating piece of legislation, potentially sweeping away generations of tradition and subtle social contact. Furthermore, it was to be put in place at great speed. The new law immediately became the subject of much heated discussion around the *Stammtische* in the Hirsch tavern and its like.

Consequently no one could be in any doubt that, since the March election, Germany was a very different country. The 'iron broom' Charlotte Stirius had once wished for was now a permanent presence in the villagers' lives. Unsettling rumours of what happened to those taken into 'protective custody' or of dismissed officials being forced on their knees to clean streets with 'bath brick and scrubbing brushes'[2] were hard to ignore. Meanwhile, in the village itself the intense propaganda, loud military music and stream of new rules and regulations issuing from the town hall may have pleased some but were felt by many others to violate their former freedom. Even street names were changed, although such was Hitler's continued popularity that renaming 'Station Square' 'Adolf-Hitler-Platz' may well have been one innovation that did meet with general approval.

On 21 April, only six weeks after the March election, the democratically elected municipal council met for the last time. The occasion was charged with emotion. Mayor Neidhart opened the meeting with a short speech. Then councillor Hermann Schallhammer stood to address his colleagues:

> You will understand that I find it difficult to speak to you on this occasion with my usual spontaneity. I am deeply moved by the changes that have taken place here in our

circle, where we have stood firmly on our native soil and always done our duty. Our heartfelt thanks go to Mayor Neidhart, who has worked unceasingly not only in the village's best interests, but also for both the greatest and the least among us.[3]

Neidhart thanked everyone for the selfless and enthusiastic way in which they had carried out their duties before concluding the meeting with these words:

> I now close this last public meeting of the outgoing municipal council and put the fate of our village into the hands of the new men. We part in the comforting knowledge that our work has been inspired by one desire only, namely to achieve the best possible outcome for our beloved Oberstdorf. I express the hope that the new council will contribute to the improvement of our economy, to the advance of the Fatherland, and not least to our beautiful Oberstdorf.[4]

Although still technically mayor, Neidhart knew that his time was up. Before leaving the room, he solemnly shook hands with each councillor.[5]

The new municipal council was soon in place. In line with the Equalisation Act, it now consisted of ten Nazi councillors, including Hermann Hoyer, a number of self-employed craftsmen and the director of the Nebelhorn Cable Car Company. Just five non-Nazi councillors remained, including Schallhammer and Neidhart. On 24 April the new council met for the first time. Its immediate task was to elect a mayor – a duty that used to be entrusted to the people of the village, but which was now to be carried out behind closed doors.

Schallhammer, after referring politely to Hitler's ambitious plans for national renewal, made the point that a village council should never be a forum for national politics since its primary duty was to promote the local economy. He continued:

> While he was Mayor of Oberstdorf, Herr Neidhart understood that. He won the trust of the village and did his duty. As a token of gratitude, I think it appropriate to propose him again. Mayor Neidhart was elected by a majority of the people who live here, the rural population who have always elected most of the councillors but can no longer do so because of the Equalisation Act.[6]

This was not a speech to win favour with the Nazis. In any case, as Schallhammer knew perfectly well, there was not the slightest possibility of restoring either Neidhart as mayor or the villagers' democratic right to elect their own councillors.

In fact, the result was already a foregone conclusion. The village's Nazi leader, Ernst Zettler, would be the next mayor. Zettler, a Septemberling who had only joined the NSDAP in August 1931, had replaced Rudolf Scheller as leader of the local Nazis, with Hermann Hoyer as his deputy, much to the fury of the Old Fighters in the party. A devout believer in the new Germany, Zettler was a man on a mission. Competent, arrogant, single-minded, he was not prepared to allow the injured egos of a few Old Fighters or superannuated village leaders to impede the revolution or, for that matter, his own career. The exact circumstances of how or when Zettler came to Oberstdorf are not known, but it is likely that he was talent-spotted by the two most senior Nazis in the region, Gauleiter (regional leader) Karl Wahl and Kreisleiter (district leader) Dr Fritz Kalhammer,* who, recognising the importance of Oberstdorf as a successful resort, were keen to replace Mayor Neidhart with a strong party man.

Schallhammer, having made his point, knew when to give in gracefully. 'There is no good reason not to vote for Herr Zettler,' he stated. 'He is a conscientious Reich official with an important job. We must of course support his nomination.'[7] Zettler was duly elected Oberstdorf's new mayor with just one dissenting vote. As a Bavarian state civil servant in the Customs service, he had a very different background from that of his predecessors. Aged forty-eight, he was neither a farmer nor a businessman. Nor was he a craftsman, hotelier, tradesman nor even a Catholic. Worst of all in the eyes of the villagers, he was an outsider. However, on the plus side he had had a 'good war', ending it as an officer with the Iron Cross first and second class. He was unquestionably able and his success as head of the district Customs office was widely recognised. Another mark in his favour was his deep knowledge of the surrounding mountains – his guide to the Allgäu Alps (1936) is still highly regarded.[8]

When, a few days later, the municipal council met to elect the new deputy mayor, Zettler was already firmly in charge. He opened proceedings by acknowledging that the Equalisation Act had not been widely popular:

> We understand very well that we do not have universal support in every town, including Oberstdorf. We take office

---

* A *Gauleiter* was the party leader of a particular region and in the Nazi hierarchy ranked only two below the Führer himself. Immediately senior to the *Gauleiter* were the *Reichsleiter* (imperial leaders), while the *Kreisleiter* occupied the next rank down.

today in the hope that at the end of this parliamentary term it will be possible to return Oberstdorf's affairs to the men to whom it was previously entrusted. But during our four-year term of office, it is vital that we gain acceptance for the measures Adolf Hitler wants put in place. They will not please everyone because they are serious and demanding.[9]

He then presented a fellow outsider, Hans Müller, director of the Oberstdorf branch of the Bayerische Vereinsbank (Bavarian Association Bank), as his candidate for deputy mayor. One of the non-Nazi councillors, Dr Otto Witzgall (noted for wearing lederhosen throughout the winter), remarked how the village would have much preferred to see a native Oberstdorfer in the job. But, like Schallhammer, he knew that such protests were useless. Müller was elected unanimously.[10] Zettler then gave the councillors a stern warning. 'Throughout the Fatherland progress continues in leaps and bounds,' he said, 'and it must not be allowed to falter here in Oberstdorf. After all the unrest and bitterness of the last weeks, peace and quiet must return.' He closed the meeting with the triple *Heil*: 'To the people and Fatherland, to our beloved *Reichspräsident* Hindenburg, and our Chancellor Adolf Hitler.'[11] Normally the mayor, together with councillors from the different village factions, signed the minutes but on this occasion only one signature appeared – that of Ernst Zettler.[12]

Schallhammer's bold words in support of Thomas Neidhart's record as mayor and democracy had done little to improve his standing with the new mayor, who already regarded him as a troublemaker. Schallhammer's determined opposition to the Münchmeyer event more than two years earlier had not been forgotten, while his reputation as a prominent supporter of the village's Jewish visitors was even more damning. By the summer of 1933, Schallhammer's job as director of the tourist office was hanging by a thread. His position was further threatened when Hermann Hoyer was appointed chairman of the tourist office board of directors. Shortly afterwards the inevitable happened. Schallhammer was accused of embezzlement and sacked.* But just when it looked as if the Nazis had conducted another successful attack on an Oberstdorf institution, the old tourist office board (of which former Mayor Hochfeichter was a member) launched a counter-attack by claiming that the resolution rubber-stamping Schallhammer's dismissal was legally invalid due to not having followed correct procedure. This was fighting talk.

The AGM that followed was a lively event at which the Nazis were eliminated from the board by means of a secret ballot. In light of the Equalisation Act, this marked a momentous victory for Oberstdorf's old guard and one that must have infuriated the Nazis. Why they did not simply overrule it is hard to explain. Perhaps Zettler decided that with village anger palpably rising, this was not an issue worth fighting over and so made a tactical retreat. For those villagers who already regretted having voted for the new regime, it was a heartening sign that it was still possible to make at least token resistance to the tidal wave of National Socialism now sweeping over the village. Significantly, the minutes of this meeting do not record a single *Heil*. But Schallhammer's fate remained sealed. In November he left Oberstdorf for a new job in Oberammergau, seventy miles away.

* Schallhammer was in fact acquitted of this charge in September 1933 by the Sonthofen court that still retained some judicial independence.

Oberstdorf's other key institution, the commons council, was just as vulnerable to Nazi takeover. The villagers were simply informed that party members had replaced many of the former councillors. After twenty-two years of impeccable service as its leader, Ludwig Brutscher was dismissed with no official word of thanks, not even from the *OGF*. Then, on 14 July 1933, a law was passed making the NSDAP the only legal political party in Germany. Thomas Neidhart and Dr Witzgall promptly resigned from the municipal council while the other councillors joined the Nazis.

With both village councils now thoroughly Nazified and Schallhammer removed from the tourist office, Zettler had every reason to feel pleased. As the very model of a modern Nazi mayor, his political future was looking rosy.

It was not just the formal administrative bodies that were expected to transform themselves into Nazi machines by the end of April 1933. Germany was a country of clubs, societies and associations (in Oberstdorf there were around fifty) and the new authority demanded that their governing boards also conform to the Equalisation Act.

One of Oberstdorf's most prominent organisations was the Music Society, whose origins went back to 1833. The fact that, despite the economic hardship of the early 1920s, 10,000 Marks had been raised to buy wind instruments underlines how much the band meant to the village. Concerts took place at the marketplace several times a week, and daily during the tourist season. The unashamedly popular repertoire of marches, waltzes and excerpts from operettas gave enormous pleasure to villagers and holidaymakers alike.

The new deputy mayor, Hans Müller, however, decided

to assert his authority by devising a programme for the 1933 summer season in line with his own more sophisticated tastes, replacing the band with an ensemble of young professional musicians drawn together from all over Germany. The new orchestra played Weber, Mozart and Strauss (Richard, not Johann). The *OGF* was impressed, calling it 'a magnificent orchestra. With their impressive technique, they are true masters of their instruments.'[13] Even more humiliatingly, the Überlingen Singers, a group from Lake Constance's eastern shore that performed each year in the village, were no longer invited. Instead, it was either the Lake Constance *Hitler-Jugend* (Hitler Youth) or the Tettnang's Labour Service Male Chorus that now serenaded Oberstdorf's summer visitors.

For many villagers, even those who supported the Nazis, this was taking 'Equalisation' too far. The time had come for a showdown. When confronted, Zettler was surprisingly concili-atory. An intelligent man, he was well aware that the new Nazi regulations were deeply unpopular in the village. Nevertheless, he had implemented them swiftly and successfully. Having thus demonstrated National Socialism's iron fist, he could now afford a little diplomacy, especially when it involved no threat to Nazi doctrine. As a result the new ensemble was given its marching orders. On 1 October the old village band, together with its conductor Josef Walter (owner of Oberstdorf's cigar shop) were officially reinstated. The *OGF* reported that the municipal council and the tourist office had thus 'acknowl-edged the excellence of our own music society. It is to be hoped that all former misunderstandings are now resolved.'[14]

In fact, most of Oberstdorf's societies (including those dedicated to bee-keeping, gliding and the zither) had simply re-elected their old boards. But once reinstalled, the more sig-nificant among them were careful to adjust their statutes to conform to the Equalisation Act. Thus even Christian gatherings now took place under a swastika, while every meeting or event invariably concluded with the 'Horst Wessel' song and the triple *Heil* to Hindenburg, Hitler and the Fatherland. But if outwardly such societies could now present themselves as properly Nazified, in essence most probably continued to conduct their affairs in much the same way as before.

One new regulation each group was expected rigorously to enforce was that of barring Jews from membership. Although Oberstdorf had never shown itself to be particularly anti-Semitic, its various societies appear to have complied with this rule, the so-called 'Aryan paragraph', without protest – except for one. On 6 April the fishing society, with only thirty-two members, met at the Hirsch tavern. After greeting everyone with his customary charm, the chairman, Dr Otto Reh, turned to the agenda. Damage to the fisheries roof, and the success of the Christlessee breeding pond were considered before the old board was unanimously re-elected. So far so good. But then the meeting took an unpleasant turn.[15] Anton Merz, who owned the cinema, submitted a proposal banning Jews. Although a majority of those present adopted the motion, Reh at once resigned. Not because he wished to protect existing Jewish members – the society had none. But, as he made very clear, he had no desire to chair any society that discriminated against his fellow citizens in such a manner. The *OGF* reported simply that Reh's resignation was 'due to a misunderstanding'.[16]

Reh's moral stand was all the more courageous since it was made immediately after the nationwide boycott of Jewish shops that took place on 1 April 1933. Extraordinarily precise instructions on how to conduct the boycott (it was to begin at exactly 10 a.m.) were distributed throughout the country and published in every local newspaper. The *OGF*, having apparently forgotten that only a couple years earlier it had condemned anti-Semitism, printed the regulations without comment:

> The Action Committees (whose members may not have any ties with Jews) will decide which shops, department stores, law firms, etc. are Jewish. This boycott concerns businesses that are run by Jews. Religion doesn't matter. Catholic or Protestant businessmen or descendents of the Jewish race are also counted as Jews for the purposes of this order. Companies in which Jews are only financially involved fall under a regulation still to be determined. If the spouse of a non-Jewish business owner is Jewish, the business is considered Jewish. The same is true when the owner is Jewish and the spouse is not Jewish. At the same time, the following banners on lorries or, even better, on furniture trucks must be driven through the streets in the following order: *To prevent Jewish atrocities and boycotts! Boycott all Jewish businesses! Don't buy in Jewish department stores! Don't go to Jewish lawyers! Don't go to Jewish doctors! The Jews are our downfall!*[17]

What Hofmann and Stirius really thought about the boycott is impossible to know. But they would certainly have been aware of the fate that befell the socialist newspaper, the *Münchener Post*, three weeks earlier. As part of the Nazis' systematic elimination of hostile media, it had been closed down and many of its staff imprisoned. The SA had then moved into its offices, destroying the printing presses and burning all the files.

In Berlin on 1 April, the SA blocked shop entrances all along Kurfürstendamm, the capital's most famous street. Windows were plastered with bright-yellow posters bearing

anti-Semitic slogans and embellished with a caricature of
a Jewish nose. But in Oberstdorf there was little evidence
of the boycott. A banner slung across the newly named
Hindenburgstrasse bore the inscriptions 'Keep away from
Jews', 'Do not buy from Jews', while a few SA men distributed anti-Semitic posters. This low-key response was not,
however, because Oberstdorfers necessarily shared Dr Reh's
moral outrage, but for the simple reason that the village had
no Jewish shopkeepers. When the Nazis first came to power
in 1933 there were roughly 40,000 Jews in Bavaria, about half
a per cent of the total population.[18] In Swabia the figure was
even lower. According to the Sonthofen district office, only
one Jew was registered in Oberstdorf although, to use Nazi
terminology, there were also resident there a number of half-
Jews, quarter-Jews and Jews who had converted to Christianity.

Despite Oberstdorf's apparent lack of anti-Semitic fervour, hints of underlying prejudice did occasionally surface. On
3 March Mayor Neidhart's municipal council had turned down
an application for a Jewish guesthouse while in July the OGF
printed a notice from someone wanting a room who signed
themselves 'a Christian'. Another subscriber advertised for an
'Aryan' housekeeper. A Sonthofen SA announcement printed
a year later also carries the clear implication that Oberstdorf
was not without its share of dedicated anti-Semites: 'Warning!
Under threat of punishment, the people of Oberstdorf are
forbidden to continue to claim that one of the doctors from
Oberstdorf is of Jewish origin. The family tree of the physician
in question has been checked by the SA leadership and found
to be faultless.'[19]

But as 1933 wore on, the 'Jewish question' was for
the great majority of villagers a minor issue compared with the
problem of their lost autonomy. And the man they blamed for

that was not Hitler but Ernst Zettler. In a remarkably short
time, the mayor and his colleagues had won the distinction of
being bitterly disliked by almost every Oberstdorfer whatever
his or her politics. The truth was that when they voted for
Hitler on 5 March, it had never occurred to them that the
strong government for which they had so long yearned would
result in loss of control over their own affairs. Oberstdorfers
had run their village with creditable success for generations.
Now these arrogant Nazi outsiders, the Septemberlings who
had been thrust on them willy-nilly, behaved as if they owned
the village. Riding roughshod over local opinion, they deliberately ignored and humiliated the men who had for so long
and so conscientiously guided Oberstdorf through the difficult
post-war years. Within three months of the election, these new
men occupied all the leading positions in the village. They were
intolerable – and Ernst Zettler worst of all.

6

Nazi versus Nazi

Zettler's achievement in alienating Oberstdorfers so comprehensively after only three months in office is all the more remarkable given how solidly the villagers had voted for the Nazis in recent elections. But if Zettler saw himself as an irresistible force, it was soon clear that in Oberstdorf he had met an immoveable object. His leadership was resented by two disparate factions – the old village elite who had run Oberstdorf's affairs for so long, and the small clutch of Old Fighters whose resistance to the new mayor was to result in a long-drawn-out legal battle. The surviving documents relating to this case not only reveal deep divides within the NSDAP, but also the arbitrariness of its various courts. The only issue that really mattered was preserving control and order within the party. There was no attempt to deliver 'justice', only total commitment to the regime's interests.

It is worth stepping outside Oberstdorf's chronological narrative to look at this dispute in some detail because it so vividly exposes the Nazis' internal disarray, their priorities, values and obsessions. As it turned out, with the permanent removal from Oberstdorf of two of the prime antagonists,

Zettler and Weinlein, the only real victor to emerge from the litigation was the village itself.

The curtain rose on Oberstdorf's particular Nazi drama – the case of Zettler & Hoyer versus Weinlein & Scheller – after the Münchmeyer meeting in January 1931 when Old Fighter Weinlein accused Septemberling Hoyer of not being a committed anti-Semite. After Zettler became mayor in 1933 (having replaced Rudolf Scheller as local party leader) and filled the municipal council with brand-new Nazi members, tensions between the factions escalated until they reached breaking point.

Weinlein began stirring things up by accusing Oberstdorf's new Nazi councillors of not taking the Jewish problem seriously. He took his grievances to what had become one of the most important authorities in Germany: the *Untersuchungs- und Schlichtungsausschuss* (Investigation and Settlement Committee), or Uschla for short. The Uschla was a Nazi tribunal system established by Hitler in 1926 to settle internal problems and disputes. The Reichs Uschla, the highest of this four-tiered Nazi court, was based in the Munich Braunes Haus* under the chairmanship of Walter Buch, an extreme anti-Semite. Buch also happened to be the father-in-law of Martin Bormann, at the time Hess's chief of staff, later Hitler's private secretary.

Mayor Zettler, so Weinlein claimed in a letter to the Munich court, favoured party members who consorted with Jews, while his deputy mayor, Hans Müller, had even been spotted buying goods in a Jewish shop. 'It is no good complaining about this to the district council,' Weinlein went on,

---

* The 'Brown House' in Munich became Nazi headquarters in 1930.

'because its leader Kreisleiter Dr Fritz Kalhammer is a bastard with Jewish half-siblings.'[1]

The complaint against Zettler and the new municipal council was not, however, primarily about anti-Semitism. The real root of the Old Fighters' anger was laid bare when Weinlein wrote to the Munich court only a few weeks after Zettler had been installed as mayor. 'I hereby state that some of the local councillors still do not own a party membership book and only joined on 5 May.'[2] Behind those few words lay a deep well of pent-up frustration. The NSDAP had given Karl Weinlein a stature and a sense of purpose normally well beyond the reach of a rural assistant postman. He now saw himself as a hero, a founder of the party who had his revered low membership number to prove it. Also, had he not loyally supported the party in its darkest hour when others had deserted? And at a time when no one in Oberstdorf was showing the slightest interest in the Nazis, had he not painstakingly created and built up the village branch of the NSDAP from scratch? But now that the Nazis were actually in power, instead of enjoying the fruits of his hard work and unstinting loyalty, he was ignored, trashed and humiliated by a bunch of Jew-loving Freemasons. Karl Weinlein was by no means unique in harbouring such sentiments; his like was to be found in communities across the Reich.

Things finally came to a head on 4 July 1933. The village's NSDAP branch had gathered at the Nebelhorn Station Hotel (formerly the Trettach Hotel) for a lecture by a senior Nazi judge. There was a tangible mood of expectancy in the packed room that evening, and many more uniforms than were normally seen at a village meeting. Zettler had just opened the proceedings when deputy party leader Hoyer made a dramatic intervention. Announcing that a subversive group was sitting among them, he asked all those present to show their support for Zettler by standing up. Everyone rose with the exception of Rudolf Scheller, Karl Weinlein's wife Maja, Emil Franoux (a former mayor of another town) and Herr Ostermann, a disabled veteran. Karl Weinlein and Lili Scheller were not present.

With the meeting instantly in turmoil, Zettler tried to calm things down. He invited the rebels to remain, suggesting that they might even learn something from the talk. But as soon as the judge had finished speaking, groups of outraged SS and SA started chanting 'out with them'. 'I was attacked from behind and half-strangled,' Scheller later testified.[3] Bundled out on to the street, the three men were beaten up badly enough to need medical attention. Whether or not Zettler engineered the incident is unclear, but he immediately exploited it to expel 'these troublemakers and psychopaths'[4] from the party, including Karl Weinlein and Lili Scheller, even though they had not been there. Ostermann was allowed to remain a member presumably because of his war wounds.

Expulsion from the NSDAP was such a serious matter that Zettler's ruling had to go before the Swabian Uschla. Without hearing any evidence, the tribunal confirmed Zettler's expulsion order so quickly that only three days after the fracas Weinlein and Scheller received letters signed by the *Gauleiter* of Swabia himself – Karl Wahl:

> In consultation with the chairman of the Uschla court you are hereby expelled from the N.S.D.A.P. in accordance with § 4, paragraph 3. The exceptional events caused by your behaviour at the Oberstdorf branch members' meeting on Tuesday, 4 July 1933, and the subsequent outrage directed against you, make this measure necessary in your

own interests and also in the interests of maintaining peace and order within the branch.[5]

Finding themselves so suddenly banished from the party that had become the mainspring of their existence, the five felt a despair matched only by their rage. For them this was tantamount to expulsion from the Garden of Eden. Cast into the wilderness, they now faced ostracism from their fellow Nazis, lasting damage to their careers and very possibly physical violence, and all because they had loyally defended the party's interests against these brash usurpers, mere upstarts who now had the gall to accuse *them* of being the troublemakers. With nothing to lose, they went on the offensive.

Consumed with righteous indignation, they took their case to the Reichs Uschla in Munich. Their first line of attack was to accuse Zettler and Hoyer of being members of the Schlaraffia. Although this society, founded in Prague in 1859, had elements in common with the Freemasons, it took itself much less seriously. Devoted to humour, music and satire, it was primarily an excuse for (mostly older) men to get together once a week for a spot of Teutonic fun. 'Medieval' taverns, castles, knights and a secret language all added to the merriment. By the early 1930s, there were around 150 Schlaraffia chapters throughout Germany. But from a Nazi viewpoint, such a society, no matter how benign, was a threat to Equalisation and was therefore not to be tolerated. Hitler regarded Freemasonry as part of the worldwide Jewish conspiracy, with the result that it was put under intense hostile pressure until finally abolished in 1935. Tarred by the same brush, Schlaraffia, with its mascot of an owl, symbolising 'wisdom, virtue, humour', also came under increasing scrutiny. It was soon revealed that, while paying lip service to the rule banning Jews, the society was in fact encouraging them to continue attending its events. Schlaraffia was finally shut down in 1937, its meeting rooms destroyed and its books burned. If Zettler really had been a member, it was most likely because he considered the society a useful networking tool. Nevertheless, Scheller and Weinlein were confident that the charge of Schlaraffian membership was so serious that it would destroy the mayor and at the same time restore their own reputations.

Further charges brought by the five included one against Hoyer, who, they declared, had, in direct contradiction to National Socialist policy concerning women's place in society, advised a widow with three children to find a job if the community could no longer support her. Most serious of all, it was pointed out that Hoyer's invitation to confirm their loyalty by standing up had been a breach of Nazi law. 'I put before you', wrote Scheller, 'the fact that branch deputy leader [Hoyer] employed democratic methods, by asking for a vote of confidence thus contravening the *Führerprinzip* [leader principle]* and that those who rightly refused to take part in it were attacked and maltreated.'[6]

In one of Scheller's many letters to the Reichs Uschla, he complained that the official leading the inquiry was also a Schlaraffian, adding, 'As he is a friend of Zettler's who belongs to the same lodge, I shall be attacked by the tribunal and taken into protective custody.'[7] His reference to 'protective custody' makes it plain that the five Old Fighters now risked a punishment far more deadly than expulsion. Although not much spoken of in public, everyone had heard the rumours of what

---

* The *Führerprinzip* replaced the vote as the basic principle of decision making in all bodies of public life.

happened to those who were sent to Dachau. If judged to be working against party interests, even loyal Nazis like Weinlein and Scheller could find themselves serving a spell there.

It was therefore more imperative than ever that they win their case. But on 28 August the five's appeal was rejected. Zettler must have been delighted. Having dealt decisively with these tiresome throwbacks, he could now concentrate on the task of transforming Oberstdorf into a model Nazi community. But he had underestimated the enemy. Despite this latest disappointment, the five had no intention of going quietly and at once began a new campaign. Knowing that the Uschla's mission was to resolve party internal disputes before they turned into harmful publicity, Weinlein and co. were convinced that once their side of the story had been properly understood, and the true nature of Zettler's 'crimes' exposed, the expulsion order would be immediately rescinded. But they in turn had underestimated the Nazi legal system's commitment to upholding the party's new image. Gone were the rough-and-ready early days to which Weinlein and his group looked back with such nostalgia. The party was now an all-powerful machine, ruthlessly intolerant of any opposition or threat to its control over every aspect of national and individual existence.

Anna-Lisa Thomsen, known as 'Baby', was among those who now rallied to support Zettler against the Old Fighters. One of the mayor's most enthusiastic fans, she was married to Hans Thomsen, an up-and-coming diplomat who was at the time serving as liaison officer between the Foreign Office and the Chancellery. While her husband remained in Berlin advising Hitler, Baby was in Oberstdorf seeking a cure for her shattered nerves. But instead of enjoying the peace and quiet prescribed by her doctors, she found herself pitched into the middle of a Nazi civil war. Because she was known to be one of Zettler's keenest champions, she had received an abusive letter from Weinlein whom she described as 'a deranged troublemaker'. Deeply upset by this attack, she too now threw herself into the breach.

Her pages-long letter (liberally scattered with exclamation marks and underlinings) to Walter Buch, chairman of the Munich Uschla, is worth quoting at length since it offers such a revealing insight into the Nazi mind-set. After reminding Buch of how immensely important her husband is, she explains that she cannot, however, approach him with the Weinlein problem because 'he would react very harshly' and she did not want to betray her Christian principles or her belief 'that it is wrong to harm people seriously even if they deserve it 100 times over'. 'This clique', she went on, 'has created an uproar around Mayor Zettler, a highly respectable, decent and excellent individual – far too good for Oberstdorf's wasp nest.' Even though she, Baby, was the only person in the village who had treated the Weinleins and Schellers with sympathy in respect of their early support of National Socialism, they had launched a vicious attack on her.

> Their lies are sabotaging all that [Mayor Zettler] is trying to achieve on behalf of NS. He does this with no thought of personal gain, and makes endless personal sacrifices in order to implement Hitler's vision. He is constantly fighting narrow-minded people who have only their own interests at heart, and are not the least concerned with the common good . . .

But, as Baby clearly knew exactly what went on in Dachau, and was aware that if the Weinleins and Schellers were taken into 'protective custody' that is where they would most likely end up, she was at pains to explain to the judge that she had no wish to harm them even though they were 'mentally ill', adding, 'I think of God when I reflect on Dachau.' Warming to her theme, she continued, 'Old National Socialism is committed to decency and is not a charter to attack the faults of others.' She noted that in this respect Frau Weinlein was even worse than her husband. 'She behaves appallingly in the post office building where they live. Every day she harasses the workers. Postman Xaver Lang's young wife Tilly is at the end of her tether and swears that Frau Weinlein will drive her to suicide!' After many more paragraphs in similar vein, Baby finally drew to a conclusion:

> Please, please don't quote my name, because I am greatly in fear of their vindictiveness . . . I know very little about Herr Zettler, but I am utterly convinced of this man's outstanding talent as a speaker, an exponent of Hitler's ideology, and as a self-sacrificing National Socialist! National Socialism means 'sacrifice' and when a man like Zettler tries to make bigoted people understand this, it is quite wrong that they should then turn against him out of obstinate self-interest![8]

The most striking aspect of this long letter is that while Baby regards Dachau with such horror that she would not wish even her worst enemy sent there, her enthusiasm for the political system that created it verges on the rapturous. In her moral world, despite knowing all that she did about Dachau and other Nazi practices, there is apparently no conflict between her twin altars of Christianity and National Socialism.

The day Baby's letter arrived in Buch's office the court also received a statement from postman Lang's wife Tilly:

I hereby declare that several years ago Frau Weinlein boasted that she would soon be trampling over dead bodies. Afterwards she told me that as a child she had slapped her father in the face. I can confirm this statement by oath. With her shameless lies Frau Weinlein is now attempting to sue Frau Thomsen. As I live in the same house as Frau Weinlein, I have been subject to her constant torments. I beg you to save me from a complete nervous breakdown by transferring Herr and Frau Weinlein elsewhere.[9]

This letter is a good example of how the internal dispute courts must have been constantly reduced to dealing with slanging matches between warring neighbours.

Lili Scheller, another powerful player in the drama, naturally also wanted to have her say. On 11 November 1933, she, too, wrote to the Reichs Uschla, deploying a softer, more feminine touch and pointing out that she had been the first woman in Oberstdorf to join the party:

I write to you without my husband's knowledge. – Maybe I'm wrong to do it, but what comes out of the heart can never be wrong, that's why I write . . . As a woman who is guided by her inner feelings, I would like to say a few words. From the bottom of my heart, I ask you to consider the enormity of the impact expulsion would have on us. It is a blow from which we would never recover. Please bear in mind the idealism, sacrifice and enthusiasm with which we have fought for our leader Adolf Hitler and his wonderful movement from the very beginning, and the humiliations we have had to endure, the like of which only us Old Fighters have experienced.

In her submission she tells the court of her husband's devotion to his job when he had been branch leader, of how he had done everything with the best of intentions, his only goal being to serve Hitler. 'Why would Gauleiter Wahl have so often asked my husband to remain in his post were it not for the fact that he carried out his difficult task so satisfactorily?' She reminded them that she and her husband had not infrequently risked imprisonment to carry out their duties, but had gladly embraced the danger for the sake of the broader vision. 'Do you really think that we have suddenly changed so drastically?' she asked the court. 'No, we have remained exactly the same as we were twelve years ago . . . Don't push us out of the party that has grown so deeply and firmly in our hearts . . . Everything we have done, we have done in the spirit of our great and beautiful movement.'[10]

But even this heart-felt plea failed to move the judge. On 22 January 1934 the expulsion order was again confirmed.

If Zettler thought that this time the dispute was finally resolved he could not have been more wrong. With two aces up their sleeves – Weinlein's low party membership number 4,003 for one, and Scheller's early collaboration with a founder of the NSDAP, Dietrich Eckart, another – the five immediately launched a new campaign to be reinstated. The time had come to call in the big guns, so they wrote letters to Joseph Goebbels, Propaganda Minister; Julius Streicher, *Gauleiter* of Franconia, founder of *Der Stürmer*, and architect of the 1 April boycott; Rudolf Hess, the Deputy Führer and Adolf Wagner, *Gauleiter* for Munich-Upper Bavaria.

All the while, their protests against the sins of the local Nazi leadership continued unremittingly. According to Weinlein, the SS-*Scharführer* (group leader) of Oberstdorf, Alexander Helmling, a dentist, had openly declared the Jewish

Emil Schnell to be the nicest person in Oberstdorf and under no circumstances would he ever relinquish his friendship with him.[11] Dr Philipsborn (founder of the village's climate research institute) also came under attack for allegedly having Jewish ancestry, an accusation later reinforced by Scheller, who asserted that Philipsborn was the great-grandson of a Jewish cattle-dealer called Levi.[12] Other Oberstdorf party members were accused of crimes ranging from homosexual attacks to standing next to a Jew while watching the carnival parade.

For eighteen months endless correspondence flowed between the various Nazi courts until a new hearing opened in the Oberstdorf town hall on 31 August 1935, when senior judge Dr Anton Wolf heard testimony from the five accused and fourteen witnesses. By this time Zettler had been transferred to Lindau and Weinlein to Berchtesgaden. But while their removal from the village provided a pragmatic solution to the immediate problem, it did nothing to resolve the expulsion order. Two months later the court handed down its judgment. Yet again the Weinleins and Schellers were found guilty of acting against the interests of the NSDAP, and yet again their expulsion from the party was confirmed although this time their co-defendant, Emil Franoux, was acquitted.

Weinlein immediately sent off a telegram to the Party Supreme Court in Munich, which he followed up with a fifteen-page letter. He and Scheller then lobbied everyone they knew, including the defrocked pastor Münchmeyer who refused to help. Scheller had better luck with an old comrade bearing a membership number of 6,429 who persuaded Rudolf Hess to intercede on his behalf. In December 1935, the matter came to the attention of Wilhelm Grimm, head of the Party Supreme Court's second chamber and one of sixteen *Reichsleiter* appointed by Hitler. Thus, a dispute that had started at a modest Nazi meeting in a village on the edge of the Reich over three years earlier had now reached the very pinnacle of the Nazi internal justice system.

Dr Wolf, the judge who had previously upheld the expulsion order, was asked to justify his decision to Grimm. He described the complainants as 'completely stubborn, persistent troublemakers who refused to admit that they had behaved irresponsibly in the tense revolutionary period of 1933'.[13] Nevertheless, it was decided that a new hearing would take place in Immenstadt on 21 April 1936 under yet another Supreme Court judge. Finally, after three years, five months, four days and five court hearings, the Weinleins and Schellers were vindicated. The six-page judgment ruled that Mayor Zettler was to blame for all the trouble in Oberstdorf and that the four exiles should immediately be returned to the Nazi fold.[14] What prompted this volte-face remains a mystery. But it seems plausible that Grimm simply decided enough was enough and that as the party now had such a firm grip on the country, it was counter-productive to continue excluding such fervent party members as the Weinleins and Schellers.

Some months later when the dust had settled, the deputy *Gauleiter* of Swabia, Franz Schmid, sent Zettler a sympathetic letter telling him not to feel too downcast. 'Unfortunately party law sometimes produces views that seem utterly incomprehensible to those of us who live in the real world,' he wrote. 'But remember, in the end your future career does not depend on that judgment, but rather on how you are assessed as a party comrade and political leader by the *Gauleiter*. The Supreme Court's statement has not in any way changed the *Gauleiter*'s high regard for you.'[15] Schmid was right. Zettler became a senior civil servant the following year and in 1941 was sent on further promotion to Innsbruck, where he was put in charge of border control in the Vorarlberg, Tyrol and Salzburg regions.

After a short spell in Berchtesgaden Weinlein went to live in Munich, where he acted as an observer in District Court 2. A document signed by Walter Buch and dated 18 August 1944 confirms that the former postman had in his new role 'met all the requirements expected of him'.[16] As for Buch – chairman of the Munich Reichs Uschla and father-in-law to Martin Bormann – he was sent to a labour camp after the war. Following his release on 12 November 1949, he committed suicide by slitting his wrists and throwing himself into the Ammersee. The two artists Scheller and Hoyer, meanwhile, continued to live in Oberstdorf, no doubt crossing the street whenever one caught sight of the other.

In 1938 Baby Thomsen accompanied her husband on his posting to the German Embassy in Washington, where, despite her 'nerves', she became a great social success. 'She is a delightful hostess,' wrote one gossip columnist, 'seldom have we seen so many delicious things to eat.' Elegant and energetic, Baby, with her 'dark slanting eyes and masses of dark curls', remained eccentric enough to cause a stir. 'What's that she's wearing?' wrote the same journalist. 'Could it be . . . moving? Yes, perched on her shoulder is a squirrel, a red squirrel that she brought over from Europe, an adorable little creature with tufted pointed ears and great bushy tail! His name is *Bienchen*.'[17] When the German ambassador was recalled that November after *Kristallnacht* (the 'night of shattered glass' of 9–10 November 1938, when the Nazis torched Jewish homes, businesses and synagogues), Hans Thomsen became chargé d'affaires. While continuing to do everything he could to bolster the American anti-war lobby, he and his wife were also at pains to project their image as 'good Germans'. Occasionally

the highly strung Baby was even seen to burst into tears at diplomatic receptions when some tactless guest reminded her of
the Nazis' less attractive methods. In view of her earlier efforts
to keep Weinlein and Scheller out of Dachau, this response
was perhaps more genuine than might at first be supposed.

At a quarter past eight on the morning of 11 December
1941, Thomsen delivered Germany's declaration of war to the
State Department before he and Baby set sail for Germany on
the neutral ship the SS *Drottningholm*, notable for its role in
repatriating thousands of civilians from various countries on
both sides of the war.[18] The couple spent the rest of the conflict in Stockholm and when it was all over lived in Hamburg,
where Hans became head of the city's Red Cross branch. In
1955 Baby returned to Oberstdorf for six months – still seeking that elusive cure for her nerves.

And Zettler? In 1945 he shot his teenage daughter and
wife before turning the gun on himself. Did he remain loyal to
National Socialism until the bitter end? Or did he die a disillusioned man, betrayed by the revolution that had once seemed
to him to promise Germany so much? We shall never know.

7

The New Era

For many Oberstdorfers, National Socialism unquestionably brought new excitement into their lives – the marking of the 1933 summer solstice being a case in point. All around the village the solstice was celebrated in the spirit of the new Reich. Rituals attributed to ancient Germanic tribes added a pagan intensity to the festivities, which began with the inevitable torchlight procession:

> Like a snake of fire, the column wound its way through the streets to [the neighbourhood of] Oybele where it was welcomed by the village band. Forming an immense circle, everyone stood around the blazing fire watching great sparks fly up into the starlit sky. To east and west more fires flared on the mountain peaks, forming a magnificent, awe-inspiring tableau.[1]

And the day when Swabian Gauleiter Karl Wahl, a former locksmith, visited the village was one that few would forget. On the afternoon of 27 October 1933, hundreds of people crowded into the marketplace to await Wahl, whose visit was of particular significance since he was formally representing the Führer. The *OGF*'s glowing account sets the scene:

> Long before the scheduled time, the Hitler Youth, the
> Scharnhorst Society, the National Socialist Women's Guild,
> the League of German Girls, the Queen Louise Society*
> and the Oberstdorf SA had taken up their positions on the
> marketplace. Around half past six, four huge columns of
> fire leaped skyward from large pedestals erected around the
> old war memorial. In front of the houses there ran a ribbon
> of light formed by hundreds of little lamps. The flags of the
> old empire and the new Germany flapped in the breeze.
> Shortly before the appointed hour, the SA troop 3/25, the
> Steel Helmet and the National Socialist student represent-
> atives, marched up and lit their torches from the blazing
> flames. Meanwhile, the standard-bearers of our societies,
> the civil servants, teachers, the clergy, Deputy Mayor
> Müller and the municipal councillors arrived. A large
> crowd stood around the edge of the square. The Oberstdorf
> band opened the ceremony with the Bavarian March.
> After some delay, Gauleiter Wahl arrived, accompanied
> by an honorary escort of SS, led among others by Mayor
> Zettler, Tourist Office Director Plenio, Dr Kalhammer[†] and
> H. Giesler[‡] to the lectern.[2]

---

* A German pro-monarchy women's organisation founded in 1923
that had branches all over the country. It was inspired by Louise of
Mecklenburg-Strelitz, Queen of Prussia (1776–1810) whose patriotism, beauty and devotion to her country made her a much-loved role
model for German women.

† Dr Fritz Kalhammer, *Kreisleiter* of the Sonthofen district.

‡ Hermann Giesler, second only to Albert Speer as Hitler's favourite
architect, SS head of Organisation Todt task force and brother of
Gauleiter Paul Giesler.

On a sliding scale of Nazi criminality, Wahl comes off relatively lightly. The son of a train driver, he was the youngest of thirteen children. His unglamorously high party number, his straightforward and honest appearance, his strong Christian faith and especially his commitment to social housing and the welfare of veterans mark him out as an unusually moderate *Gauleiter*, especially in comparison with his neighbour Adolf Wagner, the *Gauleiter* for Munich and Upper Bavaria. Unlike the power-hungry Wagner, who claimed personal friendship with Hitler, Wahl presented himself as a simple foot soldier, loyal to his Führer to the last. Nevertheless, despite his modest image, Wahl not only remained a deeply committed Nazi, but he was also politically astute enough to thwart Wagner's aggressive attempts to absorb Swabia into his own region.

Wahl knew how to play to a crowd. That autumn day in Oberstdorf he spoke of peace, bread, honour and justice. Of how the Fatherland would have been buried under a Bolshevist landslide had it not been for Hitler. Then he told them of the great National Socialist projects launched during the last eight months; of the party's inspiring economic plans and of how the Führer had brought to an end the disastrous parliamentary horse-trading that had so discredited Weimar democracy. He reminded Oberstdorfers of how it was thanks to Hitler that two and a quarter million unemployed were now back in work. Their Führer, Wahl told them, had only one goal:

> To serve his people. He abstains from all the usual pleasures. War is the last thing on his mind. No one who had been caught up in the war, either away or at home, has any wish to repeat ever again the sacrifices, fear and deprivations they endured then. The only fight the German people want is that for honour and a true peace.[3]

His words fell on fertile ground. The villagers may have resented Mayor Zettler and his cohorts but they had remained steadfastly loyal to Hitler. One local farmer had hung a large, illuminated swastika on the tall fir tree in front of his house while a herdsman, having bought a swastika out of his own pocket, 'proudly' flew it on the Märzle field. It had been put there, reported the OGF, 'as a pledge of this simple man's patriotism, and as a greeting to all hikers seeking the solitude of the mountains'.[4]

⁓

Once Zettler had departed in September 1934, the villagers began to settle down to some kind of normality in the new world in which they found themselves. Since the transition to Nazi control, the atmosphere in the village had changed profoundly. Shop windows that had once displayed quilts now flaunted swastikas and brown shirts. Even stores selling art supplies advertised their brushes and paints under the label 'The New Era'.

Those with a keen ear for language were quick to pick up on the military vocabulary in vogue. The OGF, for instance, referred to the jobs 'front', work 'sacrifice' and its intention 'to fight' for the hearts of the German people. A 'combat unit' for German culture was established, while a rural conservation project was launched under the banner 'Battle Week'. Not only the farmers but also their livestock were conscripted into the 'great battle' for increased productivity. Even milk-protein bread was a combatant in the 'fight' to produce healthy babies. But first prize in battle cries must surely go to Oberstdorf's new mayor, Ludwig Fink (a former chimney sweep from Sonthofen), who in December 1935 declared a 'war' for Christmas peace.[5] Despite being an outsider, Mayor Fink was surprisingly popular. His kind nature and natural diplomacy, characteristics so lacking in his predecessor, soon won over the villagers. As the Zettler debacle faded, many Oberstdorfers began to regard the village authorities with new respect.

As well as remoulding the nation's political and social organisations in their image, the Nazis were swift to announce projects designed to convince Germans that their leaders were successfully tackling the terrible scourge of unemployment. Hitler had sworn to overcome the problem in four years and the energy with which the regime appeared to set about fulfilling this promise did much to bolster its support. Money was invested in creating new businesses and funding public works – most famously the *Autobahnen* (motorways). Women were encouraged to stay at home, thereby reducing both competition for jobs and the unemployment figures. In addition, many of the jobless were forced to join the Volunteer Labour Service (*Reichsarbeitsdienst*), thus (if artificially) bringing down the numbers of unemployed yet further. Most significantly, and concealed under the label 'job creation' in order to thwart the Treaty of Versailles, vast numbers of Germans were employed in rearmament. The regime was also fortunate inasmuch as it was able to take the credit for some economic projects that had been put in place under the Weimar government but were only now coming to fruition.

Although many Nazi projects failed to live up to the extravagance of their propaganda, even in distant Oberstdorf there were by the middle of the decade tangible signs of material progress. The Nazis' housing programme, for example, so key to sustaining their credibility and support, soon bore local fruit. 'No quarter of our town has remained untouched by the great construction activity,' declared the *OGF* in November 1934. 'This year ... 18 new residential buildings alone have been completed and around 25 new buildings have been started.'[6]

Until Hitler came to power, the village's most significant development had been to the south, where villas had sprung up on broad avenues to cater for wealthy visitors. Such affluence, however, did not sit comfortably with the regime's much-vaunted pledge to put rural tradition at the heart of its housing programme. Germany was to be rebuilt on the bedrock of *Blut und Boden* (blood and soil), with its farmers, peasantry and craftsmen billed as the new 'aristocrats'. Their status would derive not from titles and estates, but from hard labour and their 'mystic' bond with the land.

Richard Darré, Reich Minister of Food and Agriculture, hammered home the point when he addressed thousands of farmers at Goslar in November 1934. The event was a week-long celebration held in the farmers' honour, at which the Oberstdorf contingent thrilled everyone present with performances of their 'Wild Man' dance.* 'Nowhere among the German people', Darré told his vast audience, 'has the purity and integrity of the German soul – uncontaminated by city or foreign influence – been better preserved than in the German peasantry':

> Your untainted, traditional way of life encompassing so much richness and diversity is the true measure of our nation's strength and creativity. Here this evening, for the first time, we will present to the German people a true portrait of the peasantry – your originality and imagination . . .

---

* This is a ritual dance dedicated to the Germanic god Thor involving thirteen men belonging to long-standing local families. The men's costumes are made from a moss that grows only in the Allgäu Alps.

we will strengthen your self-confidence and your determination to preserve and integrate your morality into our
modern world . . . Also for the first time in German history,
the racial appearance of the peasant as bearer and keeper of
the physical and emotional character of the German people is recognised. As torchbearers of the German spirit you
command our respect. Indeed, every aspect of this evening
should stimulate in the hearts of our national comrades
from all social classes a desire to pay proper tribute to you,
the guardians of our national life force.[7]

A year before Darré's Goslar address, plans had already been
set in motion to build a small housing development near
the cemetery in Oberstdorf for ten manual labourers and
their families. It was an idealistic scheme intended to contrast favourably with the urban mass housing promoted by
the Marxists. Land donated by the community, together with
financial support from the state, would enable the settlers
to build their own homes under the supervision of a master builder and with the help of their future neighbours. For
families who normally could only dream of owning a house,
this was the opportunity of a lifetime. There was, however, a
catch. Only those who could offer conclusive proof of their
Aryan pedigree and hereditary health were allowed to apply.

Although a Nazi initiative, the new development was
acceptable to the commoners, whose tenure of Oberstdorf's
original 353 houses gave them rights over the use of much
of the land surrounding the village, because it was for social
(not middle-class) housing. The doggedly independent commoners, many of them farmers, were exactly the kind of men
the regime sought to lionise. Yet during 1934 the two sides
became locked in a bitter dispute. The problem was that while

developments such as social housing generated much-needed goodwill, they were also very costly. It was hardly surprising, therefore, that both Nazi-controlled councils began to eye the large pot of gold sitting right on their doorstep, namely the Plattenbichl meadows – only a stone's throw from the village centre and tantalisingly ripe for development. For centuries the commoners had successfully managed these meadows through their own elected council in the interests of the whole community. But now, the new unelected Nazi councillors appeared determined to destroy this rich pastureland by building large villas on it for the wealthy middle class.

As the Nazis were in total control of the village, there was nothing in theory to prevent them from seizing the meadows at will. But the commoners' involvement put them in an awkward position. Party policy made it clear that such men were to be treated as national heroes, so it would hardly do if Oberstdorf were seen to be riding roughshod over its own 'heroes'. Yet it was equally unthinkable that Nazi rule should be challenged on any issue, let alone one as fundamental as land dispersal.

In December 1934 (just a few weeks after Darré's Goslar address), a stormy meeting was held in the Traube Hotel. Ludwig Brutscher who, until ousted by the Nazis the previous year had led the commons council for more than twenty years, complained bitterly that the decision to build houses for middle-class professionals on the Plattenbichl meadows had been made without his or the other commoners' agreement. He deplored the replacement of former commons councillors with Nazis and the fact that the commoners' rights were now utterly ignored. Such a tirade would normally have landed its speaker in Dachau. Instead, a Munich lawyer, Herr Vielebeck, tried to calm the meeting by repeating over and over again how the Führer had elevated farmers to the highest possible status in the Reich, and that it was in the interests of the entire nation that their traditional way of life should at all costs be preserved. It was quite out of the question, he kept reiterating, that commoners' rights should in any way be threatened.[8] Too shrewd to accept these assurances at face value, Brutscher proposed setting up a new independent cooperative to safeguard the interests of both the commoners and the villagers. In a secret ballot those staunch defenders of Oberstdorf freedoms – Ludwig Hochfeichter and Thomas Neidhart – were elected chairman and deputy chairman respectively.

This latest cooperative was formed not a moment too soon. On 1 April 1935 a new law came into force that would have given ownership of the land to the municipal council had a member of the newly formed *Rechtlerverband* (Rights Association) not taken successful legal action. Thus the commoners' rights over usage of the land were preserved. The Traube meeting was in effect Oberstdorf's High Noon. Against all the odds, the commoners' historic rights had survived and to this day remain intact.

If at a local level Nazification was a messy process marked by small acts of resistance and negotiation, overall the Nazis' stranglehold on the country increased as each month went by. The *Geheime Staatspolizei* (Gestapo), for instance, the secret state police force created by Göring in 1933, was a relatively small organisation, yet it generated a fear throughout Germany quite disproportionate to its size. And with the Night of the Long Knives on 30 June 1934, when senior SA men, including their leader Ernst Röhm and many others seen as a threat to Hitler's authority were brutally killed, it was clear that, far from mellowing now that he was chancellor, Hitler would stop at nothing to maintain his total grip on the country. Then, on 2 August 1934, President von Hindenburg died. With the revered old man gone, there was nothing to stop Hitler from combining the offices of chancellor and president. In a plebiscite held twelve days later, the country gave him an overwhelming mandate to do just that, thus making his dictatorship unassailable.

But if terror and brutality were the Nazis' default method of preserving control, they were also capable of using more subtle methods to bring 'Aryan' Germans into the fold. The most successful of these were the introduction of the *Volkswagen* (people's car) popularly known as the *Käfer* (Beetle), championed by Hitler himself, who wanted every German family to own an affordable car; and the *Kraft durch Freude* (KdF, Strength through Joy) programme that provided holidays, day trips and cultural events for around 25 million Germans between 1933 and 1939. Both initiatives were masterstrokes, opening up to workers a whole new world of pleasure and discovery that had previously only been available to the middle classes. Travelling together in huge groups, as Germans did on these KdF expeditions, was one of many ways the regime sought to foster the notion of *Volksgemeinschaft* (people's community). An essential part of this semi-religious Nazi cult was to instil into Germans the conviction that they were the master race – a racially superior tribe whose blood must at all costs remain untainted by inferior races such as Slavs, Gypsies – and Jews.

In September 1935 the Nazis enacted the Nuremberg Laws, which denied Jews citizenship, the vote and tenure of public office. Even those who had fought in the First World War and had hitherto been protected by 'front-line combatant privilege' enforced by President von Hindenburg were now dismissed from the civil service. Furthermore, the law covering 'Protection of German Blood and Honour' prohibited marriage and extramarital sex between Jews and Aryans. In Oberstdorf, however, the effect of the Nuremberg Laws was minimal. The few Jews living there either had private resources or were married to non-Jews and so were able to exist relatively inconspicuously. Whether this would have been possible without such a moderate Nazi as Mayor Fink in charge is debatable. But even if their lives did not change as dramatically as did those of their fellow Jews, they lived in increasing fear and uncertainty, waiting each day for a knock on the door by the SS or the Gestapo.

The village's most celebrated Jewish inhabitant was the opera singer Hertha Stolzenberg, although for a long time she remained an enigma within the community. Having by 1932 seen which way the wind was blowing, she had chosen to swap her international career for a low-profile existence in rural obscurity. The remoteness of the village, and the fact that Christ Church's pastor, Heinrich Seiler (himself a fine bass singer), had been a friend since they were fellow students no doubt contributed to her choice of refuge. Seiler's congregation was astonished when one Sunday this mysterious woman who had appeared out of nowhere stood to sing Mendelssohn's 'Come Let Us Worship'. She sang it so beautifully that a long silence followed before Seiler felt that he could continue the service. Eventually the villagers discovered that she was the famous soprano who, among her many roles, had sung Minnie at the Berlin premiere of Puccini's *Fanciulla del West* in 1913. They must have suspected that Hertha was Jewish but this was never publicly acknowledged. Under her direction the Christ Church choir was transformed into an exceptional body of singers that was to give much solace to the villagers in the testing times ahead.

By 1935, the only Jewish resident in Oberstdorf visibly working for his living was Julius Löwin, a dentist of Polish nationality. Other Jewish inhabitants included Dora Lemkes from Düsseldorf, whose non-Jewish husband had been sacked from his job as president of Wiesbaden's district court because he refused to divorce his wife; the single Thesy Heilbronner, who the moment Hitler became chancellor had moved to Oberstdorf from Munich; and Walter Proskauer, a prominent Göttingen lawyer and leader of the famous university town's Jewish community. Proskauer had been so fearless in his public criticism of the Nazis that his house was regularly vandalised, and it became too dangerous for him to remain in Göttingen. In 1934 he had fled to Switzerland with his wife and son, but with insufficient funds to satisfy the Swiss authorities they were unable to remain. There was no choice but to return to Germany. Friends in Oberstdorf suggested that the family move there since not only was it far from any big city, but the local Nazi leaders – Gauleiter Wahl, Kreisleiter Kalhammer and Mayor Fink – had, so far at least, governed with notable moderation.*

In September 1935, Fink gave a talk in the Traube Hotel entitled 'The Jewish Question: How they Lied, how they Deceived'. Yet only weeks before, when he had presented the

---

* The Proskauer family moved to Berlin in 1936. Margarethe Proskauer died there in 1941. Her husband was transported first to Theresienstadt in 1943 and then to Auschwitz, where he was murdered. Their son, Professor Johannes Proskauer, went to England on a *Kindertransport* and became a distinguished biologist. He emigrated to America, where he committed suicide in 1970.

Cross of Honour to the Jewish Emil Schnell, whose eldest son had been killed in the war, he had spoken movingly and with genuine sympathy. Schnell had retired to Oberstdorf in the early 1920s after selling his Augsburg textile mill. He was so much liked in the village that, as has already been noted, even one of its most prominent Nazis, Dr Helmling (in common with Kreisleiter Kalhammer) had publicly declared that he counted Schnell among the most decent men he had ever met, and that under no circumstances would he ever abandon their friendship.[9] But although traditionally there had been so little overt anti-Semitism in Oberstdorf, as the 1930s progressed the villagers' attitude to the 'Jewish problem' became more mixed, while outside pressures made the Jews' existence – even in a village as 'safe' as Oberstdorf – increasingly precarious.

By the mid-1930s Hitler's control over Germany was so far-reaching that, as one British diplomat noted, it was difficult to imagine how any political or economic event could 'shake Hitler off his perch'.[10] The Nazis' ambitious programme to transform the nation was having the desired effect as increasingly Germans were willing to entrust their future to their Führer – not least the country's youth.

8

Young, Bold and Blond

T he extraordinary extent to which Germany's youth was caught up in the Nazi movement became increasingly clear in the months following Hitler's rise to power. In many of the young, National Socialism engendered a fervent idealism and maturity beyond their years – an image curiously at odds with the more familiar one of young thugs beating up Jews or smashing shop windows. Certainly there were plenty of the latter, but for vast numbers of young people, brought up in the First World War's legacy of grief, hunger and humiliation, the Nazi vision of national renewal was a profoundly stirring one, inspiring them to serve their country with selfless determination.

If the Nazis were to succeed in building an empire lasting a thousand years, they knew that it was vital to capture the country's youth. Indeed, in no part of the Reich was the application of the Equalisation Act more crucial to its long-term success than in education. From the moment a child entered kindergarten to the day when as a boy he was fit to fight for the Fatherland, or as a girl ready to bear its children, all were expected to give themselves body and soul to National Socialism. As countless photographs of youths with shining faces and outstretched arms testify, the relentless propaganda directed at them was so effective that the majority did so eagerly. Few Oberstdorf teenagers would not have felt their hearts beat a little faster on reading the following passage in the *OGF*:

> With all their natural enthusiasm, our young are ready to place themselves at the service of the community, so that they will emerge united, constant and invincible, forever bound by a common love, a common will and a common pride. They want only to serve the people. They wear their brown uniform in honour of this principle. There is not a single Hitler Youth who does not put on his brown shirt with pride and joy. Our youth is the cream of the nation.[1]

For the young people in question, however, the Hitler Youth and the *Bund Deutscher Mädel* (League of German Girls) were, initially at least, as much about fun and games as service and sacrifice. Children joined the junior branch of their respective organisations at the age of ten, when they had the thrill of seeing their names published in the newspaper. At fourteen they moved up to the senior branch and four years later graduated to one of the adult organisations such as the SA, the National Socialist Women's League or the Labour Service.

In her book *True to Both My Selves*, Katrin Fitzherbert (who lived in northern Germany) recalled how overjoyed she was at the age of six to join the *Kindergruppe* (children's group). 'We had a sort of, semi, better-than-nothing uniform,' she wrote, 'a white blouse, navy skirt with shoulder straps and a beautiful stainless-steel swastika badge to pin on to the crosspiece in front.'[2] The leader of Oberstdorf's League of German Girls, Miss Käutel, even organised a procession to which the smallest girls were invited to bring along their dolls providing they too were dressed in the League's uniform.* For ones so young, to parade through the village in a uniform accompanied by the rousing music of a brass band was an elating experience.

Sybille von Arminsted was eight years old when, in 1928, she and her mother moved from the Baltic states to Oberstdorf because of Sybille's poor health. Lung disease was prevalent in the family (an aunt with tuberculosis was already living in the village), but her mother told Sybille never to mention this, in case the authorities came to the dangerous conclusion that she was suffering from an hereditary disease. In 1934, when Sybille was fourteen, she joined the League of German Girls. 'It was suddenly everywhere,' she recalled, 'you couldn't escape it and frankly I didn't want to.'

> Miss Käutel was our leader and although a dedicated Nazi, she was a wonderful person. She sang with us, taught us handicrafts and led us on outdoor expeditions. Having retired from teaching, she now spent all her time serving the Führer. She was very ugly – I have rarely seen anyone as plain – but because she made everything so interesting for us we really loved her. She didn't try to influence us politically. Maybe she did that later but by that time I had left. At Christmas we performed nativity plays in old people's homes and in hospitals. It was just like the Girl Guides.[3]

Through the League a wealth of new experiences opened up to Oberstdorf girls – camping, tracking animals, studying plants,

* As a child, Thea Stempfle was furious when her staunchly Catholic mother sewed a swastika on to her doll's dress the wrong way round.

gymnastics, singing patriotic songs, listening to stories round the campfire – and much else. For teenage girls who had grown up within the constraints of a rural Catholic community, this was heady stuff.

As for the boys, they were given even greater opportunities. Any lad who proved himself in training or on the sports field was entitled to wear a multitude of coloured cords, stripes, badges, epaulettes or stars to show off his rank and achievements to the world. On Sundays after training they were given free tickets to the cinema, where they watched films like *Hitlerjunge Quex* (*Hitler Youth Quex*), in which boys just like themselves performed heroic deeds for the Führer. Those who had dreamed of learning to ride horses could now do so for free at the newly founded SS riding school. In 1934 a gliding troop was set up, and the municipal council provided land for an airfield where the teenagers were soon building and flying their own machines. Best of all were the magical evenings when boys and girls met in the summer twilight at the top of the Hofmannsruh (a hill overlooking Oberstdorf) or on the banks of the River Stillach to sing Nazi songs round the campfire. Songs like 'Our Flag Beats Before Us'; 'The Ranks are Closed'; 'Feeble Bones Are Trembling'; 'Hear the Beating Drums'; 'Carry the Flame Away'; 'Beyond the Valley Stood their Tents' and, most famous of all, the 'Horst Wessel' song.

There was another aspect to membership of the youth groups that must have delighted many teenagers – release from parental authority. Farm children were used to working hard from a young age, but as the Hitler Youth and League of German Girls absorbed more and more of their lives, there was correspondingly less time for scrubbing out cowsheds. Some parents no doubt resented this kidnapping of their offspring.

Certainly, a number of the more conservative Oberstdorf farmers refused to allow their daughters to join the League, but whether this was from disapproval of the Nazis or because of an innate suspicion of change is hard to say. Whatever the views of individual families, it became increasingly difficult, even dangerous, to resist the intense pressure put on children to join these youth organisations. And as the Nazis continued to tell farmers that they were the rock on which the National Socialist revolution had been built, more of those initially resistant became persuaded.

Not, however, the Berktold sisters, members of a prominent local family whose deep distrust of the Nazis never wavered. Their father had died young, leaving his widow, a farm and thirteen children – ten of them girls – to support. When it came to spurning the League of German Girls, theirs was an acceptable alibi even by Nazi standards. This was just as well since Ida Berktold was quite clear that she 'hated the League and Miss Käutel who was 150% Nazi'. Instead she joined the more traditional Queen Louise Society. 'We wore nice blue dresses and there were no *Hitlar*.'[4]

Whether or not parents approved of their children spending so much time with either organisation was, however, largely irrelevant since their authority continued to be massively eroded by the state as the decade progressed.

In the summer of 1934, twenty Oberstdorf boys took part in a two-week Hitler Youth highland camp at Murnau, seventy miles to the north-east. Charlotte Stirius went along to report for the *OGF*. She was impressed by the discipline and order in the vast camp, and particularly by the *Thingplatz* (Thing Place), big enough for all 6,000 boys to assemble. A *Thing* was an outdoor gathering of ancient Germanic tribes and the inspiration behind the massive theatres, based on Greek amphitheatres, built by the Nazis to stage their extravaganzas. These were immense multi-media events often involving entire battalions of SA or Hitler Youth. 'From the stage of Thingplatz,' wrote Stirius, 'these words shone out over the landscape: "We are born to die for Germany! We the young, vow to follow in the footsteps of the two million who gave their lives for the Fatherland. As long as German families are willing to die for their homes and their country, Germany will live!"'[5]

A year later, Oberstdorf hosted its own mountain camp organised by the local Hitler Youth and the public welfare department. Two and a half thousand boys from the Chemnitz area (300 miles away in east Germany) stayed in the mountains for two weeks. They set up their own telephone line and post office and built a well, a trough with fresh spring water for washing, and a latrine they nicknamed the League of Nations.* Stirius's enthusiasm for all this youthful endeavour was undiminished. 'Anyone who wants to understand the young and their desires', she wrote, 'will rejoice to see this merry band preparing itself for service to the People and Fatherland.'[6]

But the crowning glory for Oberstdorf's Hitler Youth was their visit to the Nuremberg Rally in 1935. It was at this rally that the notorious Nuremberg Laws were announced that were to strip Germany's Jews of their citizenship. In view of the tramping boots and beating drums, the sweeping searchlights, flaming torches, and thousands of gigantic red and black swastikas beating in the breeze, not to mention the thunderous roar of the vast crowd's *Sieg* and *Heil* whenever the Führer

* Hitler had taken Germany out of the League of Nations in October 1933.

appeared, it is unlikely that the boys from Oberstdorf paid much attention to the fate of the Jews.

⌐

The building of one of the Nazis' *Ordensburgen* (order castles) in Sonthofen was to have a considerable impact on the surrounding region. These purpose-built fortresses – inspired and named after a medieval Teutonic order – were Nazi academies designed to produce the Third Reich's future leaders. Hitler intended that four castles were to be built, but in the end only three were completed. Sonthofen's Ordensburg – a formidable building that still dominates the town – housed one of about a dozen Adolf Hitler Schools (AHS) scattered throughout Germany. Here fourteen- to eighteen-year-old boys would undergo rigorous training to prepare them for top leadership roles in the party. Apart from their racial purity and perfect health, those chosen were the strongest, fastest and most ruthless among their peers – the cream of the Hitler Youth. From 1937 a weekly exercise in eugenics took place when carefully selected Oberstdorf girls, their blonde hair impeccably plaited, were bussed up to the castle to partner the boys for folk dancing. The headmaster, Rudolf Raab, was only twenty-five years old when he was appointed and had not even completed his teacher training. He may have been young and inexperienced, but as an early member of the SA and an Old Fighter who had joined the NSDAP at the age of seventeen, his qualifications for the job were considered beyond reproach.

The original concept was that after graduating from the AHS, spending six months in a labour camp and two years in the army, these reinvented 'Teutonic knights' would then attend in sequence all three of the Ordensburgen as each had its own focus. At Sonthofen, for instance, the young men were to be immersed in Nazi ideology and diplomacy. It was a system in which secondary school, military training and 'university' formed one cohesive block of Nazi indoctrination. In the end, preparations for war overtook the scheme so that the Sonthofen Ordensburg never fulfilled its intended function. Instead, apart from housing the AHS, it was used for conferences, mountain training and even as a hotel for Nazi officials.

Not all parents were keen for their children to have the 'privilege' of attending these institutions. In November 1937, when Hitler visited Sonthofen to inspect the recently completed Ordensburg (built by Hermann Giesler, one of his two favourite architects, Albert Speer being the other) Wilhelm Steiner's nephew, Franz Noichl, was there. Along with hundreds of other schoolchildren, who had been given the day off and a free train ticket to attend, he stood by the road waving a swastika and cheering the Führer:

> I was eight and remember standing about three metres away from the open car in which Hitler drove by with his arm raised. My father had said goodbye to me with the shocking remark that this would be a good opportunity 'to shoot the criminal' . . . At the time, I hadn't understood what he meant because everyone else was cheering and praising Hitler – our great leader who, as the school inspector had explained to us when he visited our class, had ended unemployment and wiped out the disgrace of defeat.[7]

A proud, independent forester, Franz's father Xaver Noichl was a socialist through and through. When his son later became a Hitler Youth leader and therefore entitled to wear the coveted red and white cord, Franz records how his father 'just shook his head and said that my eyes would soon be opened'.

Franz was an exceptionally bright boy and not long after the Sonthofen episode, his teacher told him that she wanted to recommend him for a place in another elite Nazi school – a *Nationalpolitische Erziehungsanstalt* (NPEA, National Political Educational Institution, better known as Napola). Organised along similar lines to the Adolf Hitler Schools, there were only about thirty of these SS-operated boarding schools in the whole country, so for a boy from Franz's background this was a great honour. 'I didn't know exactly what a Napola was,' wrote Noichl, 'but it quickly became clear to me when the young female teacher asked: "Your father is in the party, isn't he?"' When she learned that he was not, the subject was dropped and never again mentioned. Franz's cousin Thaddäus, Wilhelm Steiner's son, actually passed the Napola entrance exam but, not surprisingly, his socialist parents refused to let him go. Perhaps in more urban communities, or in a village where the mayor was more aggressively Nazi, such a refusal might have had adverse consequences for the family, but the Steiners and Noichls appear to have emerged unscathed from their unwelcome brush with Nazi elitism.

~

Whether or not they were the 'cream' selected to attend the elite schools, every young person underwent many hours studying Nazi ideology in the classroom. In 1935, the *Gauleiter* of East Bavaria and Bavarian Minister of Education, Hans Schemm, published a digest of his speeches. They reveal the astonishing extent to which this son of a cobbler and founder in 1928 of the National Socialist Teachers' Association had become obsessed with the issue of race. 'Race is God-ordained,' he wrote. 'Each sin against racial purity is a sin against God's will and the created order.' Nazi propagandists considered this 'insight' to be of such significance that it was printed on a poster and widely distributed. In another speech, while addressing German youth at large, Schemm made an equally memorable statement: 'You have been born in the greatest age of your people's history.'[8] As Minister of Education, Schemm had the final say on what was to be taught in schools throughout Bavaria, a responsibility that he (and, after he was killed in an aeroplane crash in 1935, his colleagues) took very seriously.

The level to which his detailed instructions on the teaching of Nazi ideology were carried out varied considerably from school to school. Many teachers all over Germany despised the new syllabuses but were caught in a trap. One young schoolmaster confessed to a British educationalist that he and many of his colleagues would have even preferred concentration camp to the daily torture of teaching Nazi doctrine were it not for the fact that their dependants would also be made to suffer.[9]

For years Dr Eduard Bessler, headmaster of Oberstdorf's secondary school, attempted to keep both his job and his integrity – not an easy challenge under the Nazis. In October 1935 he received a letter from the head of the local Hitler Youth congratulating him on the school's 95 per cent membership, which allowed the school to fly the Hitler Youth flag on special occasions. At the same time, however, in direct contradiction to party policy he succeeded in listing religion as the most important subject on the curriculum – even above German.[10]

Keeping his Nazi masters happy while providing as humanitarian an education for his students as possible was an extraordinarily hard feat to accomplish. Bessler had to be ever vigilant. In an environment where brainwashed children were urged to denounce any anti-Nazi behaviour on the part of their teachers, this balancing act required great skill, especially when it came to teaching sensitive subjects like history. Regina Zirkel, who had taught at the school since 1932, remembered her own children recounting how deftly Bessler dealt with questions designed to trip him up.[11] One pupil in particular, Margot Helmling, whose dentist father was an SS-*Scharführer* and therefore a highly prominent Nazi in the village, was always on the lookout for anyone infringing party dogma. 'She made life very unpleasant,' recalled Sybille von Arminsted. 'Outside school we were protected by my mother but in school it was much harder. Margot tormented us and as we were taught in small classes, we often felt trapped.'[12] When interviewed in 1947, many of Bessler's former pupils testified that, even though he was a party member, they believed that he had done his best to keep politics out of the classroom.

Nevertheless, despite Bessler's attempts to curb the effects of National Socialism on his school, the changes to the curriculum were devastating. In the examinations held in early March 1933, most students had written an essay on 'The mountains: A pleasure, a benefit or a threat?'. A year later the topic was 'Having a great leader in turbulent times is the finest benefit for a nation. (To be proven with examples from recent and especially very recent German history).'[13] Students in the two most senior classes now took part in exercises at the nearby shooting range. They also went regularly to the Rubihorn to observe the Landsberg Mountain Artillery conduct sniper training. Aeronautical engineering, a new subject on the curriculum, was optional but another, the study of race and heredity was mandatory for everyone. In 1935, the final year's science examination included the following questions:

'What do Mendel's* laws tell us about the inheritance of hidden hereditary diseases? What does the multiplication of hereditary offspring mean for a people? Explain Mendel's laws with examples.'[14]

Sybille von Arminsted has challenged the generally accepted view that anti-Semitism was not rife in Oberstdorf by maintaining it was present in the village from the earliest days of the Reich, despite the small number of Jews living there. She remembered two Jewish sisters who were constantly bullied at school:

> I have forgotten their names but I have felt guilty about them all my life. We were all so infected by race propaganda. I thought the Jews were lining their pockets too much so I, too, joined in tormenting them. Children are very cruel. They went to England and I feel so ashamed now remembering how much I wanted them to leave. They did no harm to anyone but that was the way we all felt then. I have no idea what their father did because it was of no interest to me.[15]

The fact that Oberstdorf's Jewish inhabitants were so few, and that the students lived so far from any big city, must have led many of them to regard their 'race' lessons as little more than theory. But the reality of Nazi racist policy was brought sharply home by an event that occurred in 1935, the year Jews were deprived of their citizenship. The incident was to leave a permanent scar on the then fourteen-year-old Sybille:

---

* Gregor Mendel (1822–54) was the Augustinian friar credited with founding the modern science of genetics.

Mrs Puhlschneider had a daughter called Liselotte who was in our class and a good friend of mine. She had no idea that her mother was half Jewish, especially since her mother was more Nazi than the rest of us put together. When the truth eventually came out, this lovely girl committed suicide. That was truly terrible. I often think about it. What a tragedy.[16]

Politics apart, by 1935 Bessler could look on his achievements with satisfaction. More classrooms had been added over the years, the students had access to a brand-new gymnasium and, thanks to his tireless efforts, the school was now securely funded by the state. That year he had registered 149 pupils, 40 per cent of them living outside the village. Perhaps most important of all, his students loved him despite his tendency to shout. 'Sometimes it seemed as if the whole school reverberated with his roaring,' wrote Sybille von Arminsted:

Once I locked myself in the lavatory until he had stopped yelling. But no one took it very seriously. He was essentially a kind man. I liked him as I did most of the teachers, who were nearly all young. The chemistry and geography teacher was the most active Nazi on the staff. We used to get him going on Hitler Youth so that we didn't have to do any work. We were constantly knitting for *Winterhilfe* [winter aid].[17]

At the school's leaving ceremony in 1935, almost all the pupils appeared smartly turned out in Hitler Youth or League of German Girls uniforms. Bessler, on the other hand, had squeezed himself into a shabby SA uniform (he had joined the reserves in 1933) that was much too tight. After a presentation glorifying the Fatherland, the students gave a robust rendering of the 'Horst Wessel' song. Then Bessler rose to address them. He started conventionally enough by telling his pupils how well he understood their joy at escaping school and setting out on adult life. But when he asked them to remain faithful to the religion of their forefathers and to trust their souls in whatever they chose to do, he was straying into dangerous territory. Dedicated young Aryans were not supposed to dwell on their souls. As one treatise on National Socialist education put it: 'Their bodies must be steeled, made hard and strong, so that the youth may become capable soldiers who are healthy; tough, trained, energetic, and able to bear hardships.'[18] Bessler, however, seems to have forgotten this as he continued his mild speech. He asked his students, at a time when the regime was doing its best to replace the family with the state, to show particular gratitude to their parents, who by supporting them through secondary school had given them such a good start in life.

By demonstrating his genuine sympathy with the students, and by reminding them of their fundamental humanity, Bessler was in effect offering a seditious alternative to the Nazi propaganda that bombarded the young day after day. To resounding applause, he brought the ceremony to a close – not with the usual triple *Heil*-ing – but by wishing his departing students 'the best of luck and a happy journey into their new life'.[19]

9

God and Hitler

The Nazis wasted no time in abolishing religions and religious organisations – Jehovah's Witnesses, the Seventh Day Adventists and the Salvation Army among them. Many in the leading ranks of the party would no doubt have liked to abolish the mainstream religions as well, but since Christian belief was so deeply entrenched in the country this was not a realistic option. The alternative was to remould the existing Churches in the National Socialist image to form one national Church and religion. Since much of the Nazis' support had in the recent elections derived from the country's 40 million Protestants, it was hardly surprising that many of them now flocked to the Nazified German Evangelical Church. Within this Church, a powerful division of some 600,000 dedicated Nazis became known as the German Christians. They did not, however, go unchallenged. The Confessing Church (of which Martin Niemöller and Dietrich Bonhoeffer were key founders) emerged in opposition to the German Christians in 1934, thus splitting Germany's Protestant Church in two.

According to some estimates, by the early 1930s around a fifth of all Protestant clergy held Nazi sympathies while one in four was a party member. Many showed no hesitation in 'worshipping' Hitler in their sermons and prayers.[1] Indeed, a number of German Christians were so fanatically pro-Nazi that they called for Hitler's *Mein Kampf* to replace the Bible, since it was now 'the people's most sacred text; their greatest, purest and truest moral code'.[2] One German Christian priest[3] from the Bavarian town of Mühldorf (he was to serve a second term as its mayor after the war) wrote, 'At present the image of Luther hangs in our churches but the next generation will exchange it for one of Hitler – the man who saved Germany from destruction.'[4]

Heinrich Seiler, pastor to Oberstdorf's small Protestant community, arrived in the village in 1932. His church had been inaugurated in 1906 in response to demand from the increasing numbers of Protestant visitors during the summer months. Dwarfed by the Catholics, the permanent Protestant population in the village barely reached 100 – the great majority of them women. The aristocratic Countess Ludmilla Castell-Castell led the church council while the former opera singer Hertha Stolzenberg directed the choir, providing the church's small congregation with exceptionally high-quality music. Seiler had been a fiery young man who, alongside the *Freikorps*, had fought communists in the immediate aftermath of the First World War. Now, he was equally determined to take on the Nazis and was to become a fervent member of the Confessing Church. So strong were his religious and political convictions that on 7 May 1933, in the crowded Baur Café on the marketplace, he had openly attacked the regime, despite the presence of the Nazi deputy mayor, Hans Müller.

It must have been particularly difficult for Seiler when, six months after that episode, on the anniversary of Luther's birth, he had to watch the Nazi mayors, Zettler and Müller, march into his church followed by the municipal councillors, party activists and the leaders of the Hitler Youth. The latter, holding aloft large swastikas, took up position either side of the altar. 'God has sent us Adolf Hitler today,' declared the key-note speaker, 'just as he sent Martin Luther four hundred and fifty years ago.'[5] A few months later the inevitable happened. Accused by Oberstdorf's SA leaders of misleading the villagers with his inflammatory rhetoric, Seiler was denounced to the Gestapo. It was only thanks to the intervention of Kreisleiter Kalhammer that he escaped Dachau.[6] Refusing to modify his views, Seiler did at least try to proceed with greater caution by deploying more subtle ways of defying the Nazis and thus avoiding arrest.

As for the Catholic Church, its relations with the Nazis deteriorated so rapidly in the course of the decade that its clergy were soon living under constant threat of arrest by the Gestapo. In 1933, about a third of all Germans, 70 per cent of Bavarians and almost 90 per cent of Oberstdorfers were Catholic. Despite losing their political representation, Catholics had, in the rural areas especially, remained a strong unified force, devoutly loyal to the Pope. Hitler admired the Church's strong hierarchical structure and the Pope's undisputed authority, but the fact that 20 million Germans were members of an international organisation that looked ultimately to Rome rather than Berlin for its leadership was utterly unacceptable.[7] As the rift between the Nazi authorities and the Catholic Church widened, Germans were encour-aged not just to reject the Church but also to confront it. In June 1933 eight young Oberstdorfers travelled to Munich to join the 20,000 taking part in the Catholic Journeymen's Association Congress. As they arrived by train from all over Bavaria, the SA, SS and Hitler Youth moved in and beat them up so badly that the whole event had to be aborted.[8]

In the village itself, the Franciscan nuns were one of the first groups to be seriously affected by the regime. Although few in number, they were a significant presence in Oberstdorf and from their comfortable quarters in the primary school they ran a nursery school, educated the village girls up to the age of fourteen and operated a weather station. They also received a considerable income from their highly successful sewing and knitting workshop. But for the municipal council, now focused on implementing Nazi policy to strip schools of all religious authority, such achievements counted for little.

The nuns survived the first year of the Reich, but with difficulty. Their salary, paid by the council, was almost halved, and in a particularly spiteful gesture their piano was seized (for Deputy Mayor Müller's smart new orchestra) and Sister Corbara forbidden to give music lessons.* As one of the nuns put it, 'we are trapped in a constant struggle that demands our endless patience and causes us severe nervous tension'.[9] Then abruptly in August 1934, without any warning, Müller terminated Oberstdorf's teaching contract with the nuns. Their nursery school was to close immediately, and the older children were in future to be taught by secular teachers.

As devout Catholics, Oberstdorfers were very attached to their nuns, so when news of their dismissal became public they were incensed. The district school inspector, Thomas Steidele, took up their cause. He suggested circulating a questionnaire among the parents asking if they wished the Franciscan Sisters to continue teaching their daughters. But before it could be

* Only after Sister Corbara had joined the Nazi-controlled *Reichsmusikkammer* (Reich Chamber of Music), which promoted 'good' German music and suppressed 'degenerate' music such as jazz and atonal works, was she permitted to teach music again.

distributed, the nuns received a curious piece of advice from Ludwig Fink (at that time the village's Nazi leader, who was soon to be sworn in as mayor). 'He was very helpful,' one of the nuns recorded, 'and hinted to us not to present our findings until 19 September.'[10] The reason was soon clear. On that day Fink was to be installed as the new mayor and so would then be in a position to come to the Sisters' aid. When the parents' vote came through, it was a resounding 'yes' – 266 out of 286 in favour.[11] Fink's support, together with the decisive vote, enabled the nuns to continue teaching the girls in the primary school. That Fink should have shown the slightest concern for the fate of a few politically undesirable nuns marks him out as an unusual Nazi. Furthermore, as became apparent over the course of the next decade, this was by no means the only occasion when he would act in direct opposition to party doctrine.

Anxious to avoid political censure, the five Sisters contributed generously (despite their fast-dwindling resources) to the Nazis' constant demands for 'voluntary' donations and even joined the torchlight parades that had become such a hallmark of the regime.[12] The nuns' ability to endure such a stressful existence was largely thanks to the leadership of Sister Biunda. A tall, softly spoken woman whose gentle manner belied her natural authority, she preserved a sense of calm determination within her little flock. One of her students, for whom knitting was a perpetual battle, recalled how Sister Biunda would take her tangled mess and return it within seconds looking perfect. Another remembered her virtuosic handling of a large pair of scissors. 'She cut the fabric without hesitation, trusting in her experience, skill – and God.'[13]

As the Nazis' grip on both country and village tightened, the Sisters' workshop became a much-sought-after refuge for Oberstdorf women. Here, in tranquillity, they would gather to embroider, knit and sew. Prominent among them was the mayor's devoutly Catholic wife, often accompanied by Werner, the Finks' teenage epileptic son. But the workshop, too, was under threat. The nuns' output was so prolific and of such high quality that Oberstdorf's professional seamstresses had long chafed at the competition. The current political climate with all its rules and regulations now gave them an opportunity to have the nuns put out of business permanently. The problem was that none of the Sisters possessed the qualifications required by the Nazi authorities either to market their wares or to teach sewing classes. Seizing on this, Oberstdorf's seamstresses petitioned the Augsburg Chamber of Crafts to close down the nuns' workshop. Their attempt failed, but it did little to improve the Sisters' shattered nerves.

Still the nuns struggled on, until the final blow came in January 1937 when an order from Munich insisted on the removal of all religious teachers from schools throughout Bavaria. This time not even Mayor Fink could save them. After nearly thirty years, they had no choice but to pack up and leave the school. Although they soon found temporary accommodation, their future looked bleak. One of them summed up the situation:

> Probably 90 per cent of the population of Oberstdorf is very supportive to us and wants to make sure that we do not suffer, but ordinary people cannot help much because they have so little to give, and the wealthy feel that in such uncertain economic times they must hold on to what they have.[14]

Morale rose briefly when Fräulein Flora Gschwender, co-owner of the Gschwender department store on the marketplace, offered the nuns a plot of land on which to build their own house. The plans passed through every conceivable hoop until they landed in Hermann Göring's office in Berlin. It seems scarcely credible that Göring, the second most powerful figure in the Nazi hierarchy, should have concerned himself with the housing arrangements of a handful of nuns in a far-off mountain village, but he did, or at least his officials did. The scheme did not meet with approval and so was abandoned.[15]

The nuns finally found a new home in October 1937:

On 15 October, Haug, the removal man, delivered our belongings to the house (for a second time) free of charge. Members of the Catholic Journeymen's Association . . . transported the kitchen, workshop and chapel furnishings in an equally kind manner. But we were so physically and mentally exhausted that Sister Biunda declared: 'Better to die than to move again.'

After so many years living in the spacious school, adjustment to their new, much more confined quarters was not easy:

As we are forced to accept resort visitors because of the high rent, we have to live very modestly: two bedrooms between the five of us with the kitchen serving as dining room. We need two large rooms for the workshop, a music room and somewhere to prepare candidates. A room on the first floor holds our only treasure: the Blessed Sacrament.[16]

They had only been in their new rooms a month when they were hit by yet another setback. On 18 November, the police, tipped off by the Guild of Handicrafts, arrived to shut down their workshop. This time it was not just the Oberstdorf nuns who were being targeted. Convent workshops throughout Germany were ordered to close on the grounds that, without a master craftsman's diploma, the nuns were working illegally. For the Oberstdorf Sisters it was a desperate situation since their workshop had become their main source of income.

But the intervention (prompted by Fink and others) of Oberstdorf's most famous master craftsman, Josef Schratt, saved them. Schratt's worldwide fame sprang from an unusual achievement. In 1930 he had made the biggest shoe in the world using nine cattle skins, 75 kilos of glue, 150 kilos of artificial leather and 45 metres of mountain guide rope. Schratt managed to arrange for Sister Biunda to be placed on the master craftsman register without her having to pass the examination. Thus, the nuns survived. Although it was necessary for them to take jobs in children's homes as parish clerks and music teachers to make ends meet, sewing remained at the heart of their activities. By 1938 their workshop was once again the haven of companionable enterprise on which so many village women had come to depend.

In order to survive from day to day, the nuns – like Catholic clergy everywhere – were forced throughout the 1930s to show allegiance to a regime whose ultimate aim was to abolish them. On a crisp, cold February day in 1936 the Sisters were seated in the packed church where the whole village had gathered to bid their parish priest, Father Isidor Kohl, farewell on his retirement. It was a major village event and Mayor Fink and Deputy Mayor Müller, together with other Nazi bigwigs, sat prominently in the front pew. After the splendid new organ with its forty-nine tones, nine transmission registers and sixty pipes had been inaugurated, a performance of Beethoven trios was received with 'a storm of applause'.[17]

But what must the nuns have thought when on this great occasion they heard Father Kohl declare that 'the fruitful cooperation and peaceful agreement between Church and State' ranked among his most beautiful Oberstdorf memories?[18] Kohl's words rang especially hollow since, quite apart from the nuns' own continuing struggles with the authorities, Goebbels was at that very moment whipping up a campaign against the Catholic clergy, accusing them of sexual and financial corruption. And only days before Kohl's mellifluous words, three priests had been sentenced in nearby Kempten to long terms of imprisonment for criticising the regime. In his efforts to dovetail God and Hitler, Father Kohl epitomised the dilemma facing Catholics across the country.

The priest who replaced him, Josef Rupp, was to prove less compliant than his predecessor, thus putting himself at constant risk of arrest as the Nazis' noose tightened around the Catholic Church in the late 1930s. Rupp had previously lived in Heilbronn, where his open hostility to the regime and specific criticism of the Hitler Youth had led the Gestapo to search his house. For this reason, Rupp's superiors thought it prudent to send him far away to a politically less dangerous job. He found his new parish gratifyingly devout, despite Kohl's concerns over the bad influence of tourism and the high rate of illegitimacy – one in every eight births was out of wedlock. A great solace for Rupp was the church itself – light and airy; richly adorned with carvings, paintings and colourful statues, it stood as an unfailing source of reassurance and inspiration for the whole village. Rupp's sister acted as his housekeeper, a role she carried out with such pious frugality that the village women became worried about the young curate always looking so thin and cold. Although they managed to supply him with extra bread, Fräulein Rupp immediately confiscated the small stove they had attempted to smuggle into his room.

The real battle on Rupp's hands was that of winning the hearts and minds of Oberstdorf's youth. It was a bitter struggle and one in which the Nazis pulled no punches. Despite the forced dissolution of Catholic youth groups, many of Oberstdorf's young still attended the main Mass on Sunday and a number still participated as altar boys. But there was constant pressure on them to switch their allegiance unreservedly to the Fatherland. In later years, when the leader of Franz Noichl's Hitler Youth group discovered that his protégé was also a keen altar boy, he told Franz in no uncertain terms that he would have to choose between God and Hitler – he could not serve both. 'After several sleepless nights,' recalled Franz,

> I went to the priest to explain my predicament. He told me that only I could decide. He could not do it for me. When I visited him again a few days later, I tearfully explained that I did not want to give up the Hitler Youth red and white badge, and that I would have to stop being an altar boy. Rupp comforted me and I promised him that even as a Hitler Youth leader, I would remain a good Christian.

Rupp must have known that he was fighting a losing battle. But perhaps Franz's tearful promise gave him some small measure of comfort. It was a big decision for a boy who had grown up imbued in the Catholic rituals that were such an integral part of village life. 'I especially loved Good Friday,' Franz recalled, 'because the Holy Sepulchre was covered in beautiful coloured glass balls.' The highlight of Oberstdorf's Easter celebrations was the raising of the dead Saviour from His grave. This was accomplished by means of a cogwheel that caused a statue of Christ holding a flag of victory to rise slowly up.* For the most devout among the villagers, the Nazis' 'religious' panoply of torchlight parades, tribal rituals or spectacular bonfires could never compete with such sacred moments in their own Catholic faith, which had been celebrated by countless generations before them.

Despite their enthusiasm, the altar boys did not give their priest an easy time and Father Rupp often had to endure their pranks. When it was particularly cold in the church he used to warm the Communion wine by briefly placing it in a small box heated with an electric light bulb. The altar boys, however, would contrive to leave the wine in the box much longer. Then with expressions of complete innocence, they would watch the unfortunate Rupp scald his mouth as he sipped the holy wine.[19] On one occasion another of their games resulted in the arrest of the sexton. 'U-boat alarm' was played up in the steeple, where they went regularly to ring the church bells. Using the swastika as a hammock, they would swing the largest boy (the U-boat captain) from side to side until the day it dramatically split with a loud ripping noise. They rolled it up and put it back in its usual place, but when the sexton later hoisted the flag its tattered appearance was there for all to see. It was a serious enough offence to land the sexton in Dachau, a fate he was only spared when the altar boys owned up.[20]

In such a climate of fear the smallest battles took on great significance. In 1938, Rupp wrote to his bishop in Augsburg.

* One Easter, this sacred moment was shattered by a howl of pain from an altar boy who had caught his finger in the machinery.

An awkward situation had arisen when a large swastika had been erected on the church spire without his permission. Each night over Easter, the most sacred festival in the Christian calendar, the illuminated swastika had been visible for miles around.[21] A week later, Rupp wrote again to the bishop confirming that his suspicions had proved correct. The swastika had been placed there on the instructions of Mayor Fink, who assumed that because the municipal council paid for the maintenance of the church spire it was entitled to fly a swastika on it. The good news, reported Rupp, was that 'the eight electric bulbs' did not pose any danger. The bad news was that the swastika was about to be replaced by a much bigger one.[22] The record does not relate what happened next, but on 18 May Rupp was able to inform the bishop 'that after a quiet, unemotional discussion with the authorities, the swastika has been removed from the spire'.[23] It was only a temporary victory since a year later, on Hitler's birthday, the swastika was again flying on the church spire.

Rupp, like so many other dissidents, was to become expert in appearing to conform to Nazi regulations while in fact subtly subverting them. As Oberstdorf was a large and widely dispersed village it was essential to keep parishioners informed of services and other church matters with a leaflet normally sent out by post. But in October 1938, Rupp received a letter signed by the president of the *Reichspressekammer* (Reich Press Chamber), stating that thenceforward distribution of such publications would be illegal. In response he continued to print the news sheets, but instead of posting them left them at the church door for anyone to take free of charge. A more zealous Nazi than Mayor Fink might have prevented him from doing even this, but Rupp continued to produce his leaflets unchallenged.

Then in the spring of 1939 he launched a 'Holy Mission', the first in Oberstdorf for a decade. Partly because of its very rarity, this event was considered to be one of immense significance in the life of a Catholic community. The concept was simple enough. Through additional church services, lectures, home visits and group discussions, the villagers would reinvigorate and intensify their faith in the space of a few days. The grand climax was a candle-lit procession on Easter Sunday. For Rupp to have initiated such an event marks him out as a priest of real courage, because in Nazi terms his Holy Mission was nothing more than a blatant political protest. And in any case, as he confessed to his bishop, he had little hope that it would have any lasting effect. The priest must have been acutely aware of the risk he was taking and of how lucky he was to escape arrest.

Rupp was pleased that so many women and children turned out for the Holy Mission, but disappointed at the poor showing of the male population. Given, however, that sixty-four villagers, most of them probably men, had abandoned Catholicism since Hitler came to power, this was hardly surprising.[24] In any case, the village men in general (Xaver Noichl is a good example) tended to be less enthusiastic churchgoers than the women. They, after all, had the mountains, the pub and their *Stammtische*. But for women like Frau Noichl, the church provided one of the few diversions from the daily grind. Inside the lovely interior of St John's, the women enjoyed precious moments of peace and quiet while outside they could meet and chat with their friends.

Corpus Christi, held in May or June, was another big Catholic event traditionally celebrated in Oberstdorf with a lavish procession through the village. Father Rupp again sailed dangerously close to the wind when in 1939 he allowed it to go ahead despite the Nazi ban on religious parades. Perhaps the fact that Mayor Fink's wife was a particularly pious Catholic was reassuring. Although only six years old, Wilhelm Steiner's son Thaddäus (Franz Noichl's cousin) carried the cross around the marketplace in the traditional manner. In old age he remembered the moment when he reached the church door, where a large crowd had gathered; Frau Fink came forward and said, 'Hosch guet g'macht' (dialect for 'well done') and thrust money into his hand.[25]

However devoted Frau Fink was to her husband, she remained first and foremost a loyal Catholic, consistently putting her religious faith above loyalty to the party. A photograph of the couple with their two sons shows Fink in a sympathetic light, appearing very much as the relaxed family man. With none of the paraphernalia usually to be seen in photographs of Nazi officials, it is hard to remember that this kindly-looking individual was in fact a National Socialist mayor charged with implementing Hitler's policies as ruthlessly as he saw fit. Did Fink come to the aid of the nuns, agree to remove the swastika from the church steeple and allow Father Rupp's Holy Mission to go ahead in deference to his wife? Or was it because his Nazi convictions were tempered by his own innate humanity? The Finks' intriguing domestic situation was complex, but one that must surely have been widely replicated in households across Germany.

10

Towards War

Only nine days after becoming chancellor, Hitler had outlined his rearming strategy in stark terms. 'The next five years in Germany must be devoted to the rearmament of the German people,' he had told his ministers. 'Every publicly supported job creation scheme should be judged by the criterion of whether it is necessary from the point of view of the rearmament of the German people.'[1] For example, the manufacture of iron and steel, engineering and motorway-building, were to take immediate precedence over industries that were not directly contributing to the infrastructure or machinery of war. Until 1935, these plans were kept secret, camouflaged as 'job creation' schemes, but in that year the Nazis went public by announcing the formation of the Luftwaffe along with the reintroduction of general military conscription, urgently needed for the army's thirty-six new divisions. Furthermore, on 18 June the Anglo-German Agreement was signed, allowing Germany to expand its navy beyond the strict limits imposed by the Treaty of Versailles. The *Wehrmacht* (the collective name for all the Nazi armed forces) had been well and truly launched. Then, on 7 March 1936, in breathtaking defiance of the Allies, Hitler moved his military forces into the demilitarised Rhineland. The Treaty of Versailles was dead, Germany's march to war unstoppable.

The 99th Regiment of the Mountain Brigade (*Gebirgstruppe*) formed in Garmisch-Partenkirchen (about fifty miles from Oberstdorf as the crow flies) on 15 October 1935, was an elite light infantry force composed of men who had lived and worked in the mountains all their lives. Only supremely fit individuals could operate at high altitude in such unforgiving terrain. Everything needed to sustain life had to be carried on the soldiers' backs except their weaponry, which was transported by mule – or sometimes, in the Caucasus, by camel. Scaling precipitous, icy slopes for hours, sometimes days on end in appalling weather while carrying a heavy pack was not for the faint-hearted. An exceptionally close camaraderie existed among these mountain troops. In April 1938, the 98th and 99th Regiments of the Mountain Ranger Brigade (plus the more recently formed 100th) were transferred to the newly created 1st Mountain Division under the command of Major-General Ludwig Kübler. As more of Oberstdorf's young men were to serve in these regiments during the Second World War (particularly the 99th) than in any other, the Division was to have a major impact on the village.

Despite being a forty-two-year-old war veteran, Wilhelm Steiner was drafted into the army in March 1938, denounced, or so he believed, by a work colleague who disapproved of his socialist politics. But this time Steiner's military service was to last only a few weeks while his regiment, the 99th Mountain Ranger Brigade, consisted almost entirely of fellow Bavarians. It was, therefore, the best possible unit for a man like Steiner.

With its distinctive profile, the 99th was ideally suited to play a key role in Hitler's annexation of Austria – the *Anschluss*. The idea of Germany and Austria uniting to form one nation was not a Nazi invention. Had the Allies consented to allow this to take place after the First World War, there were many citizens in both countries who would have welcomed such a merger. For the Nazis, however, unification with Austria was no mere pipe dream. It was absolutely central to their vision of a future in which the Reich's current borders would be extended to encompass all lands inhabited by ethnic Germans to form a 'Greater Germany'.

While preparing to invade Austria, Germany's armed forces made great efforts to avoid foreign scrutiny. In consequence, Corporal Steiner's regiment was ordered to walk 'discreetly' from Bad Reichenhall over the mountains to Graz, a distance of 180-odd miles. Despite his relatively mature years, there can have been few men on that rapid, demanding trek in better physical shape than Steiner, whose immense strength had once saved the life of his brother-in-law Xaver Noichl when they were logging up in the high forest. Unfazed by the rigours of surviving days in deep snow and icy conditions, he later told his son how much he had enjoyed the experience of hiking over new mountains and passes with his regiment, and how he had relished Styria's stunning peaks and forests, the deep ravines and ice-blue lakes.[2]

When the Germans poured across the border with Austria at dawn on 12 March 1938, they expected to meet resistance. Instead the soldiers were greeted with wild enthusiasm. 'The windows are open,' wrote one officer, 'everywhere is lit up and the Austrians "attack" the troops with open arms . . . They give them flowers and their horses apples.'[3] Another officer noted in his diary: 'The radiance in the eyes of the soldiers and the cheering population demonstrate that each is aware of this great historical moment.' Heinz Guderian, the famous tank general, lost his coat buttons when souvenir hunters ripped them off as he was carried shoulder-high through the streets.[4] The only casualties suffered by the German military were self-inflicted. Thirty-three men died in road accidents, many of them caused by the fact that the Austrians drove on the left. In addition, an embarrassing number of tanks ground to a halt because they had been filled up with Austrian petrol that was too low in octane for German vehicles.[5] The following day Austria was declared to exist no longer.

When Steiner and the 99th marched into Graz two days later, sanctioning the crowd's ecstatic greeting was an immense swastika flying over the town hall. But despite the city's excitement, Steiner noted that many of the shops were boarded up for fear of looters. Although he revelled in the warmth of the reception they received, nothing could change his disgust for the swastikas clutched so eagerly by the thousands of welcoming citizens. His own contribution to the *Anschluss* might easily have ended in his court martial. He somehow persuaded his comrades in the 11th company of the 99th that they could greatly increase their strength by eating tobacco. Within hours of swallowing their cigarettes, the men were incapacitated with acute diarrhoea. Was this just Steiner's quirky sense of humour, or could it have been a deliberate act of sabotage by the man who had scribbled in a book next to a defiled picture of Hitler: 'Satan, grösster Verbrecher aller Zeiten' (Satan, biggest criminal of all times)?[6] If it was a prank, his officers failed to see the joke. Steiner was sent back to Oberstdorf in disgrace. A few weeks later a sawmill accident put paid to his military career for good.[7]

The day after the *Anschluss*, Rudi Raab, headmaster of the Ordensburg AHS in Sonthofen, was motoring along a minor country road after a trip to Austria with his young family. He stopped the car at what a few hours earlier had been a small border post and with enormous satisfaction told the children how he had left orders for his students to march to the border at midnight on 12 March – the hour when the *Anschluss* became official. One minute later, the boys had torn down the post. This was the same day that the Gestapo arrested Raab's homosexual brother Gerhard in Vienna; he was later transported to the Buchenwald concentration camp, where he was murdered.[8]

A month later, on 10 April, referenda were held in Austria and Germany seeking public approval of the *Anschluss*. Both countries voted overwhelmingly to endorse it. In Germany, the Nazis' usual techniques of terror and intimidation produced a resounding victory with over 99 per cent of the population voting 'yes' to both the *Anschluss* and to their support of Hitler's leadership. In Oberstdorf the villagers turned out to vote amid unremitting propaganda, including such headlines as: 'On 10 April Upper Allgäu will thank the Führer with a joyful, unanimous "YES".'[9] A typical instance of *Anschluss* fervour was to be seen at a nearby farmhouse where cushions embroidered with 'YES' were hung from its windows.[10] On the day of the referendum, 4,491 Oberstdorfers did indeed vote 'yes'. But not Xaver Noichl, who, along with sixty-four other brave individuals, voted 'no'. A few days after the poll, Franz Noichl and his mother were walking through the village. As they approached the town hall they saw sixty-five nooses hanging from a gallows. Next to it was a message inviting the dissenters to hang themselves. It was an image that was to haunt Franz for the rest of his life.

The referendum, accompanied by jarring militarism and ugly street violence, did little to soothe the spirits of those who

were ideologically opposed to the regime, or who like Julius
Löwin had long since been targeted by it. After qualifying as a
dentist, Julius had moved to Oberstdorf in 1927 where he set
up in practice. As most of the Jews living in Oberstdorf either
had private resources or were married to non-Jews, they were
able to exist in relative obscurity. Julius Löwin was different.
Not only did he need to work, but he also bore the added
disadvantage of being Polish. Jews from the East were widely
viewed as socially inferior, and not just by Aryans. 'Assimilated'
German Jews also tended to regard their eastern brethren with
disdain. Löwin's Polish nationality was a reflection of the post-
First World War chaos. Born in Munich, he had never in fact
set foot in Poland, but because his father was native to a part
of Austria that was handed over to Poland after the war, the
whole family became Polish by default. This greatly complicated their lives, not least because his hard-up parents had to
pay double tuition fees for their six children.

The Jewish Proskauer family were among his patients,
so when Margarethe Proskauer's sister Leni arrived for an
extended holiday in May 1936, it was inevitable that in such
a small community she and Julius would meet. Leni was a
bright, independent young woman with a doctorate in law.
She had studied in Göttingen and Munich, spent a year in Paris
and while working in Berlin had represented Kurt Weill in a
copyright case.* One evening the Proskauers invited Julius to
their house, and that was it – love at first sight. Leni recalled
the evening: 'He brought cake for my sister . . . he was awfully
good-looking . . . he also brought a bouquet of carnations, and

---

* Kurt Weill was a German-Jewish composer who famously col-
laborated with Bertolt Brecht in various productions, including his
best-known work *Die Dreigroschenoper* (*The Threepenny Opera*).

I picked one and put it behind my ear. My brother-in-law thought that was dreadfully forward.'[11] Three months later, on 15 August 1936, Julius and Leni were married.

By then the Proskauers had moved to Berlin and Löwin's once-flourishing dental practice had all but come to a standstill. Since he was no longer legally permitted to work, even his most loyal patients now stayed away for fear of being denounced. Without money or influence, any hopes the couple may have once nurtured of riding out the Nazi storm grew more hopeless with each passing day.

But, as it happened, salvation was on hand in the unlikely guise of a Dutch aristocrat – Agatha Maria Henriëtte Laman Trip-de Beaufort. Hetty, as she was generally known, first visited Oberstdorf in the early 1920s with her lawyer husband. Immaculately well connected (her father had held office in the royal household and had been Mayor of The Hague, while her mother came from the patrician Van Eck family), it was almost certainly on her recommendation that Queen Wilhelmina stayed in Oberstdorf in 1930. Unlike most privately educated girls from her background, Hetty had attended university, and her curiosity about all aspects of the human condition – including left-wing politics, in which she dabbled – showed her to be an intelligent young woman with a mind of her own. When she unexpectedly received a large legacy, she and her husband decided to spend it on creating a convalescent home for sick Dutch children. Oberstdorf, where the couple had spent several pleasant holidays, seemed the ideal location. Named 'Hohes Licht' ('High Light') after a nearby mountain and opened in 1924, it was a substantial five-storey wooden chalet encircled by wide verandas on which, weather permitting, the sick children would lie for several hours each day, breathing in the clean mountain air. Only four years later, however, Hetty's husband died of a heart attack. Instead of abandoning the sanatorium the young childless widow (she was thirty-eight) decided to continue with the help of her close German friend and ally Elisabeth Dabelstein, whom she appointed its director.

In addition to being a successful convalescent home, 'Hohes Licht' increasingly became a covert focus of opposition to National Socialism. Although Hetty seems to have had complete confidence in her staff's allegiance, the threat of denunciation must have been a persistent anxiety. However, it was in their favour, as she observed after the war, that not only were the committed uniformed Nazis in the village a minority, they were also widely regarded with suspicion, even by those holding politically neutral views. 'From the very beginning we distrusted party members,' Hetty later wrote, 'those in our mountain village as much as any in Munich and Berlin. They tended to be second- or third-rate characters, adventurers, layabouts and profiteers.'[12] Of the Oberstdorfers opposed to the Nazis, she noted that 'they somehow managed not to sell out and quietly went their own way'.[13]

The complacent attitude of Hetty's fellow countrymen to the realities of National Socialism was a source of constant frustration:

In the years between 1933 and 1940 I had to listen all too often to the well-meant gibberish of the Dutch parents who sent their children to 'Hohes Licht'. Among them were the elite of Holland and the Dutch East Indies who one would have thought were intelligent people with political insight. How often did I hear them assure me when I tried to warn them of what was happening in Germany, that Holland had nothing to fear because we were so strong. 'We have a water-line,' a government minister told me, in an attempt to be reassuring. When I related my own experiences, good friends looked at me sceptically and said that I was exaggerating. I tried sending reports to Dutch newspapers; they were returned. They did not chime with the Dutch policy of neutrality.[14]

After the Nazis came to power, 'Hohes Licht' regularly accepted Jewish children but they were always registered as 'Aryan'. The risks involved in this strategy were never more apparent than when a senior SS officer and his wife invited their daughter's friend (a patient in the home) to stay at their house, not suspecting for one moment that such a delicate little fair-haired girl could possibly be Jewish. As conditions worsened in the 1930s, Hetty arranged for many of these children to be smuggled across the border to Switzerland.

Hetty was very fond of Julius Löwin, and in defiance of Nazi regulations continued to employ him as a dentist at 'Hohes Licht'. But the day after the *Anschluss*, she dramatically announced that he and Leni must get out of Germany as soon as possible. This, however, was easier said than done. By that date the obstacles facing Jews trying to emigrate were formidable. To make matters even more challenging, the Löwins now had a small baby, but, as Leni was quick to point out to Hetty – no money. However, in one vital respect they were fortunate. Leni's brother owned a shoe shop in Beaver Dam, Wisconsin and was therefore able to act as their sponsor. On 22 April the Löwins received notification that a Dutch bank had deposited $1,000 (approximately $18,000 in 2018) 'c/o Mr Jacob, Martin's shoe store' in a Milwaukee bank, to await their arrival. It was a gift from Hetty.

They also came up with an ingenious way of raising funds

from their own resources. When Hetty and Elisabeth visited Julius, they would smuggle out sheets of the platinum foil he used to bake porcelain teeth in his dental kiln by folding them to look like bookmarks. After enough of these had been accumulated, one of the enterprising young Dutch women working at 'Hohes Licht' was able to sell them to a goldsmith in the Netherlands.[15]

After long weeks of anxious preparations the couple at last reached Hamburg, where they were to board their ship. On 20 August 1938, Leni (using her 35mm Kodak Retina) snapped Julius walking down a gangplank on to the SS *St Louis*, their ten-month-old son John in his arms.* Two days later the following announcement appeared in the *Oberallgäuer Nationalzeitung* (the *Allgäuer Anzeigeblatt* had been renamed in October 1933):

One Jew less! On 1 August the Jew Löwin, who was a dentist here, finally left our beautiful Oberstdorf. The villagers are delighted to see him depart. Löwin is emigrating to America, where so many of his race who whine about the New Germany have chosen to live. Even though he was in business here for so many years, we have allowed him to go to join his kind completely unscathed. We are joyful that yet another of the 'Chosen People' is leaving us. Now only very few Jews live in the Sonthofen district. We regard the Löwins' departure as a beautiful event.[16]

* This was the last Atlantic crossing made by the SS *St Louis* before its infamous voyage in May 1939, when Captain Gustav Schröder endeavoured to find a refuge for the 937 Jewish refugees on board. Rejected by Cuba, America and Canada, Schröder refused to return to Germany until he had found European countries to take all his passengers. In 1976 this episode was turned into a film – *Voyage of the Damned*.

As they sailed across the Atlantic, Julius and Leni received several telegrams. Hetty's was an apt quote from the Bible, while Elisabeth Dabelstein sent the old Irish blessing: 'May the road rise up to meet you and the wind be always behind you.' On 1 September the *St Louis* docked at Ellis Island, from where the Löwins moved on to Milwaukee to begin their new life.

Hetty's intuition proved prescient. The Löwins had only just got out in time. Ten weeks after their departure a young Polish Jew called Herschel Grynszpan assassinated Ernst vom Rath, a German diplomat in Paris. The Nazis' response was *Kristallnacht*, when they unleashed a wave of violence against the Jews. The windows of Jewish shops and houses were smashed, synagogues burned, hundreds killed or injured and some 30,000 transported to concentration camps. Although none of this violence touched Oberstdorf, the few Jews living there must have wondered in the wake of that terrifying night how long they could remain safe even in their distant corner of the Reich.

With the *Anschluss* successfully accomplished, Hitler could then turn his attention to Czechoslovakia. Before the First World War the Sudetenland (those parts of the country bordering Moravia, Bohemia and Czech Silesia) had belonged to Austria and were mainly inhabited by ethnic German speakers. Hitler's demands that it should now be detached from Czechoslovakia and incorporated into the Reich grew increasingly strident, eventually resulting in the Munich Agreement. When news broke on 30 September 1938 that the leaders of Great Britain, France and Italy had acceded to Hitler's demands to annex the Sudetenland, there was a great outpouring of joy across the country. War had seemed inevitable but now, with peace assured, it was clear that the Führer's aggressive tactics had paid off handsomely.

In Munich huge crowds gathered outside the hotels where Prime Ministers Neville Chamberlain and Édouard Daladier were staying, shouting again and again for the statesmen to appear on their balconies. As *Oktoberfest* had just begun, beer flowed freely and people of all ages and backgrounds danced and swayed ecstatically through the night to the music of brass bands. If in Oberstdorf celebrations were less flamboyant, they were no less joyful as everyone breathed a collective sigh of relief that war had been averted.

Certainly, Oberstdorfers shared fully in public pride at Germany's growing international status and new-found confidence. Their response to the nation's military expansion was also one of general approval, but with two important provisos – first that it did not involve bloodshed (a view generally shared throughout the country), and second that it did not interfere with their tourist trade. Consequently, the village had watched with mounting unease as the neighbouring Alpine resorts of Mittenwald, Lenggries and Bad Reichenhall were garrisoned with mountain troops. Believing they had escaped this fate, it therefore came as an unpleasant shock when in the autumn of 1937 (a year before the Munich Agreement) Mayor Fink received news that a battalion of the 1st Mountain Division (about 850 men) was to be permanently garrisoned in Oberstdorf.

Fink, his deputy mayor Kögler (who had replaced Hans Müller) and the members of both councils were devastated, knowing that such a development would utterly transform the village, particularly since its population was only around 4,000. Oberstdorf could exist as a spa or a garrison, but in their view it could not be both. By the time the village authorities were made aware of the proposal, plans were so well advanced that the location of three large barracks had already been decided. With the loss of forty-six houses (including Fink's), fields, farms and grazing pasture, eighty farmers were affected, sixteen of whom would lose all their land.[17]

The Reich Office for Regional Planning supported Oberstdorf's appeal against the decision by arguing that since a number of major Alpine resorts had already been garrisoned, at least one should be spared, but to no avail. In September 1938, Rudolf Scheller (the artist) and Fritz Holzmann (the municipal council's building expert) were dispatched to Mittenwald, Lenggries and Bad Reichenhall to investigate how badly their tourist trade had been affected.

Meanwhile, Deputy Mayor Kögler sought advice from Gauleiter Wahl and Kreisleiter Kalhammer. Both men were adamant that, far from being a disaster, this was wonderful news for Oberstdorf. The villagers should welcome the battalion with open arms. Their view was echoed by the findings of Scheller and Holzmann. 'Mittenwald has had the best possible outcome imaginable,' its mayor had enthused, going on to claim that the military had stimulated rather than depressed tourism. A Bad Reichenhall economist insisted that more tourists had visited the town since the soldiers arrived than ever before.[18] In Lenggries and Bad Reichenhall, local farmers reported that despite their initial hostility (they had been forced to relinquish most of their land), they had long since come to terms with the situation and were now fully content. Still unconvinced, Kögler travelled to Berlin to consult with senior officials. But there too he consistently received the same advice: 'Oberstdorf should seize this unique opportunity and accept. The military will do more for the local economy than anything else.'[19]

It is tempting to assume that these upbeat assessments were simply the result of Nazi coercion. 'Protective custody' was a threat hanging over everyone, even mayors and farmers. The message enshrined in the well-known rhyme 'Lieber Gott, mach' mich stumm, dass ich nicht nach Dachau kumm!' ('Dear God make me dumb, so I won't to Dachau come!'), was one that everyone needed to heed before voicing any opinion.* On the other hand, the patriotic mood engulfing the country may genuinely have led visitors to regard the buzz created by the presence of so many soldiers as a holiday plus. It is hard, though, to see how the farmers could have accepted the loss of their land with such equanimity unless they had either been generously compensated or threatened with imprisonment.

Whatever the truth, Oberstdorf's officials underwent a dramatic conversion, and in September 1938 the municipal council unanimously endorsed the *Wehrmacht* proposal. Major Schrank wrote to congratulate Kögler: 'I am very happy for you and your community and for the 1st Mountain Division. Oberstdorf will now become a garrison town with your blessing.'[20] But in the end it was not to be. Quite suddenly and with no explanation, the army dropped the project. Why this happened remains a mystery. Such inexplicable reversals and turnabouts, however, were entirely typical of the confusion sown by the countless competing factions within the Nazi administrative machine.

~~

* A parody of a children's prayer, 'Lieber Gott, mach' mich fromm, dass ich in den Himmel komm' ('Dear God make me holy so that I to heaven can go').

When several months later Franz Amann, president of the Oberstdorf branch of the Alpine Club (after the *Anschluss* it was renamed the *Deutscher Alpenverein*, DAV),* addressed his members, he looked back on the year with deep satisfaction. Given the village's location right on the Austrian border, the *Anschluss* had been of particular significance locally. He noted how sixty-five years earlier their club had anticipated this historic moment when in 1873 it had become the German *and* Austrian Alpine Club. Amann recorded how as one organisation it had since then successfully 'nurtured the interests of climbers, walkers, path and hut builders, geologists, cartographers and glacier researchers', always putting the public interest first. It was therefore a matter for great celebration that the two nations had now followed the club's initiative by forming a union 'that expresses our common blood, language and culture'. And, with the return of the Sudetenland, Germans everywhere would merge into one glorious empire. The year 1938, he declared, 'was the most important in the club's history'.[21]

It is worth noting that Jews had been barred from this club's membership long before the Nazi regime. In 1921 Jewish mountaineers had felt the need to form their own 'Donauland Section' (Donauland is Austrian territory along the River Danube) within the club because of the latter's rampant anti-Semitism. Technically they remained members, but at a special meeting held three years later in Munich they were forced out altogether: 'The General Assembly', so the

---

* Until 1938 the Alpine Club was called the *Deutscher und Österreichischer Alpenverein* (DÖAV, German and Austrian Alpine Club). After the *Anschluss* it was renamed the *Deutscher Alpverein* (DAV, German Alpine Club). The Oberstdorf branch keeps its record books at its office, Karweidach 1, 87561 Oberstdorf.

Oberstdorf branch had reported at its AGM some weeks later, 'calls upon the Donauland Section to declare its resignation in order to restore calm and the peaceful development of the Association as a whole.'[22] This had all taken place nine years before Hitler became chancellor.

For the members of the DAV who heard Amann's address that evening, there was another reason why 1938 marked a significant milestone. Four months after the *Anschluss* the Nazis had been handed a stunning propaganda coup when at 3.30 p.m. on 24 July 1938, two Germans and two Austrians stood on the summit of the world-famous Eiger – the first climbers to reach it via its supremely difficult North Face. Before their successful conquest, a number of mountaineers had died in the attempt. Indeed, since it was a feat that many climbers had judged impossible, even Goebbels could not have dreamed up a more perfect public-relations stunt to mark the *Anschluss*. 'The Eiger's North Face', wrote the Governor of Austria, Arthur Seyss-Inquart, in the *Völkischer Beobachter*, 'has yielded to the irresistible force of German resolve.'[23]

The climbers' achievement attracted wide international attention, but there was also much speculation about how deeply they were in the Nazis' pocket. Some weeks before the ascent, the Germans Anderl Heckmair and Ludwig Vörg had started working at the Sonthofen Ordensburg as community leaders and mountain guides. In addition to free board and lodging, they received 250 RM per month and the prospect of promotion within the Nazi hierarchy.[24] Meanwhile one of the Austrians, Heinrich Harrer,* had even before the *Anschluss* been

* Harrer is the author of *Seven Years in Tibet* (1952) and *The White Spider: The Classic Account of the Ascent of the Eiger* (1959).

a member of the then illegal SA. Afterwards he promptly joined both the NSDAP and the SS. A year later, his fellow Austrian Fritz Kasparek wrote in his book *A Mountaineer*, 'I will never forget the Eiger North Face . . . symbol of German destiny . . . the Führer was always before our eyes . . . We could not have asked for a better teacher.'[25] But while it is a fact that Heckmair and Vörg used equipment provided by the Ordensburg, it is also true that they refused the latter's offer of further sponsorship and chose to make the ascent when they were on personal leave. They always vigorously denied any Nazi involvement.

Heckmair, who led the climb, lived in Oberstdorf from 1939 until his death in 2005, becoming one of the village's most celebrated inhabitants. His first contact with the Nazis had been through Leni Riefenstahl, Hitler's glamorous film director, whose documentaries *Triumph des Willens* (*The Triumph of the Will*, 1935) and *Olympia* (shot in 1936, released in 1938) had made her world-famous. Film-making was by no means her only talent. A professional actor and a dancer who had worked with Max Reinhardt, she was also an excellent swimmer, artist and a highly competent mountaineer. Her friendship with Heckmair began when a friend asked him to step in at short notice to take his place as her guide. 'Her feminine charm and natural exuberance dissolved my inner reservations,' Heckmair wrote in his autobiography. 'Whatever her relationship with Hitler, she was obviously a fantastic woman.'[26] She was also, to his surprise, a remarkably good climber. For her part, Riefenstahl wrote of Heckmair, 'I liked him from the moment we shook hands. He was somewhat coarse-grained, but I instantly sensed his basic sincerity . . . he climbed with the self-assurance of a cat.'[27]

Riefenstahl clearly fell for this rugged man of the mountains and perhaps he for her. Whether their mutual attraction ever led to anything more than friendship is impossible to know, but it was strong enough for Heckmair to accompany her in September 1937 to the Nuremberg Rally, where they stayed at Gauleiter Julius Streicher's residence. For a penniless climber who had grown up in an orphanage and had spent his life vagabonding from one mountain exploit to the next, this sudden exposure to the world of Leni Riefenstahl and the Nazi inner circle must have been a disorienting yet electrifying experience. Keen to show off her new acquisition, Riefenstahl took Heckmair to meet the Führer at the Deutscher Hof. Heckmair's account of their conversation over tea has much in common with those of others who recorded chats with Hitler. 'Far from being stupid,' he wrote,

> The questions he put to me were direct and to the point . . . what interested him was the 'why' of it all – what one would feel and experience on a severe climb as compared with a simple walk in the mountains . . . he bored his way relentlessly into every aspect of the subject. In all this my own person interested him not one bit. It was the facts that absorbed him; apparently he had never before spoken with a mountaineer.[28]

Heckmair then stepped on to the hotel balcony with the Führer and his entourage to watch a torchlight parade. For the first time, as he recorded in his autobiography, he raised his hand in the Hitler salute. For two hours thousands of youths shouting slogans and marching in impeccable unison passed beneath them. When in later years Heckmair claimed that he had found the spectacle 'disturbing and inexplicable', it is likely that he was speaking the truth.[29] Yet, at the same time, it was surely hard for an anonymous young climber not to be seduced by the sheer thrill of finding himself so unexpectedly at the centre of great events. Riefenstahl clearly had further plans for him as she persuaded him to return with her to Berlin after the rally. But he did not last there long. By the end of 1937 he was back in Bavaria, fully focused on his impending attempt on the North Face.

Heckmair and Vörg were barely down from the Eiger before Ordensburg officials in Nazi uniforms arrived in Switzerland to sweep them home to the Reich as national heroes. Within days Heckmair was to meet Hitler for a second time when the Führer received and decorated the four men. By then, whether they liked it or not, Heckmair and his fellow Oberstdorfer, Vörg, were international celebrities – poster-boys for the Nazi vision that had done so much to restore Germany's prestige in the eyes of its citizens.

By the end of 1938 people all over the country – even those who did not support the regime – could rejoice in the fact that Hitler had somehow created a Reich without war, triumphed over the hated Treaty of Versailles, reduced unemployment and rendered his former foes compliant. For Hitler and for millions of his adoring followers, 1938 had been a good year.

11

Blitzkrieg

The relief felt throughout Germany after the Munich Agreement was not shared by Hitler. Ever since becoming chancellor, his energies had been entirely focused on preparing the country for war – the 'heroic' conflict that would lead ultimately to Aryan domination of the world. To his great frustration Munich had forced him to put this long-nurtured plan on hold. But not for long. On 15 March 1939, German troops marched into Prague (in violation of the Munich Agreement), making it clear to Oberstdorfers, and to Germans everywhere, that war was imminent.

Two months earlier the Nazi authorities had begun their sweep of the Sonthofen district to ensure that no potential conscript slipped through the net. Following this, Mayor Fink received elaborate instructions on how to transform Oberstdorf's secondary school into an assembly point where all those eligible for military service (males between the ages of eighteen and forty-five), including tourists and apprentices, might be examined. Of the individuals processed, ninety-one passed muster and thirteen were rejected.[1] Meanwhile at Kaufbeuren, fifty miles to the north, the Luftwaffe was also busy recruiting.

For boys aged ten to eighteen, membership of the Hitler Youth had in effect been compulsory since 1936 but in 1939 this mandate was strengthened so that those failing to sign up (for what was in reality military training) risked prosecution. Any boy who did somehow manage to avoid joining later found it impossible to get a job or a place at university. On 19 April Franz Noichl, together with all the other village ten-year-olds, was inducted into the Hitler Youth's junior branch – the *Deutsches Jungvolk* (German Young People). The next morning – Hitler's fiftieth birthday – they appeared at their first public event: 'All I remember,' he wrote,

> is that I froze miserably in my shorts and thin brown shirt. My father was utterly disgusted that his children had to join the Hitler Youth. But any protest would have been useless and dangerous. The Youth Service Ordinance of 25 March 1939 stated that the Hitler Youth was henceforward in terms of service to the state on par with the labour force and the military.

Franz and his cohort were soon learning aggressive games designed to encourage fitness, camaraderie and the fighting spirit. For the older boys, life in the Hitler Youth was now deadly serious, their days filled with instruction on how to throw grenades, fire a rifle, crawl on their bellies under camouflage and survive outside for long periods in rugged conditions.

Since 1935 it had also been compulsory for every male on leaving school to serve six months in the *Reichsarbeitsdienst* (RAD, Reich Labour Service). From 1939 this also applied to women. The work was sanctified as youth's altruistic offering to the German people and (before military training took precedence) had typically consisted of land reclamation, drainage, building roads, clearing trees and helping farmers with the harvest. RAD units had also supported the *Wehrmacht* during the *Anschluss* and in the occupation of the Sudetenland and Czechoslovakia. Equipped with uniforms, bicycles and spades, which when marching they sloped over their shoulders like rifles, the young men learned to respect the virtues of physical labour while absorbing the true spirit of National Socialism. Having completed their six months in the RAD, they were then given a choice. They could either sign up immediately for their compulsory two years' military training or defer it while they acquired civilian qualifications.

On leaving school in summer 1937, two Oberstdorf school friends – Heini Klopfer and Max Maile – had chosen different paths. Klopfer, who after the war became a ski jump designer, pursued his architectural studies for two years before being drafted into the army. Maile, on the other hand, who loathed everything to do with uniforms, was so eager to have his military service over and done with that he chose the army – a decision that he was to regret all his life. By 1939, at the age of twenty-one, he had already sacrificed two and a half years for the regime. But instead of being released permanently into civilian life as he had planned, he was to find himself marching into Poland with the 99th Regiment of the 1st Mountain Division.[2]

Toughened by farm labour and accustomed to surviving outdoors in all weathers, Oberstdorf boys were better prepared than most for the rigours of war, especially since so many of them were also experienced mountain climbers and skiers. It is difficult to establish exactly how many of the village's young men joined the 98th and 99th, but it is likely that they numbered in the hundreds. There can have been few villagers who did not at some point during the war see a husband, brother, father or son go off to fight. Certainly, many of Oberstdorf's best known families are represented in the memorial chapel – Brutscher, Schratt, Berktold, Witsch, Hohenadl, Hochfeichter, Schwarz, Zwick, to name but a few. While the likes of Max Maile and Heini Klopfer detested the prospect of war, others (factory worker Fridolin Thomma among them) trusted in the Führer so completely that they willingly accepted his summons to fight.

Alfons Meinlinger, one of Max Maile's fellow 99ers who served in a communications unit, kept a war diary. Although not himself from Oberstdorf (he grew up near Kempten, twenty-five miles to the north), his record of the soldiers' daily lives, and the battles and marches they endured together, provides a vivid account of the war as experienced by his Oberstdorf comrades. On 28 August 1939, twenty-two-year-old Meinlinger wrote:

> We are prepared and for three days have been ready to go at any hour. There are daily incidents between Germany and Poland. The overall situation is not, however, only about Gdansk [Danzig] but rather about the supremacy in Europe. England not Poland will be our main enemy! A non-aggression pact has been signed between Russia and Germany. This must surely be a tactic by our Führer to put pressure on our opponents. What else could it be when the communists and National Socialists are such great political opponents?[3]

The non-aggression pact between the Soviet Union and Nazi Germany, in which the two bitter enemies agreed not to take military action against one another for ten years, had been signed on 23 August, taking the whole world by surprise. A week later, on 31 August, a so-called 'incident' took place at Gleiwitz in Upper Silesia, a few miles from the German–Polish border. This was one of several dozen such events, fabricated by the SS to look like a Polish attack in order to give Hitler a pretext for invasion. The following day, in Füssen (thirty miles north-east of Oberstdorf), where the 99th was waiting to mobilise, Meinlinger wrote, 'It is finally happening. We board our train at 6 p.m. and leave for Czechoslovakia at 11 p.m. Yesterday my family sent me 20 RM pocket money. I feel very uneasy. Where will this journey end? And what can we expect when we get there?'[4] He soon found out. On 1 September, Hitler ordered the *Wehrmacht* to invade Poland. Two days later, on 3 September, Poland's allies Britain and France declared war on Germany. The great conflict for which Hitler had waited so long had at last begun.

The sheer power of German force unleashed on Poland over the next few weeks is breathtaking. Sixty divisions (around 1.5 million men), hundreds of modern aircraft (tried and tested in the Spanish Civil War), a massive quantity of artillery and several thousand tanks were thrown against a country that, however courageous, was incapable of mounting any serious defence against such overwhelming odds. As the first example of Hitler's famous blitzkrieg tactics, the operation was a stunning success.

Germany's first key objective in the Polish campaign was to capture Lwów* (Lemberg). Now part of Ukraine, it was then the capital of Galicia and, as southern Poland's chief

---

* The city is referred to here by its Polish name, Lwów. Today it is in Ukraine and known as Lviv. When the Germans occupied it they called it Lemberg, while the Soviets referred to it as Lvov.

railway and road link, a city of vital strategic importance. Oberstdorf soldiers were in action from the start. As part of the 1st Mountain Division, the 99th Regiment (numbering about 1,000 men) began its war in the eastern Slovakian town of Prešov, roughly 600 miles east of Oberstdorf. Since Slovakia had declared its independence under Nazi Germany's protection six months earlier, it now provided the perfect launch pad for the invasion. The rapid march to Lwów was a feat of real endurance on the part of the young soldiers since they had to cover several hundred miles in a series of long, hard treks of up to forty miles a day. Starting at dawn, they tramped, ankle-deep in the sandy soil of southern Poland, along roads that were little more than cart tracks.[5] 'We marched until midnight,' wrote Meinlinger, 'I couldn't have taken another step.' Nevertheless, he had found time for a mild flirtation. 'During our rest yesterday,' he wrote on 7 September, 'I tried to chat to a pretty Polish girl who I thought had looked at me kindly but we didn't get very far as we couldn't understand one another.'[6]

The heat, lack of water and fierce attacks by Polish defenders, especially in the Carpathians, combined to make the young men's initial taste of war a sobering experience. Despite this, the 1st Mountain Division fought with verve and courage in the battle for Lwów. While attempting to retrieve one of his unit's communications cables during the action, Meinlinger was slightly wounded by a splinter. 'When I got back, first thing I did was to look at my knee,' he wrote in his diary. 'I took off my trousers and saw my underpants were filled with blood. Everyone crowded round, as I was the first to be wounded in the unit. I was under the impression that a couple of my comrades were quite envious.'[7]

But this first military success was to end in disappointment for the 1st Mountain Division. As part of the Nazi–Soviet

Pact, it had been agreed that Russia would take control of eastern Poland and on 17 September Russian troops attacked Poland from the East. As a result of the newly created border agreed between Hitler and Stalin, the 1st Mountain Division was ordered to hand over Lwów to the Russians after the city's surrender on 22 September. 'So for us the war in Poland is over,' wrote Meinlinger. 'We'll begin the march back today. Isn't it odd how National Socialism's greatest enemy is now our ally?'[8]

By 6 October the 'September Campaign' was completed, leaving three Oberstdorf soldiers dead. Hitler's first blitzkrieg had overwhelmed Poland in just five weeks. As for the country's fate under the Nazis, Hitler had made his intentions very clear in a speech to his generals shortly before the invasion began:

Our strength lies in our speed and our brutality. Genghis Khan hunted millions of women and children to their deaths, consciously and with a joyous heart ... I have issued a command ... that the aim of the war lies not in reaching particular lines but in the physical annihilation of the enemy. Thus, so far only in the East, I have put my *Totenkopfverbände* [Death's Head units]* at the ready with the command to send man, woman and child of Polish descent and language to their death, pitilessly and remorselessly ... Poland will be depopulated and settled with Germans.[9]

* These were the SS units responsible for administering the concentration and extermination camps.

After Poland's defeat, this policy was swiftly implemented with wholesale murder, the establishment of concentration camps, torture and mass executions following in the wake of the invading troops. Back home, however, few Germans at this stage can have had much inkling of the extent of these atrocities. Meanwhile, if some 99ers, having successfully emerged from their first exposure to war and tasted the thrill of victory, regarded the war with new confidence, Meinlinger was more cautious. Expressing the views of men like Max Maile, on 30 September he wrote: 'Today or tomorrow we will board a train in Slovakia. Nobody knows where we are going. It will depend on the negotiations with England and France. We hope that they will be successful otherwise this terrible war will start all over again.'

The 1st Mountain Division was not involved in the Scandinavian campaign (designed to protect Germany's supplies of iron ore), which ended in April 1940 with the Nazi occupation of Denmark and Norway, but the following month, having spent the winter months training (and skiing) in the Eifel, the hilly region west of the Rhine, the 99th was ordered to be ready to mobilise at two hours' notice. On 8 May it marched to the Belgian border and a few days later was in action in the Ardennes (about 100 miles west of Cologne) as part of the campaign that saw Germany over-run Luxembourg, the Netherlands and Belgium in six weeks. Having succeeded in the Ardennes, the 99ers were soon fighting their way on to France, which, like the Low Countries, was desperately ill-prepared to defend itself against Hitler's blitzkrieg.

Despite his doubts about the war, Meinlinger seems to have taken all this in his stride. 'The war against France is in full swing,' he wrote on 18 May. 'We arrived at St-Michel [about fifty miles north of Reims] yesterday; the surrounding forests are still occupied by the enemy. A tank was hit and crashed from a bridge into the river. The latest news is that the Maginot Line* has been broken through for 100 kilometres.' In the middle of all the fighting, however, there were some unexpected compensations. 'We requisition butter, jam, wine and champagne,' wrote Meinlinger. 'We rarely eat from the field kitchen because we have no need to. I've never drunk so much champagne in my life. The French live very well. They must have fled at great speed, because they have left so much behind.' A week later, somewhere near Laon, he and his comrades noticed in front of their billet

> a meadow with grazing cows. Because they hadn't been milked, their udders were very swollen. We needed milk to add to a dessert we had found in a local shop but couldn't get to the cows because the meadow was under enemy surveillance. Everyone agreed that as I am a farm boy, it was my job to get the milk. So I put on some women's clothes and brought a cow in from the field. Fortunately the enemy was unaware that the civilians had all fled.[10]

But it was not just champagne and dessert. Coming under heavy fire a few days later, he described how he and his friend Franz 'shut our eyes tight as with each impact we were thrown in the air. Not far away we heard terrible screaming. Four men were wounded. We went on installing the line despite heavy machine gun fire.' On 9 June, a few days after the Battle of Dunkirk during which the evacuation of the British army

---

* A line of concrete fortifications constructed along France's borders with Germany, Switzerland, Italy and Luxembourg during the 1930s to deter a German attack.

off the beaches had been successfully accomplished, the 99th
was somewhere north of Paris. '*Stukas* [dive-bombers] have
been at work. They attack in a nosedive emitting a screech-
ing siren as they descend. The effect on morale is said to be
devastating.'

By the time France capitulated, two more Oberstdorfers
had been killed. When news reached the 99ers that the French
had signed an armistice (effective from 25 June), the men were
eating their lunch near Gien on the Loire. 'A cheer went up
through the ranks,' recorded Meinlinger. 'We unloaded our
rifles and I took out one of my special cigarettes and smoked
it in celebration of peace.'[11]

The invasion of Great Britain – Operation Sea Lion –
planned for September 1940 was the next campaign in which
the 1st Mountain Division expected to take part. In prepara-
tion for this, the soldiers were sent to the French coast for
training. Many of these mountain boys had never before seen
the sea and found the amphibious exercises, often chaotic and
dangerous, particularly traumatic. It therefore came as a great
relief when in September the mountain troops learned that
Hitler had postponed operation Sea Lion indefinitely.

The 99ers were nevertheless to remain in the thick of
the war. At the end of March 1941 they marched east to
Völkermarkt in Austria (about ninety miles north of Ljubljana,
capital of Slovenia), to prepare for the attack on Yugoslavia
and Greece that took place on 6 April. Within days German
troops, supported by Hungarian and Bulgarian forces, had
occupied both countries. On 9 April, somewhere north of
Zagreb, Meinlinger made the following entry in his diary:

Our squad is ordered to connect with the forward vehicles.
We must do this quickly. We do so and in good humour. As

I got to the mule, I was told that Ferley had been wounded. We took cover and tried to rescue him from another side. What we didn't know, however, was that in the hills opposite us there was a trench occupied by the enemy so it didn't work. Then Oberjäger Brucker and Springer tried from another side and got through. Ferley stood up and got away. He had been shot through the neck. We were then attacked from all sides. Every time we ducked across the street, bullets whistled over our heads. The man next to me firing a machine gun quickly cleaned his rifle. He wants to shoot living targets. I can still see him leaving the back street with a grin on his face.[12]

Four days later on 13 April, Easter Sunday, Meinlinger wrote:

It has been so exhausting that I've been unable to write. At 10 o'clock we received the order to dismantle. I already suspected that we would have to march a long way today. Our 8-km line was soon packed up. We did it quickly so that we could get some sleep. It was still another 5 kilometres to the new command post. Our comrades had already gone. The place was called Misdorf [possibly today's Mislinjska Dobrava]. We marched another 12 kilometres further but our men were not there either. Again we marched on and after a few hours we reached our company at a mountain pass blocked with columns of soldiers. My feet were a mess. Yes, and we had to cross a pass that night. Was I still human when we arrived in Schönstein [Šonštanj]? It was still 24 kilometres, half of it uphill. It's the most exhausted I've been since the war began. We didn't have anything to eat that day either, because the field kitchen couldn't get through. The next morning we went on again with empty stomachs. Another 35 kilometres without food. Celje [fifty miles north-east of Ljubljana], where we are now resting, was our salvation. We have peace and quiet . . . Today is Easter Sunday, we are about to go to church.[13]

Thus, after the annexation of Austria in 1938 followed by that of Czechoslovakia in March 1939, the defeat of Poland in September 1939, the occupation of Norway and Denmark in April 1940, the rapid success of the Western offensive in May, the Franco–German armistice in June and the victorious campaign against Yugoslavia and Greece in April 1941, Hitler was the undisputable master of mainland Europe. For millions of Germans, his astonishing victories had wiped the slate clean. Germany was back where it belonged.

After the intense action in the Balkans, the 99ers were allowed to rest for a few days by the Austrian lake of Wörthersee before learning that they were again to be deployed in Poland. But as their troop train trundled its way east through Slovakia, this time the soldiers had every reason to believe that total victory would soon be theirs.

In the first weeks of the war, Franz Noichl had followed the *Wehrmacht*'s progress with keen interest. He personally knew some of the soldiers (many of them only a few years older than him) and was particularly close to his godfather's son – Alois Jäger, soon to join the border police. To begin with it seemed to Franz that Germany's rapid successes in Poland and Western Europe made a nonsense of his father's warnings that they were about to be engulfed in a new world war with devastating consequences. Indeed, as the war progressed and Germany notched up victory after victory, even the most sceptical Oberstdorfers were seduced into believing that this time Germany would win.

Everyday life in the village was surprisingly unchanged during the first couple of years of the war, as it was across most of Germany. The American journalist Howard K. Smith (based in Berlin 1940–41) noted that 'the mobilisation of several million soldiers to fight in Poland . . . had no more effect on the German home front than the wash of a motor-boat on a giant liner at sea'.[14] True, rationing was immediately introduced, but as everyone had long since become used to shortages of one kind or another this was not initially a major issue. Chocolate and coffee were scarce but there was plenty of wine, beer and cigarettes. The state's increasing interference in people's personal affairs was hard to ignore, as indeed was the constant military music blaring from loudspeakers and radios, particularly Hitler's favourite 'Badenweiler Marsch', but Germany's stunning military successes had done much to relieve people's underlying anxieties. Moreover, the fighting did not hinder their enjoyment of the mountains, the fresh air and wild flowers, or the quiet relishing of Germany's victories with friends over a stein of beer. Naturally the fate of their young soldiers was a constant worry, but there was also deep pride in their achievements and, compared with the First World War, losses on the battlefield were mercifully light.

While their menfolk were conquering Europe, Oberstdorf's young women were not forgotten. The fact that nearly 14 million men were engaged in the fighting created a huge labour shortage across the whole country. Forced labourers brought to Germany from the conquered territories did much to compensate for this, but women also played a vital role in sustaining the war effort. In August 1940, every eighteen-year-old girl living in Oberstdorf was ordered to present herself at the

Hotel Hirsch in Sonthofen armed with her birth certificate, evidence of her Aryan ancestry and proof that she was both healthy and a member of the League for German Girls. Having passed muster, no matter what her personal circumstances, she became the property of the Labour Service, most likely to be deployed on a farm or in an armaments factory.

Children too were involved in the war effort. At Franz's primary school, under the slogan 'Front and Home', the children wrote letters to the soldiers and airmen. Franz's schoolmate Max Müller sent one to an Oberstdorf pilot deployed over England. It was read out in class – 'Let Churchill and Chamberlain taste our German bombs'. Franz did not approve. In his view, such sentiments were un-heroic. At the time he was under the spell of Ernst Jünger, the famous First World War soldier whose account of his experiences in the trenches – *In Stahlgewittern* (*Storm of Steel*, 1920) – had won huge acclaim. Franz had borrowed the book from the village library and had been thrilled by it. At twenty-five, Jünger was the youngest ever recipient of Pour le Mérite, Germany's highest military honour. A free spirit, fearless, intelligent and willing to lay down his life in a just cause, Jünger was Franz's kind of hero. From time to time Oberstdorf's soldiers reappeared on home leave and were able to give their families and friends first-hand accounts of their own heroic deeds, thus strengthening the villagers' belief that this time Germany really would emerge victorious.

The first stages of the war made less impact on Franz's life than the fact that he had been awarded a scholarship to attend Oberstdorf's secondary school. After primary school, boys from his background normally took up an apprenticeship, became a craftsman or worked as a labourer, so secondary education was something quite new for the Noichl family. But

as the war progressed, school life began to change dramatically. Teachers called up to fight were replaced by those less
qualified. Lessons became shorter and some subjects, much
to Franz's annoyance, were dropped altogether. 'The teachers
were often unable to cover even a third of the curriculum,'
he recalled. 'We only had proper lessons in mathematics, and
from the 4th grade in physics and Latin as the second foreign
language.' Franz may have been troubled by the decline in
teaching standards, but the less academic among his fellow
students were delighted when in May 1940 boys aged fourteen
to eighteen and girls sixteen to eighteen were released from
school to help the farmers with the harvest. It was a pattern
that was to last throughout the war. The work was hard, but
infinitely preferable to being stuck in a stuffy classroom with
incompetent teachers. As well as helping on the local farms,
the children were also sent further afield to pick hops and
medicinal plants.

For Franz and his family, however, these were years of
hardship. Although Howard K. Smith maintained that 'For a
people engaged in a life-and-death war, in which absolutely
everything was in the scales, the German people for two years
of war ate amazingly well,'[15] this was not universally true and
certainly not in the Noichl household. Each individual's allo-
cation of bread, fat, sausage or sugar depended on his or her
work. Although, as foresters, brothers-in-law Xaver Noichl and
Wilhelm Steiner received a 'heavy labour' allowance, it was too
small to make much difference. Thanks however to the wood-
cutters' traditional hunting rights, they were still able to put
extra meat on the table. Despite this, Franz and his brothers
were always hungry. Soon Frau Noichl was adding potatoes to
her bread dough, while the boys meticulously measured each
slice of sausage with a ruler to make sure that they all received

exactly the same. Using every ounce of ingenuity, the family survived as best it could, often resorting to illegal methods. As those caught breaking the rules faced severe penalties, Frau Noichl lived in constant fear of being discovered, especially by their nearest neighbours whom she suspected would not hesitate to inform the police and collect their reward should they suspect her of any infringement.

From 1940, eleven-year-old Franz would regularly bicycle with his father to his maternal grandparents' farm at Bedernau, sixty miles due north of Oberstdorf. Farmers received fewer food stamps than everyone else and no flour or rice, a ruling they regarded as grossly unfair since there was little they could grow at high altitude, their livestock were strictly monitored and all their milk and eggs had to be handed over to the authorities. Nevertheless, despite their grumbling, most farmers were able to provide their families and others with illicit food, often in exchange for much-needed labour. Franz's grandparents Josef and Adelheid Zoller were no exception and were clearly generous enough to make the risky 120-mile round trip from Oberstdorf worthwhile.

A thumbnail portrait of the Zollers offers a sobering glimpse into German peasant life and is in marked contrast to the Reich's heroic view of Germany's farmworkers. Like his grandfather, Josef (born in 1873) was an occasional mercenary who would take on any employment he could find. Apart from farming, he worked as a bricklayer, a brewery labourer, a lay priest and a lackey for Count Castell at the nearby Schloss Bedernau. But however hard he applied himself, there was never enough money to feed his fourteen children. To add to his problems, Josef, who was himself born out of wedlock, had to pay alimony for an illegitimate child born a year before his marriage. Because of these grim circumstances, whenever a suitable opportunity arose the Zollers would give away one of their children. Thus at the age of five Franz's mother was sent to an aunt's house, where she was expected to look after the smaller children. When she was about fourteen she started work as a maid. This was a particularly demanding job during the First World War as all the regular servants were away fighting. In common with so many young girls in domestic service, her forlorn existence was made yet more miserable by sex predators. Franz described the effects of his mother's upbringing on her own family:

> There was no joy in the Zoller family. Every minute, every hour was a struggle to stay alive. People lived to work. Even at a ripe old age, when my mother's mind was already confused, she spoke only of earning money. She never liked useless activities, and could not bear to see her children reading or playing. From about the age of eight we could only do things that brought in something: carrying wood and coal for old people, delivering magazines and collecting the subscription money, picking up tennis balls, carrying messages, weeding, or picking mushrooms and berries. The only reason she tolerated my accordion was because I could earn money by playing it at weddings and dances.

But despite their poverty, the staunchly Catholic Josef was scrupulously honest. Even when there was no firewood at home Franz remembered how his grandfather would never pick up a fallen branch if it lay close to his neighbour's land, or harvest a strip of field if it touched the latter's furrow. Nor would he drink a drop of his beloved beer after midnight if he intended to take Communion the following day. Josef's temper could be frightening but he also had a soft heart. When the time came to leave after one of their wartime visits, Franz recalled how both grandparents would stand waving goodbye with 'tears streaming down their cheeks'.

After these illegal trips, Xaver and Franz's return journey to Oberstdorf – their panniers now crammed with contraband flour, eggs and lard – was fraught with danger. By riding cross-country they reduced the risk of meeting the police but increased their chances of damaging their bicycles. These they often had to carry when fields were too soft to ride over – a demanding task for any eleven-year-old, however strong. On one occasion when Franz had stopped to mend his saddlebag, egg yolks visibly oozing out of a box, he froze with fear at the sight of an approaching man. But, as the stranger walked past, he merely pointed out that Franz was wasting his time as the bag was obviously beyond repair. With informers always on the lookout for a potential reward, Franz was well aware that this encounter could have turned out very differently.

Encouraged by propaganda, the Gestapo and monetary reward, people had plenty of reasons to keep a close watch on their neighbours and to inform on those they did not like, or whom they suspected of breaking the rules. If this spying culture made life uncomfortable for ordinary Germans, it was infinitely more terrifying for the Jewish population. Around 300,000 Jews had emigrated before the war but those remaining were now trapped, their existence becoming more precarious and miserable with each passing day.

Despite the acute dangers involved, many tried to flee, among them Dr Kurt Weigert, who had been director of the Sonthofen hospital. A Jew who had been baptised into the Protestant faith, he was a long-standing member of Pastor

Seiler's congregation. Not wishing to abandon his patients after he was sacked from the hospital in 1936, he decided to remain in Germany even though his family had chosen to leave. Remarkably, Weigert was able to practise medicine privately for another three years, largely thanks to Kreisleiter Kalhammer's moderate policies, which continued to act as a counterbalance to the fevered Nazi atmosphere fostered by the powerful presence of the Ordensburg.

But with the outbreak of war Weigert decided the time had come to make a break for Switzerland. Together with Seiler, who insisted on accompanying him, he reckoned his best chance was to walk across the Austrian mountains to an uncontrolled section of the Austrian–Swiss border, a distance of some forty-five miles. After so many years in Oberstdorf Seiler had an intimate knowledge of the mountains, but it was still an ambitious and nerve-wracking hike. They walked by night, spending the daylight hours hidden in barns. Moving fast, so that Seiler could be home before his absence was noticed, they reached the border in two days. It was with intense relief that, after seeing his friend cross into Switzerland, the pastor returned home without incident, his mission successfully accomplished. It was only after the war that Seiler learned what had happened. After Weigert reached the 'safety' of Switzerland, he was picked up by the authorities and returned to Germany. Miraculously, he somehow escaped the camps, spending the rest of the war in Mannheim.

Other Jews were not so lucky. As Hitler's troops marched triumphantly across Europe, German Jews – their property confiscated and their jobs gone – were increasingly herded into ghettos and labour camps. Nor were they alone. The demands of war provided Hitler with just the excuse he was looking for to rid the regime not only of Jews, but also of

Gypsies, socialists, the disabled and mentally ill, homosexuals, Poles, communists, or anyone else who did not fit the National Socialist ideal. The elimination of those deemed undesirable became an issue of prime importance. No community was immune, not even one as far away from the centres of power as Oberstdorf.

12

Theodor Weissenberger In Memoriam

Between 20 January and 13 December 1940, the Nazis gassed 9,839 people at the Grafeneck 'euthanasia' centre.[1] Theodor Weissenberger was one of them. He was murdered because he was blind. Affectionately known in his family as Theodorle (little Theodor), he was born in Oberstdorf on 29 October 1921. He was the victim of a crime that even by Nazi standards is peculiarly shocking.

His family had lived in Oberstdorf for generations. His maternal grandparents, Fritz and Maria Gschwender, were one of Oberstdorf's more celebrated couples and owners of the Trettach Hotel. Theirs was a romantic story. At the age of twenty-six, Fritz had spent some weeks in Bad Cannstatt (near Stuttgart) undergoing a cure for his weak lungs. He was a fine tenor, and in an effort to ease his homesickness he joined a church choir where he met and fell in love with Maria Schäfer. Although the Gschwenders were successful (they owned the sawmill in Oberstdorf and lived in a large house opposite the church), Fritz felt that he had little to offer Maria, whose family were wealthier and more sophisticated – a view shared by her parents. Thanks, however, to the kindness of a Bad Cannstatt pharmacist who acted as the couple's clandestine postman, true love won out. The Schäfers abandoned their objections and Fritz and Maria were married in Oberstdorf in 1878. They were to remain devoted to one another throughout their long, eventful marriage.

Theodor's mother, Berta, was the youngest of the three Gschwender daughters. She was thirteen years old when Fritz was elected Mayor of Oberstdorf in January 1912. Berta and her sisters were proud of their father who, at a time when anything had seemed possible, was full of optimistic plans for the village. But over the next four years, instead of using his mayoral office to improve the villagers' lives, Fritz found himself paying repeated house calls in order that he might personally hand to the families the letter informing them that their husband, son, brother or father had been killed fighting a war hundreds of miles away for reasons that few understood.

The post-war economic turmoil, combined with the tight restrictions placed on travel and tourists, proved too much for the Trettach Hotel. In 1920 Fritz and Maria reluctantly agreed to sell. Finding a buyer was not easy, but they eventually sold it for a reasonable sum and began building a new family house in the village – Villa Gschwender. It was still unfinished when Fritz learned he had lost the proceeds from the sale of the hotel, having invested the money in Ruhr coalfields on the advice of a stranger. The situation was especially dire since winter was approaching and there was now no money to buy windows for the new house. As Berta, married with two children and heavily pregnant, and her sister Elisabeth (Lisi), a survivor of childhood polio, were also living with their parents, this was no small crisis.

Nor was it any use turning to Berta's husband Franz Weissenberger for help. The NSDAP was founded in Munich on 24 February 1920 and right from the start Franz had recognised the threat it posed to everyone and everything that he valued. Drawn irrevocably into Munich's post-war political chaos, he felt impelled to devote all his energies to resisting National Socialism. Indeed, his dedication to this cause was so consuming that he was soon on the Nazi blacklist, a fact that not only put his own life in danger but also imperilled Berta and the children. He continued to visit them sporadically in Oberstdorf, making sure that he arrived after dark and left for Munich before dawn. But in Franz's life-and-death struggle with the Nazis there was little place for the family and the couple divorced in 1925, a sad end to what had initially been a happy union.

As for Villa Gschwender, it was Maria who saved the day. The emergency over the windows demanded decisive action, so she took the train to Munich. There, having tracked down an old family friend in his favourite tavern, she climbed on to the back of his motorcycle* and together they set off to hunt for windows. After several hours riding around in the freezing cold, they hit the jackpot. Following up on a tip, they discovered a dozen high-quality double windows lying abandoned in a warehouse on the outskirts of the city. The janitor signed the necessary papers and, after arranging for the transport of the windows to Oberstdorf by train and horse and cart, Maria returned home exhausted but triumphant.

It was thus, in the recently completed Villa Gschwender, with its large, handsome windows, that Theodor Weissenberger was born a few weeks later. It was immediately apparent that

---

* It was probably a Megola motorcycle. These were produced in Munich between 1921 and 1925.

he was blind. The cause was never established, but he had screamed so long and so loudly after drops were put in his eyes just after his birth that Berta always suspected the midwife had given him the wrong ones.[2]

He was by all accounts a happy child, closely protected by his older brother and sister who loved to run their fingers through his soft, silky hair. They did their best to do his seeing for him, and before the increasing traffic made it too dangerous to play on the road in front of the house they would sit for hours there with Theodor making mud pies. As if to compensate for his lack of sight, it was soon clear that the little boy was deeply musical, a gift inherited from his grandparents. His pure, high soprano voice, heard regularly in church from when he was very young, was admired throughout the village. He would listen intently to his grandfather playing the fiddle, but during the height of hyperinflation in 1923 when the family had not eaten for several days, Fritz's violin (built by the famous seventeenth-century maker Jacob Stainer) was exchanged for a sack of potatoes, a sack of flour and two pounds of butter.

After Fritz's death in 1925, Maria could think only of dying herself and seldom left the villa. She did, however, attend the inauguration of the Nebelhorn cable car five years later, partly in homage to her husband, who had been one of the project's keenest supporters, but also out of sheer curiosity. She was not disappointed. As if by magic the cabin, hanging by a mere thread as it seemed to her, floated silently across the Trettach and up the mountain, taking her ever closer to her Fritz whom she did not for one moment doubt awaited her in heaven high above the Nebelhorn.*

---

* Maria Gschwender died on 25 November 1936.

When Theodor was seven, his mother and aunt took him to Ursberg, seventy miles to the north, where they placed him in an institution run by Franciscan nuns. Since its foundation in 1897, the nuns had greatly expanded their operation so that by the time Theodor arrived they were caring for people with all kinds of mental and physical disabilities, over a wide area. Indeed, the Dominikus Ringeisen nursing home (named after its founder, a Catholic priest) had by the early twentieth century become the largest establishment of its kind in Germany. When Berta and Lisi next visited their adored Theordorle they found a cheerful, self-confident child who with great pride showed them around the building without losing his way or needing any help. He was, Berta reported when she reached home, particularly proud of his bed and his little cupboard.

Four years later, when Theodor was eleven, the nuns told him that he was to be moved to their school for the blind at Pfaffenhausen (sixty miles west of Munich). Although at first it was a blow, he soon adjusted. In the new establishment he learned to read braille and acquire other practical skills (he won a prize for making the best brush) that would, so it was hoped, enable him to lead an independent life when one day he returned to Oberstdorf.

It is unclear exactly how long Theodor was at Pfaffenhausen, but by 1939 he had been moved to yet another institution – Schloss Schweinspoint near Donauwörth (fifty miles further north).

⸺

It was in the spring of 1939 that Hitler finally set in motion a 'racial hygiene' policy that he had wanted to pursue for many years, namely the systematic killing of those who were mentally or physically disabled. He had made his intentions clear in an address to the Nuremberg Rally ten years earlier when he had argued that if of the million or so children born each year in Germany 70,000 to 80,000 of the weakest were removed, the nation would be made correspondingly stronger.[3] Unease over possible public response to such a plan had prevented him from implementing it sooner, but now, at a time when the approaching war made purifying the nation's bloodline and streamlining its resources high priorities, earlier concerns were set aside. Secrecy, however, was vital and for this reason Hitler ordered the operation to be run directly out of his own Chancellery.

Although the organised killing of the 'incurably' sick did not start until shortly before the Second World War, a Law for the Prevention of Hereditarily Diseased Progeny had been in force since 1 January 1934. This made sterilisation compulsory for anyone judged to be suffering from hereditary disease or mental 'weakness'. In reality, it also included the terminally ill, homosexuals, tramps, alcoholics, the physically disabled or anyone else the Nazis deemed a burden on the state or a social misfit.

When it came to the treatment of mental health problems, Oberstdorf fell into the catchment area of Kaufbeuren (fifty miles to the north) where Dr Valentin Faltlhauser was in charge of the asylum – the oldest in Swabia. Not only did he authorise the sterilisation of his own patients, many of whom suffered from schizophrenia, but as a judge sitting at the hereditary health court in Kempten he would also have played a crucial role in deciding which Oberstdorfers should be prevented from having children. So great was Faltlhauser's enthusiasm for his mission that in the first year of the new law he applied to have 208 individuals in his area sterilised.[4] But this was not enough to satisfy him. In his 1934 report, he complained that his medical colleagues in the South Allgäu, either through passive resistance or a failure to understand the importance of the policy, were not implementing it strictly enough.[5] Nevertheless, between the inception of the law and the end of the Second World War it was so vigorously enforced throughout Germany that around 400,000 people were denied the possibility of having children.[6]

After preventing those they considered unsuitable from reproducing, the Nazis' next step was to kill the disabled children who already existed. So in the summer of 1939, the newly convened and top-secret Reich Committee for the Scientific Registering of Serious Hereditary and Congenital Illnesses was urgently tasked with compiling a national register of toddlers and babies with abnormalities. The latter included obvious conditions such as spina bifida, cerebral palsy, Down's syndrome, limb deformity and blindness. Epilepsy, which affected Mayor Fink's son Werner, was also on the list. In addition, vaguely defined disorders such as 'feeble-mindedness' allowed children who suffered from just about any kind of problem, however mild, to be labelled as deviant or disabled.

On 18 August 1939, registration of all such children became compulsory. Doctors and midwives were rewarded with 2 RM for each 'malformed' child they reported. The registration forms were then forwarded to Berlin, where they were examined by a panel of three doctors. Based on nothing more than these pieces of paper, the doctors decided if a child should live or die. If granted life, the form was marked with a blue minus. The condemned received a red plus. The plus forms were then sent to the appropriate public health office, which ordered the child's admission to a paediatric clinic. Once there, the victim was put in a special ward where he or she was starved to death or given a daily overdose of the sedative Luminal in their food. Within a few days the child usually developed a severe chest infection, which led to death. In order to speed up the process, the children were sometimes injected with a lethal dose of morphine.[7] After a lapse of several weeks, their parents were informed that their child was dead. A fictional illness was cited on the death certificate as the cause.

In October 1939, the 'euthanasia' project was given pseudo-legal status when Hitler signed the following letter:

> Reichsleiter Bouhler* and Dr Brandt,[†] MD are charged with the responsibility of extending the authority of certain physicians to be specifically named so that patients who, according to the best available human judgement are considered to be incurable, may, after careful diagnosis of their state of health, be granted a mercy death.[8]

Although the order was signed in October (around the time of Theodor's eighteenth birthday), Hitler had it backdated to 1 September, the day the war started. This was to support the propaganda that claimed the 'humanitarian' killing of the incurably sick was simply a pragmatic response to the war, when every available hospital bed would be needed for the wounded. As Dr Hermann Pfannmüller, an enthusiastic supporter of murdering the disabled, put it: 'The idea is unbearable to me that the best, the flower of our youth must lose its life at the front in order that the feeble-minded and irresponsible

* Philip Bouhler committed suicide in 1945 while detained in an American internment camp.
† Karl Brandt was tried at Nuremberg in the so-called 'Doctors' Trial' and hanged in 1948.

asocial elements can have a secure existence in the asylum.'[9] In this way the war acted as camouflage for a policy that was in reality driven by the Nazi doctrine that anyone unable to work was a valueless drain on society and was therefore living a 'life unworthy of life'.*

Once the means to kill children had been established, it was only a matter of months before the programme was extended to include adults living in asylums or other such institutions. Shrouded in secrecy, the adult 'euthanasia' programme, disguised under the innocent title 'Charitable Foundation for Cure and Institutional Care', was headquartered in a fine villa (seized from its former Jewish owners) at Tiergartenstrasse 4 in Berlin. The address gave the programme its name, *Aktion T-4* (Action T-4). The problem immediately facing its staff was how to kill large groups of German adults swiftly without arousing public suspicion. The starvation method hitherto used for children was considered too slow and likely to attract too many questions. The challenge was considerable, but by the time T-4 got under way at the beginning of 1940 a fast and efficient means of killing was readily available. In October 1939, a number of mentally ill patients had been herded into a specially built airtight room in a fort that served as the Posen Gestapo headquarters in Poland. The doors were locked, the taps turned on. Pure carbon monoxide flowed into the room along pipes pierced with holes. A glass window in the door enabled observers to watch the victims' death throes. The

---

* The expression first appeared in the title of a book published in 1920 by Karl Binding and Alfred Hoche: *Die Freigabe der Vernichtung lebensunwerten Lebens* (*Permitting the Destruction of Life Unworthy of Life*).

killings at Posen were the first instance of a gas chamber being used for mass murder.[10]

Six 'euthanasia' centres were then established throughout Germany, each serving a particular geographical area. Bavarians were sent to Grafeneck, a small town forty miles south of Stuttgart and about ninety miles from Oberstdorf. Schloss Grafeneck, originally used by the Dukes of Württemberg as a hunting lodge, had since the late 1920s been run by the Samaritans as a home for the disabled. Their tenure came to an abrupt end in October 1939 when, under the aegis of T-4, work to convert the Schloss into a murder facility began in earnest. There was a lot to do. Apart from the shed (disguised as a communal shower) where the victims were to be gassed, it was necessary to build a crematorium, a parking area for the buses, sleeping quarters for the staff and countless offices for the doctors, administrators, police, guards, crematorium operators and accountants.

From November 1939, all mental hospitals and institutions for the disabled throughout Germany were required to fill out a detailed questionnaire for the T-4 office in Berlin, specifying their patients' condition, whether or not they were able to work, how often they received visitors and how many. These were then sent to politically reliable doctors (Valentin Faltlhauser was one) who made the final life or death decision before returning the forms to the T-4 office in Berlin. The names of those selected to die were forwarded to the T-4 transport office, which notified the respective institutions and dispatched an official there to make the arrangements.

On 14 November 1940, two weeks and two days after his nineteenth birthday, Theodor Weissenberger was collected from Schloss Schweinspoint with his fellow victims and driven by bus to the psychiatric hospital in Günzburg. No accounts of the transports from those two institutions survive, but a nurse at Ursberg (where Theodor had lived as a child) left a graphic description of what happened there when patients were taken away. 'Even if you personally managed to stay calm,' she wrote, 'they knew exactly what was happening. It was terrible, indescribable. It was particularly bad for the girls who instinctively understood everything. They cried and screamed, clinging to the nurses, tearing off their veils. The doctors and nurses also wept.'[11]

Those to be gassed were transported in large grey buses with opaque windows euphemistically called 'charitable ambulances'. Sometimes the patients genuinely believed their carers when they were told they were going on an outing, but most were too astute to fall for the deception. Occasionally, as in Theodor's last institution at Schweinspoint, an inmate would hide when the buses appeared, only emerging after they had gone, but this was not an option for anyone who was blind. Accounts survive of agitated patients being brutally manhandled on to the bus. The most distressed were injected with a sedative to keep them quiet.

It is not known how long Theodor remained at the assembly station in the Günzburg hospital but it was probably only a matter of hours. From there, another 'charitable ambulance' drove him and his fellow victims the sixty odd miles to Grafeneck. When they arrived they were led by staff into a reception room and told to undress. After their identity was checked, they were given a brief medical examination to ascertain which of the sixty-odd illnesses the doctors had on file was the most suitable to be put on the death certificate. In Theodor's case they picked meningitis. A short paragraph accompanied each listed illness recommending in which circumstances it best fitted. The meningitis note read as follows:

Abscesses on the brain are relatively rare as such and
require a long period to develop, so that we can only consider this illness in a few very exceptional cases. It is useful
if any of the symptoms are already evident, such as a dis-
charge of pus from ears, nose or sinuses . . . every age group
can be affected by this illness.

Pneumonia, on the other hand, was 'an ideal cause of death for
our purpose, because the population at large always regards
it as a critical illness which therefore means that its life-
endangering character will be plausible . . . Pneumonia can
occur in every age group and in both sexes.'[12]

If Theodor had possessed any gold teeth a cross would
have been marked on his back. After they had been photographed, he and the others, still naked, were taken into the gas
chamber and killed. A witness to a gassing in another euthanasia centre wrote of how he had seen

40 to 50 men, pressed tightly together in the room, slowly
die. Some lay on the ground, others sank into themselves,
many had their mouths open as if gasping for air. The way
they died was so full of suffering that one cannot speak of
a humane killing. The more so since many of those killed
may well have had moments of clarity about what was
happening. I watched the procedure for about 2–3 minutes
then left, because I could not bear to look any longer and
I felt sick.[13]

It would have taken about twenty minutes for Theodor and
the others to die. Once the room had been properly ventilated,
the crematorium staff known as 'stokers' entered it to disen-
tangle the corpses and drag them to the death room. Here gold

teeth were extracted and subsequently sent to T-4 headquarters, where they were melted down into ingots or on occasion even given to the staff for use in their own teeth. Organs and brains were removed from those corpses thought to be of particular scientific interest. The dead were then placed on steel pallets and removed to the crematorium. Sometimes the stokers had to work through the night to reduce the bodies to ashes.[14] Afterwards the communal ashes were crammed into urns, although care was taken not to pack a notional child's too full. If the family wanted the urn it was sent to them by post, at an exorbitant charge.

When the families received a letter informing them that their relative had safely arrived at Grafeneck, he or she was probably already dead. Several weeks would elapse before a second letter was sent citing the invented illness as the cause of the patient's unexpected death. As well as signing the death certificates with a false name, the doctors appended the wrong date to make it look as if the patient had died weeks after their arrival rather than hours. There was also a considerable economic advantage to be derived from delaying news of the death since in the interim the families continued to pay for their relative's upkeep, thus, along with the gold teeth, handsomely augmenting T-4's coffers. Of course the administrators had to take great care not to send too many letters to the same town in the same time frame and quoting the same cause of death. To avoid this happening a large map hung on the wall at Grafeneck on which staff stuck coloured pins on the home towns of their victims. After Grafeneck was shut down in December 1940, the Schloss was used to house women and children fleeing the Allied bombing. Why exactly the centre closed after only a year is not clear, but possibly it was simply because T-4 ran out of suitable victims in the area.

By the time the Grafeneck killing centre closed, the truth had inevitably begun to leak out. People living near the euthanasia centre at Hadamar (fifty miles north of Frankfurt), for instance, noticed smoke coming out of the institution's chimneys shortly after the arrival of the grey buses. Furthermore, staff at these killing centres unsurprisingly felt the need to unburden themselves to their friends and family. A few courageous Germans tried to confront the policy, but it was not until the Bishop of Münster, Clemens August von Galen, in a series of sermons delivered in July 1941 (and widely distributed in print) forced the issue into the open that opposition to the killings gathered real momentum. Having secured a copy of one of von Galen's pamphlets, the BBC's German Service did its bit by broadcasting the content, while the RAF dropped leaflets over Germany and other European countries.[15]

In response to von Galen's attacks and mounting public anger, Hitler made the decision to terminate the whole programme in August 1941. In any case, by then a total of 70,273 people had been murdered in the six gassing centres, a figure in line with Hitler's original target.[16] Although the death facilities were closed, the killing did not stop. It did, however, cease to be centralised. Those living a 'life unworthy of life' now met their deaths in the institutions in which they resided, usually by starvation or lethal drugs.

A couple of weeks after Theodor's murder, the postman brought Berta a letter embellished with a large, formal swastika. She took it into the kitchen to read. The message was brief and to the point. Her son Theodor had died of meningitis. Lisi appeared and, seeing her sister's face, realised at once what had happened. They put on their black dresses and the black fur coats given to them by their father and went out into the snow. Sometime later Theodor's sister Bertl arrived home and saw the letter lying on the kitchen table. She knew exactly where she would find her mother and aunt. Not in the church which at such a moment seemed too large for their grief, but in the more intimate atmosphere of one of the three Loretto chapels that stood clustered together a little to the south of the village, against a backdrop of the mountains. There Bertl found her mother and aunt surrounded by candles, their hands clasped in prayer. For the rest of her life, Berta subscribed to the Ursberg newsletter that, in the absence of anything else, served as some link to her son's brief life.

For the epileptic Werner Fink there was a happier ending. Like Theodor, he too had lived with the nuns at Ursberg. But unlike Theodor's, his father was Mayor of Oberstdorf and as such knew about the T-4 programme – perhaps tipped off by his friend Kreisleiter Kalhammer. Whatever the source of their information, Werner's parents – one a devout Nazi the other a devout Catholic – were able to reach Ursberg before the grey buses, and bring their beloved son safely home.

13

Barbarossa

When on the morning of Sunday, 22 June 1941 Oberstdorfers switched on their wireless sets, they heard Joseph Goebbels make a startling announcement. Germany had in the early hours launched an assault on the Soviet Union – Operation Barbarossa. Reading from Hitler's proclamation, Goebbels informed the German people that in its extent and magnitude the new offensive was unprecedented. 'On the Eastern Front,' he declared, 'German forces range from East Prussia to the Carpathians . . . from the banks of the River Pruth along the lower reaches of the Danube to the shores of the Black Sea.'[1]

For once he was not exaggerating. The statistics are impressive. Over Hitler's new front, stretching 1,800 miles, 148 combat divisions were deployed involving some 3.3 million men. Along with a vast quantity of artillery, the German invaders had at their disposal 3,350 tanks, 600,000 vehicles, 600,000 horses and some 2,500 aircraft.[2] The campaign, asserted Goebbels, was nothing less than a crusade to deliver Europe from Bolshevism. But the defeat of communism was not Hitler's only aim. Once the Ukraine had been taken he planned to exterminate the entire Slav population, except those suitable for slave labour, before repopulating its immense expanse of agricultural land (the longed-for *Lebensraum*) with Aryan Germans. Equally vital was the capture of the Caucasian oilfields – Maikop, Grozny and Baku – to alleviate the Reich's chronic energy shortage. Without oil the war was unsustainable. 'May God help us in this battle,' Goebbels concluded.[3]

Despite the sun streaming through his window, Franz Noichl, now twelve years old, was still asleep when his father came to tell him the news. After Hitler's rapid and seemingly effortless triumphs, Franz not unreasonably assumed that Germany was invincible. In consequence, he was sceptical when his father jubilantly claimed that Hitler's defeat was now inevitable. Nor, a few days later, did he take seriously the old forester Michel who, spreading out a yellowing map on the floor of his mountain hut, asked: 'Does this Hitler know how big Russia is?' His elders' sceptical comments had less effect on Franz than the stirring fanfare from Liszt's tone poem *Les Préludes*, chosen by the Propaganda Ministry to herald official military announcements – 'The Supreme Command of the Armed Forces announces . . .'.[4]

Until the invasion of the Soviet Union, the war had seemed relatively remote to Oberstdorfers. Only five of their young men had perished, while the rapid succession of victories was for most of them – even those who did not necessarily support the Nazis – a source of deep pride. The record books of the Oberstdorf branch of the German Alpine Club (DAV), for example, resonate with optimism, as seen in this report of the 1940 annual general meeting on 4 April:

When in December 1939 the Führer was forced by Poland's conduct and by England and France's declaration of war to call his people to arms, the men of the DAV responded with enthusiasm. Today, we therefore remember first and foremost our soldiers. The glorious things we have heard of their bravery in the Polish campaign fill us with pride. We are confident that the war against England and France will also soon end in victory. Twenty-two of our members are fighting with the 1st Mountain Division. Alongside the boys stand the veterans, some proudly wearing the medals they won in the First World War. We want them to know that we will always support them. We salute them all.[5]

The AGM report a year later is equally buoyant. 'We believe utterly in victory over our enemies, who forced this war upon us, and in the creation of a great German empire. We vow that we will do everything we can to back our soldiers in the field.'[6] Little did the club secretary, Emma Maile (whose brother Max Maile was fighting with the 99th Regiment), realise as she wrote those words just how much support the soldiers on the Eastern Front were going to need.

Any complacency on the part of villagers, who like Franz had thought Hitler indestructible, was soon to be shattered. Indeed, the reality of the invasion was brought sharply home when they learned that, only hours after Goebbels' momentous radio announcement, the first Oberstdorf soldier (serving with the 99th) in the Barbarossa campaign had been killed. He was none other than Ludwig Vörg, one of the four mountaineers who had so recently scaled the North Face of the Eiger, and who was known by his fellow mountaineers as the 'bivouac king' because of his ability to sleep soundly while roped to a narrow, icy ledge thousands of feet above ground.[7]

Since that epic adventure, he like Heckmair had made his home in Oberstdorf.

In summer 1940, Vörg and Heckmair (who had also joined the 99th) had been plucked out of the *Wehrmacht* and, along with a number of Ordensburg personnel, sent to an SS camp at Falkensee near Berlin to be trained for a special task in the East. How much detail Heckmair and Vörg knew of what this entailed is impossible to know, but in any case they did not remain long at Falkensee. Discovered one day playing cards when they should have been attending a lecture given by Robert Ley, the head of the German Labour Front, they were labelled politically unreliable, reduced to the ranks and returned under a cloud to the *Wehrmacht*.[8]

By the time Vörg rejoined his regiment it was probably already in southern Poland. On 1 June, his fellow 99er Alfons Meinlinger made the following diary entry:

> We're leaving Grybów [in southern Poland] tomorrow. We're to march for six days and then on to the Russian border. The rumours are interesting. Some say we will attack the Russians, others say the Russians will grant us passage. I think it's just a ruse to fool the English. That's my guess. Germany is massing troops at the Russian border and Russia is doing the same. England thinks we are fighting each other. But really we will attack England together.

That afternoon he had watched an SS unit drive into the Grybów marketplace and round up Jews. Compelled alternately to run and lie flat on the ground, the latter were then

> forced to collect rubbish and horse manure by hand and put it in their hats. While doing this, the SS kicked their

backsides and if they were too slow hit them in the face. I watched this for a long time and thought to myself how unpleasant it was to treat defenceless people like this. I would rather shoot a Jew outright than mistreat him in this way. Neither is good. If we were here longer, we could tame the Jews.[9]

Three weeks later the 99th was camped in woods outside the village of Stare Sioło, right on the border between German and Russian-occupied Poland. Fifteen miles to the north, in the equally tiny hamlet of Stary Dzików, Oberstdorf soldiers serving in the 98th were also poised for action.

The last night of Vörg's life was warm and sultry. The men were tense. Although they had known for weeks that something big was brewing, they still had no information. But on 22 June 1941 they were woken a little after 1 a.m. and an hour later learned that they were to attack the Soviet Union. The order was couched in typical Nazi rhetoric – 'The devil stands before us! We will destroy him! Long Live the Edelweiss! Hail the Führer.'[10] According to Gabriel Kopold, a sergeant from Ebenhausen (eighty miles north of Oberstdorf), serving in the 98th, the news came as a shock. Their officer's briefing exalting Lebensraum and anti-communist crusades, noted Kopold, made rather less impression on the soldiers than the stark fact that they were about to set off on a very long march to a very uncertain destination.[11]

The men made their preparations as quietly as possible before moving out of the woods to take up position close to the German–Soviet demarcation line that had been in place since the 1939 campaign. It was an area of open ground lying between the forest and a great mass of Russian barbed wire that had already been cut by the Germans.[12] At 3.15 a.m., the two regiments moved forward. As in 1939, their immediate objective was Lwów, about sixty-five miles away. Then Russia had been their ally; now it was the enemy.

The first day of the fighting lasted sixteen hours and was the most intense that the Oberstdorfers had yet experienced. As one 99th soldier put it,

> It seemed that we fought from dawn to dusk before falling exhausted into our shallow slit trenches. The NCOs and officers kept watch while we slept. We were awakened just after 3 a.m., had a quick wash, a hasty breakfast and were on the march by dawn. Our commanding officer had been ordered to keep on the tail of the retreating enemy. We marched and marched, kilometre after kilometre. The roads were so bad and so congested with motor traffic that we preferred to walk cross-country. The weather was blindingly hot. When we marched on the roads, we were shrouded in a cloud of dust. The sandy roads were ankle-deep in a fine yellow dust that clung to our sweating faces.[13]

Vörg, aged twenty-nine, was just one among the heavy losses suffered by both regiments on that first day of the invasion. At least death spared him the shocking sight that greeted his comrades when they entered Lwów six days later. The corpses of several thousand Germans, Poles, Ukrainians and Jews, murdered by the Russians before their retreat, lay rotting in grotesque heaps around the city.[14*]

---

* Kopold's disgust at the Russians' brutality turned to revulsion against his own countrymen when a year later he was back in Lwów and ordered to escort three concentration camp inmates to their camp

After occupying Lwów, the 1st Mountain Division continued its long march east. 'Tonight we again covered about 28 kilometres,' wrote Meinlinger on 6 July. 'You drag yourself through the dark night. The roads are bad, your legs ache but you make yourself keep going – it is our duty.' Recording the numbers of dead horses and abandoned Russian equipment he saw by the side of the road, he added, 'I think they have already lost.'

In his book *Hitler's Mountain Troops* James Lucas quotes some of the impressions recorded by soldiers in the 98th and 99th Regiments as they marched through Poland and on through southern Ukraine. For Bavarians, accustomed to relatively small Alpine pastures, the vast, flat fields of maize or sunflowers, stretching in every direction as far as the eye could see, were utterly alien. One man described the 'unforgettable sight' of 'sunflowers that in the morning dip their heads so that the field is a monotonous shade of brown. But when they stand upright at midday and point to the sun, it changes to a bright yellow.' Others recorded the depressingly primitive settlements they encountered – so different from their own neat, picturesque villages back home in Bavaria. The further east they marched, the more wretched the conditions. For young Germans, brainwashed since childhood to believe in their racial superiority, here now was the evidence right before their eyes. As one soldier noted while still in eastern Poland: 'The miscellaneous wooden hovels (one could not really call them villages) were in a decrepit and verminous state. There was no sanitation, no electric light and the so-called roads were rutted

after their work in a hospital. According to Kopold, their account of their living conditions was so shocking that he allowed them to escape.

tracks in the sandy soil. We fed from the old familiar "Gulasch Cannon" and ate very well,' he wrote, adding, 'although it was strictly forbidden, we all gave food to the Polish children who hung around our campsite.'[15]

By early August, Meinlinger was even more convinced that the Soviets were about to surrender. Somewhere near Uman in southern Ukraine, he noted that 'the war is drawing to a close'. Nevertheless, he was impressed by the 'fanaticism' with which the Bolshevists fought – 'even women are at the front'. He had watched the execution of a Russian woman. 'She was made to dig her own grave,' he noted. 'Before she was shot, she looked the marksman straight in the eye. I was only surprised that she didn't give the command herself.'[16]

Meanwhile Heckmair was marching on the Soviet Union from a different direction. Why, with his reputation as one of the finest climbers in the world, he was not allowed to return to his prestigious mountain regiment after the Falkensee episode is not known. Conceivably his reluctance to become a Nazi hero was considered so serious a crime for a man of his celebrity that the authorities chose to humiliate him by removing him from the 99th and his fellow Bavarians.

A photograph shows Heckmair, chatting informally to an officer while walking east in a column of soldiers through a Polish forest. The men, looking confident and relaxed, can have had little idea of the trials that lay ahead. As part of the massive Army Group Centre (*Heeresgruppe Mitte*), their mission was to march through the Soviet Republic of Belarus behind the Panzer tank divisions, seize the Russian city of Smolensk and then move rapidly on to capture Moscow before winter set in. Another blitzkrieg – another triumph.

Although initially the German invasion had made such impressive progress, the capture of Smolensk took two months (from July to September), much longer than expected. Then on 7 October the first snow fell. It quickly melted, but it left behind a great sea of thick sticky mud that was to hold up the German advance still further.

While Heckmair was fighting with his infantry regiment at Smolensk, the 99th was some 500 miles to the south, still advancing east through Ukraine. Only two days after the snowfall, Alfons Meinlinger wrote from an undisclosed location, 'everything is working like clockwork. The enemy are surrendering in droves. We all believe it will be over in three weeks. Today was the best yet. It went so well that the Russians didn't even fire a shot. Then a loudspeaker van turned up to entertain us with popular music.'[17]

But his confidence was soon to vanish. As Hitler's master plan was based on the assumption that Moscow would fall before the cold weather set in, the men were hopelessly ill-equipped to deal with what was to prove one of the coldest European winters on record. By the time Heckmair's regiment came within range of Moscow in mid-October[18] the temperature had dropped dramatically, causing untold misery to the soldiers, many of whom developed severe frostbite.

Back home in Oberstdorf, villagers were now called upon not only to donate warm clothing but also their precious skis and ski boots. It was at this point that Franz began to wonder if his father might not have been right after all.

On 3 October 1941, thirty-eight-year-old Lieutenant Gerd Aurich, from Chemnitz in Saxony, was on a leadership course in Sonthofen when he learned that he and eight fellow lieutenants had been posted to the Eastern Front with immediate effect. A master builder by profession, Aurich was also an experienced mountaineer (he had climbed the Matterhorn by its most difficult route), which is why when war broke out he had at once headed south to join the 1st Mountain Division. Assigned to the 99th Regiment, his Alpine skills were impressive enough for him to have been appointed an instructor at the Division's high-altitude school at Sonthofen, where the several hundred Oberstdorfers serving in the 1st Mountain Division received their training.[19]

Before setting off to join the 99th at the front, Aurich was allowed a short visit home:

> I play with Karin and am also delighted by little Gerd. Then I go to church with Mother. The pastor tells us 'not to worry about anything!'. It is a thanksgiving service for harvest festival. The church is packed. The sermon touches me deeply. Many prisoners' messages are read out. Holy Communion. Cemetery. We spend more time in the garden. Ilse cooks a splendid meal. Karin is so sweet to me. In the afternoon we go for a walk and take photographs and cine films. Then we go to the station. At 6.20 p.m. the train arrives with my comrades, who give me a warm welcome.[20]

The lieutenants' journey east was no jaunt. It took a month to cover the 1,500-odd miles from Warsaw to the front at Artemovsk (Bakhmut) in south-eastern Ukraine, where by November the 99th was engaged in bitter fighting.

To begin with things were not too bad. Aurich even went sightseeing in Warsaw. He was impressed by the city's walls, towers and fortifications but shocked at the 'terrible poverty and dirt'. Six walnuts were all he could find to eat in the marketplace.[21] When they reached Lwów (250 miles south-east of Warsaw) his friends showed him where they had fought in the

1939 campaign. By now the weather had turned. 'Cold morning,' wrote Aurich, 'comfortable carriage again, second class.'[22] But that night at Kasatin (Kozyatyn) the only available billet was a cattle truck. Next morning they found seats in a carriage filled with noisy South Tyroleans. 'A lieutenant-colonel from Dresden joined us,' recorded Aurich. 'He has seen appalling atrocities – mass slaughtering of Jews. The war is terrible here in the East. We reached Mirinovka (Myronivka) in the evening.'[23]

On 10 October they arrived in Kirovograd (Kropyvnytskyi), where just ten days earlier several hundred Jews had been taken to nearby anti-tank ditches and murdered:[24]

This morning Lieutenants Mayer, Heimlich, Johannes, Huber and I went to a church destroyed by the Russians. It is already being rebuilt. We find a corner where we hold a service. We decide to meet there daily. These are precious hours of inner reflection. At noon we learn that tomorrow we go to the front. I feel calm. I know I am in God's hands. I want with all my heart to do my duty for my beloved and beautiful Fatherland. In the afternoon we visit a prison camp. The misery! Then we meet at the officers' inn. Everything is very cheap: two glasses of compote, a glass of vodka, three pieces of cake, 1 pagora: 70 Pfennigs. I'm reading W. Flex's moving book *Für dich mein Vaterland* [*For You My Fatherland*].[25] This book also gives me strength for the days ahead. A peaceful hour thinking of my loved ones at home. Sleep at 9 p.m. During the night we hear screaming and shooting from the nearby prison camp.[26]

But on 15 October they were still a long way from the front. A derailed armaments train and sabotaged railway track caused a lengthy delay. 'So we sit down in the sun, close our eyes and dream of the Allgäu mountains,' wrote Aurich. 'But then you open your eyes and see only the thick mud and a bombed-out train station.'

After another cold, sleepless night they finally reached the great Dnieper River, stretching 1,400 miles from central Russia to the Black Sea. They crossed at Kremenchuk, which the Germans had taken a month before. At this point the river is about half a mile wide, but because the new railway bridge ('a technical miracle') was not yet operational a bus carried them over on a makeshift pontoon. As they drove through the city, Aurich observed the thousands of prisoners and vast quantities of stockpiled supplies awaiting transport. Trucks took them to their next stop – Poltava. On the way they passed three prison camps. Aurich saw crowds of desperate women waiting outside, hoping to secure the release of their menfolk.

> We drive along a great wide road, *Panzerstrecke S* [Armoured Track S]. It is completely silted up. We try another road 50–60 metres wide. It is amazing that so many vehicles somehow manage to make progress through the mud, holes and ditches. There are of course hundreds lying in the mud. Also countless dead horses. It's a mess. Far away in the distance we see huge fields of corn, maize and sunflowers. The huts are poor, built out of clay and covered with straw like everywhere in Ukraine. Each house has a little oven and a draw well. Laundry is hung on a small tree. Some houses have shutters but they are dilapidated and hanging off their hinges. In fact most houses are in a state of collapse. Vast quantities of grain. Many windmills.[27]

Their proximity to the front was now palpable. Poltava had fallen to the Germans only a couple of days earlier. 'Fighting has been fierce here,' recorded Aurich. 'Burnt-out tanks on the streets. Many buildings shelled or destroyed by fire.' The lieutenants' quarters – a bare floor in a rat-infested room – offered little solace. The following evening they arrived in Pereschtschepino (Pereshchepyne), 'a small dirty place. We camp on straw in a filthy little room. Mayer has got lost.'[28] But despite the human misery, devastation and intense cold, or perhaps because of them, the next morning Aurich and his comrades stood round the village well discussing marriage and the search for God.

At 4 p.m. on 18 October, two weeks after leaving Sonthofen, they finally reached their Division command post and were able formally to report their presence. But their journey was far from over. They now had to locate the 99th, currently in the thick of the fighting around Artemovsk, still sixty miles away.

> Wake at 4.45 a.m. Wash and shave in the small lake. Our transport leaves at 7 a.m. It is a fine morning. The sun shines warmly through the windows. Our vehicle makes good progress. We overtake long lines of artillery and infantry. Soon we too will have to march like this. My thoughts are at home – Mother in church and Ilse with Karin and Gerd. God will reunite us. Our vehicle often breaks down. We improvise repairs. At noon a sabotaged bridge brings us to a halt. We drive into a large hemp field to camouflage ourselves from aeroplanes. The columns march on. There is a wireless in the vehicle. We listen to German folk music. Good country songs. We wonder what they are doing at home right now. Today I've only eaten a piece of white cabbage and some sunflower seeds. How do you learn to live on so little? Around 3 p.m. we head off. Columns of men are piling up at the makeshift bridge because the

vehicles have to be towed through the mud one by one by tractors. We have to get out of ours and run after it through the mud. Just before we reach Alexandropoli we hit another problem – a big muddy hole between two ponds. Everything is stuck again and it is already getting dark. If the Russian planes should come now! At 7 p.m. we reach Alexandropoli. We make our camp on damp straw in the school, which until noon was used as a stable. I have no blanket, only my coat. It took 12 hours to cover 60 k.[29]

Alexandropoli (Oleksandrivka), which they reached on 20 October, was about thirty miles west of Artemovsk. Heavy rain and lack of petrol kept them marooned in the small town for five days. Aurich tried to make the best of it. He struck up a friendship with a military policeman:

A quiet thoughtful man . . . he had watched the execution of a number of GPU officers [Soviet secret police] and told us how at the last moment they made a sign of the cross. Come to the front and you will learn to pray! May God grant that all Germans will learn to pray again.[30]

Some of the new arrivals, also now stranded in Alexandropoli, Aurich found worryingly arrogant. 'There's a lot of bad feeling,' he commented. 'Every day you hear remarks like: "I'm from Tölz! Kiss my ass" and "We'll show the infantry!"' The long wait in the rain got on everyone's nerves but news that Stalino (Donetsk), forty miles to the south-east, had fallen cheered up everyone. 'We Sonthofeners sit together by the radio listening to lovely folk songs until 10 p.m.' wrote Aurich.[31]

The next few days were tedious, but as usual Aurich kept himself well occupied. He observed how the townspeople liked to wear lots of cheap jewellery and to decorate their houses with pink and blue paper flowers. 'The oven takes up a quarter of the room,' he noted. 'People sleep on it. The children lie in baskets suspended from the ceiling. They all look well fed.' He did his laundry, played chess and roasted a goose. 'In the evening we sit around and talk about culture, civilisation, the world view and religion.'[32]

At last, on 25 October, the rain eased and they were able to leave:

> Up at 5 a.m. I feel weak and dizzy. 6.30 departure in two *Panjegespann* [traditional Ukrainian horse wagons]. The mud is a nightmare – we travel through corn, sunflower and hemp fields. We have to keep going. But it is impossible to push the old Ukrainian cart through the mud even when we remove our heavy backpacks. Then out of nowhere a vehicle appears and gives us a lift. Once more we're able to enjoy the wide-open spaces. It's an English jeep, captured in Greece. We are astonished at how well it goes. Around noon we reach a village. We make a short stop. I look at the people. Like everywhere else they are pathetic and stubborn. Children walk around in the cold with only a shirt that reaches to the navel. A sad scene.

That night they slept by a haystack, having taken eight hours to cover nine miles. It was a beautiful evening. 'We look west and send greetings home. To the north, not far away, machine guns hammer sporadically. Before sleeping, we make sure that our guns are at the ready.'[33]

Aurich found the next day's struggle through the relentless mud, carrying his share of their heavy equipment, particularly exhausting. And when they did finally reach a village, yet again there was nothing to eat or drink. But a surprise awaited them at the next one. 'A lieutenant offers us good food and a fine *Panjegespann*. Sergeant Weiss has only just heard that some weeks ago he became a father. He finds a bottle of sparkling wine.' Feeling much restored, Aurich and his companions now resumed their journey in style. 'Four Russian horses gallop across the steppe through the mud until we reach a farmstead at about 3 p.m. This is laid out very differently from the usual farms. We discover that it belongs to a Bavarian. We stayed there overnight. Above us an eagle circles.'[34]

By 29 October, the sound of thundering guns had grown much louder. Aurich paints an apocalyptic scene. 'We trudge through fields. The mud makes our boots so heavy we can barely move. Dense fog. East wind. Dead horses everywhere. After dousing the fields in petrol, the Russians have set them alight so we are surrounded by smouldering wheat. The rail track has been blown up.' Later that day they came across their first Soviet collective, the 'Rosa Luxemburg':

> From a distance it appeared quite pleasant. Some houses even have roof tiles. A few women look and speak German and are cleaner. But the streets and interiors of the houses are as filthy as everywhere else. So this is the Soviet paradise these people longed for. It is cold and raining.[35]

On 1 November they reached Konstantinovka (Kostyanty-nivka), an industrial city with a gigantic ironworks and population of 100,000. They were now only fifteen miles from Artemovsk.

> Almost everything here has been destroyed. Large groups of people stand on the street sullenly watching us. Misery.

They have no work and nothing to eat. How will they
survive the winter? We find quarters in a bombed-out
paper factory. Tomorrow we will join our regiment. Four
weeks ago, I was at home. What happy hours those were.
'Never mind!'

With the sound of gunfire now their constant companion,
they finally reached Artemovsk the next day. 'There is less
destruction here,' observed Aurich, 'but the shops have all been
looted. The people stare at us.'

At dusk, we reach our regimental command post at the
front. Our men have been through a lot – no cigarettes,
no mail, no laundry since 2 October. We are about to
attack. The attack is delayed. The men return to their
quarters in Artemovsk. But we stay. Pounding machine
guns. Booming artillery. A bright glare ahead – the village
is ablaze. Deafening explosions. Russian demolition squads
are constantly at work – even behind us. It is a beautiful
night with a full moon. Dispatch riders race across the
fields. Flares shoot up; the burning village turns the sky red.
So passes our first day at the front. Later we also return to
Artemovsk and find quarters in a small house. Huber and I
even find a bed to share. Here on the front line anything is
possible. Artillery and rattling machine guns keep us awake.
My thoughts go to home. At last I have time to reflect: 'The
Lord, your God is with you.'

Having endured so much together, the lieutenants bade each
other an emotional farewell the following morning as they set
out to report to their respective units. They would soon learn
exactly how their 99th comrades were faring in a campaign

that had so unexpectedly turned from triumphant advance to hellish conflict.

Assigned to the 8th company, Aurich was appointed a senior platoon leader. His new quarters were in a farmhouse about three miles west of Artemovsk. 'It all looks very dirty and there is not much space. The stench, snoring and vermin make it impossible to sleep.'[36] As he was about to discover, life at the front was mostly chaos and confusion:

> Alarm goes off. We are in action. The enemy is persistent. They counter-attack but are repelled. Alarm again. Heavy shooting. Planes come in the night. Many bombs fall close to us. It is rumoured they are Italian, but they are supposed to be well to the right of us. Much uncertainty surrounding our current situation. We think there is an attempt at encirclement – Panzer Division Kleist is supposed to be advancing from the south. Losses very high. One company has lost 103 out of 135 men. We eat well – chicken and potatoes. My platoon takes good care of me. No bread – we bake flour cakes. The Russians are only 500 metres in front of us. I walk into the village. Suddenly there is a noise like wild geese flying. Then 15 to 20 violent impacts. Shells hit the village. Nobody takes any notice. Heavy rain and hail follow. It is hard on the guards. I have our quarters thoroughly cleaned but they remain unpleasant. The men are lousy and dirty. We have a gramophone and Russian records, something to amuse us. I give the night watch their orders. 9 p.m. sleep.[37]

On 12 November, Aurich learned that the 8th company had been ordered to reconnoitre a couple of nearby villages the next day. 'I feel a great sense of peace,' he wrote that evening, 'don't worry about anything!' He also admitted to feeling excitement. After the long months of training and the hazardous journey to the front, his moment had come. He was to lead his platoon on a demanding and dangerous operation for the Fatherland:

> Get up at 5 a.m. It's freezing cold and there is a strong wind. The Big Dipper and Cassiopeia are very clear. It snowed overnight. Minus 15 degrees Celsius. At 6 a.m. I leave with my platoon. We also take along a couple of machine gunners and communications specialists. This ice storm is terrible for the radio men who have no head protection. It takes an hour to reach Balka Tschirkova. We see a brickyard ahead. There is movement. We search it but find only civilians. They tell us that there are 2 companies of Russians in Karlowka . . . We enter the village and conduct a house-to-house search. The villagers tell me that the Russians have only just left. I keep in contact with the company by radio. The Russians have taken almost everything but we find enough. It's not easy to take away the last cow from weeping women. But I have to be hard-hearted. I must carry out my orders. Anyway, the Russians would have taken the cow for themselves when they come back tomorrow. We make a farmer drive the booty (chickens, geese, 1 pig, plus bread and flour) to where the rest of the company is waiting. We also bring 2 more cows, 3 calves and 1 goat. We continue our reconnaissance. Snow crystals whip our faces.[38]

Although the men were disappointed not to have had a go at the enemy, they were thankful to be heading back to base. It was 4 p.m. and they had been on the job for ten hours. 'The cold brings tears to our eyes,' wrote Aurich. Exhausted, they stumbled back over the icy fields. But just as they had reached the edge of their own village and thought they were home and dry, they came under intense fire. 'One gun shoots directly into our company,' wrote Aurich, 'then it swings to the right and shoots into the village. The 2nd platoon received a direct hit. Three men dead. They were plucking chickens.'[39] At last, by now completely frozen and physically drained, Aurich and his men reached their quarters. After drinking hot milk, they lay down to sleep.

The following, bitterly cold, days saw Aurich in the thick of many more such skirmishes. Having now experienced the full thrust of battle and survived he was beginning to gain confidence. 'I feel a great peace,' he wrote on 15 November. 'Don't worry about anything! God has guided me wonderfully so far and will continue.' Then on 19 November, in a village called Sajzewa somewhere to the east of Artemovsk, Aurich made his last diary entry:

> I slept well until 9 a.m. We have a warm room and are given hot milk. Then I have a proper wash. The people here are very clean and hospitable. The housewife, a sprightly woman of about 40 is mothering us – she is cleanly dressed and wears jewellery – a cross and two amber beads. She even cuts my toenails and scrubs my back. She does it very well. I had just finished my bath when the alarm goes off. We are on special call. What's next?

Three days later, Aurich wrote to his wife from the Artemovsk field hospital:

> I am holding on bravely and so must you. The day before yesterday I was leading my platoon in a major attack when

a grenade was thrown at us. Shrapnel hit me in my shoulder and spine. Unfortunately I am paralysed from the waist down. It took 10 hours to transport me here across the frozen fields, under constant fire. One of my comrades was also wounded. I am now through the worst of the pain and this morning drank my first soup. The doctors are very good but overworked. The nursing is poor. The military hospital is overcrowded. There is much heartache all around. Blindness, head and stomach wounds. For me, everything is going well and I hope to move soon. They can cure the paralysis with special treatment. We must not worry. God will help us.

This field hospital is unlikely to have been more than a collection of tents and impossible to keep warm. It is little wonder that the nursing, of which Aurich complains, was of a low standard. Many of the nurses were poorly trained and had to tend their patients wearing greatcoats and gloves. Understandably, there are many things that Aurich does not mention in his letter home – the stench and cold, the rats running over the wounded as they lay on stretchers, the constant groaning and haunting screams of men in terrible pain.

Aurich died at the military hospital at Kramatorskaja (Kramatorsk) a month later on 21 December 1941. 'His death has hit us all hard,' wrote the doctor to Aurich's widow, Ilse, 'because right up until the end he was so determined to live.' He was buried in the 'Heroes' Cemetery' at Kramatorsk.

14

Turning Point

In the autumn of 1941, around 1,500 Oberstdorfers were on active service – in the Soviet Union, on the Western Front, in the Balkans and in North Africa. Apart from those serving in the 1st Mountain Division, villagers were also fighting in every arm of the *Wehrmacht* including the motorcycle corps, artillery, Luftwaffe, the pioneer regiment, the SS and even the navy. By the beginning of November, Oberstdorf had lost eighteen of its soldiers in Barbarossa alone, six of them from the 99th.

The invasion of the Soviet Union not only proved the turning point militarily for the Nazis, it also marked a dramatic plunge in public confidence. Until Barbarossa it had seemed that Hitler's promise of a quick victory followed by lasting peace was entirely possible. But once the eastern offensive stalled in the autumn of 1941 and Pearl Harbor brought America into the war on 7 December, many Germans began to suspect that a total victory was now impossible. It is hardly surprising, therefore, that when their men came home for brief spells, the villagers were eager to hear from them stories that would raise their spirits and restore their optimism.

As a mountaineer, Heckmair was better able than most to deal with the extreme conditions on the Eastern Front. Nevertheless, it must have been a relief when, thanks to the birth of his first son, he was allowed a few days' leave. On 13 November 1941 he was back in Oberstdorf giving a slide lecture on the 1938 Eiger ascent to a packed room in the station restaurant, which offered the largest space available in the village for such a gathering.[1] No doubt Vörg's recent death was the cause of many a damp eye in the audience, especially when they heard how, despite a crampon skewering his hand, Vörg had heroically held the rope when Heckmair fell off the Eiger, thus saving all four climbers from certain death.

The practice of Alpine Club members giving public talks while home on leave was already established by the time Heckmair made his presentation. Three months earlier, on 7 August 1941, Adolf Hofmann (son of the *OGF* printer Andreas Hofmann), who was serving in the 5th Mountain Division's 100th Regiment,* had spoken about his experiences in the Balkan campaign. 'This evening,' reported Emma Maile,

> Lieutenant Adolf Hofmann showed members a film of the army's triumphant march through Greece. His graphic account of the heavy fighting, in which our mountain troops were engaged around the Metaxas Line, was illustrated with photographs. He told us of how they had annihilated the Salonika army, of how they had hoisted the Swastika on the summit of Olympus, and of their great victory at Thermopylae. The Lieutenant then described the

---

* The 100th Mountain Regiment was originally part of the 1st Mountain Division but in 1940 it was transferred to the newly formed 5th Mountain Division.

Battle of Crete, in which the extraordinary courage of the
parachute and mountain troops endowed our national flag
with immortal glory.[2]

Hofmann did not only speak on military matters. Emma noted
how he also gave a vivid account of the Balkans landscape
and its people. 'What we heard and saw', she reported 'made
us truly honour our field-grey boys, and the Edelweiss which
they wear with such pride.'[3] When three months later (two
days after Heckmair's lecture) news reached Oberstdorf that
Lieutenant Hofmann had been awarded the Knight's Cross,
Germany's most prestigious medal in the Second World War,
the whole village rejoiced.

Indeed, Hofmann's honour was a much-needed boost to
morale. As 1941 became 1942, although Oberstdorf continued
to fare much better than most parts of Germany, the Allied
bombing of the medieval towns of Lübeck and Rostock in
March 1942, followed by the devastation of Cologne in May,
was a shock to Oberstdorfers, as it was to Germans everywhere.
Then on 13 November the Allies recovered the Libyan port
of Tobruk, dealing yet another blow to national confidence.

But despite such dispiriting events, a digest of Oberstdorf
news culled from the *Oberallgäuer Nationalzeitung* suggests
that the fundamental pattern of village life remained remarkably unchanged throughout 1942. In the early part of the year
(when even though the Barbarossa campaign had slowed,
Germany was still making good military progress) matters
considered worthy of note included the unseasonal drought,
a gymnastics display, the reopening of the Bauern Theater, a
new book, *Summer and Winter in Oberallgäu*, the repair of
the church organ and several spectacular avalanches. In May
a local woman was arrested for being in possession of 222 cut

gentians, while in June 300 mountain sheep were herded from the train station via Hindenburgstrasse to Loretto. 'With no dog to control them', reported the newspaper, 'the sheep became very distressed due to the unusual volume of traffic, and the large number of spectators, all of which made the shepherd's task very trying.' A month later a large number of wounded soldiers visited Oberstdorf on the same day that the Vienna Boys' Choir gave a concert in the village school. In August two climbers fell to their deaths, but toddler Otto Kreitner was saved from drowning by his four-year-old sister. In October domestic concerns included the state of the Hofacker cattle market, a lecture on 'The Beauty of the Nebelhorn in the Changing Seasons' and the traditional annual get-together of Oberstdorf's older inhabitants. It was also noted that the well-known American artist and committed Nazi Robert Curry celebrated his seventieth birthday. Apparently, nothing occurred in the village during November worth reporting, but in December the Oberstdorf Chamber Music Association gave its inaugural concert.[4]

While such reports may have given villagers a reassuring sense that life was continuing as normal, the reality of the war was inescapable and sometimes impacted on them in unexpected ways. In 1942 the regime, always in search of raw materials, lit on a readily available source of metal – the nation's church bells. As a result an order requisitioning Oberstdorf's bells was received in the spring, causing deep upset in the village. Since, however, bells of exceptional historical importance or those containing high amounts of silver were exempt, Father Rupp and his supporters came up with an ingenious scheme. They would simply raise the silver content of St Johannes Baptist's beloved bell by inserting more silver into it. One of the churchwardens, Josef Pirkl, who also happened to be a master blacksmith, offered his services and with the use of a large metal file and a few silver coins he achieved the desired, if crudely obvious, result. There followed weeks of anxious waiting while the bell was examined at the material-testing facility in Cologne. Back came the long-awaited answer: 'This bell has a silver content of 30 per cent and, in line with the current regulations, is therefore exempt.'[5] No doubt the official responsible for the decision was a Catholic Rhinelander whose sympathies lay firmly with Father Rupp. Nothing, however, could save Oberstdorf's other bells. Within weeks, having been melted down and transformed into armaments, they were on their way to the front. Some months later the church's crosses, incense burners, baptism plates and holy water vessels followed them, although miraculously its copper roof and candlesticks survived.

But if during 1942 the atmosphere in the village was still relatively calm, inevitably the appalling conditions faced by its soldiers on the Eastern Front became widely known, despite the relentlessly upbeat propaganda. At the same time rumours of German atrocities became increasingly difficult to ignore. When the soldiers returned home on leave, their public utterances had, of course, to be resolutely positive or they faced dire consequences. But what the young men may have revealed in the privacy of their own homes, in the confessional, or perhaps walking in the solitude of the mountains with a trusted friend is another matter. It is reasonable to assume that at least some unburdened themselves of the barbaric deeds they had witnessed or themselves perpetrated in the name of the Fatherland.

Crimes committed by the elite mountain regiments, particularly later in the Balkans, are fully documented in H.F. Meyer's book *Blutiges Edelweiß* (*Bloodstained Edelweiss*).

Meyer suggests that it was during the Russian campaign that the 1st Mountain Division first became desensitised to human life, estimating that in the course of their eastward advance its soldiers killed upwards of 60,000 people.[6] It raises the question of how men who in the early stages of the invasion had shared their food with Polish children were only weeks later massacring their fellow human beings on such a scale.

At least part of the explanation must lie in the string of directives distributed to the troops at the outset of Barbarossa. These made brutally clear exactly what was expected of them. 'This struggle demands a ruthless and strenuous crackdown on Bolshevist agitators, irregulars, saboteurs and Jews,' stated the order entitled *Guidelines for the Conduct of Troops in Russia* (*Leitlinien für das Verhalten der Truppen in Russland*).[7] The following is quoted from a pamphlet issued in June 1941:

> Anyone who has ever looked into the face of a Red commissar knows what the Bolshevists are. There is no need here for theoretical reflections. It would be an insult to animals if one were to call the features of these, largely Jewish, tormentors of people beasts. They are the embodiment of the infernal, the personification of an insane hatred of everything that is noble in humanity. In the shape of these commissars we witness the revolt of the subhuman against noble blood. The masses whom they are driving to their deaths with every means of icy terror and lunatic incitement would have brought all meaningful life to an end had the incursion [i.e. the communist invasion of Germany] not been prevented at the last moment.[8]

The purpose of such edicts was to indoctrinate the men into believing that their Slavic/Jewish enemy was subhuman and should be treated like vermin. The troops were especially encouraged to abuse women and children. One commander included the following advice in an order to his division: 'Youths from eleven to fourteen are commonly used to carry information, and as Russians are more afraid of beatings than guns, flogging is the recommended means of interrogation.'[9]

The *Einsatzgruppe* (Task Force) was a branch of the SS sent into Germany's occupied territories to murder Jews, Gypsies and political opponents on an industrial scale. Twenty-eight-year-old Heinz Schubert was a lieutenant in *Einsatzgruppe* D. It is estimated that this death squad alone executed over 90,000 individuals, the vast majority of them civilians.[10] In October 1941 Schubert was appointed adjutant to the commander of his unit then operating in Crimea. His wife, meanwhile, having fled the bombing in Berlin, was safe in Oberstdorf, where their first son was born. On the occasions that Schubert was able to visit his wife on leave, one wonders how much of the war he shared with her. Did he, for instance, tell her of the events that took place near the Crimean city of Simferopol on 13 December 1941? Although we can never know what passed between them, or what he may have confided to a comrade over a beer in one of Oberstdorf's many pubs, we do know what he told the court at his Nuremberg trial after the war:

> I was assigned . . . to organise and inspect the shooting of about 700 to 800 people, which was to take place in the close vicinity of Simferopol . . . I went to the gypsy quarter of [the city] and supervised the loading of the persons who were to be shot into a truck. I took care that the loading was completed as quickly as possible and that there were no disturbances or unrest by the native population.

Furthermore I took care the condemned persons were not
beaten while the loading was going on . . . For a short time,
when the people who were to be shot were already standing in their positions in the tank ditch, I supervised the
actual shooting . . . [They] were shot with sub-machine
guns and rifles. I knew that it was of the greatest importance . . . to have the persons who were to be shot killed
in the most humane and military manner possible because
otherwise, in other methods of killing, the moral strain
would have been too great for the execution squad.[11]

'We did not set out to kill,' Schubert stated at his trial, 'but
to defend Western civilisation.'[12] Given the unceasing propaganda to which he and his generation had been subjected,
perhaps he really believed this. What is clear is that neither
Schubert nor the other *Einsatzgruppe* men on trial with him
were common thugs or psychopaths. They included lawyers,
an economist, a university professor, an opera singer, even a
former priest. Schubert himself claimed ancestry from the
composer Franz Schubert, a point picked up by the prosecutor. 'Schubert's family reached back to the creator of the
"Unfinished Symphony"', he observed, 'but one must remark
with sorrow that it is a far cry from the "Unfinished Symphony"
of Vienna to the finished Christmas massacre of Simferopol.'[13]

One Oberstdorfer who did reveal to his wife the savagery
he had witnessed during the Russian campaign was the pilot
Georg Joas, who was awarded the German Cross in Gold for
multiple acts of bravery. A charming, adventurous young man
whose pre-war exploits were the stuff of Hollywood, he was
already a village hero even before the war. His Customs official
father had wanted him to pursue a career in local government
but young Georg had other ideas. Obsessed with aeroplanes,

he first qualified as a mechanic at the Junkers aircraft factory before going on to train as a pilot. After working for a Russian airline in Turkestan (where he took a leading part in a local uprising), he lived in South America, again flying for Junkers and surviving a series of hair-raising adventures. By the late 1930s he was back in Germany working for the new commercial airline Lufthansa and still flying Junkers 52s (nicknamed Auntie Ju or Iron Annie). After war broke out the Luftwaffe appropriated Joas, along with the aeroplanes.

Sometime in the spring of 1942 Joas was given command of a postal squadron on the Polish–Belarus border, 100 miles east of Warsaw. Because it had become increasingly difficult to deliver the soldiers' mail overland, on 15 April 1942 a military airmail service was created.[14] Each soldier received four airmail stamps a month: two for his own use and two to send home so that his family could write back. The system was such a success that the ration was doubled in June, enabling the soldiers to send and receive one airmail letter a week.[15]

As Biała Podlaska lay at the centre of the Eastern Front (which extended from Leningrad in the north to the Crimea, and the Kuban River in the south), and had good rail links to both Berlin and the rest of Germany, the airfield was ideally located for its purpose. By October 1942, Joas and his group of hand-picked pilots had twelve Junkers 52s at their disposal. Acutely aware that the morale of several million soldiers and their families depended on their getting the mail through, they flew thousands of miles each week, often in appalling weather and at increasing risk from enemy aeroplanes.

Ruled for many years by the Radziwiłł family, Biała Podlaska had been an important traffic junction for centuries. By the time Hitler came to power its population consisted largely of Jews (about 7,000) earning a meagre living from small businesses and manufactories. When Joas set up his postal squadron there in 1942, thousands of them had already died from disease and starvation while thousands more had been deported to Sobibor and Treblinka concentration camps. Those considered fit for work were incarcerated, along with the Russian prisoners of war, in camps flanking the airfield. Not only was Joas therefore constantly exposed to the inhuman conditions in which these people existed, but he was also expected to take part in nightly executions. When he refused he was locked up for four days. He later told his wife that he had fully expected to be shot himself. He spoke to her only once of these experiences, but she felt that they had haunted him for the rest of his life.[16]

As hundreds of other young men sporadically reappeared for a few days' leave, rumours of such atrocities began to gain ground in Oberstdorf, although many villagers, refusing to accept that there could be any truth in them, simply put the blame on enemy propaganda. The only way to cope with the death of a beloved husband, father, son or brother was to stick firmly to the belief that he had died a hero, defending his country from 'unprovoked foreign aggression'. To suggest anything else was for many people nothing short of blasphemy.

On 8 November 1942 a number of villagers gathered in the school gymnasium to remember Oberstdorf's fallen soldiers. Choosing his words with care, Mayor Fink gave his address. 'We have come together', he said, 'to honour our dead heroes who with the German people rose up to defend our country and attack its enemies. Displaying death-defying courage,' he continued, 'they went to fight with one holy hope in their hearts – to wipe clean the shame of Versailles. But having proved themselves on the battlefield, these fine young men have been tragically cut down before they could taste the fruits of final victory.'[17]

These were brave words. But as by the turn-of-the-year 'final victory' was beginning to look ever more remote if not hopeless, the villagers became increasingly pessimistic. Even the Nazi propaganda machine could not disguise the numbers of those killed, missing, wounded and captured during the year. And, in addition to the increased bombing of German cities and General Rommel's defeat in North Africa, the Battle of Stalingrad was still unresolved. In the summer of 1942, Hitler had determined to destroy the Soviet army in the south and then capture Stalingrad on his way to the Caucasian oilfields. Instead, by Christmas the frozen and exhausted German soldiers were trapped in the city, encircled by Russians and, under strict orders from Hitler, forbidden to attempt a breakout.

Meanwhile Oberstdorf had lost six more men. Then came the devastating news that the village's Knight's Cross hero, the dashing thirty-year-old Captain Adolf Hofmann, had also been killed. He died on 18 January 1943 just south of Lake Ladoga during the *Wehrmacht*'s attempt to repel a Soviet offensive.* That same day the Siege of Leningrad (begun on 8 September 1941) was partially broken when two Russian rifle divisions linked up near Gorodok, close to where Hofmann was killed.

Although the mayor was Oberstdorf's most senior Nazi, the letter sent from his office to the Hofmann family is striking for its lack of party rhetoric. Remarkably, it does not once refer to National Socialism. Instead it sympathises with the family's 'unspeakable grief' and refers to the village's reverence

---

* Operation Iskra (Spark).

for their son. There is no mention of the Führer, nor is the letter even signed with the mandatory *Heil Hitler*. Rather it concludes, 'Dear Family Hofmann . . . may our Lord God give you strength to bear your heavy suffering.'[18] As the death toll continued to rise remorselessly over the coming months, many similar letters were written to grieving families by commanding officers and comrades. But of the conviction and optimism expressed so enthusiastically in the Alpine Club record book two years earlier there is no trace.

In the twenty-two months between the start of the war and the invasion of the Soviet Union, only six of Oberstdorf's fighting men had been killed. But in the seventeen months from Barbarossa to the November memorial event, the number had risen to ninety-one – a fifteen-fold increase.[19] Among the dead were members of many well-known Oberstdorf families. Max Schratt, for instance, was the nephew of cobbler Josef Schratt, who had created the largest shoe in the world and had helped the nuns in their hour of need. Two of champion ski jumper Heini Klopfer's brothers died in the East. Councillor Karl Witsch's family lost two boys in Russia in the same month. Josef Berktold was killed near Smolensk in July 1942, and his cousin Friedrich in southern Ukraine a month later. The Köpl family lost Max in December 1941 and Wilhelm in August the following year (a third brother, Ernst, was killed towards the end of the war). Several members of the extensive Brutscher family also fell, including Hans, who died in the Russian Arctic. And so it goes on. The list of Barbarossa's Oberstdorf victims is a long one.

15

Mount Elbrus

As 1942 turned into 1943, the mood in Oberstdorf darkened. Now when the village men (those too old to fight) gathered in the pubs at their 'regular tables' to discuss the war, the atmosphere was increasingly gloomy. One recent event, however, was the cause of much village pride and continued to be avidly discussed long afterwards – the ascent of Mount Elbrus. At 11 a.m. on 21 August 1942, so the *Oberallgäuer Nationalzeitung* had reported, a crack mountain troop drawn mainly from the 1st Mountain Division planted the Reich war flag on the summit of Elbrus in the Caucasus, the highest peak in Russia and in Europe.

Among the twenty-one mountaineers to climb Elbrus's 5,642 metres (18,510 feet) were three Oberstdorfers: Kaspar Schwarz, his nephew Hans Schwarz and Otto Niederacher, a carpenter widely known in the village to be an excellent climber. Kaspar Schwarz was one of Oberstdorf's most respected mountain guides. Born into a modest farming family (the ninth of twelve children), thirty-six-year-old Schwarz was a typical Oberstdorfer of the old school. By the time he was seventeen he had climbed most of the neighbouring peaks and in 1935 had formally qualified as a guide. Out of season, he earned a living as a forester and herdsman. Schwarz's nephew Hans, like Alfons Meinlinger, served with a 1st Mountain Division communications unit. 'Only men possessed of an iron will and an unshakable belief in victory over both enemy and mountain are capable of wielding the sword so effectively,' enthused the newspaper.[1] For a brief moment, at least, the villagers were able to recapture something of their former pride and optimism. Although, in fact, the story behind the Elbrus ascent is primarily one of hubris, rivalry and misjudgement, it is also one of extraordinary endurance.*

After Lieutenant Gerd Aurich died in December 1941, the 1st Mountain Division had spent the rest of the winter dug in along the Mius River in south-eastern Ukraine. Although in terms of military action this was a relatively quiet period, the soldiers' inadequate protection against the icy temperatures caused terrible suffering. Many men simply froze to death. Alfons Meinlinger's diary entry for 27 January 1942 gives a graphic description:

> A snowstorm from the east pushes the temperature down to −53 degrees Celsius. We are ordered to lay a cable to the Richter exchange. We know what this means. It is impossible to stand still in the open. We have to walk or stomp around. The cold quickly penetrates our boots and freezes our toes. We don't even notice it, it happens so fast. Connecting the cable is also dangerous, because we have to take off our gloves. The Russian soldiers are much

---

* Predictably, there are many different versions, each with its own particular spin. Nevertheless, it is still possible to piece together a more or less accurate account of what actually happened.

better off. They wear warm quilted jackets and are used to the cold.

By May the Division had recovered enough to move once more on to the offensive. That spring the fighting was intense, but in July the Germans achieved a major breakthrough with the capture of the southern Russian city of Rostov-on-Don, 'Gateway to the Caucasus'. This success cleared the way for the 1st Mountain Division to pursue its new mission – Operation Edelweiss – under the command of General Hubert Lanz. The objective was to secure the high passes around Mount Elbrus before moving rapidly east through the Caucasus to capture the all-important oilfields.

On 7 August, Lanz instructed his thirty-six-year-old orderly officer, Captain Heinz Groth of the 99th, to recruit a high-altitude combat unit that would act as the vanguard for Operation Edelweiss. As well as being experienced moun-taineers, the men selected were all hardened soldiers who had fought with distinction throughout the war. Groth, a com-mitted Nazi since 1935, was from Sonthofen (he later lived in Oberstdorf) and before the war had been chairman of the Sonthofen National Socialist district court. In addition to car-rying out his legal duties, he had been an active reservist in the 99th Regiment and had taken part in both the *Anschluss* and the invasion of the Sudetenland. He was also a dedicated alpin-ist who had co-authored mountain guides with Oberstdorf's former Nazi mayor, Ernst Zettler. Highly educated (he col-lected Russian books), astute and superbly fit, he was the ideal officer to command this new elite unit.

Lanz had a further project up his sleeve for Groth – or possibly it was one that they cooked up together. Once the Division was in command of the passes, Groth was to lead a team up Elbrus and raise the Reich war flag on its summit. Although in military terms this was utterly pointless, Lanz argued that the image of a swastika flying over Europe's highest mountain would send such a powerful propaganda message that the effort would be more than justified. It would also reflect considerable glory on Lanz, Groth and the Division.

Once the new squad was in place, special equipment was flown in, while a caravan of mules delivered the necessary food supplies. On 11 August Groth and his predominantly Bavarian troop of 112 men set off. Morale was high. As Groth stated in a newspaper interview, 'When the men were briefed on their mission, their eyes shone with excitement in anticipation of the mountaineering adventure that lay ahead.'² Alfons Meinlinger was one of them. 'It is about 600 km to the mountains,' he wrote in his diary, 'as we have to get there as fast as possible, we are to travel by truck together with all the pack animals and equipment.'³ Compared with life on the hot, dusty steppe, the journey to Elbrus was a joy. 'Not a Russian in sight,' observed Meinlinger, 'they have all retreated to the mountains. The people are friendly, so whenever we stop at a village we go from house to house asking for eggs. After that, our steel helmets are usually full. Then we eat fried eggs – a very special treat.'⁴

Heinz Groth was equally charmed:

We passed through sunflower and maize fields into the rolling foothills of the Caucasus. The wild River Kuban was our constant companion. The sight of so many dramatic rapids made the hearts of the canoeists among us beat a little faster. But this was no time to dream of such things. Everywhere people welcomed us enthusiastically with buckets of apricots, plums and apples. Their gratitude at being liberated from the Soviet yoke could not have been more explicit. The men's wide white and black floppy hats gave them a dashing appearance. From stubble-bearded faces, their honest eyes shone with goodwill.[5]

After several days on the road they reached the Ullu-Kam valley. The trucks were sent back and the men started to climb. Having survived so much death and annihilation in recent months, they now found themselves tramping through deciduous forest along a path lined with exquisite Alpine flowers. Groth later recalled how, once they started climbing, the men were unusually quiet:

> But it was not their loads (which grew ever more oppressive as the path steepened) that caused their silence, but rather the sheer loveliness of the landscape. When we reached the end of the valley, we were rewarded with a broad vista of astonishing tranquillity. On the steep slopes, covered in fresh green, and forming a wide basin, sheep were grazing. Behind them stood the mighty snow-clad giants of the Caucasus – a vision of unforgettable beauty. For a moment it felt as if we were on holiday, but a glance at the column of men armed with carabiners and machine guns quickly brought one back to the harsh reality. Soon we reached the Chotju-Tau Pass and were again thrilled by a magnificent view. Ahead of us stood the massive ice-covered mountains with their bizarrely striking shapes. Above them all soared our objective – Elbrus. We knew there could be no turning back until our flag was flying on its summit.[6]

They crossed the River Kuban over the one bridge that the Russians had failed to destroy. Then, after a demanding march to the foot of Elbrus, they set up their base. There remained, however, one major obstacle: Hut 11. Also known as Elbrus House, it lay at 4,100 metres (13,451 feet) and was no ordinary mountain hut. For a start it had the curious appearance of a Zeppelin airship and stood three storeys high. With its running water, electricity, central heating and sewage system it was, in fact, a comfortable hotel that could accommodate over 100 people. Built by the Russian travel agency Intourist, it had opened in 1939 with the aim of attracting Western visitors. In addition, its position commanding the surrounding passes gave Hut 11 immense strategic value. It was vital that Groth's men take it.

Exactly how this was accomplished is hard to pin down since the Russian and German accounts are markedly different, but it seems that Groth took a small detachment to reconnoitre the building. As his men approached it, they realised that there were Russians inside so quickly took cover. Meanwhile Groth, who had been scouting elsewhere, mistook the Russians (mostly meteorologists) for his own men and therefore walked confidently up to Hut 11 believing it safe to enter. If surprised to find himself so suddenly a prisoner of the Soviets, his captors must have been even more astonished. However, the quick-witted Groth successfully bluffed the Russians into believing that they were completely surrounded by German troops. Their lives would only be spared, he told them, if they left immediately. The Russians fell for it and some twelve of them rapidly set off down the mountain. Four, however, chose to throw in their lot with the Germans and subsequently fought with the mountain troops as auxiliaries for the rest of the war.

On entering Hut 11, which they promptly renamed *Edelweisshütte* (Edelweiss Hut), Groth's men must have thought they had stumbled into Aladdin's cave. They found showers, storage rooms and a well-equipped kitchen. The floors were of polished parquet, while the walls and ceilings were covered in an expensive embossed material.[7] Not only were there ample supplies of food but, best of all, quantities of modern mountain equipment and clothing – far superior to their own. Groth, ever mindful of the glory that the successful ascent of Elbrus would bring his country, the 1st Mountain Division, General Lanz and, not least, himself, was now free to give the mountain his full attention.

Groth had assembled an impressive team. Among them were Herbert Leupold, an Olympic cross-country skier, and Dr Karl von Krauss, a veteran of the Himalayas. The only odd one out was the writer Josef Martin Bauer (much favoured by the Nazis) who had been foisted on to the Elbrus expedition by the Ministry of Propaganda. Groth was not pleased. As Bauer records in his book, 'It's not made clear what happens if I refuse to stay behind, but Groth informs me, smiling coldly, that he does not want to be the one to write the last paragraph of my entry in the History of Literature. I, with an equally cold smile, reply: "I can't write about what I haven't seen and surely Elbrus must be worth a few lines."'[8]

In retrospect Groth must have wished that he had gone straight for the summit instead of spending two days acclimatising his ascent team. But as he later pointed out, 'we had been marching through Poland and France for three years, always in the plains and steppes. Now we were finally in the mountains, but we had to be careful. Enthusiasm is not enough at such high altitude.'[9]

When on 19 August they made their first attempt, a storm sprang up, forcing them back. Conditions were no better the following day, and to make matters worse Groth then received a radio message from General Lanz warning him that permission for the climb was about to be withdrawn. In other words, if they did not climb Elbrus the next day they never would. But the weather forecast was appalling: so bad, in fact, that the decision whether or not to go should have been beyond question. It was grossly irresponsible to risk the men's lives on a mere propaganda stunt. But Groth was a mountaineer, a 99er, a Nazi, a patriot and by now so obsessed with the mission that he decided to go anyway. At 3 a.m. on Friday, 21 August a raucous command echoed through the dark passages of Hut 11 – 'Gipfelmannschaft – aufsteh'n!' ('Summit team, rise!').[10]

When they set out the weather was not too bad, but by the time they stopped for a rest at a hut some 320 metres (1,050 feet) short of the summit conditions were atrocious. 'The moment had come', wrote one member of the team in his report, 'to accept failure and retreat; or go on.'[11] As no one wanted to give up, they went out again into the increasingly violent blizzard and thickening fog. 'We fought our way up step by step,' remembered Groth. 'The storm was so vicious, the driving snow so intense, that the men were often blown off the steps that we had hacked out with our pickaxes.'[12] Bauer noted that 'the altitude is affecting everyone, even the weatherbeaten men who have climbed the highest peaks in the Alps. Opinions and disagreements are yelled in such a way that it often seems that we are more like enemies than friends.'[13]

By the time the flattening ridge indicated that they were approaching the top, the hurricane had reduced the men to crawling on all fours. 'More dead than alive,'[14] they at last reached what they took to be the summit. By then the Reich war flag had been ripped to pieces in the storm, but it was somehow secured in the snow together with the metal regimental pendant that rattled furiously in the gale. Although photographs were out of the question, the men did manage a brief ceremony. 'We salute the Führer, our Bavarian homeland and Germany. We salute this storm-torn peak, the highest in the Caucasus; and the men in our Mountain Divisions who are fighting in the valleys and passes. We salute the Mountain.'[15] It was a touching scene, but a far cry from Lanz's original concept, in which, bathed in brilliant sunshine, his heroic soldiers would be pictured hoisting a swastika over Europe.

If getting up the mountain had been a nightmare, the descent was even worse. Groth was now convinced that they would all perish. Two men were on the verge of collapse while another appeared to be having a heart attack. Discipline disintegrated. It was 'each man for himself', with the stronger men forging ahead and leaving their weaker comrades to fend for themselves. Only yelled threats of court martial eventually brought the group back together.[16] When the team finally reached Hut 11 at 8 p.m. after seventeen hours on the mountain, one man was discovered missing. But he reappeared the next day perfectly cheerful and in excellent shape. 'He had got lost, so settled into his tent in a crevasse for the night and ate chocolate,' Groth later explained.[17]

Apart from the miracle that no one had actually died or been seriously injured, Groth's ascent of Elbrus had achieved very little. In the absence of any film or photographs to offer Germany's propaganda machine, General Lanz opted for damage limitation. In his report to Hitler he wrote of how the men's conquest of Elbrus would be forever remembered in the annals of mountain warfare, and how their heroism now gave him the opportunity to ask the Führer's permission to rename Elbrus 'Mount Adolf Hitler'. According to Albert Speer, Lanz's transparent hyperbole failed catastrophically. 'I often saw Hitler furious,' Speer wrote in his diary on 22 August, but seldom did his anger erupt as it did when [Lanz's] report came in. He raged as if this bit of sport had ruined his entire campaign. Days later, he was still railing to all and sundry about 'those crazy mountaineers who should be court-martialled'. They pursued 'their idiotic hobbies in the middle of war', he exclaimed indignantly, 'to occupy a ridiculous peak'.[18]

In view of Hitler's violent reaction, it was even more vital for Lanz to produce images of a swastika flying on top of Elbrus. So as soon as the weather improved on 23 August (the first day of the Battle of Stalingrad), Herbert Leupold went back up the mountain with a team of eight men. When they reached the top (in sunshine), they found that the flags they had planted two days earlier were not actually on the summit but on a small rise some way short of it. Although this time photographs were successfully taken of an intact Reich war flag flying on the actual summit, the Propaganda Ministry was still not satisfied. No one, they complained, had filmed the intrepid mountain warriors actually climbing. So on 7 September yet another team was sent up Elbrus to do exactly that. At last the Ministry had the footage it needed and the story could be released. Soon film of Germany's conquest of Elbrus was on every newsreel in every cinema and photographs were splashed across newspapers and magazines nationwide.

Alfons Meinlinger provides a charming postscript to all the kerfuffle surrounding the Elbrus ascent. He was among the soldiers who remained in occupation of Hut 11 until January 1943. A few days before Christmas, he and a couple of mates decided to climb the peak themselves. The weather was perfect. 'When we stood at the summit,' he wrote in his diary, 'we felt so happy that we shouted with joy.'

With three Oberstdorfers having taken such a prominent part in the Elbrus expedition, it was a proud moment for the villagers, and one to savour in the coming months as Germany's military situation began to look increasingly precarious.

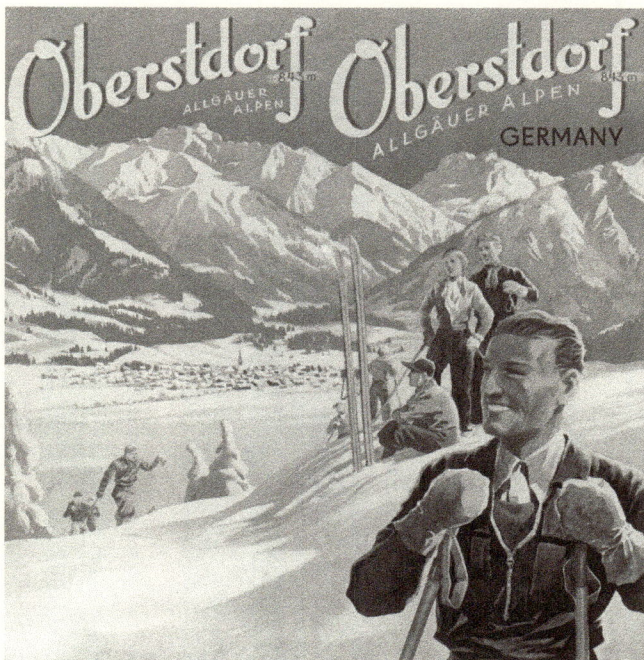

ABOVE: A travel brochure (1938) for Oberstdorf. The village was a fashionable holiday resort between the two world wars.

ABOVE: Oberstdorf, circa 1917.

ABOVE, LEFT: A studio photograph of Wilhelm Steiner, probably taken soon after his return to Oberstdorf from the First World War. He was a committed socialist with a deep disregard for authority in general and Hitler in particular.

ABOVE, RIGHT: A poster marking the 10th anniversary of the founding of Oberstdorf's branch of the Steel Helmet League of Frontline Soldiers. Originally a First World War veterans' organisation, by the 1930s it had become a right-wing paramilitary unit.

LEFT: Hoyer making a preparatory sketch of Hitler for his painting *In the Beginning was the Word* in which Hitler is depicted as the Messiah. It became one of the Third Reich's best-known images.

ABOVE, LEFT: Mayor Ludwig Fink with his wife and their two sons. Werner (left) was epileptic. His brother Erich was killed in 1944.

ABOVE, RIGHT: Theodor Weissenberger, who was born blind, with his siblings in the garden of Villa Gschwender in Oberstdorf.

LEFT: Xaver Noichl (Wilhelm Steiner's brother-in-law) with his wife and three sons, circa 1939. Franz Noichl is seated.

LEFT: Gertrud Neubaur, daughter of General Beck, whose photograph stands on the commode.

BELOW: Julius and Leni Löwin, the Jewish couple who met in Oberstdorf, with First World War hero Ernst Jünger.

ABOVE, LEFT: Hohes Licht, the Dutch children's home where a number of Jewish children were registered as Aryan and later smuggled to Switzerland.

ABOVE, RIGHT: Hetty Laman Trip-de Beaufort (left), owner of Hohes Licht, with Elisabeth Dabelstein, its director.

LEFT: Emil Schnell, a retired Jewish mill-owner. He committed suicide after receiving a summons to the Theresienstadt camp.

ABOVE: Julius Löwin, holding his baby son, boarding the SS *St Louis* in Hamburg on 20 August 1938, three months before *Kristallnacht*.

ABOVE: The Oberstdorf Hitler Youth Troop, photographed at the 1935 Nuremberg rally when Jews were deprived of their citizenship.

ABOVE: Scene of the crashed American bomber at Sonthofen on 25 February 1945. In the distance is the Ordensburg, the National Socialist stronghold frequently visited by senior Nazis. It also housed an Adolf Hitler School.

ABOVE: The identity card of Eva Noack-Mosse.

ABOVE: Hetty (centre) and Elisabeth with former inmates of the various labour camps situated around Oberstdorf. Some of the men are still in their striped uniforms. Fritz Schnell is seated in the middle row on the far left.

ABOVE, LEFT: Thomas Neidhart. Elected mayor of Oberstdorf in 1930, he was ousted by the Nazis but was again briefly mayor during the French occupation in 1945.

ABOVE, CENTRE: Georg Joas. He led a squadron of Junker 52s that delivered mail to the troops on the Eastern Front.

ABOVE, RIGHT: This photograph, published on the cover of the Swiss magazine *Sie und Er*, shows Wilhelm Steiner (centre) walking to General de Gaulle's victory parade on 14 May 1945. A Moroccan soldier beams at the camera (left).

16

Total War

On 31 January 1943, the shattering news of Germany's defeat at Stalingrad sent shock waves through the whole nation. Even Goebbels could not disguise the gravity of the disaster, nor did he seek to. Twenty months earlier Oberstdorfers had listened to him announce the invasion of Russia with characteristic swagger. Now, on 18 February, they tuned in again to hear his famous 'Total War' speech, broadcast from Berlin's Sportpalast before a carefully selected audience. Impelled to take decisive action by the Stalingrad catastrophe and Germany's continuing failure to produce enough weapons, tanks, submarines and aeroplanes, Goebbels now demanded that the nation step up the war effort to an unprecedented level. As these excerpts reveal, he was unusually candid, leaving no one in any doubt that only a superhuman effort on the part of the entire population could save the Reich – and the whole of Europe – from 'Bolshevist/Jewish enslavement':

> Stalingrad was and is fate's great alarm call to the German
> nation . . . My task is to give you an unvarnished picture
> of the situation . . . We want no more false hopes and

illusions. We want bravely to look the facts in the face, however hard and dreadful they may be . . . We know that the German people are defending their holiest possessions: their families, women and children, the beautiful and untouched countryside, their cities and villages, their two-thousand-year-old culture, everything indeed that makes life worth living . . . Total war is the demand of the hour . . . Everyone knows that if we lose, all will be destroyed . . . we can no longer make only partial and careless use of the war potential at home and in the significant parts of Europe that we control. We must use our full resources, as quickly and as thoroughly as it is organisationally and practically possible . . . Therefore a series of measures must be implemented . . . We have ordered, for example, the closing of bars and nightclubs . . . Countless luxury stores have also been closed . . . What good do shops do that no longer have anything to sell, but only use electricity, heating and human labour that is lacking everywhere else, particularly in the armaments industry? What German woman would want to ignore my appeal on behalf of those fighting at the front? Who would want to put personal comfort above national duty? Who in view of the serious threat we face would want to consider his private needs above the requirements of the war? I am firmly convinced that the German people have been deeply moved by fate's blow at Stalingrad. They have looked into the face of hard and pitiless war. They now know the awful truth, and are resolved to follow the Führer through thick and thin . . . Now, people, rise up and let the storm break![1]

If life on the home front was already grim, Goebbels had just made it chillingly clear that it was about to get a great deal worse.

As the intensified military effort engulfed the whole country, even Oberstdorf, so far from any large city, reverberated
with the sounds and sights of the war throughout 1943 and,
indeed, right up until Germany's surrender. Soldiers on leave
crowded the streets and pubs, while sporadic gunfire in the
mountains signalled that their comrades were in training or
on manoeuvres. After the announcement of Italy's surrender
to the Allies on 8 September 1943, the air raid siren on the
Nebelhorn wailed more frequently, warning first of aeroplanes
passing over Oberstdorf on their way to bomb Italy* and then
later of aeroplanes flying from Italy to bomb southern Germany.
The blare of loudspeakers was accompanied by the ceaseless
jangle of collection boxes shaken by schoolchildren as they
trailed endlessly around the village extracting money for the
Wehrmacht, Winter Aid, Swabian Victims, Mothers' Help and a
host of other causes. Nor was it any longer possible for the villagers to find respite in the beauty of their mountains since the
hiking trails and ski runs had been closed for military purposes.

Shops had little on display other than war-related items.
The Stachus department store, for instance, filled its windows
with pictures of aeroplanes, offering 'a number of wonderful
prizes' to those who could identify them all correctly.[2] 'We
have donated for our Führer', read the sign in the window of
Heimhuber's photography shop propped up next to a large
pile of boots, bed sheets, table linen, coats, blankets, belts
and socks.[3] Herr Heimhuber had good reason to advertise his

---

* Italy had the misfortune to be bombed by both the Germans and
the Allies.

generous response to the town hall's demands for donations. Anyone who failed to give adequately, like the villager who tried to get away with presenting a solitary threadbare rug, had his or her name printed in large type on a publicly displayed list of shame. Once there for all to see, only a substantial monetary donation could have it removed.[4]

Like most of rural Germany, Oberstdorf was fast filling up with evacuees fleeing the ever-expanding Allied bombing campaign. Marianne* was eleven when she arrived in Oberstdorf with her sister and pregnant mother in the summer of 1943 from Essen, which, as the biggest manufacturing centre in the Ruhr and site of the all-important Krupp armaments factory, was a prime target for the Royal Air Force. Between March and July of that year the city had been bombed incessantly, forcing the family to spend night after night in a cellar. Despite the terrifying air raids and lack of sleep, Marianne had continued to attend school and remembered salvaging aluminium from bomb fragments as she made her way there through the devastated streets.[5] After these traumatic experiences, she not surprisingly found the mountains and wild flowers of Bavaria overwhelming. Pencils and paper, barefoot children and the incomprehensible dialect were equally novel. But even in this relative haven, reminders of the war were everywhere. The family rented rooms in a house with a single lavatory on the landing, so bitterly cold that, in an attempt to provide some insulation, newspapers were laid on the floor. Each day Marianne would sit there reading the seemingly endless pages of death notices placed by the families of the soldiers killed in

---

* Between 1984 and 1994 Richard von Weizsäcker was President of the Federal Republic of Germany both before and after reunification. Marianne was his wife for sixty-three years.

action. The house was opposite the Nebelhorn Station Hotel, which like all the village's larger hotels had been converted into a military hospital. The hotel rooms, so recently occupied by tourists in search of peace and natural beauty, now accommodated young men maimed and scarred by war. The evacuees in Oberstdorf may have escaped the bombs, but they could not avoid Germany's mutilated soldiers. Marianne remembered feeling a mixture of horror and fascination as she watched men with an amputated leg play football by resting on one leg and crutch and using the other crutch to hit the ball.

The village's atmosphere had changed beyond all recognition. Every year, the *Viehscheid* (cattle separation) marked the end of the summer and was one of the great holidays in the Oberstdorf calendar. Everyone loved to watch the thousand or so young cattle being brought down from the high pastures where they had roamed freely all summer. If they had survived in the mountains without casualty (in July 1941 eight cows were struck by lightning) and if they had been spared foot-and-mouth disease, there was even more reason to celebrate. The festive atmosphere was usually made yet merrier by the elaborate floral wreaths adorning the horns of the leading cows. Escorted by farmers wearing their traditional *Gamsbart* (chamois beard) hats and lederhosen, the creatures would trot along the road back to Oberstdorf and on to the village meadows. Once safely there, the mooing of the cows and the tinkling from the massive bells hanging around their necks became deafening. When the cattle had finally been sorted and reclaimed by their owners, the village band would strike up and everyone would tuck into sausages and beer.

Now, however, when the rationed beer and sausage could only be bought with stamps, the *Viehscheid* was a sad affair. Hetty Laman Trip-de Beaufort described the 1943 event:

On St Matthew's Day the cows came off the Alp, then
the sheep – a few thousand. In the old days they were serenaded by brass band music. The shepherds wore their felt
hats at a jaunty angle and decorated them with mountain
flowers. But now they are mostly very old or very young.
I asked a couple of them in long trousers how old they
were – one is 15, the other 5. Children work now instead
of playing.[6]

As people's despair grew along with the shortages of food,
clothing, fuel and the loss of any hope that the nightmare
would soon end, the authorities cracked down even more
heavily on criticism of the regime. That summer, the dangers
of dissent were brought home to Oberstdorfers when one of
the village's regular visitors was guillotined at the Plötzensee
Prison in Berlin. Albert Schuler lived in Göppingen (twenty-
five miles east of Stuttgart), where he was technical director of
his family's engineering business. A dashing, charismatic young
man, he often stayed in Oberstdorf, where he liked to go fishing with his friends, brothers Ernst and Karl from the village's
prominent Richter family, and local architect Willi Huber.

Schuler was both profoundly anti-regime and recklessly
outspoken – a dangerous combination. In the early summer
of 1943 he spent a short holiday at Oberstdorf's Stillachhaus
Sanatorium. He had only been back home a few days when
on 3 July the Stuttgart Gestapo arrested him on the charge of
spreading 'defeatist enemy propaganda and planning high treason'. Schuler was put on trial at the *Volksgerichtshof* (People's
Court) in Berlin three months later. He was quoted, no doubt
accurately, by an anonymous informer as having said, 'We
have only one goal and that is to overthrow the government.

We are all just waiting for the Führer to be killed.' Although the denouncer was never identified, suspicion fell on a doctor at the Stillachhaus.

The young engineer was further damned by his connection with a member of the *Weisse Rose* (White Rose) resistance group, Christoph Probst (they were alumni of the same boarding school), who had been executed earlier that year. The group was led by a number of intellectual, non-violent students from the University of Munich who started an anonymous leaflet and graffiti campaign calling for people to resist the Nazis. Whether or not Schuler was part of this group is not recorded, nor do we know if any of his Oberstdorf friends shared his views.

Schuler's family was refused permission for a last visit, but a few weeks later his mother received a bill for the cost of her son's imprisonment and execution.[7]

Blaming enemy propaganda, as they did for most things, the Nazis saw the 'enemy within' as a serious threat. In consequence, Oberstdorfers, like millions of others in the Reich, perceived that their most immediate danger came not from Jews and Bolshevists but from informers inside their own communities. Although successful denunciations were in fact rare, they were an insidious, ever-present menace that left many people (especially the likes of Frau Noichl with her outspoken socialist husband Xaver) living in a perpetual state of fear. With conditions continuing to deteriorate, people's dread of denunciation grew more acute as the authorities intensified their vigilance.

The historian Richard J. Evans suggests that the enemy in this context was not primarily ordinary Germans, family members or friends; nor even the Gestapo, a relatively small organisation,[8] but rather the legions of low-level Nazi functionaries and hard-core believers who existed in every city, town, village and apartment block along with Labour Front officials, *Blockleiter* (block wardens) and Hitler Youth leaders.[9] Postman Karl Weinlein (the fanatic who had become embroiled in a dispute with Mayor Ernst Zettler) is a good example of the type.

Any accusation, however trivial, was potentially dangerous because of the pre-war legislation that included the *Heimtückegesetz* (Law Against Treacherous Attacks on the State and Party and for the Protection of Party Uniforms), enacted on 20 December 1934. This law was later expanded to impose even more restrictions on freedom of expression. Criticising the regime, making derogatory remarks about its leaders, spreading rumours, engaging in malicious gossip and telling jokes about Hitler were among the multitude of criminal offences that could lead to a long prison sentence, concentration camp or even execution. The highest court in the system was the People's Court[10] in Berlin, but elsewhere denunciations were heard in *Sondergerichte* (Special Courts) that had been set up in 1933 in the wake of the Reichstag fire. For the vast majority of those unlucky enough to be convicted there was no appeal. The verdict was final.

Inevitably this sinister law offered an open door to anyone with a score to settle, or who wanted to be rid of an unsatisfactory spouse or business rival. In consequence, the authorities were forced to spend an excessive amount of time weeding out accusations made purely from spite. The fact that letters could be opened, telephones tapped and people detained in 'protective custody' indefinitely without a court order greatly added to the psychological pressure on everyone.

Given the extraordinary climate of fear generated by informers, the relatively small number of denunciations recorded in the surviving data comes as a surprise. Oberstdorf's own statistics fit with the wider picture. Between 1936 and 1945 only nineteen villagers (out of a population ranging from about 4,000 at the beginning of the war to roughly 8,000 by the end) were brought before the Special Court in Munich and seven of their cases were dropped.

Mayor Fink undoubtedly used his discretionary powers to prevent many more denunciations going further than the town hall. Even so, enough of them resulted in conviction to make the villagers acutely aware of the need to be wary at all times, especially when talking to a stranger or when visiting Oberstdorf's most notorious danger spots – the post office and the office of Nebelhorn cable car. Heard in the wrong ears, a harmless joke, amusing anecdote or throw-away line could have terrifying consequences.

While most of the denunciation cases brought against Oberstdorfers were trifling, there was considerable variation in their outcomes. In 1936, for instance, the first villager (an unskilled labourer) to go before a Special Court was sentenced to four months for making offensive remarks about the government.[11] But when the following year a train driver was accused of alluding to 'sexual misconduct' between the Hitler Youth and the League of German Girls, he was let off.[12] Similarly, two years later a waitress was given three months for 'grumbling' about the government,[13] yet shortly afterwards the case against a farmer's wife accused of making unfavourable comments about the *Anschluss* was abandoned.[14] A young bicycle repairman, overheard in the ticket office of the Nebelhorn cable car station calling Robert Ley (head of the Labour Front) a 'Jew boy', was lucky to escape with a reprimand.[15] Equally fortunate were the maid accused of insulting Hitler and the cook from Breitscheid (twenty-five miles south of Bonn) who reported that anti-Nazi views in her home town were wide-spread.[16] On the other hand, another cook was put in prison for voicing pessimism about the Russian campaign while the Polish maid Maria Chuda, caught listening to a foreign radio station, was sent to a concentration camp for a year.[17] The arbitrariness of the Special Court sentencing is illustrated by the fate of two Oberstdorfers, each with a sense of humour. One of them, a master electrician, told an anti-regime joke to the wrong person and ended up in prison for six months. But the other, a farmer who carved on his cart loaded with manure in large letters 'KV' (short for *kriegsverwendungsfähig*, 'fit for war service') got off scot-free.[18]

Franz Noichl's godfather Anton Jäger fell foul of an offi-cious low-level Nazi. As well as being the landlord of the Adler inn, Jäger owned a farm and a slaughterhouse. Although the illegal slaughtering of animals was rife, most villagers man-aged to get away with it. Not Jäger, however. The man who denounced him was Wilhelm Herzog, who, until the Nazis came to power, had been an unsuccessful shoemaker of little standing in the village. But this all changed when he became head of the local SA and then a meat inspector. In common with so many other minor Nazi officials, his promotion led to a new sense of purpose and self-importance.

Jäger was sent for trial in Munich on 28 March 1942, accused of illegally killing six pigs and seventeen calves over a period of seventeen months. It was a serious crime, but in a letter sent from Mayor Fink's office a long list of mitigat-ing circumstances was presented to the court. The diligent and generous-hearted Jäger, Fink contended, had fought bravely and been seriously wounded in the First World War, he had eight young children to support and when he had taken on the inn from his wife's family it was already in considerable debt. He had only one labourer to help him, a Polish woman, and, as if those were not enough problems, his wife was an alcoholic who habitually gave too much meat to their guests. Furthermore, as a result of bureaucratic confusion, Jäger had twice been sent a slaughter certificate for a calf instead of the pig he had requested, thus leaving him with no meat to offer the inn's guests over Christmas.

Despite this catalogue of woes, he was sentenced to ten months' imprisonment and given a hefty fine.[19] However, there is an unusually happy ending to this particular story. Although very few appeals succeeded, one was sent on Jäger's behalf, supported by Fink, to the Central Office of Clemency Appeals in Berlin, located in the Führer's Chancellery. Three months later back came the response – a pardon. Jäger was a lucky man, but his desperate circumstances remained unchanged and within days of his reprieve he was again slaughtering animals illegally.[20]

The denunciation that had the most serious consequences for an Oberstdorfer occurred in 1942. It involved Hans Seeweg, a stonemason and poet who was also something of a local celebrity. A man of arresting appearance, Seeweg had a character to match. He was an extrovert who loved to spin a good yarn, although one of his favourite stories – how he had torn Hitler's portrait from the wall in the Adler inn and flung it out of the window – is probably untrue.

Before the war he was employed at the Ordensburg in Sonthofen. According to his own testimony, he was present at Hitler's visit there in 1937. By refusing to applaud the Führer on that occasion he had immediately drawn attention to himself as troublemaker.[21] The Munich Special Court records confirm that he was indicted and sentenced to five years' imprisonment in August 1942. The most disturbing aspect of his case, and the one that underlines why everyone was so haunted by fear of denunciation, was that he was arrested on the word of a stranger with whom he had been sitting in a friend's kitchen one day having a 'harmless' chat. Although the exact nature of Seeweg's crime is not clear, they had discussed various matters relating to the black market and Seeweg had spoken with particular vehemence about the 'filthy' beer served at the Adler, adding that 'Hitler should be forced to pour the muck down his own throat.'[22] The stranger turned out to have been a Gestapo official, who on his return to Essen reported the unfortunate stonemason. Luckily Seeweg was not without influence. In 1939 he had made friends with the film producer Walter Leckebusch while the latter was shooting *Hochzeit im Walsertal* (*Wedding in the Walser Valley*) and had been taken on as a film extra. In desperation after her husband's arrest, Frau Seeweg turned to Leckebusch who, in league with Mayor Fink, the local police and a leading innkeeper, saved Seeweg from execution.

Apart from dealing on the black market, the most common 'crime' committed by the villagers, and by Germans everywhere, was that of listening to foreign broadcasts. Because wireless sets played such a vital role in delivering propaganda there were generous subsidies to help with cost and each household, however modest its circumstances, was expected to acquire one. But as they also gave Germans access to the outside world they created a flaw in the Nazis' control system that even their intrusive policing was unable to eliminate. The authorities' only effective deterrent was fear – fear of denunciation and the harsh punishment that would follow.

According to Franz, the Noichls possessed a 'monster' wireless to which they listened avidly despite the risks. Unlike the sets in many other Oberstdorf households, theirs could receive both short and medium waves, thus providing them with good reception of the BBC. The Corporation's Lindley Fraser, whose fluent Edinburgh-accented German was familiar to many thousands of listeners across the Reich, became for many Germans a regular part of family life. But the foreign station most trusted by the Noichls, and by Oberstdorfers generally, was not the BBC but Radio Beromünster, transmitted from a small town near Lucerne in neutral Switzerland. Its programme *Weltchronik* (*World Chronicle*), written and presented by Professor Jean-Rudolph von Salis, went out every Friday evening between 7.10 and 7.25. Although as a neutral Swiss national von Salis had to abide by some modest censorship, his programmes contained enough accurate information to infuriate the Nazi authorities, who regularly demanded his removal. Meanwhile, von Salis's listeners had learned to trust him early in the war when, even though so clearly an opponent to the regime, he had not tried to disguise Germany's successes nor underestimate the Allies' defeats.

Von Salis's programmes rarely touched on anti-Semitism, but if Oberstdorfers had tuned into *Weltchronik* on Friday, 27 February 1942 they would have heard him reporting a speech made by Hitler three days earlier on the twenty-second anniversary of the NSDAP in which Hitler referred to the extermination of the Jews. What von Salis could not have known then was that at the Wannsee conference held five weeks before, on 20 January 1942, the decision to implement the 'Final Solution' had been approved by senior Nazis.

Summarising Hitler's speech for his listeners, von Salis informed them that

> Despite the winter storms, the German soldiers and their
> allies had held up, and now that the snow was beginning

to melt in the Crimea and southern Russia, preparations
were being made for the final battle and the destruction of
the enemy. The aim of the war, the chancellor stated, was
to prevent the extinction of Aryans by a Jewish alliance
of capitalists and communists. As a result of the conflict,
it was not the Aryans who would be exterminated, but
the Jews.[23]

From von Salis, Oberstdorfers would also have learned of the
brutal reprisals inflicted by the Germans on French civilians
in retaliation to attacks by the French resistance. He reported
that on 10 July 1942 a decree was issued informing the
French that if saboteurs and assassins did not voluntarily surrender to the French or German police within ten days of
their hostile action, every close male relative in the ascending
line, as well as brothers-in-law and cousins over the age of
eighteen, would be shot. All women similarly related would
be sentenced to forced labour, and every child up to the age
of eighteen placed in a custodial institution.[24]

What exactly the villagers made of such reports is difficult to assess. But the information was so valuable that they
kept on tuning in despite the dangers. It was hard, however,
to remain permanently on guard and children in particular,
even if thoroughly schooled, were alarmingly unpredictable.
Franz Noichl remembered his mother turning sheet-white in
the marketplace when his eight-year-old brother Schorschl
started jumping up and down shouting 'padatata padatata'
– the jingle that introduced the news on a forbidden French
radio station. Then one evening when Franz had just turned
up the volume because of bad reception, there was a loud,
officious-sounding rap on the shutter. 'My mother fled into
the bedroom,' he recalled, 'convinced that she was about to

be arrested.' On opening the door, Franz found their neighbour chuckling at his own joke, having come to borrow a snow shovel.

Anderl Heckmair's widow Trudl (they were married after the war) remembers how her father, Franz Amann (chairman of the Oberstdorf branch of the DAV), would come home from his office and, without even pausing to kiss her, close the curtains and go straight to the wireless. Before switching off, he would be sure to reposition the dial so that no prying eyes could see that it had been tuned to a foreign station.[25]

For those villagers prepared to accept the risks, Radio Beromünster's bulletins provided a much-needed corrective to the stream of Nazi propaganda blasted daily out of loudspeakers in schools, shops, offices and in the marketplace. But for anyone with family or friends fighting at the front, von Salis's war reports were becoming more depressing every day.

After retreating from the Soviet Union in March 1943, the 1st Mountain Division, still under the command of General Hubert Lanz, was sent to fight in the Balkans and Greece where, in the darkest chapter of its history, its soldiers committed a series of well-documented war crimes.

On 16 August 1943 an act of shocking barbarity took place in the Greek village of Kommeno. Soldiers from the 98th massacred 317 Greeks, many of them young children.[26] A few weeks later the 98th was also heavily involved in the infamous atrocity that occurred on the island of Cephalonia, when thousands of Italian soldiers (who had until 3 September been the Germans' allies) were murdered after they had surrendered.[27] Although his regiment did not take part in either of these war crimes, Alfons Meinlinger has left a vivid account of its actions a few months later in north-western Greece, just south of Corfu:

> Partisans attacked the 7th Company last night. Orders have been issued that a number of villages are to be burned. The guerrillas don't take prisoners in such raids. Anyone they capture is shot. The war is becoming much crueller. We came across one of the burning villages while dismantling our communications line. I felt sorry for these people. Women and children ran from house to house, dragging what little they had with them. Everything was burning, the children were crying, the women ran about, praying. It is terrible to witness all this. It is cold and they have no shelter. These people are so poor! It is those who are least guilty who suffer most. The perpetrators of this attack are no doubt sitting safely somewhere in the dry. What can we do? We fight these people because they keep attacking us. The peasants could live in peace if only they would stop fighting. I was sad when we left that place, so full of horror. But then, as we marched away, I reflected on the misery back home in Germany: don't they suffer even more? Do not bombs fall on our cities and burn our homes? Do they not wound and kill women and children? Yes, the suffering of our loved ones at home is even worse.[28]

Many Germans, Oberstdorfers among them, may have continued to believe in Hitler's superhuman powers as the war turned against Germany, but few can have been unaware of the atrocities that were being perpetrated in their name – or that their own future was now looking increasingly bleak.

17

Camps

Ever since the Nazis came to power, camps had been an intrinsic part of national life. From the age of ten, when children entered the junior branches of the Hitler Youth or the League of German Girls, through their teenage years to when as young adults they joined the Labour Service or the armed forces, young Germans expected to spend weeks if not months every year in a camp learning how to be dedicated National Socialists. So when during the war many more camps of various kinds sprang up all over the country, including those for foreign labourers, prisoners of war, political prisoners and of course countless *Wehrmacht* training camps, they were neither a strange nor a new phenomenon.

Dachau, however, was a camp to strike fear into the heart of even the most law-abiding citizen. Not only did anyone sent there have no recourse to the law (such as it was), but they also had to endure the torment of never knowing when or if ever they would be released. So, although realistically Dachau and its like were only a distant threat for the great majority of Germans, the dread of being woken in the middle of the night by the Gestapo pounding on the door never entirely went away. Indeed, this is what happened to

Count Joachim von Alvensleben, a German aristocrat and owner of a 30,000-acre estate in Poland, whose divorced wife (the Polish Countess Katarzyna Bnińska) had moved to Oberstdorf in 1929. Count Joachim was arrested in Poland by the SS at his magnificent Ostrometzko house and sent first to Dachau and then to Buchenwald, thus making it clear that no German – even one from such a noble family as the count's – was immune to Nazi 'justice'.*

Dachau spawned over 120 sub-camps, two of which were located right on Oberstdorf's doorstep. The nearest, situated between Oberstdorf and Fischen, was only two miles north of the village, while Birgsau, lying six miles to the south, was a hamlet located on what had before the *Anschluss* been the border with Austria. A third satellite camp, in which around 700 Dutch, Russian, French and German prisoners were held, was built at Blaichach, close to Sonthofen. Overlooked by watchtowers, surrounded with barbed wire and guarded by SS Death's Head units, the Blaichach camp must have presented a forbidding image to the local population.

Birgsau was the first to be established. In August 1943, sixteen prisoners were transported from Dachau to this beauty spot at the foot of the Bavarian Alps in order to build a training camp for *Waffen*-SS mountain troops. It was staffed by Nazis who during the last years of the war trained batches of 300 boys a time, fresh from the Hitler Youth, giving them four weeks of intensive instruction before sending them off to the front. The presence of the camp so close to Oberstdorf meant

---

* Count Joachim was eventually released and spent the rest of his life in Oberstdorf trying to retrieve his lost estate.

a substantial rise in the number of hard-core Nazis to be seen around the village.

Among the Dachau prisoners detailed to construct and then maintain the new camp was eighteen-year-old Andrzej Burzawa, who had been abducted from his village in Poland and brought to Germany as a forced labourer. Some scholars estimate that between 10 and 15 million foreign civilians worked in Germany during the war, the vast majority of them deported there against their will.[1] By 1942 over a million Poles were in this unenviable position, mostly working as farm labourers since the Nazis considered them too inferior for other employment.[2] By filling the growing gap created by Germans who had either abandoned agriculture for the towns or more recently been drafted into the *Wehrmacht* (between the summers of 1941 and 1944 some 60,000 German soldiers a month were being killed on the Eastern Front), the Poles, along with the Slavic nationalities – Russians, Ukrainians, Belarusians and of course the Jews – were forced to play a significant role in keeping the Reich's agriculture, construction work and factories going. These millions of foreign labourers were generally treated no better than slaves. For the Poles, conditions were particularly unpleasant. Their wages were lower than those of other foreigners doing the same work, yet they had to pay special taxes. They were not allowed to enter pubs or restaurants or to use the same churches as German Catholics. Sex with a German woman was punishable by death. Poor performance at work or, indeed, any minor infringement would land them in a concentration camp. Furthermore they had to wear a badge, making their despised nationality and serf status plain for all to see.[3]

In Andrzej's case, the police had turned up at his home in Jadowniki Mokre (between Kraków and Lwów) on 24 April

1940. They had come to the village to arrest twelve men, including Andrzej's father, and deport them to Germany. However, as Wladislaus Burzawa was not there the police seized his fifteen-year-old son instead. 'They wouldn't even let me get dressed,' recalled Andrzej in a letter written fifty-six years later.[4] On the document authorising his deportation he saw that his father's first name had been crossed out and his own inserted. The birthdate, however, had been left unchanged. By the time their Jadowniki Mokre group reached Tarnów, twenty miles away, the number of Polish men and women abducted from villages in the region had swollen to more than 500.

Andrzej was sent to Schmieh, a small village in the Black Forest. 'The peasants were waiting for us,' he remembered. 'Each took "his" Pole from the list.' Crucially, the Schmieh farmers were not Nazis. They expected the Poles to work hard (Andrzej's hands suffered badly from too much scything), but no harder than they did themselves. Thus for his first two years in Germany Andrzej survived reasonably well. But one day in April 1942 a policeman turned up on a motorbike and without any explanation took him to Calw, the local market town, for interrogation. He never learned the reason for his arrest, but as he was closely questioned about his family in Poland, it is possible that one or more of them had joined the Polish resistance.

Eventually, on 14 January 1943, along with a large batch of other prisoners, he arrived at Dachau. 'We had to form up in six lines and march through the town. It was a clean, quiet little place with several churches.' They entered the camp through the iron gate bearing the infamous words *'Arbeit macht frei'* ('Work Sets You Free'). As soon as they had assembled on the roll-call square for registration, SS guards walked between their ranks inspecting the new intake, 'looking for priests, Jews and Gypsies'. The prisoners had to stand all night in the freezing cold while they were being processed. Andrzej noticed a slogan written in large letters on the roof of one of the buildings: 'There is only one way to freedom and the milestones are: sacrifice, truth, diligence, cleanliness, sobriety and love of the Fatherland.' But within minutes of entering Dachau, he realised that in reality the only way to freedom was 'through the chimney of the crematorium'.

Each day spent in Dachau was one of acute suffering. Andrzej, now eighteen years old, survived a typhus epidemic, a severe beating, hard labour in a gravel pit, and starvation rations. Then one evening in early August 1943, his block warden shouted out his number, 42307, and told him to be ready to leave early next morning. Sixteen prisoners lined up on the roll-call square at 4 a.m. The fact that they were issued with new clothes and clogs offered some reassurance that they were not about to be executed. A truck and unfamiliar guards arrived to take them to Munich, where they boarded a train heading south. 'The behaviour of the SS men was very odd,' remembered Andrzej. 'They didn't shout and allowed us to smoke. They even talked to us and told us that we were going to Birgsau, near Oberstdorf.' Andrzej noticed the Edelweiss badges on their caps and lapels identifying them as *Waffen*-SS Mountain Division soldiers. They explained to the prisoners that a long spell on the Eastern Front had left them only fit for guard duty.

Birgsau had little to offer except an inn, a couple of farms, a small chapel, three defunct Customs houses (built to deter smugglers) and magnificent Alpine views. The prisoners – from Russia, Yugoslavia, Romania, Czechoslovakia, Poland, Spain and Germany – were quartered in the cellars of the former Customs buildings. Their first job the next morning was to clear debris left by an avalanche – not an easy task in wooden clogs. The camp commandant, SS-Obersturmbannführer (Lieutenant-Colonel) Willi Baumgärtner, a decent man, noticed this and had them issued with proper leather boots.

The work was hard and living conditions basic, but life at Birgsau under Baumgärtner was immeasurably better than at Dachau. 'Nobody beat us and we had 200 grams more bread every day,' recorded Andrzej, adding, 'in Birgsau there were no murderers wearing the *Totenkopf* badge.' In fact, for much of the time, not only were they left unguarded but also supplied with extra food. On Christmas Eve 1943 they even received presents. 'We were all given two packets of biscuits, a chocolate bar, a cigar and a handful of sweets. There was also a bottle of wine for every four men. We were told that this was our reward for a job well done.' They decorated Christmas trees and put one in each accommodation hut.

Easily identified by their striped uniform, the prisoners were a familiar sight in Oberstdorf where they went frequently to collect building materials for the new camp, which slowly took shape as the men constructed barracks, a weapons store, sick-bay and kitchen. They also diverted a mountain stream to supply the camp with running water. The moment an accommodation hut was completed, a new batch of recruits – boys aged between sixteen and eighteen – moved in.

Fischen, a small village four miles north of Oberstdorf, gave its name to a huge camp for foreign forced labourers built there in 1944. The devastation caused by the Allied bombing led the aeroplane manufacturer Messerschmitt and engine producer BMW to move their operations out of Augsburg and Munich respectively. And because almost every village and town in the Allgäu had some kind of factory or warehouse suitable for conversion, soon the whole region was involved in aeroplane production. By the end of the war these improvised manufactories had delivered more than 30,000 engines to the Luftwaffe. In Oberstdorf's neighbouring valley (Kleinwalsertal), 150 women found themselves suddenly switched from milking cows to producing parts for the Me 262 – the first operational jet fighter. The bulk of Messerschmitt's workforce, however, came not from the native population but from foreign forced labourers, prisoners of war and concentration camp inmates, the latter supplied by Dachau.

In July 1944, Messerschmitt converted an old textile mill, midway between Oberstdorf and Fischen, into a factory for making precision gauges. In his book *Spuren im Wald* (*Traces in the Forest*), Kempten historian Markus Naumann reveals that by February 1945 there were over 1,000 workers at this plant, 60 per cent of whom were foreigners mainly from western and southern Europe. They were housed in a number of makeshift camps throughout the area, the biggest of which was built at Fischen. Conditions there were so insanitary that local doctors complained to Messerschmitt. But as the company's only concern was to maintain production, their protest was largely ignored. A substantial number of foreign workers were also billeted in Oberstdorf, forty of them in a specially built barracks.

Although life for these foreigners was far from pleasant, they did have a degree of freedom and were certainly much better off than the 300 prisoners from Dachau for whom Messerschmitt paid the SS a daily rate of 4 RM per head, rising to 6 RM for skilled workers. Along with several hundred prisoners of war, these inmates were confined in a separate Dachau sub-camp next to the Fischen factory. Despite their atrocious living conditions (many prisoners suffered from scurvy), only one prisoner actually perished there for the simple reason that when they became too sick to work they were sent back to die at Dachau.[5]

The sight of the workers being marched to and from the factory or wandering about in the village in their free time became part of the villagers' daily life. It was an Oberstdorf inn that provided meals for the workforce (food for the sub-camps was supplied direct from Dachau), while Messerschmitt set up an additional workshop in the Loritz garage close to the railway station and used other village buildings as repositories. There were even some locals who worked at the camps. Wilhelm Bühler was a dedicated Nazi who had joined the party while employed in the Oberstdorf post office. After leaving the *Wehrmacht*, Bühler became a block warden at Dachau's Türkheim sub-camp (sixty miles away), but by the end of the war he was one of around twenty SS men guarding Fischen.*

Although there was a certain amount of grumbling about the presence of all these strangers in the village, the fact that food and socks were regularly left by the side of the road on which the foreigners were marched to and from the factory suggests that at least some of the locals were touched by their plight. It is likely, however, that most villagers assumed the concentration camp inmates deserved their fate because they were either communists or criminals and therefore 'enemies of the state'.

---

* His wife Walburga was an equally enthusiastic *Hitlar*. After the war she worked as a waitress at the Stempfle café, where her memorable hairdo and buoyant personality made her especially popular with the customers.

There can be little doubt that Oberstdorfers were well informed about what went on in Dachau and its sub-camps. They also had first-hand knowledge of the treatment of the foreign labourers: the appalling sanitation, the crippling working hours and poor-quality food that combined to make their existence barely tolerable. But no matter how much sympathy individual villagers may have felt for the inmates of these assorted camps, it is likely that most of them concluded their welfare was either none of their business or beyond their control.

If a majority of villagers regarded these foreigners as an unfortunate fact of life and of no direct concern to them, Hetty Laman Trip-de Beaufort took the opposite view. The Hohes Licht Sanatorium that she had founded in 1924 for sick Dutch children became an effective source of aid for some of the estimated 350,000 Dutch citizens who found themselves trapped in Nazi Germany,[6] and of whom several hundred were living in the camps around Oberstdorf. In addition to the Dutch working in the Messerschmitt and BMW factories, there were yet more Dutch nationals employed locally on farms, in hotels or in domestic service.

Hetty (who, as mentioned, had helped Julius and Leni Löwin escape to America shortly before *Kristallnacht*) worked tirelessly for her fellow countrymen throughout the war, as well as continuing to smuggle Jewish children out of the country whenever possible. She did so alongside the German director of the home, Elisabeth Dabelstein, who had always detested the Nazis. In later years Elisabeth commented that, for Germans who like her had opposed Hitler from the start, National Socialism had felt like a terrible cancer spreading within their own bodies. 'But for the occupied countries,' she added, 'the death and destruction came from outside, and that, I believe, is ultimately easier to deal with.'[7]

With the outbreak of war, Hetty's original plan had been to flee to Switzerland as soon as Germany invaded the Netherlands. But when the invasion took place on 10 May 1940, she decided instead to remain in Oberstdorf in the belief that Hohes Licht could play an important role supporting Dutch captives and other 'kindred spirits'. She trusted her staff completely, especially Elisabeth. 'We formed a sort of secret society,' Hetty wrote, 'we could communicate perfectly with half a word, a minute gesture or a sideways glance.' When, years later, Hetty was asked if she and Elisabeth had ever been frightened of betrayal, she replied, 'We must have been, of course, but the villagers were mostly good people and we developed a kind of sixth sense about where people's loyalties lay.'[8]

In 1942 Hetty returned to the Netherlands to research a book that she had long wanted to write. While there, she tried to convince her friends that there still existed legions of decent Germans many of whom were themselves in concentration camps. Overwhelmed, however, by the reality of the Nazi occupation, few in Hetty's circle were prepared to show much sympathy for Hitler's German victims. Six months later Hetty returned to Oberstdorf. Although it was strictly forbidden to travel with papers or letters, she carried a briefcase full of her research material:

I had brought with me as a decoy one of Shakespeare's sonnets . . . I obediently declared the letter at Emmerikon on the border. The sergeant fetched a lieutenant and the lieutenant fetched a major, with whom I stood in the train compartment shamelessly translating 'Let me not to the marriage of true minds admit impediments'. The major said he had heard of Shakespeare but didn't speak English. He stared at it blankly. When the whistle blew signalling our departure, he snatched my letter and put it in his pocket, at which point I felt it necessary to let out a hysterical sob. As the train gathered speed, I looked up at my briefcase, untouched in the net, and full to the brim with notes for my Hogendorp biography!*[9]

Hetty's patrician background had given her a natural confidence and authority. This, combined with the fact that she was middle-aged and had owned the Oberstdorf children's home for nearly twenty years, allowed her considerable licence under Nazi rule. She used it to great effect. She and Elisabeth soon made contact with prisoners and forced labourers in the camps. 'We helped them with visits, money and all kinds of necessities. We also passed on information from the BBC. In this way we managed to make their lives a little better.'[10] She responded to one group of prisoners who had requested books to cheer them up by sending the comedy *Till Eulenspiegel*.[†] 'They told me that they laughed until their bellies ached.'[11]

Together with Elisabeth and their Dutch and German staff, Hetty managed to locate former Hohes Licht patients and send them 'clothes, spectacles or magnifying glasses, and food'. She also regularly filled a large rucksack with supplies that she would personally deliver to Dutch prisoners or forced labourers in the nearby camps. Sometimes she went as far as

* Gijsbert Karel, Count van Hogendorp was a nineteenth-century Dutch statesman.
† The prankster from north Germany whose adventures first appeared in print in 1515.

Kempten to the Kottern camp, where a large number of Dutch were among 1,500-odd prisoners guarded by thirty-five SS guards and a pack of dogs. In addition, Kottern was surrounded by a high-voltage fence and at night swept continuously by searchlight. Hetty was undeterred:

> I myself went to Kottern and to Fischen, Dachau offshoots close to Oberstdorf. A German courier used to smuggle reports in and out of Kottern for me. As for Fischen, I would pay an official call on the camp commandant [Erich Schmidt] and then on my way out look for a familiar face peering through the hedge. We would exchange a quick word or through intense eye contact convey a universe of meaning.[12]

She was also helped by a young Dutch gardener she employed at Hohes Licht. 'He's an exemplary young man who even helps me deliver Dutch reading matter to the Dutch labourers in the camps – and show them Dutch films etc. They are so uprooted.' She went on:

> They have nothing. Catholics can go to Mass even though they don't understand the German but Protestants are in a void. They are desperate for books. Recently, a barber from Amsterdam married a French girl from the Alsace. On a misty Tuesday morning they walked across the Oberstdorf market square from the town hall to the parish church with another barber, a waiter and me in tow as the only witnesses. On Boxing Day, I showed a group of Dutch a colour film – flowering fields of Holland, the dunes of Zeeland, city and town vistas. All the workers hoped that their own city would pop up on to the screen.[13]

The French, Dutch and Scandinavian forced labourers were in general treated much better than the Slavic races. French civilians in particular seem to have enjoyed considerable freedom. When the Hohes Licht wireless set broke down, it was a French engineer who went there one evening to mend it. 'He had to be back in his camp by 11 p.m. or there would have been dreadful consequences,' recalled Hetty. 'After he fixed the radio, we asked him if he wanted to listen quickly to the London news. "Non Madame, mais une petite chanson de Paris, je vous en prie!"' ('No Madame, but, please, a little song from Paris!')[14]

If Hetty was courageous, so indeed was Elisabeth. Before the war she had made a name for herself as an alpinist and with Josef Aschauer, one of the Allgäu's most respected mountaineers, tackled some of Germany's toughest climbs. A Dutch journalist interviewing the two women after the war described Elisabeth as having intelligent brown eyes and a strong, friendly face. Glancing from her to Hetty, he decided that, although they looked nothing alike physically, they nevertheless bore a strong resemblance to each other. He attributed this to an 'inner decency and the open, clear gaze of those who have learned the hard way what makes life worthwhile and what renders it unbearable'.[15]

Despite the enormous strain under which the two women lived during the war, they were still able to find pleasure in the natural beauty of their surroundings. As Hetty wrote,

In the midst of all this tumult our mountains were pure heaven. Every plant and animal continued to live its quiet existence. We looked after the cows and the calves. We watched felled trees being brought down from the mountains on sledges. We looked after man and beast, even a tiny kitten that we found warming itself on a horse blanket in the stables. It would sometimes amuse itself by hanging off one of the horses' tails and swinging from side to side. We went for long walks. And all the time, I never stopped thinking about my country.[16]

18

To the Bitter End

Following their defeat at Stalingrad in February 1943, the Germans suffered a series of disasters on the Eastern Front. In July they lost the Battle of Kursk, and two months later the Russians recaptured Smolensk. Not only was the *Wehrmacht* now unable to stem the Soviet advance through Ukraine, but in January 1944 the Siege of Leningrad, which had lasted nearly two and a half years, was finally lifted. By August the Russians had entered East Prussia, prompting those in their path to flee in terror. As the resolve of Germany's fighting men began to evaporate, so too did that of Hitler's allies. Italy had already gone, but in August 1944 Turkey broke off diplomatic relations with Hitler and Romania joined the Allies. Shortly afterwards Bulgaria also declared war on its former ally and by the end of the year Hungary had been over-run by Soviet troops. Nor was the outlook any less depressing for Germany on the Western Front. On 6 June Allied troops landed on the Normandy beaches and were soon – like the Russians from the East – heading for Berlin. Despite its inadequate resources, an utterly demoralised civilian population and too many soldiers who had lost the will to go on, Germany now had no choice but to fight the war on two major fronts.

On 20 July 1944, Franz Noichl was bicycling home. On his way he stopped at the Adler inn, owned by his godfather Anton Jäger, where he heard some extraordinary news on the wireless. A few hours earlier there had been a failed attempt to assassinate Hitler at his Eastern Front military headquarters – the Wolf's Lair – deep in the East Prussian forest. As it had never occurred to Franz that an organised resistance even existed, his first reaction was one of total astonishment quickly followed by deep disappointment. With Hitler still alive there was no hope of reprieve; the war would have to be fought to the bitter end. While Franz listened to the dramatic news, he thought of how easy it would have been for him to shoot Hitler when, at the age of eight, he had stood by the roadside in Sonthofen – his arm raised in the Nazi salute – only three metres from the open car in which Hitler had stood, rigid and impassive, as he was slowly driven through the cheering crowds to the Ordensburg.

What Franz did not know was that at a house in Oberstdorf on the Plattenbichl, a short distance from the Adler, a young woman called Gertrud Neubaur also sat glued to the wireless. Her father was General Ludwig Beck and, although she almost certainly had no knowledge of this at the time, he was one of the bomb plot conspirators of whom the most prominent was Colonel Claus von Stauffenberg. It was von Stauffenberg who had personally planted the bomb that failed to kill Hitler. Had the assassination attempt succeeded, Gertrud might at that moment have been listening to her father addressing the nation as its new head of state. In fact, by the time she heard the news Beck was probably already dead. Arrested immediately after the failed coup, he had tried to kill himself. When that also failed, a soldier finished the job by shooting him in the back of his neck.[1]

Gertrud and her small daughter had some months earlier escaped the bombing in Berlin to find refuge in Oberstdorf. Although only twenty-seven, she had already experienced more than her fair share of misfortune. Her mother Amalie suffered from tuberculosis and as a girl had been a patient at the Stillachhaus Sanatorium in Oberstdorf under the care of Dr Saathoff. He had initially advised Amalie never to have children, but after she married Beck in 1916 he changed his mind, with fatal consequences. Nine months after giving birth to her daughter Gertrud, Amalie died at his sanatorium. Beck, a professional soldier, was at the time serving as a staff officer on the Western Front and had therefore little opportunity to grieve for his dead wife or to give much thought to his infant daughter. Thus, at the age of five, Gertrud was put into the care of the authoritarian Dr Saathoff. As he already had five children of his own as well as several foster children, this was not ideal. But whatever the difficulties of her Oberstdorf childhood, Gertrud did at least remember the school and its headmaster, Dr Bessler, with affection.

It wasn't until she was fourteen that Gertrud went to live permanently with her father, a stern military man brought up in the Prussian tradition. Because he kept moving from one army posting to the next her education suffered, and it was not easy for her to make lasting friendships. But life improved when they began living in Berlin and father and daughter could share their love of horses. Each morning they would ride out together before he left for the office and she for school.

In 1935 Beck was appointed Chief of Staff of the *Wehrmacht*. Initially he had been a keen supporter of the Nazis, believing that Hitler had the ability both to expunge the shame of the Treaty of Versailles and to transform Germany into a great power. But his enthusiasm did not last and in 1938 he resigned.

When war broke out, in order to avoid being sent to a labour service camp, Gertrud stayed on a forestry estate in East Prussia belonging to family friends. It was there on the tennis court that she first met a young officer called Günther Neubaur. Although for them it was love at first sight, his parents did not approve. They thought Günther too immature for marriage, and in any case he was already engaged to another girl whom they liked. Nevertheless, Günther and Gertrud married in 1940 and their daughter was born the following January. But Gertrud's new-found happiness was to be tragically short-lived. In February 1942, Günther was shot in the stomach near Leningrad and died on his way to hospital. His younger brother was at the time stationed in Africa, and when he learned of Günther's death he requested a transfer to Russia. Four weeks later he was also dead.

In 1944, Beck decided that Berlin was too dangerous and sent Gertrud and her daughter to her Neubaur in-laws in Oberstdorf. In July, six days after the assassination attempt, Gertrud wrote to her uncle Wilhelm Beck from the village, desperate for news of her father but probably knowing in her heart that he was dead:

> I am deeply worried about father. I've not had any news since the 19th although he usually writes to me every two days. My letters to him are returned marked 'recipient travelling indefinitely. No forwarding address.' You know yourself that Father never travels and he never mentioned anything about a trip to me. It is all very strange and worrying. Have you heard any more details? I would love to come to you for a couple of days, if only it were not so difficult to travel. Could you possibly send me a telegram to enable me to get a travel permit first to you and then to Berlin?[2]

A few days later two Gestapo officials arrived in Oberstdorf to arrest Gertrud. Her sister-in-law Annemarie, who worked as a nurse at the Stillachhaus, reacted swiftly. She suggested that, as it was so late, they might like to have dinner at the Schützenhaus in Faltenbach, a short walk away, where they could also stay the night. The men needed little persuading. As soon as they had gone Annemarie took the child to a neighbour's house. Then the two young women collected all the letters and documents they could find and burned them.

The next morning the men returned and took Gertrud into custody. The journey to Munich was grim. Within two and a half years Gertrud had lost her husband and father in terrible circumstances; she lived with in-laws who while attentive to her needs did not love her, and now, forced to abandon her three-year-old daughter, she was under Gestapo arrest with no idea of what lay in store. When they arrived in Munich, the political prison was so full that she had to share a cell with ordinary criminals. Later she was held with people also related to bomb plot conspirators, a number of whom she knew. Eventually the Gestapo decided that this apparently unsophisticated young woman was not a threat to the regime and allowed her to return to Oberstdorf. In the feverish aftermath of the bomb plot, around 7,000 people were arrested and some 5,000 executed.[3] As friends and family of those directly involved were an obvious target, Gertrud was lucky to get off so lightly.

Public reaction to the assassination attempt varied enormously. Many citizens, like the Noichls, were deeply disappointed that the plot had failed but were careful not to show this in public for fear of arrest. The reaction of a group of Bavarian farmers who heard the news in their local inn was no doubt mirrored all over Germany. After listening in 'rapt attention', a local report noted, they sat silently at their tables, none of them daring to say a word.[4] Nazi sympathisers, on the other hand, were naturally anxious to establish their unfailing loyalty to the Führer. Other Germans were incensed that so many aristocrats and high-ranking *Wehrmacht* officers had been involved in the plot and wanted to know whether these men were also to blame for Germany's recent military failures – a suggestion that Goebbels was only too happy to encourage.

For young people who, like Franz, had spent their entire lives under National Socialism, the world was now changing fast. The 1944 harvest and the annual expedition to the Hallertau region north of Munich for hop-picking were therefore reassuringly familiar events. Because there was so much grassland in the Allgäu, haymaking lasted several months from around mid-June until the end of August. It was hard work, but for the teenagers it was also a cheerful time full of fun and mild flirtations. In the summer of 1944, Franz and his friends quite literally made hay while the sun shone. As one of the hop pickers, Franz remembered how they 'ate roast pork and dumplings each day' and

> drank red or green lemonade with a piece of brown bread and slept in the hay. Our top pickers, later praised by the school, picked ten baskets a day. I managed four and occasionally five. We were paid 50 Pfennigs for each basket, not that you could buy anything with that.

But those relatively carefree days were not to last. The war could not be ignored and everyone – young and old alike – lived in deep dread of the Red Army, now advancing with alarming speed. The farmer employing Franz and his school-mates that summer made no attempt to hide his views. 'If only the Americans were already here and the Russians weren't coming,' he said, despite risking Dachau or execution had one of the boys chosen to denounce him.

In the last months of the war some two and a half million Germans fled from Eastern Europe ahead of the advancing Soviet forces. A great many died on the journey. Women were particularly at risk, since when it came to rape there were no holds barred. In an Order of the Day issued in early January 1945, General Gyorgy Zhukov urged his troops 'to remember our brothers and sisters, our mothers and fathers, our wives and children tortured to death by the Germans'. He called on the soldiers 'to avenge those burned in the devil's ovens, to avenge those who suffocated in gas chambers, to avenge the murdered and martyred'. And there could be no doubt in anyone's mind that when Zhukov stated in the same order 'We shall exact a brutal revenge for everything', he meant every word.[5]

Not only were the Russians an imminent and terrifying threat, but tensions in the village were also heightened by the endless flood of evacuees and refugees. By 1944 there were about 4,000 of them living in Oberstdorf, doubling the village's pre-war population. The majority of the earlier evacuees had come from the Ruhr, but later, when the Allies were capable of flying greater distances and bombing Augsburg and Munich, many more were to emerge from those two cities. The absorption of so many disparate and traumatised people into the village was never going to be easy and for Oberstdorfers, with their innate suspicion of outsiders (unless they were paying visitors), it was particularly hard. The pressures from over-crowding, food shortages and, above all, the alien ways of these 'outsiders' put a heavy strain on everyone.

One group that aroused particular dislike consisted of the so-called *Mukis*. These were pregnant women and young mothers who were evacuated in special trains to Oberstdorf by the *Hilfswerk Mutter und Kind* (Mothers and Children Relief Organisation), hence the name. In 1944 they gave birth to nearly 700 babies in the village. The fact that they received special treatment and state funding caused deep resentment among the locals, particularly as it was widely held that *Mukis* did nothing but lounge about (or worse), leaving the village women to do all the work. A senior official in Sonthofen summed up the general view when he accused *Mukis* of 'adultery, idleness, drunkenness and a passionate addiction to cigarettes'.[6] Further annoyance was caused by the free meals to which *Mukis* were entitled and which created yet more logistical headaches for the village authorities.

Mukis were not the only evacuee women to merit Oberstdorf's disapproval. Hans Schnell's mother had a miserable time there – not because she had married into a Jewish family (she was Emil Schnell's daughter-in-law) but simply because she was a *Bombenweib* (bomb woman). The Schnell family also qualified for free rations, although Hans remembered 'the food cooked at the Adler inn smelled so disgusting that even the cats wouldn't touch it'.[7] On the other hand, the better-off evacuees who rented rooms in private houses or the smaller hotels were welcomed as a source of much-needed income. For struggling farmers like the Berktold family, the money earned from their wartime lodgers made a crucial difference to their survival even if it meant having to sleep in the barn.[8]

Initially there were fifty-two students in Franz's class at school, but that number rapidly increased as more and more evacuees found their way to Oberstdorf. Many of these young people, who came from all over Germany, were deeply traumatised after being bombed night after night. Not surprisingly, they were a disruptive and an often disturbing influence on the local children. 'When a student teacher criticised one boy,' Franz recalled, 'he pushed her up against the blackboard and held her there with her arms spread, as if nailed to the cross.' The fact that the north German girls were more sexually advanced than the village children created yet further pressures. At the same time the qualified teachers (most had willingly joined the Nazi Party) had disappeared off to the war, with the result that the children's education was reduced to shortened lessons in fewer subjects delivered by substitute teachers who knew little more than their pupils. The *Notabitur*, introduced at the beginning of the war, was a rudimentary alternative to the *Abitur*, (the equivalent to English A-Levels), which before the National Socialists took control of education had been widely respected for its depth and rigour. But by offering the watered-down version, which did not involve a written examination, it was possible to funnel young men from school to the front more rapidly.

After the school was turned into a hospital in 1944, lessons, such as they were, took place all over the village in the railway station restaurant, the dairy, wine cellars, various pubs and even the Stempfle food factory. With so many children left unsupervised for long periods it did not take much for the violence simmering beneath the surface to erupt. Windows were broken and furniture smashed. 'When on one occasion there was yet again pandemonium in the classroom,' Franz wrote, 'I was suddenly overcome with fury and knocked down a boy from the Ruhr whom everyone thought particularly tough. This did a great deal for my reputation.'

At the end of June 1944, the Jägers' eldest son Alois came home for a few days' leave. He was popular in the village and much admired as a virtuoso accordion player. He had taught Franz how to play, and although he was five years older the two had become close friends. As they worked together in the hayfields that summer, Franz brought up the subject of the Allied landings in Normandy a couple of weeks earlier; and of how Germany's defeat must now surely be only months away. Alois's furious response came as a shock. 'The Americans and English were going down like flies,' he retorted, 'and it was the same in Russia. Germany's final victory was certain.' A few days later, when Franz accompanied his friend to the railway station, he could think of little to say. As the train carrying Alois back to the Eastern Front pulled out, he waved him goodbye for the last time. Four months later, on 22 October 1944, Alois was killed in East Prussia. He was twenty years old.

On 15 November, three weeks and three days after Alois Jäger's death, the villagers gathered in the parish church to remember their fallen heroes. Next to the church stood the memorial chapel, designed originally to commemorate the dead of the 'war to end all wars'. Now it was scarcely big enough to contain the names of all those killed in this new one, let alone the abundance of crosses and wreaths covering every available space. With so many Nazis and bereaved families assembled in his church, Father Rupp chose his words with particular care. This was not the moment to express his true emotions even though by this stage of the war they were probably shared by the majority of villagers: that Alois and all the young men whose sacrifice they were there to 'celebrate' had not, in fact, fallen gloriously for the Fatherland but had died terribly in a war that was about to be catastrophically lost.

Throughout the war Oberstdorf's municipal council had continued to exist in name but in practice was nothing more than an empty shell. In the first three years of the conflict it had met a dozen times but in 1943 only once, and again once the following year. At its last wartime meeting in 1944 there were only two items on the agenda – the budget and the bestowal of an honorary citizenship on the ailing former mayor, Ludwig Hochfeichter. Having served the village so loyally through many testing times, Hochfeichter had survived only to see the inevitability of a second defeat for Germany and the death of his only son Michael, killed on the Eastern Front. As for the council with which Hochfeichter had been so long involved, it seems to have been entirely impotent in the war. There is not a single mention in the council papers of any of the issues that were affecting village life so profoundly: evacuees, resources, compulsory purchase, military hospitals, the Dachau sub-camps, rationing, forced labourers – and, of course, the dead.

The general gloom in the village was shared by many of the wounded soldiers convalescing in Oberstdorf who, after years of fighting for their country, had no desire to sacrifice their lives in these final stages of the war. Fortunately, one of the doctors in Oberstdorf, Dr Gassmann, having lost a leg in Russia, now devoted his energies to saving as many young lives as he could – and not just by medical intervention.

A number of the soldiers under Gassmann's care were in the *Waffen*-SS. But many had been drafted into this military wing of the SS against their will simply because they were tall and blond. It was the practice to brand *Waffen*-SS men on the upper underside of their arm with the letters of their blood group so that even those who despised the regime were thus indelibly marked as true believers. As such, they feared the Allies would treat them more harshly than ordinary soldiers.

Dr Gassmann had no difficulty differentiating between genuine Nazis and those who had been forced into SS uniform, and to the latter he surreptitiously offered surgery to remove their incriminating tattoos.

Karl Ruhrberg was one of many Eastern Front veterans in hospital in Oberstdorf and had no intention of being sent back if he could possibly help it.[9] Fortunately Dr Gassmann was of like mind. When he saw that Karl's blood pressure had disobligingly returned to normal, he announced that the apparatus must be at fault. He would come back later and test it again. Karl knew exactly what he had to do – press-ups. When Dr Gassmann returned he found that Karl's blood pressure was again dangerously high. But both men knew that this was a risky strategy. Oberstdorf's hospitals were full of medics, patients, orderlies and nurses whose views on such subterfuge sharply differed. Had Gassmann's actions been uncovered by a Nazi sympathiser and reported to the SS, both he and Ruhrberg could have been summarily executed. The danger of denunciation was particularly acute for Karl, since a committed Nazi lieutenant occupied the room next to his. Every day Karl could hear him issuing denunciations, either directly to the SS on the telephone or dictating them to a secretary on the balcony that ran past both their rooms.[10]

Indeed, the whole village had become a minefield since it now swarmed with people of all political persuasions, ranging from those who wanted to surrender to the Allies at the first possible opportunity to fanatical Nazis sworn to fight on to the bitter end – and beyond.

In a last-ditch attempt to swell the ranks of Germany's defenders, the *Volkssturm* (People's Storm) was established and officially launched on 18 October 1944. Every male between the ages of sixteen and sixty not already involved in the war was to be conscripted. In this way Hitler hoped to pour a further 6 million fighters into Germany's defence. The men and boys in question were poorly armed and received virtually no training. As well as digging tank trenches, erecting barriers and blasting bridges, these hopelessly equipped 'soldiers', who were not even given a uniform, were deployed on the front line against battle-hardened Allied troops. Not surprisingly, many thousands were killed.[11]

Knowing that Franz too would soon be sent off to fight, his parents watched developments with mounting anxiety, desperate for the Allies to clinch victory. Unlike many of his classmates, Franz had long been disillusioned with the Nazis. Formerly an enthusiastic junior Hitler Youth leader, when he had turned fourteen he had moved up into the Hitler Youth proper. The red and white cord that he had previously worn was now exchanged for epaulettes adorned with stripes and stars. But despite his rise up the ranks, Franz had still attended early Sunday Mass. When, however, the free film shown on Sunday mornings was deliberately brought forward to coincide with the church service, it had become impossible for him to go to both. For Franz, this final clash between God and the Führer brought his love affair with the Hitler Youth to an end. For some months he kept his change of heart a secret. But it had all come to a head one day in 1943 when his leader instructed him to collect some boys from the church (where they were making their confession) and march them to roll call. 'This was the moment of truth,' Franz records. 'I refused to carry out the order. Shortly afterwards I was formally demoted in front of the whole group. I regarded this as an honour. From then on, I no longer held any leadership role and only did enough to avoid attracting attention.' By joining the glider section he managed to find an activity that interested him but also allowed him to maintain a low profile.

Nevertheless, Franz was still expected to train hard. By autumn 1944 he and his schoolmates had been undergoing military exercises for months, but these now became more intense and, because the sergeant in charge was a bully, deeply unpleasant. The sergeant enjoyed humiliating the boys and Franz was several times forced to stand in a pile of manure calling out 'cock-a-doodle-doo'. By declaring that it had been his lifelong ambition to join one of the mountain regiments such as the 98th or 99th, he hoped to escape the *Waffen*-SS whose training camp lay so close to the village. But most of all he wanted to avoid the war altogether.

Unlike Franz, however, many teenagers, having been primed since childhood to regard fighting for the Fatherland as their glorious destiny, were only too keen join the defenders. In February 1945, Theo Sommer* was a fifteen-year-old student in the Adolf Hitler School at the Sonthofen Ordensburg. In his memoir he recalls how, for many local boys, 22 February was their first taste of war. That evening the sudden wailing of air raid sirens was followed by a series of explosions. Sommer was among the boys who raced down the hill to the town, where they found buildings collapsing everywhere in flames. 'The nursing home had taken the biggest hit,' he remembered. 'Wearing gas masks, we entered the smoking ruins and helped to put out the fires. But we found no one alive, only the shrunken corpses of old people who had suffocated and been burned beyond recognition.'[12]

---

* Sommer was later editor of *Die Zeit*.

Three days later Sonthofen experienced another drama. It was 1.30 p.m. and Theo's cohort had just begun their afternoon training session when the boys keeping watch on the roof of the Ordensburg raised the alarm. A mile away an American Flying Fortress, its engines stuttering, was making an emergency landing on the meadows near the town, eight miles north of Oberstdorf. 'We set off immediately,' recalled Sommer,

> running past Altstädten, to the Illerwiesen where it had landed. There the mighty bird lay on her stomach, silvery in the sun, her chassis smashed. Ten men in fur-lined flying suits stood in front of it with raised hands and surrendered to us. They were strapping young lads, fresh-faced and well fed, unlike the emaciated fathers who when on leave would sometimes visit their sons at the Ordensburg.[13]

The boys stayed with the American crew until soldiers from the Sonthofen barracks arrived to take charge. While they were waiting, Sommer managed to climb inside the B-17 bomber and have a good look around. 'The bomb bay, with its capacity for a 4,000-pound load, occupied the middle of the aircraft and was empty. The jumble of cables and electronic equipment astonished us. Our spoils of war were a few Hershey bars, the first American chocolate I ever tasted. We felt like real heroes.'[14] The aircraft, which had flown out that day from England, had been hit by flak. The pilot, needing to be rid of the bombs before making his emergency landing, had managed to drop them in open country, creating several large craters but causing no damage to the local population.*

---

* To this day the area is still known as *Bombenlöcher* (Bomb Holes). Sonja Karnath, Public Relations Office, Sonthofen, 2019.

The schoolboys were not the only ones to have gained unauthorised access to the bomber. By the time the *Wehrmacht* arrived on the scene to take charge, pistols, parachutes and petrol had all mysteriously disappeared. As the reporting sergeant noted, 'According to my information, there should have been eleven parachutes. An unidentified civilian was seen leaving the aircraft with a parachute under his arm. I retrieved one but was unable to discover what happened to the others.'[15] But at least the town received a substantial windfall in the shape of 700 litres of oil that Kreisleiter Kalhammer ordered to be siphoned from the bomber and presented to Sonthofen's transport department.[16]

For these young and enthusiastic *Hitlars*, brought up to believe in the glory of war, this was a great event and, as the Allies drew closer, many of them were keen to taste battle at first hand. Sommer was himself still too young to serve in the *Volkssturm* but, as he recalled, 'We knew it was our sacred mission to serve the German Reich in the same way that Etonians had for centuries served the British Empire.'[17] Sadly, in the final months of the war too many boys were given that opportunity.

19

The Jews

As the war entered its final stage, despite the relentless bombing and apocalyptic destruction of Germany's cities, despite the Allies' advance on Berlin from the west and the Russians' from the east, the Gestapo chose to hunt down a few thousand Jews of mixed blood or mixed marriage. The small number of Jews living in Oberstdorf during the last couple of years of the war nearly all fell into one of two groups – those who were only part-Jewish, described by the Nazis as *Mischlinge* (half-breeds), and those who were married to non-Jews. Although they had so far escaped the camps, they nevertheless lived a precarious existence in constant fear of a summons by the Gestapo. As the war drew to a close, that long-dreaded reckoning finally came.

Even though the 1935 Nuremberg Laws had made matrimony between Jews and non-Jews illegal, the Nazis did not go so far as to outlaw those unions already in existence. Perhaps they hoped in this way to avoid alienating the large numbers of Aryan family members connected to such marriages. They did, however, find plenty of ways to pressurise non-Jewish spouses into voluntarily divorcing their Jewish partners, such as by making it impossible for them to work. Individuals still in a mixed marriage after 1935 were subject to a complicated set of rules. Their status depended on whether or not their children were being brought up as Jews. If they were not, the Jewish partner (usually the husband) was classed as 'privileged'. If there were no children and the husband was Aryan, his Jewish wife was also 'privileged', but only for as long as he remained alive. Privileged Jews did not have to wear the Star of David, nor were they deported to camps until this policy changed shortly before the end of the war. *Mischlinge* were also placed in categories. Two Jewish grandparents labelled a person a first-degree *Mischling*, one Jewish grandparent second-degree. But although these rules theoretically offered protection, there was no knowing from one day to the next how they would be interpreted or for how long they would last. Rumours endlessly circulated. One of the more persistent claimed that the law forcibly separating mixed couples had already been signed and was sitting in Göring's desk drawer.[1]

The fact that Oberstdorf's Jews continued to live in relative security under Nazi rule was largely thanks to Mayor Fink. Remarkably, despite Fink's 'impassioned Nazi speeches and big bombastic gestures',[2] he readily granted resident permits to Jews seeking refuge in the village.* Every Jew in the Reich who did not already bear one of the approved Jewish names on the Nazis' list had in 1938 been forced to adopt the additional name of 'Israel' or 'Sara'. But when, for instance, the Jewish Helene Mayser registered as a resident in the village, 'Sara' was omitted by the mayor's office – a crime carrying severe

---

* Fink also granted a residency permit to Count Joachim von Alvensleben, even though the latter was an 'enemy of the people' who had erected a monument on his estate to the despised Polish people.

penalties. And when the elderly parents of the famous playwright Carl Zuckmayer arrived in Oberstdorf in 1943 having
fled their bombed-out house in Mainz, Fink similarly ignored
the fact that Frau Zuckmayer was Jewish. Meanwhile the half-
Jewish opera singer Hertha Stolzenberg, who had first come
to the village in 1932, continued to live there with her Jewish
mother under Fink's authority.

Oberstdorf's Jews, however, were still subject to the same
restrictions as everywhere else. Several young couples in the
village wanted to marry but were unable to do so because
one of them was a *Mischling*. Johannes (Hannes) Trautloft,
credited with destroying fifty-eight Allied aircraft, was one of
the Luftwaffe's star fighter pilots. He was twenty-seven when
the war began and had already made a name for himself by
shooting down five Republican aeroplanes in the Spanish
Civil War. Handsome, ebullient and brave, he possessed all
the qualities of an Aryan hero except for one – his fiancée was
half-Jewish. Marga Mayser's family made hats – very stylish
ones – and had been doing so ever since 1800 when their company was founded in Ulm. She and Hannes became engaged
in their early twenties but were unable to marry because
her mother (Helene) was Jewish, thus making Marga a first-
degree *Mischling*. So while Hannes was fighting heroically in
Poland, France, the Battle of Britain and Russia, the Maysers
were keeping a low profile in Oberstdorf. A surviving cine-film
shows Marga and Hannes with two of his fellow ace pilots[3]
enjoying a picnic and fooling around in the summer of 1944.
The fact that the lives of this young couple were under mortal
threat from both the Nazis and the Allies gives these brief
moments of happiness caught on film a particular poignancy.[4]

Among the other Jews to benefit from Fink's shielding was
Emil Schnell, a well-known and respected figure in Oberstdorf

who had lived there since the 1920s. Schnell's grandson Hans recalled how walking through the village with his grandfather always took much longer than usual because everyone wanted to stop and chat to him.[5] Indeed, Schnell's reputation was so well established that even leading local Nazis like Kreisleiter Kalhammer and Dr Alexander Helmling (as we have already seen) were openly friendly to him. Schnell's social life also crossed class barriers. Despite the fact that he and Countess Ludmilla zu Castell-Castell (a pillar of the Protestant church) were equally deaf, Hans remembered them roaring with laughter at each other's jokes. As time went on, a number of villagers, including Fink, made sure that the increasingly frail Schnell did not lack for essentials by keeping him well supplied with firewood even though this was strictly illegal.

Emil's grandson Hans was thirteen years old when his family moved from Leverkusen to his widowed grandfather's house in Oberstdorf to escape the bombing. The house, decorated in the art nouveau style and filled with van de Velde furniture, was comfortable despite being in the grip of a tyrannical housekeeper. As Hans observed, 'Jews were not allowed to have attractive servants.'* He grew close to his grandfather, with whom he shared an attic bedroom for two years. He remembered him as 'small, modest and good-natured with a typically Jewish sense of humour'.[6] Although Schnell had converted to Protestantism when he married, according to his grandson he always kept a box of Jewish blessings by his bed. No one, it seems, complained when he failed to wear the compulsory Jewish star. This is not so surprising, since

---

* In order to prevent 'racial impurity', no Aryan servant under forty-five was allowed to work in a Jewish household.

its introduction had in fact proved unpopular throughout Germany. Nor was it only the yellow star to which so
many Germans objected. There was also widespread aversion
to the rounding up and deportation of Jews to the East.[7]

The Schnells had four sons. Emil, the eldest, had been
killed in the First World War. A large picture of him, his Iron
Cross pinned prominently to his uniform, hung in Schnell's
house. The portrait was a precious reminder of a dead son,
but it also offered protection since for the first few years of
Nazi rule the parents of fallen Jewish soldiers were spared
persecution.

Another son, Hermann (Hans's father), was a senior
engineer at the Altötting chemical plant (a subsidiary of
I.G. Farben) and so the fact that he was half Jewish was conveniently ignored. Schnell's youngest son Fritz, however, was
a mere musician, and so, even though he and his brother were
both first-degree *Mischlinge*, their treatment by the Nazis
was very different. Fritz, having been sacked from his job as
Kapellmeister in Augsburg, was made homeless, and with practically no income (he earned a little by playing the organ in
the parish church and giving singing lessons) he moved into
his father's cellar. It was not long before Fritz became engaged
to Henny, one of the young Dutch women employed at the
Hohes Licht children's home, although of course his Jewish
blood made it impossible for them to marry.

In addition to his family, Emil Schnell had a lodger under
his roof – Thesy Heilbronner. She too was Jewish, and although
still married to her non-Jewish husband – a manufacturer in
Berlin – the couple lived permanently apart. Thesy was a small,
stooped woman who kept herself to herself. Unlike Schnell,
she did wear the yellow star. Villagers remembered her trying
to conceal it by clutching a large handbag close to her chest.[8]

Bertl Wirtz (Theodor Weissenberger's sister) recalled how as a young girl she used to shout '*Judenweib*' ('Jew-woman') after Thesy in the street, safe in the knowledge that no one would rebuke her.[9] Although Pauli Rössle (née Lang), whose father Xaver Lang was a postman and a leading local Nazi, remembered seeing Thesy only once, the image of that 'pitiable creature trying to make herself invisible' was one, she recalled, that she would never forget.[10]

In contrast, Dora Lemkes, also Jewish and married to a non-Jew, retained her natural flamboyance. After her husband Hermann Lemkes lost his job as president of Wiesbaden's district court for refusing to divorce her, they too had found sanctuary in Oberstdorf. Elfriede Bierbichler, niece of Wilhelm Herzog, another prominent village Nazi, remembered Frau Lemkes as a highly visible presence. 'She had distinctive Jewish looks and greeted her friends in the street with loud shrieks of delight. We saw her everywhere – even at the cinema, although Jews were strictly forbidden to go there.'[11]

The Lemkes were neighbours of the Noichls, their two houses only separated by a meadow. Franz recalled them as 'a charming elderly couple, always very friendly to us children'. He and his brothers would sometimes run errands for them. When he was about twelve he noticed Mrs Lemkes had begun to wear a large yellow star. Then, towards the end of the war, she suddenly disappeared. Franz's father explained that the Gestapo had taken her away to kill her. 'What is more,' he told Franz, 'her teeth will be broken out to get the gold from the fillings, her hair will be shaved off, her scalp made into lampshades and her bones into soap.' 'We children shuddered,' wrote Franz. 'From then on I never wanted to use soap.'

When an acquaintance of Dora's friend Dr Hanna Witzgall remarked on how sad she had been at Dora's sudden departure,

Hanna replied, 'Didn't you know that the Jews are transported to camps and murdered?'[12]

⟶

During the war some 3 million Jews died in the extermination camps; 700,000 were killed in mobile gas-vans while SS Task Forces, police units and similar organisations murdered 1.3 million. Another million Jews were either shot or died of hunger, disease or SS brutality in the concentration camps and in the ghettos that the Nazis established in the occupied territories.[13] How much of all this did Oberstdorfers know at the time?

With thousands of evacuees pouring into Oberstdorf from all over the country, and with others drafted into the region to work for Messerschmitt or BMW, the village was far from isolated. SS guards from the nearby Dachau sub-camps may have discussed the Final Solution over their beer in the local pubs while soldiers home on leave from the Eastern Front could report on the mass killing of Jews that they had seen with their own eyes or had even themselves taken part in. From December 1942 the Allies ran a campaign to inform Germans about the extermination camps by bombarding them with broadcast information and dropping pamphlets from aeroplanes. And, as we have seen, von Salis's reports also gave Oberstdorf listeners hints as to what was going on. The villagers themselves continued to travel for one reason or another and could have picked up rumours about the systematic murder of Jews from numerous sources. Furthermore, in May 1944 detailed discussion of the Final Solution took place only ten miles from Oberstdorf when on several occasions Heinrich Himmler briefed senior *Wehrmacht* officers at the Sonthofen Ordensburg. It seems unlikely that no word of these speeches leaked out into the town and beyond.

More generally it is argued that the sheer number of ordinary Germans involved in the mechanics of the Holocaust – the civil servants, train drivers, transport personnel, bureaucrats, housing officials, registry clerks, secretaries and suchlike – would have made it impossible for news of the death camps not to have spread into the wider public domain.[14] In the case of the gas chambers, however, located in relatively remote places, behind barbed wire and out of the sight of ordinary German soldiers, it was far harder for people to know exactly what was happening.[15] Rumours, clues and odd bits of information did not necessarily add up to the kind of hard evidence that would have presented the public with unequivocal facts.[16] Nevertheless, it is fair to say that by the end of 1942, knowledge of the mass killing of Jews was widespread throughout Germany.

But while most Germans failed to become rabid anti-Semites despite the regime's best efforts, neither did they attempt any resistance to the genocide. In *Hitler, the Germans, and the Final Solution*, Ian Kershaw suggests that this lack of reaction was largely because the fate of the Jews or, indeed, any other racial, ethnic or religious minority, was not a high priority.[17] Kershaw also makes a telling point when he writes: 'Whether the passivity of the majority reflected moral indifference, bad conscience, suppression of uncomfortable knowledge, fear of the consequences, or tacit approval for what was being done seems to me, truth to tell, impossible to establish.'[18]

In late October 1944, Emil Schnell received a recorded letter stamped with multiple swastikas. It was an order to report to the Gestapo in Augsburg before transportation to the Theresienstadt ghetto. He was instructed to bring underwear and a spoon. It emerged after the war that Mayor Fink had warned Schnell the letter was on its way. In any case, as Schnell had always expected the summons would come one day he had long been prepared.

He had an understanding with Dr Otto Witzgall about what to do should these circumstances arise. Witzgall was one of the villagers who had been consistently opposed to the Nazis from the start. A highly intelligent if eccentric individual, he had served on the municipal council until forced to resign after its Nazification in 1933. Hanna, his former wife and also a medical doctor, was equally hostile to the regime.

Witzgall provided a prescription for the barbiturate Veronal and Fritz's fiancée Henny fetched it from the chemist. Hanna Witzgall did the same for Thesy Heilbronner. That evening Schnell surprised his grandson by saying, 'Hans, I have to tell you something. It doesn't matter if you are a Christian, a Jew, a Buddhist or a Mohammedan, the main thing is that you are a decent human being.'[19]

Hans did not sleep in the same room as his grandfather that night. The next morning, 1 November 1944, Emil Schnell and Thesy Heilbronner were found dead.

That same day Fritz and Hans went to the Oberstdorf police station to hand in all Schnell's possessions and clothes as the law dictated. 'But the police were visibly uncomfortable,' remembered Hans, 'and told us to take my grandfather's things back home.'

A Protestant priest buried Schnell at the edge of the cemetery. Standing by the graveside, Hans remembered his mother's anger and his father's tears. He also remembered that his uncle Fritz, by then working in Sonthofen at an armaments factory, was deeply anxious, knowing that he too could expect a letter from the Gestapo any day. A few days after his father's death, the dreaded letter arrived:

You are summoned herewith to report for urgent work
service at Organisation Todt on 24 November 1944 by
the latest at 10 o'clock at the Geheime Staatspolizei-
Staatspolizeistelle [Gestapo] Augsburg, Prinzregentenstr. 11.
You must bring: food for three days, strong clothes for
work, sturdy shoes, one or two woollen blankets, as well
as some tools such as a saw, axe, shovel and spade . . .
Non-compliance in respect of this order will carry the
heaviest consequences. It is your duty to observe uncondi-
tionally the indicated dates.[20]

Fritz was sent to a camp 300 miles away near Kamsdorf in
Thuringia. The town was in an extensive mining area in which
thousands of concentration camp inmates, mainly from Eastern
Europe, were forced to work underground in nightmarish conditions. Their task was to expand the existing system of mining
tunnels into a vast factory for the manufacture of Me 262
jet aircraft. Named after Reichsmarschall Hermann Göring,
this massive plant was known as REIMAHG. By the time
Fritz arrived in Kamsdorf, the military engineering company
Organisation Todt (OT) had taken charge of production.*

Fritz Schnell had the relative good fortune to end up in a
camp especially designated for *Mischlinge* and was thus spared
from having to labour underground. Instead, he and his fellow
inmates were put to work building a barracks and a cinema
for Luftwaffe officers. The Gestapo rules originally stated that

* OT was a military engineering company named after Fritz Todt,
the construction engineer who before the war had masterminded the
building of Germany's Autobahns. At the time of his death in 1942 in
a mysterious aeroplane crash, he was Reich Minister for Armaments
and Ammunition.

Mischlinge were to be treated as 'voluntary' workers, not prisoners but by the time Fritz arrived at Kamsdorf conditions had become more stringent. Now inmates could only leave the camp under guard and were no longer allowed to receive visits from their wives or families.[21] However, the Gestapo had not reckoned with Henny – 'one of those blonde, tough, blue-eyed women who refuse to take no for an answer', as one friend described her.[22] Having often visited the Dutch forced labourers living around Oberstdorf as a member of the Hohes Licht team, she was familiar with a wide variety of camps and the different ways in which they operated. Overcoming some formidable obstacles (not least the 600-mile round trip), she turned up one night at Fritz's camp, climbed through the barbed wire and found her way to the hut he shared with sixteen others. Perhaps by this late stage of the war the OT guards had lost interest in maintaining tight security, or possibly Henny bribed them. How long she stayed or how often she visited the camp is not recorded, but by nursing Fritz, who had become seriously ill, and feeding him soup and puréed vegetables she may well have saved his life. She also washed, cleaned and mended for his room-mates.

Surviving documents later revealed that Fritz and his fellow captives had been selected for 'departure' to the Ohrdruf concentration camp forty-five miles away. In other words, they had been put on a death list.[23] Fortunately the Allies arrived in time to liberate them before they could be moved.

~

Once Fritz had been deported to Thuringia, his friend Eva Noack-Mosse knew that it was only a matter of time before she too received a letter from the Gestapo. Married to the non-Jewish Moritz Noack, Eva was forty-two and came from a distinguished Jewish family. Her grandfather had founded one of Berlin's finest clothing stores; her father was a medical professor. An uncle had owned a particularly grand house on Potsdamer Platz until it was appropriated by the Nazis and turned into the Academy of German Law. Eva and Moritz, together with his two daughters, moved from Berlin to Oberstdorf in 1941. As Eva wrote in her memoir, 'we had only one aim: to stay alive during the Third Reich'.[24] Again the village authorities demonstrated their relaxed attitude to Jews by ignoring the fact that she failed to register the name 'Sara'.

To begin with, Eva and her family lived in the village without incident. But difficulties arose when she began to receive letters from Berlin addressing her as Eva Sara Noack. The 'Sara' did not go unnoticed by the other occupants in the house, among them Dr Otto Stahmer, the lawyer who after the war was to defend Hermann Göring at the Nuremberg trials. The fact that Eva's 'adorable' terrier had a tendency to bark and bite did not help. However, the landlord was so irritated by the behaviour of his Nazi tenants that he evicted them instead, allowing the 'privileged' Eva and her family to continue living under his roof.

It was not until 6 February 1945 that the letter from the Gestapo finally arrived. 'I knew right away I was lost,' wrote Eva, 'goodbye to family, goodbye to a freshly changed bed, goodbye to everything, really everything.'[25] The Gestapo led Eva to believe that as a privileged Jew she would, like Fritz Schnell, be sent to an OT camp in Thuringia where she would be employed in office work. This prospect was grim enough, but it was not as frightening as the Theresienstadt ghetto where so many of Eva's relatives had already been incarcerated.

There remained one slim hope of avoiding deportation. At the time she was suffering from an infection that a sympathetic doctor could have used as grounds to exempt her from forced labour. However, as the 'young, cold, soulless, cruel and sadistic' doctor in Oberstdorf who examined her turned out to be a committed Nazi, that hope was quickly extinguished. Soon the whole village knew of Eva's fate. So many people came up to her in the street wanting to help that it all became too much. 'I hardly ever went out,' she recalled, 'I couldn't bear hearing the same words of sympathy expressed over and over again.'

Deciding what to pack for a Nazi labour camp was not straightforward, especially since Eva realised that there was no hope of returning home before the end of the war and, although the Allies were making rapid progress, no one could tell when precisely that would be:

> Thus I took a little bit of everything: my winter dress, since it was very practical; ski trousers, because I didn't know whether I would have to work outside; a skirt with a dark, heavy blouse, and another dark silk one – because even in a camp there would be Sundays. I packed sewing necessities and shoe polish, some thumbtacks, a rope for lingerie, hooks to bind it on the wall, candles, and a pocket light. I sewed a nugget of gold into a piece of clothing . . . because I assumed that, after the unconditional surrender, I would need gold to pay for a truck ride in all the confusion.[26]

It seemed foolhardy to set out across a devastated Germany in the middle of winter without cash, so she decided to take a substantial amount. She also packed linen sheets, freshly laundered by her husband. To lighten her rucksack, she chose coupons rather than actual food in the expectation that she would find a village near the OT camp where she could exchange them. Shortly before her departure, she spent three hours at the hairdresser's having a permanent wave – 'it seemed important to me to look at least half decent'.[27] She was distressed by how everyone in the village appeared to be watching her, including the town hall civil servants anxious to see if she would hand in her food coupons before her departure.

As instructed, on 20 February she reported to the Gestapo headquarters in Augsburg. There were twenty-four people in her group but two, whose non-Jewish spouses had recently died and who had therefore lost their privileged status, were informed that they were being sent to Theresienstadt. 'We felt great pity for them,' Eva recalled. The rest still had no idea where they were going, but at least the train carriage in which they were to spend the next three days was heated and surprisingly roomy. Having expected to travel north to Thuringia, they were puzzled not only to find their train heading north-east towards Czechoslovakia but that the two people earmarked for Theresienstadt were still with them. They all wrote postcards, and when the train stopped at a station one of the group distracted the SS guards while the cards were quickly thrust into the hand of a trustworthy-looking individual on the platform. All six of the postcards Eva sent in this manner reached her husband. 'Little by little the mountains disappear, the landscape becomes hilly, the farmers' houses poorer, simpler less well kept . . . we pass by Pilsen, grey and dusty; bombed-out sites everywhere.'[28] During the second night their train crept round Prague, stopping sometimes for hours before being attached to another train. The city's numerous towers appeared to Eva 'strange and ghost-like against the black sky'. The next day, painfully stiff from sitting so long on hard wooden benches, she and her companions stared out of the window at the bleak winter landscape, realising with mounting dread that they were approaching Theresienstadt.

They finally disembarked at a deserted station. 'A railway employee passes by. I ask in a whisper "Theresienstadt?" He nods cautiously and whispers back "yes". Now I know for certain.'[29] After the long train journey she found 'marching together' along a country road in light rain not unpleasant, although the wretched houses, the drab landscape and penetrating cold did little to lift their spirits. Half an hour later they were walking through a thick, thirty-foot-high wall into Theresienstadt, the chilling words 'Arbeit macht frei' painted above the door.

The Theresienstadt ghetto-cum-concentration camp was located in a fortress town built in the eighteenth century, forty miles north of Prague. Ironically, it had originally been conceived as a holiday resort for Czech nobility. After the Nazis turned it into a ghetto in 1941, it was deployed in a number of different ways. One ruse was to present a carefully doctored image of Theresienstadt to international organisations such as the Red Cross to demonstrate how well the Nazis were treating the Jews, many of whom were scholars, musicians, philosophers, artists, scientists, engineers and highly skilled craftsmen. Elderly Jews were also sent there in great numbers. In truth, the appalling conditions – massive overcrowding, malnutrition, lack of medicine and sadistic treatment – caused the death of some 33,000 inmates in the four years of the ghetto's existence. By the time Eva arrived, 17,000 people were living there. This already seemed to her appallingly overcrowded but at its height the ghetto's population had risen to 60,000.[30] Although no gas chambers were built at Theresienstadt, it served as a transit camp from where 90,000 Jews were deported to death camps such as Auschwitz, Treblinka and Sobibór. These deportations continued until October 1944. In January 1945 the Nazis began the death marches from key camps like Auschwitz to Germany's interior to prevent the inmates from falling into the Allies' hands.

Predictably, everything of value that Eva had so carefully chosen to bring with her had been removed from her luggage by the time she recovered it ten days after her arrival. She did, however, manage to retrieve a tiny diamond hidden in her lipstick and her mother's gold watch wrapped in a crumpled paper bag. The fact that the Jews themselves administered Theresienstadt meant that certain aspects of life there were rather better than might be expected. It was possible, for instance, with the camp currency to buy a hot shower or to have clothes washed. Everyone under sixty-five was made to work. Because Eva could type she was employed for ten hours a day in the main administration office. Her job consisted of typing interminable lists and filling out multiple index cards for new arrivals. It was grindingly dull work and, with the war about to end, utterly pointless. On her first day in the office she was surprised to find her female colleagues smartly dressed, wearing lipstick, their faces freshly powdered. The Czech women in particular took great trouble with their clothes. Eva also admired the way they could create 'the fanciest hairdos with just a few hairpins'.[31] To keep up a presentable appearance in such squalid circumstances required a superhuman effort. But it was how thousands of women in Theresienstadt retained their self-respect and kept some sense of control over their lives. One old woman told Eva with pride how for two years she had polished her shoes every day.

By the time Eva arrived, the inmates were allowed to walk on the town walls, where, in her precious few hours of leisure, she would sit with her cousin Martha Mosse soaking up the beauty of the Bohemian countryside now blossoming in the unfolding spring. Nevertheless, Theresienstadt was vile.

Life was an endless battle against hunger, filth, lice, cruelty, disease and depression. The last weeks at Theresienstadt were agonising because, although everyone knew the war was coming to an end, there was a deep fear that the Nazis would murder them all before the Allies arrived. Fortunately they did not have long to wait.

20

Collapse

On 30 January 1945, the day that marked the twelfth anniversary of Hitler's appointment as chancellor, Oberstdorfers tuned into their wireless sets to hear him give what, as it turned out, was to be his last speech. If any of the villagers had hoped for an inspirational message from their Führer, they were to be disappointed. He had nothing to offer them. There was no more talk of the wonder weapons that would turn the war around, only his usual rant against the 'Jewish international conspiracy'. By the time Hitler gave this speech, Germany's last major offensive of the war – the Battle of the Bulge – had ground to a halt. In February most of Hungary was lost to the Russians, and then on 22 March the Americans crossed the Rhine. But as Hitler's statement (recorded by his ADC, Nicolaus von Below) makes crystal-clear, he had no thought of surrender. 'We'll not capitulate. Never. We can go down but we'll take a world with us.'[1] On 19 March Hitler announced his so-called 'Nero Decree' in which his commanders were ordered to blow up everything that might be of use to the advancing enemy – in other words, the country's entire infrastructure. If, like the Valhalla of Hitler's beloved Wagner, the Third Reich was to collapse in a fiery furnace, it was because the German people had ultimately lacked the steel and resolve to grasp the visionary future that he, their Führer, had laid before them. Now they too must perish in the conflagration. Without him, without National Socialism, there was no Germany.

Even before the Allies arrived, the country was in chaos. Sybille von Arminsted, who had spent so much of her childhood in Oberstdorf, was one of the many thousands of Germans fleeing west as the Soviets advanced. She and her mother were living in Poznań in western-central Poland, where she had been allocated an office job in General Command headquarters, while her mother worked as a voluntary nurse in the Luftwaffe hospital. In 1939, at the beginning of the German occupation, there were only some 5,000 Germans in the city, Sybille's family among them, but by 1944 this figure had risen to 95,000.[2] When Sybille's unit received orders to evacuate at the end of January 1945, she remembered how by then the city was 'totally empty', its civilian population having already fled. 'We left at night in four-wheel drive vehicles heading west,' recalled Sybille, who had had no option but to leave her mother behind. 'We ended up on the eastern bank of the Oder, close to Frankfurt.'[3] It was only then that her group discovered that the military personnel and wounded soldiers accompanying them were meant to have remained in Poznań as Hitler had declared the city a *Festung* – a stronghold that was to be defended to the last. 'We caught sight of our chief of staff (he had been awarded the Golden Medal of Honour for bravery) being transported back to Poznań, where he was executed by the SS for leading the retreat.'

Now the problem facing Sybille and her female colleagues was how to cross the River Oder. 'Suddenly a truck loaded with barrels turned up so we crawled behind the barrels and were carried over the bridge to Frankfurt.' From there they boarded a train to Berlin, fifty miles away, which came to a halt at the city's central cattle yard in the middle of an air raid:

> We were totally filthy. It was impossible to wash and there were no sanitary towels. It was terrible. My girlfriend Bärbel, who had an aunt in Berlin, said that maybe we could have a bath there. So we set off but were caught in the massive air raid and had to shelter in a cellar. When we came out we couldn't make out where we were. Nothing was left. There were no houses, only the smoke and intense heat. We tied cloths over our faces and eventually found our way back to the cattle yard where we were met with cries of delight as everyone assumed that we had been killed. Then a train arrived and took us to Potsdam, where it stopped for several hours.[4]

Bärbel's mother happened to live in Potsdam so, still determined to have their bath, the young women made their way to her apartment. 'To be clean again', remembered Sybille, 'was the most exquisite experience of my life.' They returned to the station relieved to find their train still there.

From Potsdam Sybille and her colleagues journeyed fifty miles west to Rathenow, a garrison town where she continued to work for the military, duplicating endless files. Fortunately, the general in charge was a kind man and he managed to track down news of Sybille's mother. It was not encouraging. She had not been evacuated with other hospital staff because as a volunteer she did not belong to any particular organisation and so had been left behind. Consumed with anxiety for her, by the end of March Sybille had had enough and, with the

approval of the general, decided the time had come to abandon
her job. Astonishingly, the telegraph service was still working
so she sent a telegram to her grandmother, who had bought a
farm near Dingolfing (a small town sixty miles north-east of
Munich), where she hoped to offer her far-flung family a safe
haven as the world unravelled around them. Back came the
reply that Sybille's mother had already arrived, having been
squeezed on to the last train out of Poznań with the help of
a kindly conductor:

> A great rush of relief. Then the terrible journey to
> Dingolfing – overcrowded trains, hunger, no food stamps.
> I was pushed through the window into one train with my
> suitcases and rucksack, landing up between some Luftwaffe
> men. To my astonishment, one of them unpacked an unim-
> aginable feast – sandwiches made of white bread thickly
> spread with butter and filled with chicken. I thought I was
> hallucinating. 'Do you want one?' he asked.

When they reached Jena, Sybille's birthplace, the air raid sirens
sounded 'so we all got out and lay on the tracks under the
train. "Born in Jena died in Jena", was the phrase that kept
going round and round in my head. We were terrified that the
train would leave while we were still under it.' They finally
reached Nuremberg, from where Sybille hiked and hitched
rides to Fürth before catching another train to Dingolfing. She
walked the last three miles carrying her suitcases and rucksack.
When her grandmother opened the door, the first thing she
said was, 'My goodness you've grown', a remark, remembered
Sybille, 'that at the age of twenty-four I found rather annoy-
ing'.[5] The relief and joy of being reunited with her family did
not last long. Apart from lack of food and having to sleep on

a straw bed, Sybille, like Germans everywhere, was now living in constant fear of what would happen to them all when the Allies finally arrived.

⌒

In March 1945, Elfriede Bierbichler, a native Oberstdorfer, found herself trapped in Austria with the Allies drawing closer every day. Elfriede's uncle was none other than Wilhelm Herzog, the meat inspector who had denounced Anton Jäger and who was recognised as one of the village's most devoted Nazis. Elfriede did not share her uncle's politics and by the end of 1944 all she had wanted, like so many others, was for the war to end as quickly as possible. In November, however, she received orders to report to a labour camp in Austria. The fact that the Nazis pursued a policy of sending the girls as far away from their homes as possible did not make this unpleasant news any more palatable. 'My friend was smarter,' Elfriede recalled, 'she pretended to be ill so her service was postponed for six months by which time the war was over.'[6]

When Elfriede arrived at the camp in Styria it was lying under deep snow. Forty girls lived in an unheated barracks so poorly built that the wind blew through cracks in the walls. After spending the freezing nights in bug-infested bunks they would rise at 5 a.m. and dress in their brown uniform and unlined leather boots. Although uncomfortably heavy, the horsehair jackets with which they were issued offered little protection against the cold. After roll call the girls stood holding hands around the camp flag singing Nazi songs – a ceremony that was repeated in the evening. Elfriede was assigned to a farm where her chores included doing the laundry in an icy stream and making beds, but only after she had first trapped the fleas. 'Everything was disgusting,' Elfriede remembered, 'particularly the slobbering old grandfather.' Her only means of escape was to perform so incompetently that her employers would want to be rid of her. It worked. A few days later she was sent away. Her subsequent sewing job was an improvement, but life at the remote camp remained immeasurably bleak.

In March 1945, the girls were moved thirty miles east to Mürzzuschlag, some 300 miles from Oberstdorf and close to a camp in which 4,000 foreign forced labourers were incarcerated. By now the Russians were only forty miles away – 'we could hear the gunfire', recalled Elfriede. The prospect of what might happen to them once the Russians arrived and the foreign prisoners were released was enough to decide her and three others to make a break for it. Their opportunity came next day when they were sent to register with the local authorities. Fortunately they were not in uniform, and Elfriede had prudently preserved some cash and a food parcel sent by her mother. So instead of returning to the camp, the girls managed to find their way to the station and board a freight train. As they had no idea where it was going, when it stopped a few hours later in a forest they jumped off. Almost immediately they met a friendly soldier who put them on a northbound road. 'We were twelve days on the road, sometimes walking and sometimes hitching a lift in military trucks. When I think about it now,' Elfriede remarked in 2019,

> it seems astonishing that we were so little afraid of being raped by the soldiers we met, even though they were also fleeing and had had no women for such a long time. For some reason it never occurred to us. At night we slept in barns. We soon discovered that straw is cold but hay is wonderfully warm and cosy.

When they reached Innsbruck the girls separated and Elfriede made her way west to Oberstdorf by train, fearful that despite holding valid papers she would be arrested for absconding from her camp. She walked the final couple of miles to the village through the woods in the dark. 'I was terrified that I would bump into someone I knew or, even worse, a Nazi official.' Three weeks before the end of the war, she finally reached home.

━

Soldiers, too, were by now desperate to give up and go home. By the spring of 1945 Alfons Meinlinger had been fighting with the 99th Regiment for five and a half years with little respite. Apart from a brief sally into Hungary, the 1st Mountain Division had remained in Greece and the Balkans until the autumn of 1944, when the Russians encircled what was left of it in Belgrade. On 18 October the Germans managed to break out but suffered terrible losses in the process. The survivors went on to fight their now hopeless cause in the region between Dravograd (in Slovenia) and Lake Balaton (in Hungary).

On 19 March, the day of Hitler's 'Nero Decree', Meinlinger made the following diary entry:

> Tomorrow is the first day of spring. I have already seen some flowers sticking their heads out of the earth. They shame us humans with their purity and peace. The sun is warm again. The meadows are turning green. Our hearts could be so full of joy if only this mutual slaughter would end.

In the evening, a fellow communications sergeant approached him with a proposition. The war was lost, he said, and it was time to go home. He planned to lead his platoon the 300-odd miles back to Bavaria; would Meinlinger join them? The two men had fought together since the beginning of the war and were close friends. But it would have meant Meinlinger abandoning his own unit, and that he was not prepared to do:

> My men are all good lads except Alois, my second muleteer who can't even count to ten. Eder Schorsch is hard-working and courageous. Unfortunately he was slightly wounded during the last engagement and will be out of action for a while. Kammerloher is a bit slow but is also diligent and very reliable. Lambach, from Innsbruck, is older but I can always depend on him. Despite his stomach troubles, he tries really hard and manages to perform as well as the others. He has a wife and two children but often volunteers for dangerous jobs even though, as a family man, he is only required to do so in an emergency. Then comes Illmer Karl, my senior pack animal man, a very reliable soldier. My beasts are always in good shape. Yes, it's easy being the leader of such a squad, and I am pleased to say that they also like and trust me. Our officer Lieutenant Wagner is excellent. He stands up for us but because he is so eager, he always gives us a lot to do.

The next day, following their orders, Meinlinger and his unit joined about thirty of their fellow 99ers to march to Mürzzuschlag – the Austrian town where Elfriede Bierbichler had only a few days earlier absconded from her League of German Girls camp. When the men drew close, they sent a scout ahead to see what was happening. He returned to report Russian tanks on the main road and villagers who had told him how they had seen officers changing into civilian clothes before melting away into the countryside. 'We knew then that we could expect nothing more from our officers,' Meinlinger later wrote. 'We were on our own.'

> We had to act quickly before the Russians caught us. We asked Thoma Emil from Hinterzarten in the Black Forest to be our leader. We still numbered about thirty. First we unsaddled our pack animals and set them free. Then we distributed the food – bread and cheese powder, which could be mixed with water. We then made our backpacks as light as possible as we had no idea how long we would have to carry them. We kept our pistols so we could defend ourselves in an emergency. We knew that we would have to keep to the side roads and avoid villages.

Somehow they managed to evade the Russians on their long hike from Mürzzuschlag to Innsbruck – a distance of 250 miles. Once in Innsbruck, however, they felt dangerously exposed as they tramped in broad daylight through the streets still in uniform. Their biggest problem was how to cross the River Inn. Some locals told them where to find an unguarded foot-bridge so, 'without looking right or left, we marched through the city and across the bridge. There were American vehicles everywhere, but they took no notice of us.' Meinlinger and his fellow 99ers breathed a deep sigh of relief knowing that, whatever happened to them now, they had at least escaped capture by the Russians.

While Meinlinger and many thousands of his fellow sol-diers wanted only to put down their weapons and go home, Oberstdorf's boys and old men were still being ordered to the front. On 1 February 1945 Franz Noichl turned sixteen and shortly afterwards received his call-up papers. '10 April was a warm spring day when we Oberstdorfers were ordered to report to a military unit seven miles away. We walked there and back, our usual exuberance tempered by a certain gallows humour.' After passing his medical examination he was given a chit stating that he was 'fit for war service'. By then the Battle of Berlin had begun, Vienna was under Russian control, the Americans were on the banks of the Elbe and the French had entered Karlsruhe.

As it seemed impossible the war could last more than a couple of weeks, Franz and his father decided that he should ignore the conscription order. The problem was that the SS remained in tight control regionally. Deserters and those ducking conscription were summarily shot or hanged as a deterrent, no matter how young or old. Such was the fate of Franz's uncle, Hans Zoller, who on 21 April was executed by the SS for having said that he wanted to stop fighting and go home. His death announcement read 'For the People and the Fatherland'.

Franz then had an extraordinary piece of luck. He caught a cold. 'I drank a lot of hot tea, went to bed, covered myself in blankets and began to sweat.' Dr Witzgall, the inveterate anti-Nazi, came to see him. He diagnosed flu and prescribed bed rest. But still the war dragged on. A few days later, an Oberstdorf shopkeeper who had been given the task of checking up on boys like Franz appeared unannounced at the Noichls' house. Fortunately he found Franz in bed, but as he left he delivered a chilling parting shot – if Franz was faking his illness both he and his father would hang. It was not until the last week of April that his visits finally ceased and Franz could feel safe.

One of his classmates was not so lucky. Claudius Asal, conscripted into the *Volkssturm*, was thrown into battle against the Americans without any training. He was killed on 26 April, twelve days before the end of the war. At sixteen he was the youngest Oberstdorfer to perish in action.

In Theresienstadt, Eva Noack Mosse witnessed an influx of some 12,000 people in the last weeks of the war – prisoners who had been taken out of concentration camps from all over Eastern Europe. Some were brought to Theresienstadt in cattle trucks; others had been forced to walk hundreds of miles on what came to be known as the death marches. 'I see them advance along the street,' wrote Eva on 22 April. 'They walk slowly, barely able to put one foot in front of the other . . . the stink of humans who have not washed for weeks overwhelms us. We realise that we have been living in luxury compared with them.' Over the next few days the victims kept arriving. 'Their skulls were the size of children's,' noted Eva. 'They had no flesh, only bones covered by skin of a greenish, yellow colour.' She joined with other Theresienstadt inmates in trying to feed them bread and sugar but as this immediately triggered brawls they were forced to abandon the effort. 'They were no longer human beings,' Eva wrote, 'they had become wild animals.'[7]

For the Nazis at Theresienstadt, however, it was all over. On 22 April, despite the continuing presence of the SS, the Red Cross formally took control of it. Hitler shot himself on 30 April but his death was not officially announced to the inmates until three days later. 'The SS have lowered the swastika to half-mast,' wrote Eva. 'It is grotesque, almost unbelievable . . . to mourn Hitler's death at Theresienstadt.' Then, finally, the SS were gone. 'At last it is real,' wrote Eva. 'The pessimists begin to breathe.'[8]

She remained in the ghetto long enough to watch Nazi women, themselves now prisoners, cleaning the foul lavatories. 'The Russians did not let them have much to eat,' she recorded, 'but their good-natured Jewish supervisor gave them some bread whenever she could.'[9] Eva's last weeks at Theresienstadt were spent responding to the thousands of telegrams sent by people from all over the world frantically seeking their relatives. It would still be some weeks before Eva could start the long journey back to Oberstdorf.

In Oberstdorf itself, the villagers watched their nation disintegrate with mounting fear and not just because of the Allies' imminent victory. During the last nine months of the war there were roughly 3,000 foreign civilians forced to labour for the Reich within a twenty-five-mile radius of Oberstdorf. With the end of the war in sight, no one could guess how these people would respond to the fast-changing circumstances. Given everything that they had suffered at the hands of Germans, it seemed entirely possible that they might rise up as one and murder all the villagers in their beds.

To make matters worse, as the Allies tightened their grip on Germany in the spring of 1945, thousands of SS men, Gestapo, Nazi officials and concentration camp guards fled south towards the mountains, where the most fervent among them intended to operate as 'werewolves' in a guerrilla force set up by an SS general[10] six months earlier. Their resolve had been reinforced by a speech Goebbels had delivered on 23 March in which he urged every German to fight to the death. Eight days later, *Radio Werwolf* began its brief existence calling for perseverance and promising miracle weapons that would instantly turn the war around. A song sung by 'Werwolf Lily' went: 'My werewolf teeth bite the enemy / And then he's done and then he's gone'.[11] As operation Werwolf failed to materialise in any meaningful way, this was pure wishful thinking. Nevertheless, it had tragic consequences inasmuch as it persuaded many Germans to continue a fight that had long since become futile. And, by convincing Allied soldiers that a fanatic Nazi lurked behind every tree, Werwolf was also the cause of many unnecessary deaths.

In addition to the mountains, both the Ordensburg – that potent symbol of National Socialism – and the SS training camp at Birgsau acted as magnets for fleeing Nazis, thus drawing a steady stream of devoted Hitlars into Oberstdorf's immediate orbit. In the last weeks of the war Birgsau became a staging post for would-be partisans and for those hoping to escape to South America.

Many, however, did not make it past the Allied forces. On 1 May 1945, Hauptbannführer (Brigadier) Rudi Raab, the thirty-four-year-old former headmaster of Ordensburg's Adolf Hitler School, was using every ounce of ingenuity to dodge the Allies as he led his men through Bavaria towards the mountains. He rode in the sidecar of a motorcycle driven by one of his soldiers:

> It was very foggy and we nearly didn't spot the old farmer in the gloom. I asked him, 'Have you seen the enemy?' He was dressed in shabby clothes and carried a long staff. 'Yes,' he replied, not bothering to stop, 'the enemy are all around us.' Reaching the top of a rise, I told the driver to turn off the engine and we silently coasted down the hill. When we reached the bottom the fog lifted and there right

in front of us was an American tank. The soldier sitting on top of it fired a burst from his machine gun, killing my driver instantly. But because we were so close to the tank, he couldn't position it low enough to shoot me.

Raab jumped out of the sidecar, threw down his gun and put his hands up. For him the war was over.[12]

By now, all that most Oberstdorfers wanted was for the war to end as quickly as possible, so the possibility that the surrounding mountains were full of Nazi extremists was deeply unnerving. Furthermore, there were still enough committed Nazis in the village itself to present a serious threat to anyone who deserted or talked of surrender, particularly since Himmler had issued an order on 3 April that all males inhabiting a house displaying a white flag were to be shot on the spot.

As tension escalated between those villagers wanting to hang white flags out of their windows and the fanatic Nazis prepared to murder them for doing so, some Oberstdorfers began to explore how they might make contact with the Allies and save the village from bombardment. They knew full well, however, that one false move or careless comment could leave them hanging from the nearest tree or lamp-post.

21

Surrender

The story of Oberstdorf's anti-Nazi resistance movement, or the *Heimatschutz* (Homeland Security) as it
was called, is for many reasons a complicated one. In
the light of post-war sentiment it would seem obvious that
those who took part in it, thus saving the village from bombardment, looting and rape, would be unreservedly regarded
as heroes. But, as the events that engulfed Oberstdorf in
late April and early May 1945 illustrate so well, the world
is rarely that simple. By then the villagers' conflicting affilia-
tions and motives, their fears, egos and emotions, had created
a situation of such complexity that the role played by the
Heimatschutz in Oberstdorf's surrender, and particularly in
its aftermath, was to remain a source of strife among them
for decades.

The driving force behind the resistance movement
was Karl Richter, whose father, the brewer and property owner
Karl Richter senior, was Oberstdorf's most successful businessman. As a prisoner of the French in the First World War,
Hubert Richter (young Karl's older brother) had made a daring escape with Hermann Hoyer. It was this friendship, forged
in extreme adversity, that had brought the one-armed Hoyer

to Oberstdorf when the Richter family offered him land on which to build a house. During the 1920s, the younger Karl and his brother Ernst had a reputation for sporting daredevilry. Rich and privileged but possessing great charm, they were also known to have a ruthless streak and were not above waking the villagers in the middle of the night by firing off their hunting guns in a fit of high spirits. Ernst, who had subsequently settled down and become a dentist, was also a key player in the *Heimatschutz*, as was their mutual mountaineering friend Dr Franz Pfister, a Munich lawyer.

Although the three men had by November 1944 already begun secret discussions with soldiers who were stationed nearby, convalescent or on home leave, it was not until the following February that they launched their resistance movement in earnest.[1] By then Lieutenant Karl Richter was based at the Ordensburg, instructing soldiers on high-altitude warfare to prepare them for their werewolf existence in the so-called 'Alpine Fortress'. The job provided Richter with a perfect cover for his underground operations, but it was a high-wire act fraught with danger. Knowing that he might at any moment be betrayed, he nevertheless went on to recruit a significant number of soldiers for the *Heimatschutz*. Under the pretext of mountain training, he stationed about forty of them in the nearby Oytal valley and began stockpiling weapons there and in a farmhouse belonging to his family. By mid-April everything appeared to be going to plan apart from the increasing numbers of SS men gathering in Sonthofen and Birgsau, their presence hanging like the Sword of Damocles over Oberstdorf's future.

Other conspirators, most notably Ernst Richter and Franz Pfister, were busy plotting in another nearby valley, the Kleinwalsertal. It was their task to draft and print the leaflets that, at the right moment, would be distributed among Oberstdorfers and other locals in the region, informing them of *Heimatschutz* objectives and calling on everyone to join together in preventing an Allied attack on Oberstdorf. The leader of the Kleinwalsertal group was Peter Meusburger, a master butcher and a man of considerable courage. Three times he drove his truck through various police checks into his valley and three times the policemen failed to spot the guns concealed behind carcasses of meat.[2]

On 24 April, it looked as though all the *Heimatschutz* plans were falling neatly into place when Karl Richter learned that an SS brigade, under the command of Standartenführer (Colonel) Hans Thumser, was on its way from Donauwörth to Sonthofen with enough tanks and heavy artillery to pose a serious threat to any plans for a peaceful surrender. Should this SS unit coincide with the arrival of the Allies, Richter knew that all would be lost. He therefore arranged to meet Thumser in Sonthofen and was able, so he claimed subsequently, to convince the colonel that instead of lingering in Sonthofen he should set off at once for the Tyrol via Hindelang and the Oberjoch, on a route that would take the SS unit well to the north and east of Oberstdorf. It was a nail-biting encounter, but Thumser eventually agreed to the plan. Richter, however, was not yet done. With remarkable audacity, he then extracted a signed order from the colonel requiring the SS commander of the Birgsau camp to hand over to Richter six machine guns. Within a few hours of Thumser's departure, Richter was not only in possession of six more machine guns but the Birgsau SS had six fewer.[3]

As Thumser's tanks trundled off to the Tyrol to fight the Americans there, Richter must have breathed a deep sigh of relief. But the stakes were still unbearably high and the pressure on him over the next few days unremitting. Could all the soldiers in the Oytal be trusted? Had the *Heimatschutz* enough men to bring off the coup? And, most worrying of all, why, two days after he had collected the machine guns from Birgsau, had his commander in Sonthofen sent orders for him to dismantle the Oytal training base and report back immediately? This last instruction Richter wisely ignored, choosing to stay with his men. However it was clear that they were living on borrowed time and must strike soon. Everything now depended on the Allies. But where were they?

In fact, French tanks were rumbling south towards Immenstadt along the west side of the River Iller, while the Americans headed down its east bank to Kempten. Meeting no resistance, the US army entered the town, the largest in the Allgäu, on 27 April 1945.

The night of 27 April was bitterly cold, and the moonlight reflecting off the snow-covered mountains made it eerily bright.[4] With the Allies now so close to Oberstdorf, all the villagers – Nazis and non-Nazis alike – were in a state of high tension. That evening a member of the *Heimatschutz*, a local forester and hunter called Hans Stadler, had returned from Oberstdorf to the Birgsau SS training camp, where he had living quarters in one of the old Customs houses that had been incorporated into the SS complex. By this time it was only a shadow of its former strength. The Dachau prisoners, including Andrzej Burzawa, were still there, but for many weeks had been left to their own devices. Andrzej described how he and his fellow prisoners had watched discipline in the camp disintegrate as the Allies drew closer, and how the SS men had increasingly turned to binge-drinking to drown their sorrows.

'No one bothered to guard us so I went alone to find food and supplies.'[5] By the end of April almost all the officers had fled, abandoning the boy soldiers under their charge, some as young as fifteen. According to Andrzej, 300 of these teenagers had several weeks earlier been sent direct from the camp to the front line, at the time located near Lake Constance. Fewer than 100 had returned.[6]

Officially Stadler was still a serving soldier, but for some while had been on sick leave. Because he lived in the camp he was able to supply Karl Richter with regular intelligence reports. Earlier that night he had met his resistance comrades in Oberstdorf and briefed them on how the camp was being stripped and dismantled ahead of the arrival of the Allies, expected any day. Stadler made it clear that he intended to steal weapons from the camp later that night and deliver them direct to the *Heimatschutz*.[7]

After returning to Birgsau, Stadler sat for a long time drinking at the inn located just across the meadow from the camp and the chapel. Shortly before midnight he told the inn-keeper, Frau Mayer, that he was going home and left to walk the couple of hundred metres back to the camp. Sometime later, in the early hours of 28 April, he reappeared, and with the help of several locals loaded a number of crates on to a horse-drawn wagon.[8] Stadler then set off with the wagon, but had only gone a short distance when Sergeant Josef Berghuber appeared unexpectedly and ordered him to halt. Although the pair knew each other well, there was no love lost between them. The two men now confronted each other in mutual hostility – one refusing to accept that the Nazis were finished, the other determined on surrendering Oberstdorf peacefully to the Allies. Berghuber summoned the few remaining boys still living at the camp and told them to break open the crates, while ordering Stadler and his friends not to move. But Stadler, perhaps too proud or too contemptuous to comply, turned his back on the sergeant and started walking towards the chapel. Giving Stadler no word of warning, Berghuber raised his gun and shot him dead.[9]*

When news reached Oberstdorf of Stadler's death it had a profound emotional impact on the villagers. In fact, the struggle between diehard Nazis and those wanting to surrender was having tragic consequences across the region. A few hours after Stadler was killed, the *Gauleiter* of Munich, Paul Giesler, brutally put down a resistance movement, the 'Bavarian Freedom Campaign', with the execution of fifty-eight people. The following day in Penzberg, thirty miles south of Munich, fourteen 'defeatists', including a pregnant woman, were also shot or hanged after a failed attempt to overthrow the town's Nazi mayor. It was in these volatile conditions, when any individual might be killed by anyone for any reason, that Karl Richter had to decide when to strike. On 30 April, the day Hitler killed himself, the French entered Immenstadt. This prompted Richter to test the mood in the village by asking his men to raise a white flag on the church spire. Although Mayor Fink had it quickly taken down, he made no attempt to have anyone arrested or executed.

With the French now only fifteen miles away, Richter decided that the moment had finally come. It was time for action. Word went out to the *Heimatschutz* – in the Oytal, the Kleinwalsertal and in Oberstdorf itself – to don their armbands. At dusk on 30 April, Max Schraudolf (who after the war

---

* Because this is still a sensitive issue in Oberstdorf, the men's real names have not been used.

won fame as a virtuoso zither player) collected some of the
Oytal-based soldiers in an armoured truck and drove them to
Kühberg at the eastern edge of Oberstdorf.[10] Around midnight
they slid silently into the village. Moving from one house to
the next, they proceeded to arrest around fifty of the village's
most prominent Nazis.

Among them were Mayor Fink and his officials, SS and
SA men, the artists Hermann Hoyer and Rudolf Scheller,
propaganda leader and meat inspector Wilhelm Herzog and
Frau Helmling, together with her daughter Margot, the school
bully. Also taken into custody were Herr Schweizer from the
National Socialist People's Welfare office in Sonthofen, who
had had the misfortune to be staying that night in Oberstdorf,
Herr Kaiser the baker's son, the carpenter Schaem's son-in-law
Herb, and the highly respected Dr Knöckel, who had brought
Franz Noichl into the world. Postman Xaver Lang, a former
leader of the local SA, was forced to walk barefoot through
the snow in his pyjamas while his wife Tilly and daughter
Pauli were detained with other Nazi-tainted women in the
Stempfle café, among them the wife and daughter of Gauleiter
Karl Wahl. Pauli remembered how they had all 'trembled with
fear when the Richter brothers appeared in their long grey
coats'. But no harm came to them and the hairdresser Frau
Stenger, whose husband was a member of the *Heimatschutz*,
even made sure they had something to eat.[11] 'Soon all our little "darlings" were locked up in the town hall cellars', wrote
Elisabeth Dabelstein to a friend a few weeks later.[12] It was a
cataclysmic event – the moment when National Socialism in
Oberstdorf was definitively crushed.

While the arrests were taking place, another seventy or
so supporters, also wearing blue and white armbands, had
emerged out of the darkness to join the action. Given that

the men involved in the coup were a mixed group coming from varied backgrounds and different parts of the surrounding area, it seems nothing short of a miracle that the tight security surrounding the coup was maintained right up to the last moment. But everyone taking part was highly motivated and united by one clear objective – to surrender to the Allies and save Oberstdorf from destruction.

Otmar Schuster, one of the *Heimatschutz* men based in Oberstdorf, left a vivid impression of the atmosphere that night:

> At half past one in the morning, Franz Seiler, the barman at the Weinklause, woke me and told me to go immediately to the town hall. When I got there, I was given a blue and white armband with the inscription '*Heimatschutz*'. Some of the Nazis had already been locked up in the cellar. At half past three, we were all summoned to a meeting with the leaders. Karl Richter wanted to hang a Nazi from the ash tree at the entrance of the village as a deterrent. He suggested a number of different people as possible victims. There was a lot of discussion during which Richter made it clear that he did not like being contradicted. But I then spoke up and said, 'If you hang someone now, you will one day in the future face a court of law for murder.' After that, despite Richter's irritation, the idea was dropped.*

---

* This account was supplied by Schuster's son. Subsequently others present in the town hall that night also claimed to have prevented the execution of a Nazi from taking place.

'So,' wrote Elisabeth Dabelstein, 'little Oberstdorf had its own St Bartholomew's Night* but without shedding a drop of blood.'[13]

The key village buildings, including the railway station, the fire station and the post office, were swiftly occupied. Richter had worried that the *Volkssturm* might cause trouble, but in the event the reverse was true as most of the old soldiers declared themselves only too happy to switch their allegiance to the *Heimatschutz*. When dawn broke on 1 May, a white flag could be seen flying again from the church spire. 'White flags then sprang up everywhere,' recorded Dabelstein, 'it was as if the village had just done a gigantic wash!'[14]

The coup had not only triumphed, it had done so without loss of life. Yet tension remained high, fuelled by fear that Nazi fanatics still lurked in the Birgsau valley waiting to attack. Such was the reputation of the SS that even though the majority of its men had in fact already left the area, it was still widely believed that as many as 400 remained in the immediate vicinity prepared to defend Oberstdorf from the Allies at any cost. Another sinister rumour claimed that the SS had a list of villagers they intended to liquidate.

Events were now moving fast. In the early hours of 1 May, the leader of the Kleinwalsertal *Heimatschutz*, Peter Meusburger, went on an urgent mission to the Ifen Hotel located in the small village of Hirschegg. It was here, in this luxurious hotel opened in 1936, that the former French Ambassador to Berlin, André François-Poncet, had been interned since 24 November 1943. He was later joined by an

* Catholics murdered thousands of Huguenots on the night of 23–4 August 1572, the eve of the Feast of St Bartholomew.

assortment of foreign civilians including such grand person-
ages as the Duchess of Aosta and Princess Anne of France.
Senior Nazis also stayed at the hotel, either on holiday or, if
they had been made homeless by bombing, for much longer
periods. This curious mix of people, who all ate together in
the same dining room, were fed extremely well and even on
occasion supplied with wine and champagne. The internees
were allowed to walk in the valley, to receive letters and par-
cels and were also supplied with books from the Red Cross.
But despite such relatively comfortable conditions, the volatile
atmosphere, intense boredom, lack of any real news and, above
all, the agonising uncertainty over their future combined to
make their existence far from pleasant.*

When Meusburger reached the hotel at 5.30 a.m. he
immediately woke the ambassador and asked him to provide a letter that could be presented to the Allies when they
arrived. As at that stage it was still not clear whether it
would be the French or the Americans, François-Poncet (by
now deeply fearful that the internees would all be murdered
by their SS guards before the Allies could free them) wrote
the letter in both French and English.[15] It was headed 'A Cry
for Help':

> On behalf of thirty civilian internees who have been
> detained in Hirschegg for the last two years, I request help!
> Germans determined to resist the occupation of this val-
> ley remain a serious threat. It is essential that the army

---

* Crown Prince Wilhelm of Prussia (the former Kaiser's eldest son)
took refuge in a small hunting lodge close to the Ifen Hotel where
several of his cousins, including the Duchess of Aosta, were interned.
After Oberstdorf's surrender he was arrested by Moroccan troops.

intervene as soon as possible. The Allied forces can give Lieutenant Richter, the bearer of this letter, their full trust as he is contacting you on my instructions and will clarify the situation. He is leader of a group of partisans anxious to protect the valley. His members wear a blue and white armband on their left arm. They stand ready to support the Allied troops. If it is not possible to contact us personally, we can be reached by telephone at Riezlern 23.[16]

Hiding the letter in his shoe, Meusburger (whose calm manner throughout was much admired by François-Poncet) immediately drove the nine miles to Oberstdorf, where he handed the ambassador's letter to Richter. On his return to Kleinwalsertal he rallied thirty men with whom he managed to capture the Riezlern town hall and depose the Nazi mayor. By 11.30 that morning, the number of *Heimatschutz* supporters in Kleinwalsertal had risen to 120.[17]

But when by lunchtime on that cold, snowy day there was still no sign of the Allies, the levels of anxiety in Oberstdorf began to rise sharply. Needless to say, Frau Noichl's nerves were in tatters. 'My mother', Franz recalled, 'was convinced that the SS had already shot my father,' Xaver, of course, being a keen member of the *Heimatschutz*:

> I was sent to look for him. I didn't have to go far. I found him in Sonthofener Strasse. He was sitting on the bonnet of a truck, pistol in hand, directing the SS officer at the wheel. I was amazed to see my father with a gun. He was such a bad shot that his friends never allowed him to have a rifle when they went poaching together. Fortunately, his bluff worked. The SS officer offered no resistance and was led away to imprisonment.

It was not until the late afternoon that at last eight French tanks slowly emerged out of the blizzard. Two miles north of the village, Richter was waiting to greet them at the Breitach bridge with a white flag. After presenting François-Poncet's letter to the French commander, Richter introduced him to the man he had provisionally appointed Oberstdorf's new mayor. This was none other than Thomas Neidhart, the village's former mayor whom the Nazis had so unceremoniously dumped exactly twelve years earlier on 24 April 1933.[18]

Franz Noichl first became aware of the French tanks when he heard the sound of their rattling chains as they made their way along Sonthofener Strasse, the main road leading from the north into Oberstdorf. Elisabeth Dabelstein recalled her excitement on hearing the news:

> Shortly before 5 p.m. we heard a mighty roar – Frau Noichl was with us and we all shouted 'The tanks! The tanks!' Frau Noichl rushed off because she didn't want to miss anything! I went straight up to the attic to fetch our Dutch flag, which we immediately flew over the house. It was really unbelievable! Twelve years that had seemed more like a thousand were finally over! I can't remember having ever experienced a more beautiful moment! Then, of course I also hurried to the marketplace, driven by exactly the same urge as Frau Noichl! There were eight French tanks parked there in a circle. Everywhere people were beaming. The secret organisation, now calling itself *Heimatschutz*, wore white-blue armbands and rifles and looked enormously proud. This was their finest hour ... So now we are all French![19]

When everyone later gathered in the town hall, Richter

received formal authorisation from the French commander to maintain order in the village and permission for his men to keep their weapons. For Richter this was a moment to relish, especially when the Frenchman stated that he would not have hesitated to destroy Oberstdorf with his heavy artillery had even one shot been fired in its defence. Satisfied that with Richter and the *Heimatschutz* now under his direct control he could leave the village in safe hands, the French commander ordered his tanks to return to Sonthofen. Their departure so soon after their arrival sent a shiver of fear down the spines of those Oberstdorfers still afraid that the SS might yet launch some desperate last-ditch attack.

But the French were not gone long. The next day, 2 May, the villagers witnessed one of the more bizarre episodes in Oberstdorf's long history when black Moroccan troops wearing red fezzes or turbans marched into the village. Their reception was understandably mixed. For members of the *Heimatschutz* and their followers, for socialists and boys like Franz who had been in hiding from the *Volkssturm*, for the foreign forced labourers, miscellany of prisoners and the handful of Jews, or for those who simply longed for it all to be over, reaction to their unlikely liberators was either one of unalloyed joy or relief tempered by anxiety as to how the German inhabitants would be treated by these alien troops. But for anyone with Nazi sympathies (many of them now locked up) it was, of course, a day of profound bitterness: men like Hermann Hoyer who, in common with so many other Oberstdorfers and millions of his fellow countrymen, had trusted in Hitler's promise to lead Germany back to its rightful place in the sun, and to create an empire that would last 1,000 years. Now the appearance of these despised conquerors meant that those dreams had been shattered forever, and that for the second time in his fifty-three years Hoyer was compelled to endure the misery of defeat and humiliation. Given his harrowing experiences in France and North Africa during the First World War, that it should be Moroccans occupying Oberstdorf under a French flag was an additional twist of the knife. Meanwhile other villagers, even if they had long ceased to support the regime, were so convinced by years of Nazi propaganda that the Allies were fiends from whom they could expect no mercy that they too anticipated the French occupation with the deepest dread. Nor can there have been many women in Oberstdorf that day who – regardless of their political persuasion – did not fear rape at the hands of their new masters.

With the village now fully occupied, the imposition of curfews and multiple restrictions, the seizure of goods and property, the spot searches and general inconveniences left villagers in no doubt that they were far from free. The following day, 3 May, Mayor Neidhart was required to publish a list of the new regulations signed by the French commander:

1. No citizen is permitted to be outside between 8 p.m. and 6 a.m. with the exception of doctors, nurses, the police, and in certain exceptional cases.

2. No German officer or soldier may be on the street at any time.

3. The German wounded must remain in the military hospitals.

4. All weapons, ammunition, cameras, binoculars and radios must be delivered to the town hall.

5. A list of all Oberstdorf *Wehrmacht* and *Volkssturm* members is to be delivered to the Commander on 4 May by 10 p.m.

6. Anyone sheltering a member of the *Wehrmacht* in uniform or in civilian clothes who is not on the list of wounded in the military hospitals may be punished with death.

7. The mayor is responsible for the implementation of these regulations.

8. The chief of police is under the authority of the Commander.

9. Gatherings of more than three people on the street are forbidden.[20]

Amid all the turmoil, one fact was plain: for Oberstdorf the war was over. Or was it? Many villagers remained convinced that Nazi fanatics still hid in the mountains waiting to strike, while Stadler's comrades had at his grave sworn to exact revenge on his killer.

By 3 May it was apparent that, despite all earlier fears to the contrary, the Birgsau camp had been abandoned. The commandant, Lieutenant-Colonel Lindemann, however, unlike his subordinates, had chosen to remain at his post. That evening Richter telephoned him demanding that he hand over any weapons still remaining at the camp. Lindemann's response was not helpful. If Richter wanted them, he replied, he would have to come and get them. As a result, the French commanding officer commissioned Richter's men to collect the weapons the following day and at the same time to round up any stray Nazis in the area.[21]

Thus on 4 May, two days after the surrender, forty *Heimatschutz* men drove in two trucks up the mountain road to Birgsau to carry out these orders. When Xaver Noichl had told his wife that he planned to go with them she had become distraught, convinced that her husband would take part in the revenge on Stadler's killer. But to her great relief

Xaver unexpectedly returned home, having missed the transport. Josef Geiger, a member of the militia, gave the following
account of what took place:

> We first searched the SS camp but found it already aban-
> doned. The SS men had initially retreated to the Buchrainer
> Alpe, then to Peter's Älpele [mountain huts]. We went
> after them and demanded their surrender. They fired on
> us so we surrounded the hut and attacked it. Shortly after-
> wards they came out with their hands up. We disarmed
> them and they were taken away. When we entered the
> hut, we found slogans plastered over walls: 'To the last
> drop of blood for the Führer' and 'For the People and the
> Fatherland'.[22]

The precise circumstances of what followed remain unclear,
but when the *Heimatschutz* detachment returned to Birgsau
after capturing the SS men, another member of the Noichl
clan and several other *Heimatschutz* colleagues were told
where to find Sergeant Berghuber. They tracked him down,
confronted him and then, according to Josef Geiger, brought
him to a garage next to the Birgsau inn where, in a shocking
act of revenge, they beat him to death with their rifle butts.[23]

  Significantly, the villagers' response to this murder
depended less on their pro- or anti-Nazi sympathies than
their personal allegiances. As the greatest conflict in human
history neared its end, the issues that divided them, therefore, focused on such matters as whether or not Stadler had
been looting goods for the black market, or if Berghuber (who
was not an Oberstdorfer) had simply been doing his duty. In
the context of a war in which it is estimated some 80 million
people died, it might seem that the deaths of these two minor

players are of little consequence. Yet among all the hideous crimes committed in the Third Reich, it is these specific acts of violence that were to polarise the villagers more intensely than any other. The cold-blooded killing of Stadler, followed by the savage clubbing to death of Berghuber, had happened within the villagers' own community to men anyone might have spoken to hours before they were slain. It was as if all the barbarity, butchery and horror of the war, all the misery, the grief and suffering had been encapsulated in the deaths of these two men.

It was at the temporary Allied headquarters in Reims, in the nondescript red-brick Collège Moderne et Technique, that General Jodl signed his country's unconditional surrender on behalf of the German High Command. The time was 2.41 on the morning of 7 May 1945. The next day, Germany's highest-ranking officer, Field Marshal Keitel, signed a second surrender at a former engineering school in Berlin shortly before midnight. The war was over. The Third Reich had ceased to exist. In Oberstdorf a sixteen-year-old girl wrote in her diary, 'Complete surrender! The whole of Europe is cheering except us.'[24]

The following Sunday, 13 May, a priest arrived in Birgsau to celebrate Mass at the little chapel dedicated to St Wendelin, the patron saint of herdsmen. It was just outside this chapel, standing so picturesquely at the foot of the mountains, that Hans Stadler had been fatally shot only two weeks earlier. The buildings of the SS camp, now deserted except for the former Dachau prisoners who remained because they had nowhere else to go, lay sprawled across the adjacent meadow. One of the former prisoners, a Ukrainian, had become so attached to Birgsau that he decided to stay and a few weeks later married a local German girl. Although it had been a particularly cold spring in the Allgäu, there was just enough warmth that day to remind everyone that summer was on the way. The chapel was so small that it could barely hold thirty people, but on this occasion many more had managed to squeeze in, filling every conceivable space. Seated among the Birgsau locals and the few families who had come up from Oberstdorf were the former Dachau prisoners, still wearing their striped uniforms. Four of them served at the altar. A heavy silence followed the service. At last the war was over, but there was little to celebrate.[25]

22

Aftermath

Oberstdorf was still reeling from the events of the previous two weeks when on 14 May 1945 France's new head of state, General Charles de Gaulle, arrived in the village to preside over a victory parade. He was accompanied by his war minister, André Diethelm, and commander-in-chief General de Lattre de Tassigny, who only a week earlier had represented France at the signing of Germany's surrender in Reims. With so little time to organise the parade, preparations were intense. The French commander had to cope with countless logistic challenges (such as finding enough flagpoles), while the Moroccans billeted in the Amann household begged Trudl's mother to help them make their 'Vive La France' banner. At the same time Sister Biunda and her flock were working round the clock to produce the hundreds of pairs of white gloves and gaiters required to add a touch of chic to the soldiers' appearance at the big event.[1]

On the day itself, there was a great flurry of activity. Couriers rushed about, guards patrolled the streets and, despite the ban on fraternisation, French soldiers danced with German girls to music from a scratchy gramophone. The marching Moroccans, clattering tanks and jeeps squealing round corners all added to the sense of occasion as people made their way out to the parade ground on the western edge of the village.[2] A journalist covering the story for the Swiss magazine *Sie und Er* (*Her and Him*) noted how 'girls dressed in their Sunday best, men in lederhosen and rugged peasants, their hunters' hats decorated with chamois beards, mingled amicably with the French and Moroccan soldiers'.[3] A photographer happened to snap Wilhelm Steiner as he was walking to the parade – a chance incident with a happy outcome. His sister Anna, who had lived in Switzerland throughout the war, was desperate for news of Oberstdorf and her family. She had seen images of the terrible destruction in Germany and feared the worst. Then she bought a copy of *Sie und Er* and to her astonishment found herself staring at pictures of her brother and of Oberstdorf – both looking reassuringly the same.[4]

Once everyone had assembled at the parade ground there was a long wait until a fanfare of trumpets brought the soldiers smartly to attention. The crowd fell silent.

> General De Gaulle's motorcade drove slowly down the winding mountain road and pulled up on the square. The General . . . walked silently down the lines of soldiers, looking them straight in the eye. The Moroccan band's stirring rendering of the 'Marseillaise' echoed across the parade ground. We could sense the troops' suppressed emotion. Awed, astonished, curious and maybe also confused, the villagers looked on.[5]

After the regiments, tanks and artillery had paraded past de Gaulle, the climax of the afternoon came with an awesome display of French firepower as the artillery loosed off its big guns in the direction of the Rubihorn. The barrage provided

AFTERMATH
347

such a graphic illustration of what would have happened to Oberstdorf had the *Heimatschutz* coup failed that, according to the Swiss journalist, a collective shudder passed through the crowd of watching villagers.[6]

The French military had planned to lodge their VIPs overnight in the Hohes Licht children's home but were thwarted when Hetty refused them point-blank on the grounds that the house was the private property of the Netherlands. After much toing and froing, de Gaulle and his entourage were finally put up at the hotel in Kleinwalsertal in which Ambassador François-Poncet had been interned. That evening, local singing groups and members of the Oberstdorf traditional costume society dressed in their most colourful creations, entertained the French delegation. By all accounts it was a merry evening enjoyed by victors and vanquished alike. 'There is no sign of hostility towards the foreign soldiers,' reported *Sie und Er*. 'They are all just thankful that the war is over and have only good things to say about the French.'[7] Meanwhile in Oberstdorf the day ended with a military concert, which, as Mayor Neidhart noted in his thank-you letter to the French commander, 'attracted sustained applause and much enthusiasm among those present'.[8]

～

Despite the obvious fears and difficulties under which both occupiers and occupied existed, their relations in the last days of the war and in the two and a half months until the Americans took over in July were surprisingly friendly. 'We had 800 men here,' wrote Elisabeth Dabelstein,

> Berbers, Kabyles and Schellus, handsome lads on the whole and picturesque in their white or red turbans. They had

strange voices and wild looks but were quite harmless. The village soon made friends with them. Of course there were lootings and rapes in the remoter houses, but here in the village the reverse was true. Everything was impeccable. The white French, especially the officers, were naturally much more difficult. After their country had suffered five years of German occupation, no wonder! There was a hustle and bustle of cars, much honking and squealing of brakes, indescribable![9]

The few rapes that did take place were punished with such severity that the villagers' confidence in the French authorities' commitment to an orderly and just occupation grew accordingly. By promising voluntarily to provide accommodation and provisions for their occupiers, the *Heimatschutz* leaders had also persuaded the French to forego the usual plundering. On delivering this commitment, the *Heimatschutz* made sure that the heaviest burden fell on the village's Nazi supporters.

The Moroccan soldiers' mild manners and kindness to children certainly did much to ease tensions. Trudl Amann (who later became Anderl Heckmair's second wife) was thirteen years old at the time. She paints a remarkably benign picture of what it was like to share her home with nine Moroccan soldiers:

We were just women in the house. The old ladies who owned it lived on the top floor while my mother and I and a cousin, a bomb refugee from Nuremberg, occupied the ground floor. Nothing untoward ever happened. We were allowed to sleep in our own beds while the soldiers slept in the living room or the cellar. They cooked for themselves but invited us to eat with them. They made delicious white bread from corn flour. How I would love to eat that again! They shared everything with us. Mother spoke French, which made things a bit easier although their own French wasn't very good. They should have confiscated our radio but it remained sitting in its usual place in the cupboard and we ended up all listening to it together.[10]

Indeed, so good were relations that the soldiers (employed as drivers for the French officers billeted in the Sonne Hotel) asked Trudl's widowed mother to look after their pay. While such fraternising was officially forbidden, 'paternising', as Dabelstein called it, was sanctioned with the establishment of a brothel in one of the Plattenbichl houses.[11]

But if overall the occupation was relatively unthreatening, nothing could detract from the misery experienced by the villagers as they looked on helplessly while their wounded, demoralised soldiers were removed from hospital and various hiding places to be dispatched to captivity in France. And because the procedure in those chaotic post-surrender days was so arbitrary, men who had detested the regime were condemned to an indefinite term of imprisonment from which some never returned, while others who had been enthusiastic Nazis avoided the same fate by joining the *Heimatschutz* or hiding in the mountains.

On 6 May, 800 soldiers were put on trains to France, making it an especially wretched day for the villagers. Among them was their Protestant pastor, Paul Friedrich. Although still suffering from wounds sustained in Russia, in a death-defying feat he had walked through thick snow over the mountains from Holzgau to Oberstdorf. On reaching the village he had been immediately admitted to hospital but was not there long. Neither his wounds nor his consistent anti-Nazi

record could save him from a lengthy spell in a prison camp
near Nice.[12]

⌐

But while there was no shortage of grief and tragedy in
Oberstdorf in the immediate aftermath of the war, the steady
stream of individuals who managed to find their way safely
home provided a much-needed boost to village morale. Luck
naturally played a big part in who succeeded and who did
not. In Anderl Heckmair's case it was primarily his intimate
knowledge of the mountains that brought him safely back
to Oberstdorf.[13] Having in 1943 secured a transfer from the
Eastern Front to the high-altitude training school at Fulpmes
in the Austrian Tyrol, Heckmair was still working there as an
instructor in the last days of the war. He always attributed the
fact that he had managed to survive eighteen months in Russia
to the fast reactions and quick wits he had perfected as a
mountaineer. 'I might have been killed not just once but ump-
teen times if my sharpened perceptions had not enabled me to
head for cover at the last moment,' he wrote in his memoir.[14]
Sometime in late April 1945, when the Americans were only
seventy miles away, Heckmair decided the time had come to
leave his post. He agreed to take a fellow Oberstdorfer[15] with
him, despite the fact that the young man had minimal mountaineering experience and therefore posed a considerable risk.

They set out to cross the formidable obstacles of mountains and rivers that lay between Fulpmes and Oberstdorf
wearing uniform but carrying neither papers nor weapons.
In an unguarded moment they had the misfortune to run into
an American soldier, who ordered them to join a group of
German prisoners at a rallying point further down the road.
Instead, as soon as they were out of sight they fled back to the

mountains, which were still covered in deep snow. Somehow they managed to climb through the difficult Märzle corridor without ropes or crampons, but Heckmair realised that the only way to descend through such thick snow was literally to leap down. 'I was worried that Heini would be too scared,' he recalled decades later, 'so I pushed him first and then jumped myself.' When they reached a mountain hut on the Traufberg belonging to Oberstdorf's master butcher, Franz Becherer, they knew they were home.

After a couple of days resting in the hut, sustained by schnapps and the twenty-five pairs of sausages they found hanging from the ceiling, they made their final descent into Oberstdorf after dark. When Heckmair reached his house, he looked through the window to see his wife surrounded by Moroccan soldiers. Fortunately Heckmair knew Morocco well, having climbed extensively in the Atlas Mountains in 1932. Soon the homesick soldiers were poring over his photographs of Rabat, Fez and Marrakech. No doubt concluding that after such an amicable evening it would have been bad manners to arrest him, the Moroccans left Heckmair in peace to sleep in his own bed. On 6 May, the day that hundreds of German soldiers were rounded up and sent to France, Heckmair again slipped away to a mountain hut where he lay low for some weeks. When the coast was clear he returned to Oberstdorf unnoticed. The luck and skill that had seen him survive the Eiger North Face, Barbarossa and the long years of conflict had kept him safe until the end.

Many 99ers also managed to make it home. Although, after evading the Russians in Austria, Alfons Meinlinger ceased writing his diary for a while, we know that at some point he was detained by the Americans and spent a short spell at Landeck, a camp in Austria about seventy miles south of his home village.[16] His last diary entry was written on 2 June 1945, a little more than three weeks after Germany's surrender. 'I was dropped off in the middle of Kempten,' he wrote. 'I am a free man.'

Others, like Fridolin Thomma, were not so fortunate. Thomma (who had begun supporting Hitler after the disastrous 1923 strike at the local textile factory) had remained loyal to him throughout. He worked as an aircraft mechanic during the war until January 1945, when, because there were no longer any aeroplanes to service, he had been drafted into the army. In April he was in Immenstadt with his unit and so close to Oberstdorf that he could easily have deserted and hidden in his sister-in-law's house. But, even as the world collapsed around him, he refused to dishonour the oath of allegiance he had sworn to Hitler. After the war he was sent to a camp in France where he was put to work clearing mines. When one of these exploded he died of his injuries a few days later.[17]

Oberstdorf's surviving Jews fared better than might have been expected. In May 1945 Hannes Trautloft, the Luftwaffe pilot engaged to the *Mischling* Marga Mayser, had by the end of the war fallen from grace as a result to his involvement in the 'fighter pilots' revolt', in which he and other ace pilots had confronted Göring over his disastrous air strategy. This had not gone down well. Trautloft was relieved of his command and ended the war as an instructor in Strasbourg.* When he reckoned Germany's surrender to be imminent, he stole a small

---

* In late 1944, Trautloft was responsible for rescuing around 160 Allied airmen wrongfully imprisoned by the SS in Buchenwald concentration camp. They were transferred to Stalag Luft III shortly before they were due to be executed.

aircraft and landed it on a meadow between Blaichach and Sonthofen. He and Marga (who, unlike Eva Noack-Mosse and Fritz Schnell, had for some unknown reason been spared the SS summons to a camp) hid first in a mountain hut belonging to a family friend and then, like Heckmair, in the Becherer hut.[18] When it was finally safe for Trautloft to emerge, he and Marga became the first Oberstdorf couple to be married after the war.

Marga was not the only Jewish Oberstdorfer whose story ended well. The day after Germany's surrender in Reims, Dora Lemkes miraculously emerged in perfect health despite Xaver Noichl's dire predictions. In evidence given after the war, her husband revealed that a town hall official had warned him that Dora was about to be deported to Theresienstadt and advised him to hide her, which is exactly what he did.[19] The playwright Carl Zuckmayer's Jewish mother, who with her husband had come to Oberstdorf on the advice of Eva Noack-Mosse, also survived unscathed. Fritz Schnell, having found his way safely back to Oberstdorf, married his Henny. And Hertha Stolzenberg, who had lived with her Jewish mother unmolested in Oberstdorf for so long, continued to conduct the Protestant church choir for many years to come.

On 2 July a vehicle was finally found to drive Eva Noack-Mosse and twenty others from Theresienstadt back to Augsburg. Although Oberstdorf was only 400 miles from the ghetto/concentration camp, it was to be another five days before Eva reached home. As they drove through 'grey provincial Pilsen', she spotted her first American soldier. 'He was directing the traffic but at the same time having lots of fun tossing an orange up in the air and catching it.'[20] While Eva was in Augsburg awaiting further transport she went to the hairdresser – 'soap, warm water, hot hair dryer, clean towels, all on the house because I am a concentration camp returnee'. The final lap of the journey to Oberstdorf, undertaken in a rickety old paddy wagon, took forever because Eva's fellow former inmates all had to be dropped off at their various homes first. But on 7 July, just as the church bell struck five o'clock in the afternoon, she at last stood outside her own front door.

⁓

'In general Bavaria is a paradise compared with the rest of destroyed, starving and miserable Germany,' observed the *Sie und Er* reporter. And of Oberstdorf in particular he commented, 'No air raids have ruined this pretty village; nor have any of its residents been killed in tank battles and street fighting.'* But Oberstdorfers still had to deal with an avalanche of problems, both practical and emotional, in those first weeks and months of peace, not least the hundreds of villagers grieving for their dead or for those still missing. For them the word 'peace' would have a hollow ring for many years to come. Furthermore, joy over the end of the war was soon dulled by the grim realisation that the Allies, despite their competing agendas, were united on one issue – that Germany must be rendered harmless and made to pay for the terrible suffering it had caused. As President Truman put it, 'Germany was occupied not for the purpose of its liberation but as a defeated enemy state.'[21]

It was now the responsibility of Oberstdorf's new 'old' leaders, relatively untainted by National Socialism, to make sure that somehow – despite the hunger and curfews, the

---

* In fact, Oberstdorf suffered one air raid when six bombs fell on the outskirts of the village causing much panic but little damage. The only casualties were two mules.

overcrowding, the closed shops and schools, the lack of news-papers, the disbanded societies and dead telephones, the non-functioning postal service, disarmed police, the travel ban and the absence of male labour – life went on. The mass of files and memoranda preserved in the Oberstdorf archives bear witness to the frantic efforts to find enough mattresses, blankets, washing powder, cribs, clothes, etc. for the 8,000 peo-ple living in the village, half of them refugees, evacuees or displaced persons; '300 blankets and straw sacks have been col-lected from the Birgsau camp in a truck provided by the River Engineering Office,' records one scrap of paper. Another notes that '200 HJ shirts and 100 HJ trousers from the *Volkssturm* training camp have been handed out to needy children'.[22]

Understandably, the liberated foreign labourers and prison-ers felt little inhibition when it came to stealing, while scores of traumatised teenagers began arriving back from labour camps and other Nazi institutions. As it had been deliberate policy to send these young people to camps hundreds of miles from their villages and towns, many of them had suffered great hard-ship on the hazardous journey home. Meanwhile, Oberstdorf children took to the perilous practice of diving into lakes and rivers in search of jettisoned guns.

But of all the intractable problems facing Oberstdorf in the immediate aftermath of the war, none was more pressing than food – or rather lack of it. Hunger made every other hardship pale in comparison. It was all that anyone could think about. This dire situation was not helped by the Moroccans' love of roast meat, which led them to seize chickens and sheep at every opportunity. They cooked their bounty over hundreds of small fires that they lit in and around the village and over which they desperately huddled in their losing battle against the cold.

Two days after the parade, Mayor Neidhart made clear to the French commander just how desperate the situation had become. As a result, matters improved a little, but not enough to prevent many villagers hovering dangerously close to starvation. In July Elisabeth Dabelstein recorded her relief that there were no longer any children at the home, because she would have been unable to feed them. 'Young Wolfgang and my nephew, for example, are just skeletons and you would not recognise little Dorle and Jutta.'[23]

The ever-resourceful Xaver Noichl, aided by Franz, managed to smuggle tins of sausage, lard and processed cheese from SS stores hidden in the Rappenalp valley. But since these caches were high in the mountains and a fifteen-mile bicycle ride away it was no easy matter to retrieve them, especially as the curfew was strictly enforced and backpacks rigorously checked. Another problem was the state of their bicycles, for, as Franz noted, 'by that stage our tyres consisted of little more than patches wrapped in string'. In one mountain hut Xaver found a large stash of guns left behind by the SS. But when he brought several home, Frau Noichl was so horrified that she made him throw them in the River Stillach in the dead of night.

The task of providing enough food for Oberstdorf was made even more challenging by the enormous transport difficulties. Only nine trucks and two tractors were in regular service during the French occupation. These were run not on petrol or diesel, which were anyway unavailable, but on timber. The converted carburettors and wood fuel took up so much space in the vehicle that there was hardly any room left for the load. In addition, the dangerous roads, unpredictable behaviour of the occupying forces and ever-changing permit regulations were enough to turn each journey into a full-scale adventure. One villager remembered being dispatched regularly to Munich to buy food from the wholesale market, a round trip that took about twenty hours. 'Once the French sent me to Bad Reichenhall to fetch salt,' he recalled. 'As the only truck available was still covered in SS graffiti, I was arrested twice – once by the Americans in Bad Tölz and then in Rettenberg by the French.'[24]

In spite of such obstacles, most villagers believed the biggest problem with their transport system was the fact that it was controlled by the *Heimatschutz*, which since the spectacular success of the coup had, in Elisabeth Dabelstein's words, 'degenerated into a band of robbers' and was now popularly dubbed *Heimatschmutz* (Home Dirt).[25] After Germany's surrender, the French authorities continued to delegate authority to the militia to such an extent that the Richter brothers felt licensed to act like warlords. It was they who decided who was or was not a Nazi and they who picked which house or mountain hut to raid in search of hoarded supplies. But instead of turning confiscated goods over to the French for the public benefit, the *Heimatschutz* men, so it was widely believed, kept the loot themselves or sold it on the flourishing black market. Moreover, in a deeply unpopular move, but one nevertheless backed by the French, Karl Richter pressured Mayor Neidhart into appointing him deputy mayor. Thus, from being hailed as Oberstdorf's saviours, the *Heimatschutz* and its leaders within a remarkably short time became the village's hated enemies. All this, however, was about to change with the arrival of the Americans.

In February 1945 Churchill, Roosevelt and Stalin had agreed at the Yalta Conference that Germany would be divided into four zones of occupation and for the first two years the British, French and American zones were run more or less independently of each other. On 7 July 1945, US troops entered Oberstdorf under the command of Captain John F. Purdum. Although at the time America's strategy for dealing with its defeated enemy was unequivocally hard-line (the Marshall Plan was not implemented until 1948), it was not as draconian as that originally proposed by Henry Morgenthau Jr, the US Secretary of the Treasury. In the autumn of 1944, when it was clear that Germany had lost the war, President Roosevelt and Morgenthau had sought to formulate a policy that would prevent Germany from ever posing a military threat again. The idea was to turn the whole of the Ruhr region, the so-called cauldron of German aggression, into harmless agricultural land. Additionally, much of the country's infrastructure was to be removed or destroyed and its mines flooded, with the aim of reducing Germany to a primitive agrarian society. Unfortunately for the Allies, this controversial plan was leaked, thereby handing Goebbels an invaluable propaganda tool for the last seven months of the war. Armed with this devastating information, he urged Germans to fight on whatever the cost because if they faltered now the 'American Jew Morgenthau' would turn their beloved Fatherland into a potato field'.[26]

As far as Oberstdorf was concerned, it was clear from the start that the American occupation was going to be very different from that of the French, not least because, to everyone's relief, there were only 300 of them. 'We couldn't have lasted much longer under the French,' Elisabeth Dabelstein wrote to a friend. 'Long-term occupation by them would have been a catastrophe. One-sixth of our entire livestock disappeared in two months, either consumed here or sent to France. Except for chamois, we have no game left, the forest is utterly depleted.'[27] Underlining Dabelstein's point, the departing French loaded several hundred head of cattle on to a train bound for France. It had only got as far as Kempten, however, when the incoming Americans – fearful that the food problem would worsen on their watch – turned it round and sent it back to Oberstdorf.[28]*

If food was the top priority for the French, for the Americans it was housing. The Moroccans had mostly been billeted in barns, which while acceptable in the summer months was not an option for their successors. In consequence, over eighty of the best village houses were requisitioned, including all those on the Plattenbichl. Not, however, Hohes Licht, which after many battles finally won exemption thanks to Captain Purdum's personal intervention. Others were not so lucky. It was too soon for the Americans to distinguish between supporters and opponents of the Nazi regime – a problem that would never in fact be satisfactorily resolved – so that even Gertrud Neubaur, whose father had died trying to kill Hitler, had to give up her home to Oberstdorf's new masters.

The withdrawal of the French also spelled the end of the Richter brothers' reign. Since there was no question of the Americans countenancing a German militia operating autonomously on their patch, and because they remained so fearful of the non-existent *Werwolf* threat, Karl and Ernst Richter faded out of the picture to become embroiled in legal matters and family disputes. The Americans also took up the case of the murdered Sergeant Berghuber. The men involved in beating him to death were arrested but then later freed. The case

* In 1946 eighty Oberstdorf farmers received compensation from the Occupation Costs Office for cattle removed by the French.

was so complicated and so beset with conflicting evidence that several years after the war it was finally dropped. But even though Berghuber's killers went free it was by no means the end of the saga, since the deep animosities triggered by the crime continued to fester for many years. As for the Richter brothers, their story ends tragically. Karl committed suicide in 1955, as did Ernst several years later.

Enshrined in American post-war policy was the notion that democracy should be home-grown in Bavaria rather than imposed by its conquerors. As a result, political parties, strictly under American supervision, were re-established in the autumn of 1945. The following January, in the first free elections held since 1932, Bavarians were invited to vote for their municipal representatives; 83.3 per cent of Oberstdorfers went to the polls, casting their votes overwhelmingly for the centre-right *Christlich-Soziale Union* (CSU, Christian Socialist Union) candidates. It was only a few weeks later, on 5 March, that Winston Churchill gave his famous speech at the small Midwestern town of Fulton, Missouri. 'From Stettin in the Baltic to Trieste in the Adriatic,' he said on that memorable occasion, 'an iron curtain has descended across the continent.'

As a result of Bavaria's municipal elections, the farmers and master craftsmen who had served Oberstdorf so well before Nazification were once again in charge at the town hall. One of these, a farmer named Hans Gehring, was elected the new mayor. An educated man and widely admired for his fundamental decency, he in many ways resembled Ludwig Hochfeichter, who had served Oberstdorf with such distinction after the First World War. Gehring's immediate and unenviable task was to build consensus between the American military, his hard-pressed villagers and the several thousand lost souls washed up in Oberstdorf by the war.

In no area were Gehring's diplomatic skills tested more acutely than in his dealings with the United Nations Relief and Rehabilitation Administration (UNRRA). By the end of the war there were nearly half a million deeply traumatised displaced persons in Bavaria, mostly Russians and Poles. Among them were concentration camp survivors, prisoners of war, forced labourers and of course Jews – in other words, the very people whom Oberstdorfers had for so long been brainwashed to regard as subhuman. Now they were swarming all over the village, living in the best hotels and spending their days playing table tennis in private houses requisitioned especially for their recreation.

By this stage, few villagers can have been unaware of the appalling suffering Germans had inflicted on these individuals, but the sight of so many of them receiving preferential treatment while they, the native inhabitants, continued to starve was a particularly bitter pill to swallow. Certainly, Oberstdorfers found the photographs and newsreels of concentration camp victims profoundly shocking, but there is little evidence to suggest that these revelations led to any widespread feelings of collective guilt. On the contrary, the continual pressure on the villagers to supply UNRRA with goods that they themselves needed so badly such as bicycles, radios, irons, light bulbs, thermometers, chessboards, files and mousetraps only fuelled their own sense of victimhood. Such items were essential, not so much for their intrinsic desirability but because, until the Deutsche Mark (DM) was introduced on 20 June 1948, they formed the only viable currency. So although the villagers were in theory compensated by UNRRA for any goods received, since payment was in cash it was effectively useless. Without 'stuff', particularly cigarettes, to barter it was very hard to survive.

Franz Noichl (now eighteen) had become an accomplished accordion player and was able to earn valuable American cigarettes by playing at UNRRA events, thereby making a substantial contribution to the family coffers. A notice that appeared in the *Allgäuer Anzeigeblatt* (it had reverted to its pre-Nazi name) on 8 October 1948, pleading for light bulbs for the school as it currently only had two, is a telling example of just how much everyone needed everything.[29] It was against this emotionally charged background that Mayor Gehring did his best to keep UNRRA supplied and the villagers compliant. When the stock of skis at the abandoned Birgsau camp ran out, he turned to the local ski shops – Schratt, Zobel and Seeweg for help:

> It is vital in the interests of the village to maintain good relations with UNRRA so I intend to send at least a few pairs of new skis with Kandahar bindings to them by Christmas. I would therefore be very grateful if you could provide me with at least one such pair. Perhaps you could refurbish some old *Wehrmacht* skis?[30]

To the villagers, therefore, it seemed that any attempt to rebuild their lives was constantly undermined by the sheer numbers and endless needs of these unwelcome immigrants. The fact that the Commissioner of Refugees found it necessary to circulate a directive to all local councils in Bavaria, making it clear that it was unacceptable to bury displaced persons outside the cemetery walls, indicates the depth of hostility felt by native populations towards their unfortunate visitors.[31]

It was not just the Russians and Poles who caused such antagonism. Oberstdorfers were also still finding it difficult to absorb all the German refugees and evacuees (in many respects as alien as the foreigners) still living in the village. People like the Stowinskis and Burbas, who were among the 12 million or so Germans made homeless between 1945 and 1950 because they had been expelled from East Prussia, were fleeing the Russians from Poland, Czechoslovakia (where many had lived for several generations) or from some other former Nazi-occupied territory. Nearly 2 million of these refugees ended up in Bavaria and about 26,000 in the Oberallgäu. Four-year-old Sigmar Stowinski from Ragnit in East Prussia (now Neman in Russia) arrived in Oberstdorf on 30 March 1945 with his mother and one-year-old brother on a special refugee train from the Pirna reception camp near Dresden. By the time they reached Oberstdorf, they had been on the move for six months and had just one suitcase left, all their other belongings having been lost or stolen. Although Sigmar was German, he was intensely aware of being different from the village children and longed to have a local name like Brutscher, Schraudolph, or Gschwender. Nineteen-year-old Egon Burba was deaf and had also escaped from Ragnit together with his mother, grandmother, aunt and two cousins. When the Oberstdorf reception committee greeted them at the station, he remembered his mother holding tight to the precious sewing machine she had at the last minute turned back to rescue, even as the Russians were entering Ragnit. Miraculously, it had survived their 1,000-mile journey and now offered some means of supporting the family in their uncertain future.

But no matter how touching these individual stories, as far as the villagers were concerned there were just too many refugees for them to cope with. As one American officer observed, 'In Bavaria and perhaps in the whole of Germany no distinction is made between Nazi and anti-Nazi, Black or Red, Catholic or Protestant. The only difference that matters is that between natives and refugees.'[32]

Carl Zuckmayer, who had spent the war exiled in America but had finally managed to visit his elderly parents in Oberstdorf in 1946, was entirely realistic when in a report for the Americans he wrote, 'It will not be possible to eradicate anti-Semitism in Germany until an international solution to the displaced person problem is found.'[33]

He was also right when he added that the black market would remain indispensable until there was monetary reform. In Oberstdorf the black market was regarded as part of everyday life, whereas prostitution, another means of acquiring the necessities of life, was universally condemned. Indeed, so little did black-market offences blemish a villager's reputation that not long after councillor and bricklayer Hans Klopfer emerged from a seven-month prison sentence for killing a pig in his garage, he was unanimously elected to lead the municipal council's most exacting office – housing. Nonetheless, as nosy neighbours and denunciators had failed to vanish along with the Third Reich, it was still vital to remain vigilant in any under-the-counter dealings.

As the food situation worsened during 1946 and 1947, the desperate plight of German civilians began to receive increasing attention in America and in Britain. Here the publisher Victor Gollancz, of Polish-Jewish background, was a frontrunner in highlighting the suffering of ordinary German people, particularly women and children. 'I am never likely to forget the unspeakable wickedness of which the Nazis were guilty,' he wrote on return from a visit to Germany soon after the war:

But when I see the swollen bodies and living skeletons in hospitals here and elsewhere; when I look at the miserable 'shoes' of boys and girls in the schools, and find that they have come to their lessons without even a dry piece of bread for breakfast; when I go down into a one-roomed cellar where a mother is struggling, and struggling very bravely, to do her best for a husband and four or five children – then I think not of Germans, but of men and women.[34]

Many Oberstdorfers read about Gollancz's humanitarian gesture to the German people in their *Allgäuer Anzeigeblatt* and were understandably moved.[35]

As a result of such publicity, foreign aid began to trickle into Germany. Then, on 3 April 1948, President Truman signed the European Recovery Program, better known as the Marshall Plan, which was to pump some $1.3 billion (the equivalent of $14 billion in 2020) into (West) Germany over the next four years. Even before the Marshall Plan took effect new businesses were being registered in Oberstdorf, among them the former Staehely factory that went seamlessly from producing aeroplane parts for Messerschmitt to manufacturing frying pans, saucepans and stoves. By the latter half of 1948, thanks to the Deutsche Mark (which saw the black market disappear overnight) and the Marshall Plan, green shoots began springing up all over the village. A number of refugees, evacuees and displaced persons decided to stay in Oberstdorf and set up businesses. Thus the Pohl pharmacy, Iflander fruit shop and Jost tobacco store, along with several tailoring shops and Rudi Stannat's taxi service, sprang into existence. Just three years after the war Gerda Grabner was doing well enough to employ eleven people at her pottery. But as the villagers looked forward to 1949 with renewed hope, the *Allgäuer Anzeigeblatt* struck a sobering note three days before Christmas by reminding everyone that 200 Oberstdorf families were still waiting for their men to return from captivity, while hope for the 132 missing soldiers had all but vanished.[36]

23

The Reckoning

'Have you heard of the "Spruchkammer"?' Eva Noack-Mosse asked Carl Zuckmayer in a letter she wrote to him while he was still in America. 'It's a new kind of tribunal, which is supposed to separate the Nazis from the non-Nazis.'[1]

The task of identifying and removing Nazis from all levels of German society was monumental and, as those involved soon discovered, beset with problems at every turn. The ambiguities attached to pinning down exactly who was and who was not a Nazi were legion. Was someone guilty, for instance, if he had joined the party only in order to protect his job and family? Or if, despite having his name inscribed on a plate of honour at the local NSDAP headquarters, he had gone out of his way to help a Jewish neighbour? Should a normally zealous Nazi official who had occasionally acted against the regime in the interests of his community be treated more leniently than others? If a headmaster wearing SA uniform harangued his pupils with Nazi rhetoric but allowed Jewish children to remain in his school unmolested, was he an activist? How much was an individual's apparent loyalty to the regime driven by fear of denunciation? To what degree was a soldier culpable when, after witnessing the murder, torture and rape of thousands of innocent civilians, he went on fighting for a German victory? And how on earth was it possible to know who was speaking the truth and who was lying through their teeth? For that matter, where *were* all the Nazis? As Eva Noack-Mosse commented to Zuckmayer, 'You can spin around and stand on your head but you won't find a Nazi anywhere.'[2]

It is not hard to understand why the Americans – still haunted by pre-war images of the Nuremberg Rallies and convinced that SS fanatics lurked round every corner – were not in the mood to take on board such subtleties. Yet the more perceptive among them could see that in practice most Germans were utterly disillusioned with National Socialism, deeply weary of conflict and – far from plotting guerrilla warfare – were thinking only of where to find the next meal.

By the end of 1945, the Americans had imprisoned or interned around 120,000 Germans in their sector – SS personnel, NSDAP group leaders and their deputies, schoolteachers, the staff of the Ordensburg, Napolas and Adolf Hitler Schools, local policemen, leaders of paramilitary organisations and senior civil servants who had been appointed or promoted after 1 March 1939.[3] These initial categories were soon expanded, with the result that the number of Germans under investigation in Bavaria rapidly reached the hundreds of thousands. Every German male over the age of eighteen was legally required to fill out a registration form detailing his association with Nazi organisations and any benefits he may have received from the party. Food ration cards were only issued to those who could prove they had completed the form. In March 1946, the overwhelming demands of denazification, plus the emergence of more pressing issues, led the Americans to hand

over the whole process – now conducted in civilian tribunals
– to the Germans themselves.

The *Spruchkammer*, as these courts were called, were
charged with removing all Nazis from public office and from
responsible positions in the private sector. After undergoing
examination, the suspects were placed in one of five categories: (1) Major Offenders; (2) Offenders; (3) Lesser Offenders;
(4) Followers; (5) Exonerated Persons. The original intention
was to appoint legally qualified Germans, untarnished by
National Socialism, to act as chairmen, each aided by two
assessors with equally impeccable anti-Nazi credentials. But as
the legal profession had been dovetailed so flawlessly into the
regime for so long, it was impossible to find enough qualified
candidates who were politically clean. As a result, the 'judges'
often had no previous legal experience, but despite this lack
received little guidance or support.

The role of the tribunals was to examine documents and
to hear witness statements before deciding in which category a
suspect belonged. Unlike the Nazis on trial in Nuremberg, the
defendants who came before these courts were rarely accused
of specific crimes. Rather it was the extent of their association with National Socialism and the manner in which they
had wielded power over those around them that was under
scrutiny – an altogether more nebulous proposition. The work
of the *Spruchkammer* was not made easier by the fact that
they had to operate under enormous time pressures and in the
knowledge that they were deeply unpopular, since the general
public believed that they failed to provide justice either for
the guilty or for the victims. Indeed, cynics began to talk of
'renazification through denazification'. In a joke doing the
rounds in 1947, a man goes to the local police station to register. 'I am a Nazi,' he declares. 'If you are a Nazi, you should

have registered eighteen months ago,' replies the policeman. 'But I wasn't a Nazi then,' says the man.[4]

Oberstdorfers under investigation were sent to the Sonthofen *Spruchkammer*, where Dr Otto Witzgall was appointed its first chairman despite his lack of legal knowledge. Those summoned were required to produce their own witnesses and supporting documents, and because these naturally presented the accused in the best possible light such affidavits became known as *Persilschein* (Persil tickets).[5] By October 1946, the Sonthofen court had received 46,175 registration forms from the surrounding district. After those exonerated or cleared by the youth amnesty (which the Americans applied to those born after 1 January 1919) had been weeded out, this left around 11,000 individuals with a case to answer. As they were forbidden to work or take part in public life while awaiting their hearing, they had plenty of time to reflect on their past deeds.[6]

An incomplete list of Oberstdorf's Nazis, compiled from various sources after the war, has 445 names on it, roughly 10 per cent of the village's 1933 population and therefore consistent with the rest of the country.[7] These party members came from a wide range of occupations, but it was the post office, with at least thirty party members, that harboured the biggest group, followed respectively by innkeepers, farmers, railwaymen and craftsmen. Naturally, no one wanted to find themselves on the Americans' list, which did not include women and made no distinction between the village's hardcore Nazis, the opportunists or those who had joined simply to keep their jobs and safeguard their families. A few had believed they could lessen the worst effects of the regime by working within it rather than remaining outside, while others had signed up on the 'if you can't beat them join them' principle, or because they thought that by doing so they stood a better chance of survival in a dangerous world. The fake Nazis included villagers such as Anton Jäger, who, denounced by Herzog, had so narrowly avoided imprisonment, Mayor Thomas Neidhart, a leading opponent of the Nazi takeover in the early 1930s, and Max Schraudolf, a member of the *Heimatschutz*, who, like Jäger, had delayed joining the party until 1940. Such men were in stark contrast to true believers such as SA leader Wilhelm Herzog, the extreme anti-Semite Rudolf Scheller, activist Hermann Hoyer and cinema proprietor Anton Merz.

By the time those on the list were called before the *Spruchkammer* in late 1946 and 1947, there had been a shift in attitude to denazification. Now the emphasis was less on punishment and more on rehabilitation, with the result that out of the 397 accused villagers, all but ten were placed in the fourth category of 'Followers' and allowed to return to their former occupations.[8]* Only one man merited the second most serious category of 'Offender', and that was Heinz Schubert. The death sentence he received at his trial in Nuremberg in 1948 was commuted to ten years' imprisonment, although he was in fact released in 1951. It was not quite over, however. A few months later he was brought before the Munich *Spruchkammer*, which handed down the following judgment:

As far as the three-month labour camp sentence is concerned, this is regarded as having already been served. The fine of DM 100 appears to be appropriate when taking

* This is why the *Spruchkammer* was nicknamed *Mitläuferfabrik* (follower factory).

into consideration the lengthy imprisonment of the person concerned [Schubert], the loss of his property and
the undoubted mental anguish he suffered during the long
period he was living under sentence of death.[9]

The thirty-eight-year-old Schubert was therefore allowed to
return to Oberstdorf a free man and, unlike the 700 victims
whose death he had supervised in the Ukraine, could together
with his wife look forward to a future watching his young sons
grow up.

The case of Oberstdorf's headmaster, Dr Eduard Bessler,
is a good example of the difficulties permeating the denazification process. As a teacher promoted to headmaster by
the regime, he came under the 'automatic arrest' rule and in
August 1945 was interned in a camp near Schongau. Thanks,
however, to the intervention of Mayor Gehring he was released
the following April and permitted to return to Oberstdorf,
where he found some unskilled work. In May 1947 he was
summoned before the Sonthofen *Spruchkammer*. A Dr Wenger
was by then chairman, assisted by Eva Noack-Mosse – the only
Oberstdorf woman ever appointed to the tribunal. The public
prosecutor had demanded that Bessler be placed in category
three, the 'Lesser Offender' group, which would have meant
a 3,000 RM fine, working unpaid for the community two days a
week, disenfranchisement, living in the lowest legal level of
accommodation and being forbidden to hold a driving, fishing or hunting licence. Fortunately for Dr Bessler there were
many people eager to testify on his behalf. Parents, former
pupils, teachers and clergy all asserted that his outward display
of Nazi enthusiasm had only been to deflect attention from
the humane culture that he was really trying to establish in the
school. Despite the Nazis' tight grip on all aspects of education,

the tribunal learned that Bessler had done his best to enable his pupils, including the Jewish children, to learn as freely as was possible under such binding constraints. But as committed Nazis like Frau Helmling and her daughter Margot were always watching his every move, his role as headmaster had inevitably turned into in a messy compromise. Nonetheless, by outwardly conforming to the regime he had managed to survive, thus preventing a real Nazi from taking over. The court accepted this and Bessler, like the great majority of Oberstdorf's Nazis, was classed as a 'Follower' in the fourth category. As such he was fined 1,000 RM and forbidden to return to his former job as headmaster for three years.

Of all the different characters that have appeared in these pages, arguably the most intriguing are Ludwig Fink and Fritz Kalhammer. This is because both men were ardent Nazis in senior positions of power and influence, yet it seems that they were also decent human beings – a rare combination. Fink, the older of the two by half a generation, and in charge of all the chimney sweeps in the region, became a member of the NSDAP in 1929 at the age of forty-one. When the twenty-eight-year-old Kalhammer signed up the following year he was already an established doctor in Blaichach. Both men had joined the party for ideological reasons at a time when, deeply disturbed by the state of their country, they were convinced that only National Socialism, with its forthright policies and strong leadership, could give Germany the future it deserved.

Kalhammer's rise in the party was so meteoric that just a year after joining it he was appointed Sonthofen's *Kreisleiter*, or district leader. In addition he became chief medical officer to the SA, held an honorary rank in the SS and, as a member of the elite 'speakers circle', gave more than 500 speeches on behalf of the party. In other words, his Nazi credentials were second to none. Yet when after the war he claimed at his *Spruchkammer* trial in Baden-Württemberg (where he was interned) that he had never promoted the violence so intrinsic to National Socialism, nor sought to put pressure on his political opponents, the record confirms he was telling the truth.[10] In 1934, when both men were living in Sonthofen, Kalhammer recognised in Fink a kindred spirit and a man capable of restoring the party's reputation in Oberstdorf after the village's bruising encounter with its first Nazi mayor, Ernst Zettler. It was on his recommendation that Fink was appointed the new mayor.

We can, of course, only guess at the two men's evolving attitude towards the NSDAP, but their conduct suggests that, with the darkening political scene, their enthusiasm for each and every aspect of party policy began to wane. We have already seen how Fink helped Sister Biunda and her nuns and how he protected the Jews and other persecuted individuals under his jurisdiction; how he not only helped to ensure that the elderly Emil Schnell was adequately provisioned, but had also warned him of his imminent deportation. The delicacy of his position as a moderate Nazi mayor is illustrated by an anecdote that recounts how during the war he publicly reprimanded a woman for criticising the regime but then privately advised her just to be careful not to say such things to him when others were present. In addition, Fink was widely respected for not ducking the miserable task of informing families of the deaths of their men in person (his own son Erich was killed in France in August 1944). His refusal to resist the French as ordered by the SS was entirely consistent with his eleven-year record as mayor. Carl Zuckmayer described him as the 'unknown man wearing the mask of evil' who had protected his Jewish mother.[11]

After the war Fink was interned in a camp near Würzburg. Although his original *Spruchkammer* file is lost, the partial certified copy that survives provides some useful information. At his trial on 15 April 1948, when he was sixty years old, the prosecutor asked that he be placed in the highest category of 'Major Offenders'. While some witnesses tried to paint him as a Nazi fanatic, others produced more convincing evidence that in his mayoral capacity Fink had never committed a crime, had always dealt with people fairly and had not been afraid to stand up to the regional authorities in defending those wrongfully accused or discriminated against. The initial court judgment placed him in the third group as a 'Lesser Offender', but on appeal eight months later, and with the help of Carl Zuckmayer's testimony, he was downgraded to a 'Follower' and allowed to go home.[12]

Dr Kalhammer's *Spruchkammer* file does survive and gives us a real sense of the man. One credible witness after another came forward to commend the district leader's modest lifestyle, his tolerant attitude to political opponents and religious matters, and his willingness to put himself in danger in order to help others, as on the day of the Sonthofen air raid, when he cared for the injured regardless of his own welfare. Those who spoke on his behalf agreed that, as district leader, Kalhammer had treated the general public with moderation, had shown particular consideration to soldiers' wives and paid proper attention to social work. An important point in his favour, as far as the locals were concerned, was that he had also stopped Robert Ley (the head of the German Labour Front, who committed suicide while awaiting trial at Nuremberg) from destroying Sonthofen's meadows with his plans to build a large hotel and airfield for visitors to the Ordensburg. And, despite the continuing SS presence at the Ordensburg, as the French approached in May 1945 he had ordered the tank traps to be disabled and the *Volkssturm* to stand down. As such a prominent Nazi Kalhammer might well have tried to escape over the mountains, but instead he continued to treat the sick up until the moment he was arrested. Even minor episodes, such as when he asked his children to greet his fellow high-ranking Nazis with the traditional Bavarian greeting *Grüss Gott* instead of the mandatory *Heil Hitler*, were noted down by the court.

The long list of virtues attributed to this unusual *Kreisleiter* (who by 1940 had perhaps as many as 500 officials under his control) was therefore impressive. But it was the Jewish doctor Kurt Weigert, the former director of Sonthofen's hospital, who presented the court with the most striking evidence. In May 1933 Weigert had been forced to inform Kalhammer that he was Jewish. Kalhammer (who had a Jewish stepbrother) advised him to keep this quiet as he felt certain that before long the party would adopt a milder approach to the 'Jewish question'. Despite Kalhammer's support, Weigert was sacked on 31 July 1935. But as he told the court,

> Dr Kalhammer nevertheless continued to treat me as a valued colleague until my medical licence expired three years later (according to the 4th decree of the Reich Citizenship Law) and I was forced to leave . . . [He] had the power to cause great harm to me and to my family but instead, as the facts demonstrate, he spared me as much as possible and I gratefully acknowledge this.[13]*

* Weigert also told the court that some individuals in Blaichach claimed they had been sent to concentration camps by Kalhammer but Weigert had been unable to verify this.

The court responded to all this positive evidence by treating Kalhammer (who had already been detained four and a half years in an internment camp) with considerable leniency. Notwithstanding his senior rank, he was judged a Lesser Offender, ordered to pay 25,000 DM legal costs and a fine of 1,000 DM.[14] He was also banned from any political activity for five years. But because of the shortage of doctors in Sonthofen he was allowed to resume his medical practice – a major concession.

While we know there were plenty of 'good Germans' in the Third Reich, the concept of 'good Nazis' is hard to swallow. Yet the conduct of Kalhammer and Fink suggests that there were at least some Nazis in top jobs capable of putting morality before the party and behaving honourably, even as their colleagues committed the most horrific crimes against humanity. So why, once it was clear that the National Socialist vision of a better world was nothing more than a grotesque mirage, when hope of the party's extremist policies subsiding had vanished, and when it was no longer possible to ignore the criminal reality of Nazi rule, did men of the calibre of Fink and Kalhammer remain loyal to the regime?

This is of course a question that should have been asked and debated immediately after the war. But at that point it was the last thing anyone wanted to talk about. When, on his return to Oberstdorf in 1945, master tailor Georg Vogler burned everything that reminded him of the Nazis, he was just one of millions of Germans intent on repressing all memory of the Third Reich. Frau Noichl would not let Franz keep the copy of Hitler's *Mein Kampf* given him by a neighbour, thrusting it vigorously into the flames of the kitchen stove. If Oberstdorfers did get round to discussing the war – perhaps at their regular *Stammtisch* – they tended to focus on who was to blame for the military defeat or whether the terrible fate visited upon the German people had been a punishment for abandoning Christian values, rather than exploring notions of racism, gullibility, compliance and collective guilt.[15] Fink's daughter (born in 1943) had excellent memories of her father, remembering him as a kind, generous and intelligent man. But she did not meet him until she was an adult and by then, as she points out, they were more interested in discussing family affairs. By the time people did want to talk about the Nazi period, it was too late. Too many of those who could have shed light on these agonisingly difficult questions were dead. But in any case, arguably the best way for the Germans to restore their equilibrium in the raw aftermath of the war was, as Richard Evans suggests, 'not by exorcising Hitler, but by forgetting him'.[16]

In view of the well-documented record of their professional conduct, it seems inconceivable that Fink and Kalhammer, even at a relatively early stage, did not have doubts about the party they had joined with such high expectations. Fink knew perfectly well that his epileptic son Werner would have been gassed had he not been in a position to save him.[17] As for Kalhammer, he was much too senior a figure not to have been aware of the multiple evils perpetrated in the name of National Socialism and especially since he lived in Sonthofen, a town dominated by the Ordensburg. But what, in practice, could men in their position have done? Of course millions of Germans were similarly trapped, but high-ranking figures like Fink and Kalhammer were in a particularly vulnerable situation. Either they kept going, thereby protecting their families (Kalhammer had five young children) and mitigating the worst effects of the regime where they could; or resign in protest and end up in a concentration camp, guillotined or hanging from a meat hook. There was no middle road, no turning back. But if this is a valid point in their defence, why did they not deploy it at their post-war trials? Was it a matter of pride, or did they still retain some lingering loyalty to the National Socialism of their youthful dreams? Did they perhaps believe that, had the party's leaders not betrayed it so catastrophically, it might even have succeeded? These are questions to which, like so many others concerning the Finks and Kalhammers of the Nazi world, we shall never now have satisfactory answers.

~

While the *Spruchkammer* toiled away at the thankless task of denazification, global politics were changing fast. On 23 May 1949, four years after the end of the war, the three Western zones formally joined together to form the Federal Republic of Germany. Then, on 7 October, the German Democratic Republic also came into being. With the emergence of the Cold War the focus on punishing Nazis became less important than transforming Germany into a prosperous and reliable ally capable of playing a central role in protecting Western Europe from the Soviet Union. As denazification was the cause of so much resentment in Germany, this seemed the right moment to change tack. In 1952 hundreds of Nazis serving life sentences were therefore released, while countless more still at large were never even brought to trial. These people, who had caused such unspeakable misery to so many millions of their fellow human beings, were now free to build new lives in a democratic and increasingly affluent country.

On 30 March 1955 the *Anzeiger Anzeigeblatt* announced that all the houses confiscated by the Americans were to be released back to their owners over the next few weeks – a moment of great joy for the whole village. At noon on

Thursday, 5 May 1955, 'The full authority of a sovereign state' was granted to the Federal Republic of Germany under the Bonn–Paris conventions, thus formally ending the Allied military occupation and drawing a definitive line between Germany's Nazi past and the future. Mayor Gehring, who had so skilfully steered Oberstdorf through the difficult early months of the occupation, died only a few days later, no doubt comforted in the knowledge that at long last his country and village were set fair on their new course. Nevertheless, the 'Homecoming Cross' placed in the Oberstdorf churchyard was a constant reminder to everyone that, while they could look forward to a bright new future, thousands of German soldiers still remained in Russian captivity.

As for the villagers, they continued to rebuild their lives. Ludwig Fink returned to his old job overseeing the region's chimney sweeps, while Eduard Bessler resumed his headmastership of the school. Hermann Schallhammer reappeared after the war and at the age of seventy fulfilled his long-held ambition of becoming Oberstdorf's mayor. The issue of who owned and controlled the use of the land around the village was successfully resolved between the two councils, while Anderl Heckmair went on climbing mountains and regularly meeting his anti-Semite friend Rudolf Scheller. The nuns maintained a presence in the village and Toni Brutscher (a member of one of Oberstdorf's oldest families), who at the age of seventeen had been so badly wounded that he was not expected to walk again, became an international ski jump champion. Sybille von Arminsted replaced Charlotte Stirius as Oberstdorf's representative on the *Anzeiger Anzeigeblatt*, while the East Prussian refugee Egon Burba ran a successful upholstery business and lived in the village until his death in 2021 at the age of ninety-five. Franz Noichl, having decided not to be ordained a Catholic priest, qualified as a teacher and had a distinguished career in the Bavarian ministry of education. Meanwhile his cousin Thaddäus Steiner studied for a PhD in history. Reassuringly, their free-spirited fathers Xaver Noichl and Wilhelm Steiner remained true men of the mountains.

In 1955 it was exactly forty years since Wilhelm had left Oberstdorf to fight in the First World War: four decades dominated by turmoil and grief, for which the villagers, despite being hardened to all that nature could throw at them, had been quite unprepared. Today the only visible sign of those tragic years is to be found in the memorial chapel next to the church, where the names of the 286 Oberstdorf men killed in the Second World War are carved in stone. But the invisible scars of the Third Reich will be part of the village's history forever.

A Village in the Third Reich: The Back Story

Julia Boyd

The story of this book really begins in January 2006 when Oberstdorf's municipal council, under the leadership of Mayor Thomas Müller, decided the time had come to write Volume Five of the village's official history. This was no small decision since the period in question, 1918–52, covers the twelve years of the Third Reich. And even though six decades had passed since the end of the war, sensitivities were still acute. After all, many children and grandchildren of those who had lived through the National Socialist years were themselves now living in Oberstdorf, and not necessarily keen to dig up matters that had long since been laid to rest. Nor, indeed, did everyone wish to discover exactly what part his or her own family had played in those painful times. Nevertheless, the municipal council believed it their duty to produce a formal account of the period before those who had actually experienced it were all gone. And, because German law requires every town council to maintain a detailed and up-to-date record of its community's history, there was no shortage of material in Oberstdorf's archives to fuel the project.

So, without more ado, a Volume Five Committee was set up. Because all those selected to serve on it had close personal ties with Oberstdorf, its members were well aware of the challenge they faced in maintaining the committee's objectivity. Two individuals came from socialist families, while another colleague's grandfather had been a member of the Nazi Party. The oldest in the group was born in 1929, the youngest in 1969. But however diverse their ancestry, age and professional life, all on the committee were united in their determination to achieve as objective and historically accurate a picture of Oberstdorf during those years as was possible. Although nationally Germany has been exemplary in examining its Nazi past, debatably there is still more work to be done at the local level, thus giving this chapter of Oberstdorf's history added significance.

The job of researching and writing Volume Five fell to Angelika (Cati) Patel who, with the committee's support, spent four years on the task. Cati's father was descended from the Gschwenders, one of the village's oldest and most distinguished families, while her mother was a third-generation Oberstdorfer. Cati was born in August 1949, three months after the Federal Republic of West Germany came into being, and two months before the Allied occupation ended. She grew up on Walserstrasse, where her parents owned the Stempfle café, famous for its excellent pastries. It was not until she was an adult that she first saw the photograph of a swastika on her parents' house that prompted her resolve to get to grips with the Nazi era. How had it been possible? And how in particular had it affected Oberstdorf?

By the end of 2010, Volume Five of Oberstdorf's official history had turned into *Ein Dorf im Spiegel seiner Zeit: Oberstdorf 1918–1952 (A Village in the Mirror of its Time: Oberstdorf 1918–*

1952), an exhaustive account of Oberstdorf from the end of the First World War until 1952, the year when thousands of Nazis were released from prison. When Cati began her research she had, like most of us, regarded the Third Reich in stark terms of good versus evil. But she soon realised that the complexities and inconsistencies of those years made this approach too simplistic. So, although she had no intention of whitewashing the village's Nazi history, she also wanted to record its shades of grey. Her book draws on many different local, national and international sources but is particularly interesting for the interviews she conducted with various villagers who had lived through the Third Reich, most of them known to her personally. The result is a remarkable record of Oberstdorf's collective memory and an invaluable source for anyone interested in grassroots history during the Nazi period.

Having completed the book, it occurred to Cati, who was by then living in London with her late husband Peter Patel, that Oberstdorf's story might be of interest to a wider public, which is where I come in. Cati and I first met at a party. At the time I was working on *Travellers in the Third Reich* so we had plenty to talk about. Shortly afterwards, she asked me if I could be tempted to write about the village, using her research as a starting point but expanding on the material to produce a completely new book that would interest even those readers who knew little about Germany, let alone Oberstdorf. Initially I was not enthusiastic. For a start, it seemed to me that as a Brit who (until I met Cati) had never even heard of Oberstdorf, it was the height of arrogance to imagine that I could just waltz in and write about such a tightly knit community during the most sensitive period of its history. But some months later, having finished *Travellers*, I was restless and ready for a new project. So we began to explore the idea in earnest.

My first and most obvious step was to visit Oberstdorf – Germany's southernmost village. Throughout its long history it has always been referred to as a 'village', although with a current population of around 10,000 inhabitants, today it is more aptly described as a small town. Nevertheless, as you walk from the station along the main street towards the marketplace, it has all the atmosphere and charm of a traditional Alpine village. The wooden houses and taverns, the spectacular mountain views, the sight of villagers chatting on street corners or tourists shouldering skies as they head for the Nebelhorn cable car are images that have changed little since the 1930s.

I spent my first day in Oberstdorf just wandering around getting the feel of the place. I visualised the swastikas that had once adorned the town hall, the hotels, the church spire – and also, of course, many private houses. I pictured the noisy Nazi showpieces that had taken place in the market square, the storm troopers shouting anti-Jewish slogans, the raucous Horst Wessel song, the tramping boots, assorted uniforms, torchlight processions and the Nazi propaganda relentlessly spewing out of the public address system. Sitting in the Catholic parish church of St John the Baptist, so full of light and colour, I tried to imagine myself a farmer's widow who, having lost her husband in the first war, had just received the news that her only son had been killed in this second one, and as a devout Catholic had come to seek succour from her faith. Right next to St John's is the small chapel dedicated to Oberstdorf's dead of the two world wars. I sat there too for a long while, looking at the four-hundred-odd carved names and feeling the deep sadness we all experience when contemplating the death of the young.

Yet during that initial exploration of Oberstdorf, it was also possible to conjure happier images – of cattle being driven through the village streets by herdsmen in lederhosen; of taverns crowded with foresters and farmers, all with strong opinions on the way of world; of children skiing fearlessly down terrifying slopes, their homemade skis fastened on with string, or in summer helping harvest the grass-rich meadows surrounding the village. Equally, the much cherished festivals and religious parades came to mind, not to mention the village brass band that in summer gave regular concerts on the marketplace. Then there were the women: capable, stalwart, turning their hand to any challenge, however demanding, as they raised their families in defiance of all that nature, war and poverty could throw at them. And, as this rural outpost had been transformed into a fashionable holiday resort by the time Hitler came to power, I also envisaged the wealthy visitors from northern Germany – Protestants, Jews, aristocrats, artists and industrialists relishing Oberstdorf's natural beauty and winter sports, or in summer, when not hiking in the mountains, perhaps enjoying *Kaffee und Kuchen* at the Stempfle café.

By the end of that first day in Oberstdorf my initial reservations had melted away. I was hooked and eager to begin work. Apart from anything else, I wanted to try to understand how it was possible that decent, hard-working people like the Oberstdorfers could have fallen for Hitler. I did not expect to find definitive answers, but I hoped that by examining the minutiae of village life, I might at least uncover some clues. But most of all, I saw the potential in Oberstdorf's story to write a different kind of book about the Nazis, one in which the intimate and detailed stories of the villagers' lives could be set against the vast canvas of the Third Reich.

With Cati as my guide and mentor, the first port of call clearly had to be the village archives, which like the church is located on the marketplace. Cati had told me enough about the man who was in charge at the time, Eugen Thomma (born in 1931, two years before Hitler came to power; he died in 2022), to make me a little nervous. Eugen was a substantial figure in every respect. He had lived in Oberstdorf all his life and remembered the Nazi years vividly. Nothing about him was casual or spontaneous. Each sentence he uttered was carefully considered and had probably been repeated many times. He had been the village's archivist for forty years so I assumed he would have strong views on the documents in his charge and how they should be deployed. I wasn't at all sure if he would be prepared to open up to me or if would he regard me as an outsider, an enemy alien.

When we met, he spoke in dialect (which Cati translated), answering all my questions without hesitation. He spoke movingly about his factory-worker parents who had remained fiercely loyal to Hitler even as Germany descended into Armageddon, of his family's poverty, his father's death as a prisoner in France, and of his own childhood memories of the war. Because his mother had to work all day in a factory kitchen, Eugen's baby brother was left with a neighbour. His bitterness at having to collect the child after school, push him home in a pram and change his nappies while his school friends went off skiing, was still palpable. But although his responses to my searching questions were immaculate and detailed, I left the archives with no real sense of what he personally thought about the Third Reich. Had I won him over? I couldn't be sure, but I had at least made a start.

Our next call was on Oberstdorf's most senior civil servant, Thomas Kretschmer. The moment we entered his office in the town hall (also on the marketplace) I knew I was in the presence of a man who likes to make things happen.

A young-looking forty-something, he exuded energy and enthusiasm. In flawless English he swept away all my worries about how Oberstdorfers might react to having some random Englishwoman poking around in their Nazi past. 'Think about it like this,' he said, 'how many other Bavarian towns and villages have attracted so much outside interest in their history?' His confidence was reassuring, as indeed were the various officials who popped their heads round the door, smiling their encouragement.

After meeting Thomas, Cati and I were in need of lunch and so joined her brother Gustl Stempfle in what had once been the family café but is now a restaurant. Gustl is a tall, fine-looking man whom one can easily picture skiing stylishly down Oberstdorf's more formidable runs. He was the fourth master pastry chef in the family, and had run the café for many years before it became a restaurant. He is also a former municipal councillor and remains an enthusiastic contributor to village life at many levels. A warm, generous man, he was to prove a key ally, always ready to research any questions we threw at him, always coming back with the answers.

That afternoon we visited Trudl Heckmair, widow of Anderl Heckmair, the mountaineer who in 1938 led the first successful ascent of the North Face of the Eiger. A diminutive figure, Trudl steered us into her *gemütliche* (cosy) sitting room, with its carved panelling, Bavarian furniture, ornaments and tiled table – beautifully set with china cups and saucers. It all made me feel as though I were stepping back into the Oberstdorf of the 1930s. Several Rudolf Scheller paintings hung on the walls, including one depicting an idealised German peasant couple – exactly the kind of subject so beloved by the Nazis. Indeed, Hitler had admired Scheller's work enough to buy one his pictures. Both Scheller and his wife were ardent

National Socialists and among the very first Oberstdorfers to join the Nazi Party. Although Heckmair was never himself a member of the party, he and Scheller became close friends and had spent a good deal of time walking together in the mountains in their later years.

As we sat there drinking Trudl's excellent coffee, she told us how in the last days of the war (when she was thirteen) she had watched the village's Nazis being led through the snow – still in their pyjamas – to imprisonment in the town hall cellars. Perhaps surprisingly, she also remembers with real affection the Moroccan troops who occupied Oberstdorf immediately after the war. A number of them were billeted in her mother's house and Trudl was especially fond of 'the wonderful white bread' they made from cornflour. For some reason, our conversation then turned to Leni Riefenstahl, Hitler's notorious propagandist, whose films of the 1936 Olympic games and the Nuremberg rallies made such an impact on the world. Suddenly, Trudl got up and climbed onto a chair over by a bookcase. Then, standing precariously on tiptoe, she reached up to the top shelf and extracted a large album. She opened it to reveal dramatic photographs, now a little faded, of Riefenstahl climbing vertical rock faces while roped to Heckmair. 'She was a very fine mountaineer,' reflected Trudl. After more absorbing chat about Trudl's childhood memories of the war, it was time to leave. Pressing me to return soon, Trudl waved us off with her gentle smile.

On subsequent trips to Oberstdorf I started to explore further afield, walking south along the River Trettach and catching glimpses of the mountains through the trees. Depending on the weather, this river can change dramatically from crystal clarity one day to a chalky green or a deep chocolatey brown the next. After some searching, I located the spot where the

Trettach Hotel, one of Oberstdorf's earliest and most promi-nent resort hotels, had once stood on the riverbank, but which has long since gone. Another excursion took me up the wind-ing road to Birgsau, about six miles south of Oberstdorf at the foot of the mountains and on the border with Austria. Apart from the fact there is no longer a Waffen SS training camp there, it hasn't changed much since National Socialist times. The inn across the meadow from the picturesque little chapel is still there, while the River Stillach flows close by. The only clue that this tranquil and beautiful place was, in the last days of the war, the scene of two brutal murders – of Germans by Germans – is a small monument marking the spot where one of the victims was shot. But these days it no longer refers to his violent death, recording only his name and the dates of his short life. As I was soon to learn, this double murder, even when set against the unspeakable horror of the war, was to be a source of anguish and conflict in the village for decades.

In a book of this kind, luck inevitably plays a major role. One exceptional piece of good fortune to come our way was Cati's discovery of the Meinlinger diary. This happened by pure chance when at the airport one day on her way back to London, she picked up a free copy of a local newspaper and read an article by someone whose soldier uncle had kept a diary throughout the war. She made contact with the dia-ry's owner who not only let us quote extensively from the journal, but also told us about another diary written by a lieu-tenant who had fought on the Eastern Front. Thanks to that chance encounter with a newspaper, we soon had access to two exceptional unpublished testimonies by soldiers of the 99th regiment of the 1st Mountain Division, the same regi-ment in which so many Oberstdorfers had fought and died in the Second World War.

Hunting down new sources was an endless quest and one in which we received help from a number of individuals. Lisa Luther-Heckel (who was at school with Cati) is a member of Mensa and it is her whom we have to thank for compiling the list of villagers who joined the Nazi Party. The Americans unwittingly made this task much harder when, during their occupation of Bavaria, they decided to abandon local records and lump all members of the NSDAP together alphabetically in one vast national list. And without Lisa's guidance, I would still be irretrievably lost in the labyrinth of Bundesarchiv references. Another hero is Dr Otto Nübel, whose book on the Protestant Church in Oberstdorf is a tour de force and a prime source of information about the village and church matters. Gerhard Klein is a meticulous historian, and as head of all the archives in the region was an invaluable guide in our search for relevant material. One of the most rewarding parts of this project has been my involvement with local people like Lisa, Gustl, Otto, Gerhard and of course Cati, the instigator, whose ceaseless efforts to understand their country's Nazi past has won my deep respect.

The purpose of this book was now clear to me. Building on Cati's work and enlarging on her research, I would aim not merely to present a factual account of how one German community had fared under Hitler, but to make these people – with all their problems, dreams, hopes and foibles, their compromises and contradictions – come alive on the page. I would also try to follow the village's young men as they fought Hitler's war across Europe and on the Eastern Front. In other words, while sticking strictly to the sources, I would attempt a narrative that allowed readers to live and breathe Oberstdorf's history; to sense what it had actually been like to be alive in this particular village at this particular time.

Of course many months were to pass before I felt that I was at last beginning to get under the skin of the place. But I realised just how far I had come when one day, three years after my first visit, I was again sitting in the memorial chapel. This time, however, as I looked at the names of the soldiers they were no longer just Gothic letters on a stone tablet. Now I knew so many of them personally. Some had committed atrocities, others acts of heroism, but all had died young in terrible circumstances. The name that held my gaze the longest was that of Claudius Asal, killed on 26 April 1945, twelve days before the end of the war. He was sixteen.

As is usually the case with human endeavour, more knowledge breeds more questions and my mission to gain a better grasp of the Nazis through the experiences of one village is no exception. Nevertheless, for me personally this study of Oberstdorf has been enormously enriching, and if there are still aspects of ordinary people's responses to Hitler that are incomprehensible, I can only hope that Oberstdorf's saga – together with the stories of other villages and small towns – will combine to shed greater light on the Third Reich and what is arguably the most far-reaching tragedy in human history.

Uncovering
Oberstdorf's Past

Angelika (Cati) Patel

S kiing and friendship were the unlikely triggers for my turn to local history.

I was born and raised in Oberstdorf, a summer and winter resort on the edge of the Bavarian Alps. Despite its undoubted beauty, I had left in 1968 at the age of nineteen, craving new experiences, foreign countries and cultures. Moving to London with my half-Indian, half-German-Jewish husband and our two young daughters in the early 1980s was the fulfilment of my wildest dreams. But we regularly returned to Oberstdorf to visit my family and friends.

One of those friends was of my parents' generation, Max Maile, who was born in 1918. Max was a crack skier and over the years he and I shared many happy hours on the slopes of the Nebelhorn mountain.

One day Max told me he had been a member of the *Heimatschutz* (Homeland Security). At the time, I had no idea what that was, and he explained it was a resistance group that had formed to defy the Nazis as the war drew to a close surrender to the Allies, which was ultimately successful but not without deadly bloodshed.

I was surprised that I had never heard anything about it, despite having grown up in an old local family, and I became curious. I soon discovered that the indisputably heroic early actions of the *Heimatschutz* had been followed by less heroic ones, which is why the organisation had become known as *Heimatschmutz* (Home Dirt). Decades ago its actions had been reported in the local paper, but gradually the topic had been swept under the carpet as it had caused deep divisions in the village.

Max had no children. He never said so directly but I felt that he wanted me to write down the *Heimatschutz* story as his legacy.

I started talking to others who had witnessed the events. I met Franz Noichl, a senior civil servant in the ministry of education in Munich whose uncle – also a member of the *Heimatschutz* – had later been charged with murder. This had fuelled Franz's meticulous research on the topic. He gave me his material with the warning that there was little chance of publication. The topic was still highly controversial and there was strong local opposition against bringing it up again.

My brother Gustl Stempfle came to help. He had remained living in Oberstdorf, where he had been a local councillor and, unlike me, had always been interested in local history. Under his chairmanship, the *Verschönerungsverein* (the association that started furthering tourism in the nineteenth century) had founded the biannual magazine *Unser Oberstdorf*, which covered historical and cultural topics. With my brother's help, my matter-of-fact, non-judgemental and non-emotional account of the last days of the war and subsequent events was published there in 2000 under the title 'Der Umsturz in

Oberstdorf' ('The Revolution in Oberstdorf'). The magazine sold out within days and the reaction on the whole was positive. People also came forward with their own experiences to add to the overall picture.

I had always been interested in the Third Reich but I had thought – rather arrogantly, as it turned out – that I knew more than enough about it. This project, which had started as a favour to my friend Max, inspired me to delve much more deeply into that history and thus became a turning point in my life.

At school we had been confronted with the Third Reich in the most shocking and life-changing way by reading *Die Ermittlung* (*The Investigation*), a play by Peter Weiss, based on the Frankfurt Auschwitz trials. Neither I nor my school friends would ever forget the shame and horror we felt on reading about the atrocities that had been instigated by the people of our country.

After the silence of the 1950s and the early 1960s, the Auschwitz trials had started an avalanche of *Vergangenheitsbewältigung* ('dealing with the past'). Suddenly, there was no shortage of books, documentaries, plays, original newsreel footage or films dealing with the twelve most horrifying years in German history. I read and watched lots of them but my mind didn't connect these accounts and events with my parents or grandparents and their friends. They were ordinary, decent people; it was Adolf Hitler, Hermann Göring or Josef Goebbels who were the monsters. These men also came across as ridiculous, with their pompous strutting and marching, their mad gesticulating and their screaming voices. And the roaring crowds shouting 'YES' in one voice for total war? Completely incomprehensible, but nothing to do with the people I knew.

But now the *Heimatschutz* project had shown me a tangible connection between our little village and the big wide world where history was made.

And as an empty nester I had the time and energy to take a closer look.

My next research concentrated on the fates of two Jewish women living in Oberstdorf during the Third Reich: Amalie Zuckmayer, the mother of the playwright Carl Zuckmayer, who survived the Nazi years in Oberstdorf not least thanks to its Nazi mayor; and Eva Noack-Mosse, who was deported to the Theresienstadt camp in February 1945.* I wrote an article about the experiences of the two women in 2006, again published in *Unser Oberstdorf*.

By that time the local council had decided that it was time for Oberstdorf's own *Vergangenheitsbewältigung*. Two enormously knowledgeable and competent men – Eugen Thomma, the archivist and walking memory of Oberstdorf, and the historian Dr Thaddäus Steiner, author of several publications on various aspects of local history – were offered the commission for researching and writing Oberstdorf's local history of the first half of the twentieth century, but both declined. My brother suggested me to the good and great of Oberstdorf, whom Mayor Thomas Müller had gathered to answer the question 'Do we really want to tackle this project?' The answer was yes and I was entrusted with the task.

* After her liberation and return to Oberstdorf, Eva described in excruciating detail the horrors of the camp in her *Tagebuch aus Theresienstadt* ('Diary from Theresienstadt'). It has since been translated into English, but at the time I found the German original on a microfilm in the Wiener Library in London thanks to the enthusiastic support of the archivist Howard Falksohn.

With hindsight, the most crucial aspect for the successful research and publication of my book *Ein Dorf im Spiegel seiner Zeit (A Village in the Mirror of Its Time)*, *Oberstdorf 1918–1952* was the establishment of a support group for my work. Eugen Thomma and Dr Steiner agreed to join, as did Franz Noichl and Albert Vogler, who had been involved in local government for decades, both as deputy mayor and as a councillor. Heidi Bromberger, who still runs the mayor's office, joined the group from the town hall as did the head of administration, Thomas Kretschmer. Thanks to this group, diverse in both age and political outlook, I can say with confidence that *Ein Dorf im Spiegel seiner Zeit* represents the collective memory of Oberstdorf's history during the Third Reich.

Max Maile took great interest in the project as well, offering plenty of helpful contributions. He was the first to see the proofs of the book. Sitting at his dining table we went through every page. He nodded his approval and was pleased to find an Eduard Thöny* cartoon depicting himself and Thöny's son as children in its pages. His story – and that of his generation – had finally been told.

A true gentleman he insisted on walking me home. He died a few weeks later aged ninety-two.

Exploring the Third Reich among the people I grew up with – not anonymous monsters – taught me how fragile civilisation is. It also taught me that humble individuals can – and do – create pockets of humanity in inhuman times and circumstances.

Last, but very much not least, I understood how lucky I was to be born after the war.

---

* Eduard Thöny was a famous caricaturist for *Simplizissimus*, the weekly satirical magazine. His son and Max used to deliver Thöny's cartoons to the train station every week to be transported to Berlin.

Acknowledgements

First we would like to thank the people of Oberstdorf for their openness, candour and willingness to confront the Nazi years. We owe a great debt to Oberstdorf's archivist Eugen Thomma who, having looked after the municipal archive for more than four decades, had an unrivalled knowledge of Oberstdorf's history. That he was able to retrieve answers to even the most obscure questions is testimony to the exceptional quality of this village archive. It was with great sadness we learned of his death in June 2022. Elisabeth Luther-Heckel is a formidable researcher whose eagle eye for detail and ability to tease out relevant material from a mass of impenetrable data is endlessly impressive. She also read an early draft of the book and made many perceptive suggestions. Heartfelt thanks go to Gustl Stempfle whose deep understanding of the village and its inhabitants has been an unfailingly valuable source. As adviser, path-smoother, checker of facts and much else, he has played an essential role. Our thanks also go to Thomas Kretschmer for ensuring the town hall's continued support, and to Heidi Bromberger for so brilliantly sourcing the photographs. Dr Caroline Neubaur, granddaughter of General Ludwig Beck, has been extraordinarily generous in sharing her family's personal history and in allowing the publication of a letter written by her mother a few days after the 20 July bomb plot. She was also kind enough to read the manuscript in draft and contributed many thoughtful observations. We owe very special thanks to Dr Paul Hoser for his guidance in accessing elusive archive material and for sharing his vast knowledge of Bavarian history. Franz Noichl's son, Klaus Noichl, has made an invaluable contribution by allowing his father's unpublished memoir to be quoted so extensively. Equally, thanks go to Herbert Prenzel for permitting liberal use of his father-in-law Lieutenant Gerd Aurich's unpublished diary, and to the family of Sergeant Alfons Meinlinger whose journal, also unpublished, takes us from the very first day of the war right through to the end. Dr Theo Sommer, a former editor of *Die Zeit*, was also kind enough to share extracts from his memoir. Ingrid Weissenberger (Theodor Weissenberger's niece) has been an enthusiastic supporter from the outset, while her own book, *Das Trettach Hotel*, provided many intriguing insights. It is a great sadness that John Lowin did not live to see the book in print, although he had read much of it in draft. His extensive input and enthusiasm for the project are greatly appreciated. Our correspondence – initiated because his Jewish parents lived in Oberstdorf when he was born in 1938 – grew into a regular and always fascinating exchange. Jenny Willis, a gifted Germanist, has produced a number of excellent translations and given much wise advice. She also contributed valuable feedback having read a draft of the book. Emily Wilson threw herself into the task of translating the Dutch material with great skill and energy, becoming a dear friend in the process.

We would also like to thank the following individuals for the help they have given us in many different ways: Anna Katarina Hefferon von Alvensleben, Carole Angier, Willem H. de Beaufort, Franz Becherer, Phoebe Bentinck, Gerd Bischoff, Professor Sir Robert Boyd, Sir Rodric Braithwaite, Sir Nicholas Brooksbank Bt., Harriet Crawley (who set the book in motion by introducing us to one another), Richard Dorment, Frieda van Essen, Howard Falksohn (Wiener Library), Clare Ferguson, Julie Freestone, Dr Thomas Gayda, Hugh Geddes, Francis Hazeel, Trudl Heckmair, Susanne Hilbrand, Peter and Otto Jäger, Gerhard Klein, Margaret Mair, Gunther le Maire, Angus W. McGeoch, Ute Menzel, Dr Otto Nübel, Matthew Olex-Szczytowski, Dr Burkhard Quessel (British Library), Rudi Raab Jr, the late Alex Rössle, Elfriede Ruhrberg, Dr Nancy Sahli, Theo van der Sande (Utrecht Archives), Dr Jacques Schuhmacher, Otmar Schuster Jr., the late Dr Thaddäus Steiner.

I (JB) would like to add personal thanks to Dr Piers Brendon who has given me so much help with this book. He has been my friend and mentor for twenty-five years and without his patient tutoring and willingness to share his wisdom about this period and so much else, I would never have found the courage to start writing, let alone persevere. To be privy to his sharp, witty, astute and always original take on the world has been a constant delight.

In the course of our two collaborations I have learned so much from Jennie Condell, our brilliant and impeccable editor. Completely unflappable, she is a joy to work with. I deeply value her professionalism – and her friendship. Warmest possible thanks go to everyone at Elliott & Thompson – Lorne Forsyth, Pippa Crane, Sarah Rigby, Marianne Thorndahl, Robin Harvie, Amy Greaves – for all the flair, energy and enthusiasm they have put into producing this book, as well as to all of the external team who have worked so diligently on it: Emma Finnigan, Linden Lawson, Jon Asbury, Mark Swan, John Plumer, Kate Inskip and Marie Doherty.

The Villagers

Alvensleben-Schönborn, Count Joachim von (1877–1969)
After losing Ostrometzko, the family estate lying between Berlin
and Warsaw, and surviving spells in Dachau and Buchenwald,
the count lived in Oberstdorf with his former wife, the Polish
Countess Katarzyna Bninska. One of his sons joined the SS, the
other served briefly in the Polish reserves.

Amann, Franz (1897–1940)
Chairman of the Oberstdorf branch of the German Alpine Club.
His daughter Trudl became the mountaineer Anderl Heckmair's
second wife.

Arminsted, Sybille von (1921–2012)
Her mother first brought her to Oberstdorf when she was eight
years old to improve her health. Much of her childhood was
spent in the village, where she attended school and enjoyed the
various activities organised by the League for German Girls.
She returned to Oberstdorf after the war, where she replaced
Charlotte Stirius as the leading local journalist and became
private secretary of the Catholic poet and novelist Gertrud
von Le Fort.

Aurich, Lieutenant Paul Gerd (1903–41)
A master builder from Chemnitz in Saxony, he was also an
accomplished mountaineer who at the outbreak of war travelled
to Sonthofen to join the 99th Regiment of the 1st Mountain

Division. He fought alongside Oberstdorf soldiers with this regiment until he was killed on the Eastern Front.

Bessler, Dr Eduard (1899–1974)
Headmaster of Oberstdorf's secondary school since the 1920s, he had difficulty in steering a middle course between Nazi doctrine and his own humanitarian principles. Despite his habitual shouting, he was much liked by his students, many of whom spoke up for him at his denazification trial after the war.

Bierbichler, Elfriede (1928–)
Although her uncle, Wilhelm Herzog, was one of the most prominent Nazis in Oberstdorf, Elfriede did not herself support the regime. She was sent to an obligatory labour service camp for girls in 1944, but managed to abscond successfully and make her way back home before the end of the war. She married Professor Karl Ruhrberg.

Biunda, Mother Superior Maria (1891–1972)
She was in charge of the small flock of Franciscan nuns that had been based in Oberstdorf since 1907. The Sisters ran a nursery school, taught the village girls up to the age of fourteen and operated a sewing workshop until new Nazi laws curtailed their activities in the mid-1930s. With the help of Mayor Ludwig Fink and other villagers, the nuns survived the war and (in 2021) still have a presence in the village.

Burzawa, Andrzej (1925–?)
A Polish forced labourer abducted from his village at the age of fifteen to work on a farm in the Black Forest. Later incarcerated in Dachau, he was then among a batch of prisoners sent to Birgsau, just south of Oberstdorf, to build and maintain an SS training camp. After the war he returned to his village, married and had a family.

Dabelstein, Elisabeth (1895–1976)
Mountaineer and director of Hohes Licht children's home,
founded by Henriette Laman Trip-de Beaufort in 1924. She
consistently opposed the Nazis and was after the war awarded
the Order of Orange-Nassau by the Netherlands government
for her resistance work.

Fink, Ludwig (1888–1974)
Before he was appointed mayor of Oberstdorf in 1934, Fink was
leader of the district's chimney sweeps. Apparently a devoted
Nazi, Fink is nevertheless noted for having protected the Jews
living under his jurisdiction, for helping the nuns survive during
the Third Reich and for supporting villagers brought before the
Nazi courts. He was well liked locally even by those who did
not share his politics.

Groth, Heinz (1906–94)
A committed Nazi, he was a district judge in Sonthofen and an
officer in the 99th Regiment of the 1st Mountain Division. He
fought in Russia and led a propaganda expedition to the summit
of Mount Elbrus in 1942. He lived first in Oberstdorf after the
war, but then settled in Sonthofen. In 1936 he co-authored a
guide to the Allgäu mountains with Ernst Zettler.

Gschwender, Fritz (1851–1925)
Owner of the Trettach Hotel until it was sold it 1920. He was
Mayor of Oberstdorf 1912–19. His nineteen-year-old grandson,
Theodor Weissenberger, was gassed in the Nazis' 'euthanasia'
programme because he was blind.

Heckmair, Anderl (1906–2005)
A mountaineer who won global fame when he led a fellow
German and two Austrians on the first successful ascent of the
North Face of the Eiger in 1938. He met Hitler twice and was a

friend of the regime's most famous film-maker, Leni Riefenstahl. At the outbreak of war he was working at the Ordensburg in Sonthofen. He later joined an infantry regiment with which he spent eighteen months on the Eastern Front before being posted as instructor to the Fulpmes mountain training school in Austria. After the war he married Trudl Amann and was to spend the rest of his life in Oberstdorf.

Heckmair, Trudl (1931–)
Daughter of Franz Amann, chairman of the Oberstdorf branch of the German Alpine Club who after the war became Anderl Heckmair's second wife. During the French occupation Moroccan troops were billeted in her home.

Helmling, Dr Alexander (1892–?)
A dentist and as an SS-*Scharführer* was one of the village's leading Nazis. His wife shared his politics and his daughter Margot was known to be a school bully.

Herzog, Wilhelm (1893–1961)
An unsuccessful cobbler, Herzog was an enthusiastic member of the Nazi Party in charge of local propaganda. He was also appointed a meat inspector, in which capacity he denounced Anton Jäger, landlord of the Adler inn, for slaughtering animals illegally.

Hochfeichter, Ludwig (1875–1949)
A farmer who was Mayor of Oberstdorf from 1919 to 1924 and who did much to steer the village successfully through the difficult post-First World War years. He also played a major part in the building of the Nebelhorn cable car and the Moor swimming pool. His only son Michael was killed in action in 1944.

Hofmann, Andreas (1874–1953)
Bookseller and publisher of the *Oberstdorfer Gemeinde- und Fremdenblatt*. For a long time the newspaper refused to acknowledge the rise of the Nazis but changed its policy after the Reichstag was burned down in 1933. Also father of Adolf Hofmann, who was awarded the prestigious Knight's Cross before he was killed in Russia in 1943.

Hoyer, Hermann Otto, (1893–1968)
A prisoner of war in the First World War, he lost his right arm while trying to escape. After teaching himself how to paint with his left hand, he became a popular artist in the Nazi period much admired by Hitler. A print of his original painting *In the Beginning was the Word* was widely distributed, becoming one of the most famous images of the Third Reich. He subsequently lived in Oberstdorf, where he was an active member of the NSDAP.

Jäger, Anton (1895–1972)
Owner of the Adler inn, farmer and godfather to Franz Noichl. Denounced by the meat inspector for illegally slaughtering animals, he was lucky to escape imprisonment. His son Alois was killed in East Prussia in 1944.

Kalhammer, Dr Fritz (1902–68)
A medical doctor who rose swiftly through the party ranks to become the Sonthofen *Kreisleiter*. It was on his recommendation that Ludwig Fink was appointed Mayor of Oberstdorf. Despite his senior party role, he was a moderate administrator who on occasion protected Jews and sought to take good care of the people under his jurisdiction.

Laman Trip-de Beaufort, Agatha Maria Henriëtte
(1890–1992)
Known as Hetty, she was a Dutch aristocrat who in 1924 established a home for sick children in Oberstdorf called Hohes Licht. During the war she and the director of the home, Elisabeth Dabelstein, smuggled Jewish children over the Swiss border to safety and also provided assistance for Dutch forced labourers held in nearby camps.

Lang, Xaver (1894–1974)
Like many of his fellow postmen, he was an enthusiastic member of the Nazi Party and for a time leader of the village SA. Husband of Tilly and father of a daughter, Pauli.

Löwin, Julius (1904–97)
A Polish Jew who set up a dental practice in Oberstdorf in 1927. Although initially successful, by 1938 only the Hohes Licht children's home continued to employ him. In August 1938, shortly before *Kristallnacht*, he and his wife emigrated to America with their baby son John.

Löwin, Leni (1903–95)
Wife of Julius, she grew up in Göttingen and held a doctorate in law. She met Julius in 1936 while visiting her sister and brother-in-law who were temporarily living in Oberstdorf.

Maile, Max (1918–2010)
Reluctantly caught up in the Nazi war machine, Maile went straight from school into the Labour Service and then into the 99th Regiment of the 1st Mountain Division. By the end of the war, he was back in Oberstdorf and thus able to join the *Heimatschutz* resistance movement. An excellent skier and sportsman, he ran a successful electrical business after the war. He made a major contribution to recording Oberstdorf's Third

Reich history. His sister, Emma, was secretary to the Oberstdorf branch of the German Alpine Club.

Meinlinger, Alfons (1917–98)
Born on a farm near Kempten (about thirty miles north of Oberstdorf), he fought throughout the Second World War with the 99th Regiment of the 1st Mountain Division. He served in a communications unit initially as a private but ending the war as an NCO. After a brief spell in an American internment camp, he returned home and enjoyed a fulfilling family and professional life until his death.

Merz, Anton (1896–1968)
As the owner of one of Oberstdorf's original 353 houses he held rights as a 'commoner' and served as an elected member of the commons council after the First World War. A Nazi supporter, he opened Oberstdorf's first cinema in 1927.

Neidhart, Thomas (1887–1960)
A master baker who first became mayor of Oberstdorf in 1930. Forced to resign in the wake of the Nazis' Equalisation Act in 1933, he was briefly mayor again during the French occupation from May to October 1945.

Neubaur, Gertrud (1917–2008)
Daughter of General Ludwig Beck, wife of Lieutenant Günther Neubaur. After her husband was killed in Russia in 1942, she went with her small daughter to live in Oberstdorf, where she had been born and where she had spent much of her childhood. Beck was one of the conspirators in the plot to assassinate Hitler on 20 July 1944 and, had it succeeded, would have become head of state. He committed suicide immediately after it failed. After being briefly imprisoned by the Gestapo, Gertrud was allowed to return to Oberstdorf where she spent the rest of her life.

Noack-Mosse, Eva (1902–98)
She came from a distinguished Jewish family but as she was married to an 'Aryan' received 'privileged' status. She, her husband and two stepdaughters sought refuge in Oberstdorf, where they were able to live unmolested until she was sent to Theresienstadt in February 1945. She returned safely after the war and served for a while as an assistant assessor at the Sonthofen denazification tribunal. She was a close friend of the playwright Carl Zuckmayer.

Noichl, Xaver (1892–1974)
Forester and socialist. Consistently opposed to the Nazis, he was an active member of the *Heimatschutz*. Married to Therese (née Zoller), he was Franz Noichl's father.

Noichl, Franz (1929–2019)
Xaver and Therese Noichl's eldest son. As a child he was initially an enthusiastic participant in the Hitler Youth but grew to despise everything to do with the regime. His unpublished memoir is an important source.

Raab, Rudi (1912–93)
An avid Nazi who at the age of twenty-five was appointed headmaster of the Adolf Hitler School in the Sonthofen Ordensburg. He ended the war as a brigadier and was captured by the Americans while attempting to escape with his men to the mountains south of Oberstdorf.

Richter, Karl (1901–55)
As leader of the *Heimatschutz* he masterminded the coup that saved Oberstdorf from Allied attack on 1 May 1945. However, during the French occupation, the *Heimatschutz* fell into disrepute and Richter became deeply unpopular. He committed suicide in 1955.

Richter, Ernst (1908–60)
Like his older brother Karl, as a young man Ernst had a reputation for being a tearaway but later became a dentist. While
his brother led the military side of the coup, Ernst (with the
lawyer Pfister) was responsible for organising the logistics. He
also committed suicide.

Rupp, Father Josef (1884–1966)
He succeeded Father Isidor Kohl as Oberstdorf's parish priest in
1936 and remained in the post until 1955. As a member of the
Confessing Church, he was deeply opposed to the Nazi regime
and often dangerously outspoken.

Schallhammer, Hermann (1883–1980)
Oberstdorf's pioneer director of tourism during the 1920s. After
he was sacked by the Nazis in 1933, he moved to Oberammergau
and later Bad Tölz but returned to Oberstdorf after the war. He
was mayor 1952–60.

Scheller, Rudolf (1889–1984)
A dedicated Nazi and anti-Semite, he was a successful artist
whose work was admired by Hitler. His wife Lili was the first
woman in Oberstdorf to join the NSDAP. He and the mountaineer Anderl Heckmair were close friends.

Schnell, Emil (1859–1945)
The Jewish owner of a textile mill in Ulm, he retired with his
Protestant wife to Oberstdorf to become a much-respected
member of the community. As a widower, he was protected
during the war by Mayor Fink and cared for by other villagers.
He committed suicide after receiving a letter from the Gestapo
informing him that he was to be sent to the Theresienstadt
ghetto where his brother had died in 1943.

Schnell, Fritz (*c.*1895–?)
Emil's youngest son and a professional musician. Sent to a labour camp in 1945, he survived the war to return to Oberstdorf and marry Henny (one of the Dutch women working at the children's home, Hohes Licht) and to resume a successful musical career.

Schnell, Hans (*c.*1930–?)
Grandson of Emil Schnell with whom, as a teenager, he shared a room for several years before Emil's suicide. As his father (Emil's second son, also Hans) was a leading engineer, the fact that he was half Jewish was ignored by the Nazis.

Schratt, Josef (1886–1969)
A shoemaker and master craftsman famous for making the largest shoe in the world. He supported the nuns when the Nazis threatened their sewing workshop with closure. The Schratts were one of Oberstdorf's many large extended families. Four members of the family were killed in the Second World War.

Schubert, Heinz (1914–87)
An SS officer who as a member of *Einsatzgruppe* D organised the massacre of over 700 people (many of them Gypsies) at Simferopol in the Crimea in 1941. Although condemned to death at his Nuremberg trial, he was released from prison in 1952. He then joined his wife in Oberstdorf, where she had been sent early in the war to have her first child.

Schuster, Otmar (1914–2007)
A master tailor who did not fight in the war because of a childhood leg injury. He took a leading part in the *Heimatschutz* coup on 1 May 1945.

Steiner, Dr Thaddäus (1933–2017)
Historian and son of Wilhelm and Genovefa Steiner. He and
Franz Noichl were first cousins.

Steiner, Wilhelm (1895–1971)
Forester, soldier, socialist and sportsman. Married to Genovefa
Zoller, Frau Noichl's sister.

Stirius, Charlotte (1895–1971)
A journalist who worked for many years on the *Oberstdorfer
Gemeinde- und Fremdenblatt*. Afterwards she was the local editor
of the *Allgäuer Anzeigeblatt* until her retirement in 1958.

Stolzenberg, Hertha (1889–1960)
Half Jewish, she gave up a successful career as an opera singer
in 1932 to live in Oberstdorf with her wholly Jewish mother
where she hoped to escape the rising anti-Semitism. As a member of the village's Protestant church, she trained its choir to a
high level of excellence. Although it was probably known that
she and her mother were Jewish, the two women survived the
war unharmed.

Thomma, Fridolin (d. 1945) and Eugenie-
Workers in a local textile factory. They began supporting Hitler
after their lives were devastated by the effects of the 1923
hyperinflation and they lost faith in the unions. They remained
loyal to Hitler throughout the war. After the German surrender,
Fridolin was imprisoned in France where he died from injuries
sustained while clearing mines.

Thomsen, Anna-Lisa
A regular visitor to Oberstdorf in search of a cure for her
'nerves', she became embroiled in the Weinlein, Scheller v.

Zettler case. She was married to Hans Thomsen, a senior diplomat whom she accompanied to Washington DC. Thomsen
became chargé d'affaires after *Kristallnacht* and it was he who
presented Germany's declaration of war to the State Department
on 8 December 1941, the day after Pearl Harbor.

Vörg, Ludwig (1911–41)
One of four climbers who in 1938 were the first to make a
successful ascent of the North Face of the Eiger. He saved
his companions from death when he held Heckmair in a fall
despite his hand having been pierced by a crampon. He worked
with Heckmair at the Sonthofen Ordensburg until joining the
99th Regiment of the 1st Mountain Division at the outbreak
of war. Like Heckmair, he had by then made his home in
Oberstdorf. He was killed in Poland on 22 June 1941, the first
day of Operation Barbarossa.

Wahl, Karl (1892–1981)
Gauleiter of Swabia 1928–45. He joined the Nazi Party in 1922
soon after it was founded, becoming leader of the Swabian SA
the following year. In comparison with many other *Gauleiter*,
most notably Adolf Wagner, *Gauleiter* of Munich, Wahl was considered a moderate Nazi. His wife and daughter were among
those imprisoned in Oberstdorf during the *Heimatschutz* coup
on 1 May 1945.

Weigert, Dr Kurt (1881–1978)
A medical doctor and head of the Sonthofen Hospital who
because he was Jewish fled over the mountains to Switzerland
in 1940. Forced by the Swiss to return to Germany, he survived
the war in Mannheim. Afterwards he returned to Sonthofen
and gave evidence in support of Kreisleiter Dr Fritz Kalhammer
who, despite his high Nazi rank, had tried to protect Weigert.

Weinlein, Karl (1896–?)
Dedicated Nazi and anti-Semite. A veteran of the First World War, he joined the NSDAP soon after it was founded and held the prized low party membership number of 4,003. A postman by profession, he was sent to Oberstdorf in 1927 where he set up an NSDAP branch. His wife, Maja, was an equally devout Nazi. After quarrelling with Oberstdorf's first Nazi mayor, Ernst Zettler, he and his wife together with Rudolf and Lilli Scheller were expelled from the party. They made constant appeals through the courts and were finally reinstated in 1936.

Weissenberger, Theodor (1921–40)
Grandson of Mayor Fritz Gschwender and his wife Maria, the highly musical Theodor was born in Oberstdorf to the Gschwenders' youngest daughter. He was murdered by the Nazis as part of their 'euthanasia' programme because he was blind.

Witzgall, Dr Hanna (1892–1974)
A medical doctor strongly opposed to the Nazis. She assisted Thesy Heilbronner to commit suicide. She was divorced from Dr Otto Witzgall.

Witzgall, Dr Otto (1888–64)
Also a medical doctor opposed to the Nazis. He was forced to resign from the municipal council after they took power. He assisted the Jewish Emil Schnell to commit suicide. After the war he was briefly appointed a judge at the denazification court in Sonthofen.

Zettler, Ernst (1885–1945)
He became Oberstdorf's first Nazi mayor in April 1933. Responsible for implementing the National Socialist Equalisation Law that was to impact so heavily on the village,

he was deeply unpopular. Responsible for having Karl Weinlein, Rudolf Scheller and their wives expelled from the NSDAP, he became embroiled in the long-lasting court case that eventually vindicated his opponents. He left Oberstdorf on promotion in 1934. Two years later he published a guide to the Allgäu mountains in collaboration with Heinz Groth, who was to lead the ascent of Mount Elbrus in 1942. He committed suicide in May 1945 after shooting his wife and daughter.

Notes

Introduction

1 *Oberstdorfer Gemeinde- und Fremdenblatt* (OGF) (*Oberstdorf Village and Tourist News*), 6 March 1933.

2 Weinlein to Goebbels, 14 March 1934, Bundesarchiv Berlin, Oberstes Partei Gericht (OPG) (Supreme Party Court), Parteiausschlussverfahren gegen Weinlein, Scheller Franoux und Ehefrauen (Party Expulsion Proceedings against Weinlein, Scheller, Franoux and their wives), File R 9361/I 41628, pp. 84–7.

Chapter 1

1 Information provided by Wilhelm Steiner's son Dr Thaddäus Steiner, interview, 22 July 2017.

2 Ingrid Weissenberger, *Das Trettach Hotel* (Hamburg: Tredition, 2018), p. 332.

3 Ibid., pp. 329–30.

4 Ibid., p. 334.

5 *OGF*, 28 January 1919.

6 Ibid., 5 October 1919.

7 Joseph Buck, *Handbuch für Reisende im Algäu* [sic], *Lechtal und Bregenzerwald* (*Guidebook for Travellers in the Algäu* [sic], *Lechtal and Bregenzerwald*) (Kempten: Dannheimer, 1866), p. 149.

8 See Daniel Ritter von Pitrof, *Gegen Spartakus in München und im Allgäu* (*Fighting Spartacus in Munich and the Allgäu*) (Munich: C. Gerber, 1937), p. 25 f.

9 Archiv Marktgemeinde Oberstdorf, population statistics, Box 13 D.

10 *OGF*, 1 October 1919.

11 *OGF*, 16 February 1921.

12 *OGF*, 3 January 1920.

13 *OGF*, 1 October 1919.

14 *OGF*, 15 November 1919.

15 *OGF*, 20 March 1920.

16 *OGF*, 7 April 1920.

17 *OGF*, 30 October 1920.

Chapter 2

1 OGF, 19 May 1920.
2 Völkischer Beobachter, No. 71, 8 August 1920, p. 5.
3 OGF, 18 August 1920.
4 Oberstdorfer Heimat- und Fremdblatt (OHF), 1 September 1923. The OHF was founded in 1923 after the OGF folded as a result of hyperinflation.
5 The Spectator, 18 August 1923.
6 OHF, 19 September 1923.
7 OHF, 10 November 1923.
8 Allgäuer Anzeigeblatt (AA), 10 November 1923.
9 OHF, 29 March 1924.
10 Lothar Gruchmann and Reinhard Weber with Otto von Gritschneder (eds), Der Hitler-Prozess 1924: Wortlaut der Hauptverhandlung vor dem Volksgericht München I (The Hitler Trial 1924: Text of the Main Hearing before the People's Court, Munich I) (Munich: Institut für Zeitgeschichte, 1997–9), pp. 1232–3.
11 OGF, 21 January 1920.
12 Karl Baum to Westermayer, 1 July 1925, Landeskirchliches Archiv der Evangelisch-Lutherischen Kirche in Bayern (LAELKB KrD, München) 866, quoted in Otto Nübel, Die Oberstdorfer Christuskirche im Dritten Reich – ein Beitrag zur Geschichte der Bekennenden Kirche im Oberallgäu (Oberstdorf's Christ Church in the Third Reich – A Contribution to the History of the Confessing Church in the Oberallgäu) (Oberstdorf: Evangelische Kirchengemeinde, 2017), p. 14.
13 OHF, 19 November 1924.
14 OGF, 1 April 1926.
15 OGF, 25 May 1926.
16 OGF, 22 June 1926.
17 OGF, 3 July 1926.

Chapter 3

1 Weinlein to Goebbels, 14 March 1934, Bundesarchiv Berlin, Oberstes Partei Gericht (OPG) (Supreme Party Court), Parteiausschlussverfahren gegen Weinlein, Scheller und Ehefrauen, Franoux, (Party Expulsion Proceedings against Weinlein, Scheller and their wives, Franoux), File R 9361/I 41628, pp. 84–7.
2 OGF, 9 November 1933.
3 OGF, 19 July 1930.
4 Detlef Mühlberger, Hitler's Voice: The Völkischer Beobachter, 1920–1933, Vol. 1 (Peter Lang, n.p. 2005), p. 399.
5 OGF, 17 April 1930.

6   *OGF*, 9 September 1930.
7   Interview with Eugen Thomma, son of Fridolin and Eugenie, Oberstdorf, March 2018.
8   *OGF*, 16 September 1930.
9   Hermann Otto Hoyer, unpublished manuscript, private collection. Given to the owner (who wishes to remain anonymous) by Hoyer's daughter and sent to Julia Boyd electronically.
10 Weinlein to Goebbels, ibid. op cit.
11 *OGF*, 5 January 1931.
12 Ibid.
13 *OGF*, 3 March 1931.
14 Bundesarchiv, 17 October 1935, OPG, R9361/1 141629, p. 334, Rudolf Scheller to *Gaugericht* (Regional Court).

Chapter 4

1   Interview with the late Thea Stempfle, 2008.
2   *OGF*, 13 October 1931.
3   *OGF*, 21 June 1932.
4   *OGF*, 30 June 1932.
5   *OGF*, 10 March 1932.
6   Ibid.
7   *OGF*, 7 November 1931.
8   *OGF*, 25 July 1931.
9   See Wikipedia https://en.wikipedia.org/wiki/Bavarian_Landtag_elections _in_the_Weimar_Republic
10 *OGF*, 2 August 1932.
11 *OGF*, 8 November 1932.
12 Constantia Rumbold, daughter of the British Ambassador Sir Horace Rumbold, n.d. private collection.
13 *OGF*, 7 March 1933.
14 Ibid.
15 *OGF*, 25 March 1933.
16 *OGF*, 4 March 1933.
17 *OGF*, 23 March 1933.
18 *AA*, 14 March 1933.

Chapter 5

1   Erich Ebermayer, 21 March 1933, *Denn heute gehört uns Deutschland: Persönliches und politisches Tagebuch* (*Because Today Germany Belongs to Us: Personal and Political Diary*) (Hamburg and Vienna: Paul Zsolnay, 1959), quoted in *The Nazi German Sourcebook*, ed. Roderick Stackelberg (London: Routledge, 2002), p. 46.

2 Madeleine Kent, *I Married a German* (New York: Harper & Brothers, 1939), p. 172.
3 *OGF*, 22 April 1933.
4 Municipal Council Record Book 1933, Archiv Marktgemeinde Oberstdorf, p. 92.
5 Ibid., p. 93.
6 Ibid., p. 94.
7 Ibid.
8 Ernst Zettler and Heinz Groth, *Allgäuer Alpen: Ein Führer für Täler, Hütten und Berge* (*Allgäuer Alps: A Guide to the Valleys, Huts and Mountains*) (Berlin: Deutsche Union 1936), various subsequent editions.
9 Municipal Council Record Book 1933, p. 94.
10 Frau Trudl Heckmair (widow of the mountaineer Anderl Heckmair, who with a fellow German and two Austrians was the first to climb the north face of the Eiger) worked for Müller as a sixteen-year-old bank clerk after the war. She remembered him as a 'small, mousey man – easily overlooked'. Her contract stipulated that she finish work at 1 p.m. on Saturdays. But Müller would read his newspaper all morning until the clock struck one, at which point he would summon Trudl for several hours' dictation. Interview with Trudl Heckmair, 7 March 2018.
11 *OGF*, 2 May 1933.
12 Municipal Council Record Book 1933, p. 98.
13 *OGF*, 7 September 1933.
14 *OGF*, 30 September 1933.
15 *OGF*, 8 April, 1933.
16 Protokollbuch Fischerei-Verein (Fishing Society Record Book), 8 July 1925–28 April 1942, private archive, Dr Michael Klotz, p. 92.
17 *OGF*, 1 April, 1933.
18 See 'Bavaria Germany', Jewish Virtual Library.
19 Bundesarchiv, Berlin, OPG R 9361/I 41628 S.56/57.

Chapter 6

1 Weinlein to Reichs Uschla, 25 May 1933, Bundesarchiv Berlin, OPG R 9361/1 41628, p. 1.
2 Ibid.
3 Scheller to Reichs Uschla, n.d., July 1933, Bundesarchiv Berlin, OPG R 9361/1 41628, p. 17.
4 Zettler to Swabian Court, 30 June 1935, Bundesarchiv Berlin, OPG R 9361/1 41629, p. 226.
5 Karl Wahl to Weinlein, 7 July 1933, Bundesarchiv Berlin, OPG R 9361/1 41628, p. 8.

6   Scheller to Reichs Uschla, n.d., July 1933, ibid., p. 17.

7   Ibid., 11 July 1933, p. 13.

8   Anna-Lisa Thomsen to Walter Buch, 2 October 1933, Bundesarchiv Berlin, OPG R 9361/1 41628, p. 50.

9   Statement by Tilly Lang, 9 October 1933, ibid., p. 55.

10 Lili Scheller to Reichs Uschla, 11 November 1933, ibid., p. 61.

11 Weinlein to Goebbels, 14 March 1934, ibid., p. 85.

12 Scheller to Dannhauer, 18 October 1935, Bundesarchiv Berlin, OPG R 9361/1 41630, p. 140.

13 Wolf to OPG, Court II, 7 November 1935, Bundesarchiv Berlin, OPG R 9361/1 41630, p. 87.

14 OPG, Court III: Statement of Reasons, 7 July 1936, ibid., pp. 202–9.

15 Schmid to Zettler (via Dr Hartwig), 19 October 1936, ibid., p. 241.

16 Weinlein personal file, ibid., Bundesarchiv Berlin, OPG R 9361/1 58681.

17 Harvey Solomon, *Such Splendid Prisons: Diplomatic Detainment in America During World War II* (Sterling, VA: Potomac Books, 2020), pp. 13–14.

18 Paul Starobin, 'Fake News and Election Meddling 1940s Style', https://www.historynet.com/fake-news-1940s-style.htm

Chapter 7

1   *OGF*, 26 June 1933.

2   *OGF*, 28 October 1933.

3   Ibid.

4   *OGF*, 12 September 1933.

5   *OGF*, 17 December 1935.

6   *OGF*, 8 November 1934.

7   Pamphlet, *Deutsches Bauerntum* (*German Farmers*), 11–18 November 1934, Archiv Marktgemeinde Oberstdorf.

8   *OGF*, 15 December 1934.

9   Weinlein to Goebbels, 14 March 1934, Bundesarchiv, Berlin, R/9361/I 41628, pp. 84–5.

10 Ivone Kirkpatrick to R.F. Wigram, 17 September 1935, NA FO/371/18858.

Chapter 8

1   *OGF*, 13 February 1934.

2   Katrin Fitzherbert, *True to Both My Selves* (London: Virago Press, 1997), p. 58.

3   Sybille von Arminsted, unpublished memoir, and interview 13 January 2008.

4   Interview with the Berktold sisters, 2008.

5   *OGF*, 14 August 1934.

6   *OGF*, 20 July 1935.

7   Franz Noichl, 'Warten was kommt: Wahrheiten aus meinem Leben' ('Waiting to See What Happens: Truths from my Life'), unpublished memoir. All subsequent quotes from Noichl come from this source.

8   G. Kahl-Furthmann (ed.), *Hans Schemm spricht: Seine Reden und Sein Werk* (*Hans Schemm Speaks: His Speeches and his Work*) (Bayreuth: Gauverlag Bayerische Ostmark, 1935) translated by Randall Bytwerk, https://research.calvin.edu/german-propaganda-archive/schemm.htm

9   Amy Buller, *Darkness Over Germany* (London: The Right Book Club, 1945), p. 4.

10 Privat-Realschule Oberstdorf, *Jahresbericht* (annual report) 1935/36, p. 17.

11 State Archive Augsburg (St AA), Spruchkammer Sonthofen, B, 159/58.

12 von Arminsted interview, 19 February 2001.

13 *OGF*, 11 March 1934.

14 *OGF*, 5 March 1935.

15 von Arminsted interview.

16 Ibid.

17 Ibid.

18 'Die Erziehungsgrundsätze des neuen Deutschlands' ('The Educational Principles of the New Germany'), 22 (1936/37), pp. 692–3, https://research.calvin.edu/german-propaganda-archive/frau01.htm

19 *OGF*, 6 April 1935.

Chapter 9

1   Nübel, p. 32.

2   Immenstadt Parish archive, *Kirchenkampf* (*The Church's Struggle*), PAI, 1938, 18/102; quoted in Nübel, p. 27.

3   Hans Gollwitzer.

4   Lindau Parish archive, St Stephan, Pastor Kühn to Landeskirchenrat LKR (Regional Church Council), 11 March 1935, PAL, L 18; quoted in Nübel, p. 32.

5   *OGF*, 21 November 1933.

6   Nübel, p. 98.

7   See Richard J. Evans, *The Third Reich in Power* (London: Penguin, 2005), p. 234.

8   Donald J. Dietrich, *Catholic Citizens in the Third Reich* (New Brunswick: Transaction Publishers, 1988), p. 103.

9   Chronik des Schulklosters (Nuns' record book), 1934, Haus Tanneck, Oberstdorf.

10 Ibid.

11 *OGF*, 2 October 1934.

12 See Alexander Rössle, *Unser Oberstdorf*, '100 Jahre Volkschule' ('100 Years of Primary School on Ludwigstrasse'), 1 December 2007, issue 51.

13 Related by Angelika Patel.

14 Nuns' record book.

15 Ibid.

16 Ibid.

17 *OGF*, 18 February 1936.

18 Ibid.

19 Dr T. Steiner, *Wörterbuch der Oberstdorfer Mundart, 2003* (*Dictionary of the Oberstdorf Dialect*), CD, *A Minischtranteg'schichtle* (A Little Story)

20 Ibid.

21 Archiv des Bistums Augsburg (Archive of the Diocese of Augsburg), ABA GV PfAkt Oberstdorf.

22 Ibid.

23 Ibid.

24 Oberstdorf Registry Office.

25 Interview with Dr Thaddäus Steiner, 22 July 2017.

Chapter 10

1 Quoted in Evans, p. 337.

2 T. Steiner.

3 'Österreichs Anschluss an das Deutsche Reich März 1938' ('Austrian Union with the German Reich in March 1938'), *Der Spiegel*, 1 February 1988.

4 Ibid.

5 Ibid.

6 T. Steiner

7 Ibid.

8 Information provided by Raab's son, Rudi Raab in 2020. See also Rudi Raab and Julie Freestone, *Stumbling Stone* (Richmond, CA: Alvarado Press, 2015), Part III, *Gerhard's Stumbling Stone*.

9 *Oberallgäuer Nationalzeitung*, 17 April 1938.

10 Interview with Eugen Thomma.

11 Helen Löwin interview, 15 July 1983, Marquette University, Libraries Department, Special Collections and Archives.

12 Henriëtte Laman Trip-de Beaufort, *Gisteren en Vandaag* (*Yesterday and Today*) (Haarlem: H.D. Tjeenk Willink & Zoon, 1961), p. 21.

13 Ibid., p. 23.

14 Ibid., p. 21.

15 'Jot' to Julius Löwin, 21 September 1921, letter in possession of the widow of Julius's son John Löwin.
16 *Oberallgäuer Nationalzeitung*, 3 August 1938.
17 Archiv Marktgemeinde Oberstdorf, letter dated 11 November 1937, Box 108/3.
18 See copy of unsigned letter, 19 November 1937, and transcript of report signed by Deputy Mayor Hans Kögler, 24 September 1938, Archiv Marktgemeinde Oberstdorf, Box 108/3.
19 Ibid.
20 Major Schrank to Deputy Mayor Kögler, n.d., Archiv Marktgemeinde Oberstdorf, Box 108/3.
21 DAV Record Books (1–3), p. 277.
22 DÖAV AGM, 24 January 1924, Record Book (1).
23 Quoted in *St Galler Tagblatt*, 24 July 2013.
24 *Berg Heil! Alpenverein und Bergsteigen 1918–1945* (*Hail the Mountain! Alpine and Mountaineering Club 1918–1945*) (Vienna: Böhlau, 2011), p. 142.
25 Fritz Kasparek, *A Mountaineer* (Salzburg: Bergland Books, 1939), p. 224. This passage was omitted in later editions.
26 Anderl Heckmair, *My Life* (Seattle: Mountaineers Books, 2002), p. 104.
27 Leni Riefenstahl, *Leni Riefenstahl, A Memoir* (New York: Picador USA, 1995), pp. 214–15.
28 Heckmair, p. 109.
29 Ibid.

Chapter 11

1 Archiv Marktgemeinde Oberstdorf, Box 13 E.
2 Information supplied by Angelika Patel, a close friend of Max Maile.
3 Alfons Meinlinger, unpublished diary, 28 August 1939, private collection. Meinlinger is not the soldier's real name as his family wish him to remain anonymous.
4 Ibid., 31 August 1939.
5 James Lucas, *Hitler's Mountain Troops* (London: Cassell, 1992), p. 20.
6 Meinlinger, 7 September 1939.
7 Ibid., 13 September 1939.
8 Ibid., 21 September 1939.
9 Quoted in Evans, p. 11.
10 Meinlinger, 27 May 1940.
11 Ibid., 26 June 1940.
12 Ibid., 9 April 1941.
13 Ibid., 13 April 1941.

14 Howard K. Smith, *Last Train from Berlin* (London: Cresset Press, 1942), p. 38.
15 Ibid., pp. 84–5.

Chapter 12
1 Michael Burleigh, *Death and Deliverance* (London: Pan Books, 2002), p. 154.
2 The material concerning Theodor and the Gschwender family has come either directly from Ingrid Weissenberger, Theodor's niece, or from her book *Das Trettach Hotel* (Hamburg: Tredition GmbH, 2018).
3 Evans, p. 77.
4 Burleigh, p. 67.
5 Michael von Cranach (ed.), *Psychiatrie im Nationalsozialismus, Die Bayerischen Heil- und Pflegeanstalten zwischen 1933 und 1945* (*Psychiatry under National Socialism: The Bavarian Sanatoria and Nursing Homes Between 1933 and 1945*) (Munich: R. Oldenbourg, 1999), pp. 270–71.
6 Ibid., p. 61
7 Evans, p. 81.
8 *The Nuremberg Trial Against the Chief War Criminals from 14 November 1945 to 1 October 1946: Documents and other Evidence*, Vol. XXVI, first published Nuremberg, 1947 (Munich: Delphin, 1989), Official Text German Edition, No. 405-PS to No. 1063(d)-PS, document 630-PS, p. 169.
9 Quoted in Robert Jay Lifton, *The Nazi Doctors* (New York: Basic Books, 1986), p. 63.
10 Evans, p. 76.
11 Quoted in Thomas Stöckle, *Grafeneck 1940: Die Euthanasie-Verbrechen in Südwestdeutschland* (*The Euthanasia Crimes in South-West Germany*) (Tübingen: Silberburg, 2002), pp. 111–12.
12 Quoted in Burleigh, p. 147.
13 Quoted in Evans, p. 87.
14 See ibid., p. 89.
15 Ibid., pp. 90–98.
16 See Burleigh, p. 154.

Chapter 13
1 'Der Führer an das deutsche Volk 22. Juni 1941' ('The Führer to the German People'), in Philipp Bouhler (ed.), *Der grossdeutsche Freiheitskampf, Reden Adolf Hilters* (*Greater Germany's Freedom Fight: Speeches by Adolf Hitler*), Vol. 3 (Munich: Franz Eher, 1942), pp. 51–61.
2 Jonathan Dimbleby, *Barbarossa*, p. 134.

3 Bouhler, pp. 51–61.
4 Noichl.
5 DAV Record Book, 4 April 1940.
6 Ibid., 1941.
7 Harrer, *The White Spider*, p. 84.
8 Heckmair, pp. 163–4.
9 Meinlinger, 1 June 1941.
10 'Tagesbefehl, unterzeichnet von Lanz' ('Order of the Day, signed by Lanz'), NA: T-315/39-1247, Divisions 21 June 1941. Quoted in H.F. Meyer, *Blutiges Edelweiß: Die 1 Gebirgsdivision im Zweiten Weltkrieg* (*Bloodstained Edelweiss: The 1st Mountain Division in the Second World War*) (Berlin: Ch. Links Verlag, 2007), p. 53.
11 Ray Merriam (ed.), *Gebirgsjäger: Germany's Mountain Troops* (Bennington, VT: Merriam Press, 2015), p. 28.
12 Ibid., pp. 28–9 and Lucas, p. 89.
13 Lucas, p. 88.
14 Merriam, p. 28.
15 Quoted in Lucas, pp. 88–9.
16 Meinlinger, 7 July 1941.
17 Meinlinger, October 1941.
18 Heckmair, interview 2004.
19 Aurich's late daughter, Karin Prenzel, donated her father's diary to the Gebirgsjäger museum in Sonthofen. This has now closed and its contents transferred to the Archiv Marktgemeinde Oberstdorf.
20 Aurich, 5 October 1941.
21 Ibid., 6 October 1941.
22 Ibid., 8 October 1941.
23 Ibid., 9 October 1941.
24 Jewish Virtual Library.
25 Walter Flex, *Für dich, mein Vaterland!* (*For You, My Fatherland!*) (Munich: C.H. Beck, 1939).
26 Aurich, 13 October 1941.
27 Ibid., 16 October 1941.
28 Ibid.
29 Ibid., 19 October 1941.
30 Ibid., 20 October 1941.
31 Ibid., 22 October 1941.
32 Ibid., 20 October 1941.
33 Ibid., 25 October 1941.
34 Ibid., 29 October 1941.
35 Ibid.

36   Ibid., 4 November 1941.
37   Ibid., 5 November 1941.
38   Ibid., 13 November 1941.
39   Ibid.

Chapter 14

1   DAV Record Book, p. 16.
2   Ibid.
3   Ibid.
4   *Unser Oberstdorf*: 'Oberstdorf vor 50 Jahren' (*Our Oberstdorf*: 'Oberstdorf 50 Years Ago'), Otmar Schuster, 1993, issue 22.
5   *Unser Oberstdorf*: 'Die Glocken der Kath. Pfarrkirche Oberstdorf' (Teil 2)' (*Our Oberstdorf*: 'The Bells of the Parish Church Oberstdorf', (Part 2)), Issue 7.
6   Meyer, p. 111.
7   Hannes Heer, Walther Manoschek, Alexander Pollak and Ruth Wodack, *The Discursive Construction of History: Remembering the Wehrmacht's War of Annihilation* (New York: Palgrave Macmillan, 2008), pp. 117–19.
8   The Wehrmacht Propaganda Department, quoted in Horst Boog, Jürgen Förster, Joachim Hoffman, Ernst Klink, Rolf-Dieter Müller and Gerd R. Ueberschär, *Germany and the Second World War* (Oxford: Clarendon Press, 1998), Vol. IV, p. 516.
9   Omer Bartov, *The Eastern Front, 1941–1945: German Troops and the Barbarization of Warfare* (London: Palgrave Macmillan, 2001), p. 49.
10   Records of the USA Nuremberg War Criminal Trials, Vol. 4, pp. 581–4.
11   Ibid., p. 582.
12   Ibid., p. 409.
13   Ibid., Prosecutor Brigadier General Telford Taylor, p. 500.
14   Camille Allaz, *The History of Air Cargo and Airmail from the 18th Century* (London: Christopher Foyle Publishing, 2005), p. 149.
15   Ibid., p. 150.
16   Interview, Thea Joas, 19 June 2008.
17   Speech by Ludwig Fink given at the 'Memorial Service for Fallen Heroes', 8 November 1942, Archiv Marktgemeinde Oberstdorf, Box 13 E.
18   Letter from the mayor's office (signed by Deputy Mayor Kögler) to the Hofmann family, 22 January 1943, Archiv Marktgemeinde Oberstdorf, Box 13 E.
19   These statistics are deduced from the names and dates inscribed in the Oberstdorf memorial chapel. Further records are to be found in the Archiv Marktgemeinde Oberstdorf, Box 13 E.

Chapter 15

1 *Oberallgäuer Nationalzeitung,* 8 and 24 September 1942.

2 *Oberallgäuer Nationalzeitung,* 8 September 1942.

3 Meinlinger, n.d., August 1942.

4 Ibid.

5 *Oberallgäuer Nationalzeitung,* 24 September 1942.

6 Ibid.

7 Ruslan Budnik, 'The Highest Soviet Hotel', *War History Online,* 31 December 2018.

8 Josef Martin Bauer, *Unternehmen 'Elbrus': Das kaukasische Abenteuer 1942 (Operation 'Elbrus': The Caucasian Adventure 1942)* (Esslingen: Bechtle, 1950), revised edition 1976, p. 85.

9 Heinz Groth, radio interview, n.d., typescript in possession of Kaspar Schwarz's family.

10 Roland Kaltenegger, *Major der Reserve Heinz Groth (Major of the Reserve Heinz Groth)* (Würzburg: Flechsig, 2016), p. 78

11 Max Gämmerler, Report, *Der Vorstoss zum Elbrus (The Advance to Elbrus),* p. 4; Militär und Gebirgstruppenarchiv Kaltenegger (Kaltenegger's Military and Mountain Troops archive), quoted in Kaltenegger, p. 77.

12 Groth, radio interview.

13 Bauer, p. 102.

14 Ibid.

15 Kaltenegger, p. 79.

16 Ibid.

17 Groth, radio interview.

18 Albert Speer, *Inside the Third Reich* (New York: Macmillan Company, 1970), p. 239.

Chapter 16

1 '"Nun, Volk steh auf, und Sturm brich los!", Rede im Berliner Sportpalast' ('"Now People Rise and Let the Storm Break!", speech at the Berlin Sports Palace'), *Der steile Aufstieg (The Steep Climb)* (Munich: Zentralverlag der NSDAP, 1944), pp. 167–204.

2 *Oberallgäuer Nationalzeitung,* 8 February 1944.

3 Ibid., 12 January 1945.

4 Interview with Eugen Thomma.

5 Interview with Marianne von Weizsäcker, 6 November 2006.

6 H. de Beaufort to Willem de Beaufort, 29 September 1943, de Beaufort family archive, Utrecht Provincial Archive (HUA).

7 See http://www.stolpersteine-gp.de and unpublished research by Pia Hellweg.

8 For example, on 1 September 1941 there were only 150 Gestapo officials in Nuremberg responsible for a population of nearly 3 million. See Robert Gellately, 'The Gestapo and German Society: Political Denunciation in the Gestapo Case Files', University of Chicago, *Journal of Modern History*, 60, December 1988, p. 687.

9 See Evans, 'Coercion and Consent in Nazi Germany', Raleigh Lecture, British Academy, 2006, *Proceedings of the British Academy*, 151 (London: The British Academy, 2007), pp. 70–71.

10 The Uschla Courts (which dealt with the Zettler case) were only for internal Nazi disputes whereas the People's Courts handled cases for the public at large.

11 Staatsarchiv München, Bestand Staatsanwalten, Sondergericht München (Munich State Archives; public prosecutors' collection, Munich Special Court), (1362) 9056.

12 Ibid., (1655) 3207.

13 Ibid., (1960) 8745.

14 Ibid., (2318) 3709.

15 Ibid., (2754) 4140.

16 Ibid., (4206) 5296 and (3943) 5060.

17 Ibid., (6368) 10560 and (7203) 11391.

18 Recounted by Eugen Thomma.

19 Munich State Archives, public prosecutors' collection; Munich District Court 2, criminal case against Jäger Anton, 10680.

20 Interview with Peter and Otto Jäger (Anton's grandsons), 2020.

21 Interview with Seeweg, 25 March 2000.

22 Munich State Archives, (8187) 12396.

23 J.R. von Salis, *Weltchronik 1939–1945* (Zurich: Orell Füssli, 1966), p. 223.

24 Ibid, p. 238.

25 Interview with Trudl Heckmair, 12 March 2018.

26 See Meyer, pp. 208–38.

27 Ibid., pp. 405–23. See also Louis de Bernières, *Captain Corelli's Mandolin* (London: Secker & Warburg, 1994).

28 Meinlinger, 21 January 1944.

Chapter 17

1 See Mark Spoerer and Jocken Fleischhacker, 'Forced Laborers in Nazi Germany: Categories, Numbers and Survivors', *Journal of Interdisciplinary History*, 33 (2) (Autumn 2002), p. 172.

2 Evans, p. 348.

3 Ibid., pp. 353–4.

4 Letter written by Andrzej Burzawa, 26 October 1999, Archive of the Dachau Concentration Camp Memorial Site, Birgsau sub-camp, ref: 34.103. This letter, together with others dated 9 November 1999 and 5 and 13 March 2000, have been collated into one document and are the source of all the material used here relating to Burzawa's experiences.

5 See Markus Naumann, *Spuren im Wald: Messerschmitt/Werkzeugbau Kottern und das KZ-Aussenlanger in Fischen* (*Traces in the Forest: Messerschmitt/Werkzeubau Kottern and the KZ Ausslanger in Fischen*) (Friedberg: Likias, 2017).

6 John C. Beyer and Stephen A. Schneider, *Forced Labour under Third Reich* (Washington, DC: Nathan Associates, 1999), https://www.google.com/search?client=safari&rls=en&q=John+C.+Beyer;+Stephen+A.+Schneider.+Forced+Labour+under+Third+Reich,+(Washington+D.C.:+Nathan+Associates,+1999)&ie=UTF-8&oe=UTF-8

7 Interview published in the Dutch newspaper *Het Parool*, 'In Het Hol van de Leeuw' ('Inside the Lion's Den'), 3 May 1963.

8 Ibid.

9 de Beaufort, pp. 22–23

10 Ibid.

11 H. de Beaufort to Willem de Beaufort, 14 August 1943, de Beaufort family archives, Utrecht Provincial Archive (HUA).

12 de Beaufort, p. 26.

13 H. de Beaufort to Willem de Beaufort, 9 January 1944.

14 *Het Parool*.

15 Ibid.

16 de Beaufort, p. 25.

Chapter 18

1 Dr Caroline Neubaur has provided the information concerning her grandfather General Beck and her mother Gertrud Neubaur.

2 Gertrud Neubaur to Wilhelm Beck, 26 July 1944, private collection.

3 Ian Kershaw, *Hitler 1936–1945: Nemesis* (W.W. Norton & Co, 2001), p. 693.

4 Martin Broszat et al. (eds), *Bayern in der NS Zeit* (*Bavaria in the National Socialist Era*) (Munich: Oldenbourg, 1977–83), Vol. 1, p. 667, quoted in Evans, p. 651.

5 German Federal Archives, Military Archive, record group H3/665, quoted in Alfred-Maurice de Zayas, *A Terrible Revenge: The Ethnic Cleansing of the East Germans 1944–1950* (New York: St Martin's Press, 1994), p. 50.

6   Quoted in Paul Erker, 'Revolution des Dorfes? Ländliche Bevölkerung zwischen Flüchtingsstrom und landwirtschftlichem Strukturwandel' ('Revolution of the Villages? The Rural Population Between the Influx of Refugees and Agricultural Structural Change', in Martin Broszat et al. (eds), *Von Stalingrad zur Währungsreform, Zur Sozialgeschichte des Umbruchs in Deutschland* (*From Stalingrad to Agricultural Reform: On the Social History of the Structural Change in Germany*) (Munich: Oldenbourg Wissenschaftsverlag, 1988), p. 378.

7   Hans Schnell, interview 14 January 2008.

8   Interview with Anneliese Titscher, née Berktold, 4 August 2008.

9   Interview with Professor Karl Ruhrberg, 17 February 2004.

10 Ibid.

11 Richard Evans estimates that 175,000 were killed; see 'Into Dust', *London Review of Books*, Vol. 33, No. 17, 8 September 2011.

12 Quoted from Theo Sommer's memoir, sent by Sommer to Julia Boyd, 13 May 2019.

13 Ibid.

14 Ibid.

15 Official report on KU 3738; see www.486th.org/Photos/Stammlager/KU3738/KU3738eng-5.htm

16 Ibid.

17 Sommer, memoir.

Chapter 19

1   Eva Noack-Mosse, *Last Days of Theresienstadt* (Madison: University of Wisconsin Press, 2018), p. 11. The original diary can be viewed on microfilm at the Wiener Holocaust Library in London, ref: 504D/1.

2   Elfriede Ruhrberg, interview 28 June 2019.

3   Günther Lützow and Wolfgang Falck.

4   https://neunundzwanzigsechs.de/luetzow-trautloft-falck-eine-fundsache/

5   Hans Schnell interview.

6   Ibid.

7   See Richard Evans's lecture, 'Ordinary Germans and the Final Solution', published on his website.

8   Ruhrberg interview.

9   Bertl Wirtz (née Weissenberger), interview 2008.

10 Pauli Rössle interview, 29 March 2006.

11 Ruhrberg interview.

12 Wirtz interview.

13 See Evans, lecture, ibid.

14 Ibid.

15 Evans, lecture, ibid.

16   See Peter Longerich, *'Davon haben wir nichts gewusst!': Die Deutschen und die Judenverfolgung 1933–1945 ('We Knew Nothing About It!': The Germans and the Persecution of the Jews 1933–1945)* (München: Pantheon, 2007), p. 148.

17   Ian Kershaw, *Hitler, Germany, and the Final Solution* (New Haven: Yale University Press, 2008), p. 140.

18   Ibid., p. 11.

19   Hans Schnell interview.

20   Noack-Mosse, p. 12.

21   See Wolf Gruner, *Jewish Forced Labor Under the Nazis: Economic Needs and Racial Aims, 1938–1944* (Cambridge: CUP, 2006), pp. 97–8.

22   Noack-Mosse, p. 13.

23   Ibid.

24   Ibid., p. 11.

25   Noack-Mosse, p. 15.

26   Ibid., p. 18.

27   Ibid.

28   Ibid., p. 24.

29   Ibid.

30   Ibid., p. 47.

31   Ibid., p. 44.

Chapter 20

1   Nicolaus von Below, *Als Hitlers Adjutant 1937–1945 (As Hitler's Adjutant, 1937–1945)* (Frankfurt am Main: Hase & Koehler, 1980), p. 398.

2   'Trial of Gauleiter Arthur Greiser', *Law Reports of Trials of War Criminals*, United Nations War Crimes Commission (New York: Wm. S. Hein Publishing, 1997), p. 86.

3   Interview with Sybille von Arminsted, 2 February 2001.

4   Ibid.

5   Ibid.

6   Interviews with Elfriede Ruhrberg (née Bierbichler), 17 February 2004 and 28 June 2019. All subsequent information regarding her experiences is from these sources.

7   Noack-Mosse, pp. 99–100.

8   Ibid., pp. 104 and 106.

9   Ibid., p. 119.

10   General Hans-Adolf Prützmann.

11   *Washington Post*, 6 April 1945, p. 1.

12   Rudolf Raab, diary, quoted in Julie Freestone and Rudi Raab Jr, *Stumbling Stone* (n.p.: Alvarado Press, 2015), pp. 165–6.

Chapter 21

1 Franz J. Pfister, letter 1 March 1946 describing the formation of the Oberstdorf Heimatschutz, Institut für Zeitgeschichte (Institute for Contemporary History), Munich, ZS/A/4 Bd. 3.

2 Alfons Köberle, 'Werden und Wirken des Walsertaler Heimatschutzes' ('Development and Work of the Walser Valley Homeland Security'), typescript copy of the lost original, n.d., Vorarlberger Landesarchiv (Vorarlberg State Archive), Bregenz.

3 Hans Falk, *Allgäuer Anzeigeblatt*, 26 July 1947.

4 Noichl.

5 Burzawa.

6 Ibid.

7 Affidavit signed by two *Heimatschutz* men, originally in a file assembled by the lawyer Dr Georg Weiss, dated 22 March 1953 and later in the possession of Hans Stadler's daughter.

8 Interview on 5 December 1994 with the then eighty-seven-year-old Maria Mayer, innkeeper at the Birgsau inn, who remembered the evening of 27 April 1945 with exceptional clarity.

9 Bayerisches Hauptstaatsarchiv (Bavarian State Archive), MJu 23459.

10 *Allgäuer Anzeigeblatt*, 3 May 1995.

11 Pauli Rössle, interview 29 March 2006.

12 Elisabeth Dabelstein to Almuth Mezger, 15 July 1945, private collection.

13 Dabelstein to Mezger.

14 Ibid.

15 See André François-Poncet, *Tagebuch eines Gefangenen* (*Diary of a Prisoner*), ed. Dr Thomas Gayda, trans. Barbara Sommer, Geneviève Unger-Forray, Konstanze Hollweg, Sybille Segovia (Berlin: Europaverlag, 2015), p. 256.

16 A photocopy of this letter is in the Archiv Marktgemeinde Oberstdorf; the original is in the Bayerisches Hauptstaatsarchiv (Bavarian State Archive).

17 Köberle.

18 Copies of handwritten statements, Bavarian State Archive, StK 11398.

19 Dabelstein to Mezger.

20 Archiv Marktgemeinde Oberstdorf, Box 108/2.

21 Noichl.

22 Josef Geiger Sr, interview, February 2001.

23 Bavarian State Archive, MJu 23459.

24 Leonore Gutermann, diary, 7 May 1945. The diary remains in the possession of Leonore Gutermann's family.

25 Burzawa.

Chapter 22

1   Interview with Thea Stempfle, 2008, whose mother was one of the village women who sewed the gloves and gaiters.

2   'De Gaulle in den Bayerischen Alpen, Teil 2' (De Gaulle in the Bavarian Alps, Part 2), *Sie und Er*, n.d., May 1945; see also Dr Thaddäus Steiner, *Unser Oberstdorf*, 1 December 2007, issue 51.

3   Ibid.

4   Ibid.

5   Ibid.

6   Ibid.

7   Ibid.

8   Thomas Neidhart to the French commander, 14 May 1945, Archiv Marktgemeinde Oberstdorf, Box 108/2.

9   Dabelstein to Mezger, ibid.

10 Interviews with Trudl Heckmair, 2004 and 2018.

11 Dabelstein to Mezger.

12 Nübel, pp. 131–2.

13 Interview with Anderl and Trudl Heckmair, 2004.

14 Heckmair, p. 164.

15 Heini Müller.

16 Information supplied by Meinlinger's nephew.

17 Interview with Fridolin's son Eugen Thomma, March 2018.

18 Information provided by the late Max Maile.

19 State Archive Augsburg, Spruchkammer, Sonthofen, L9, 12 July 1946.

20 Noack-Mosse, p. 121.

21 Rolf Steininger, *Deutsche Geschichte: Darstellung und Dokumente* (*German History: Presentation and Documents*), Vol. 1, 1945–7 (Frankfurt am Main: Fischer, 2002), p. 47 ff.

22 Undated memos, Archiv Marktgemeinde Oberstdorf, Box 108/5.

23 Dabelstein to Mezger.

24 Quoted in Angelika Patel, *Unser Oberstdorf*, 'Der Umsturz in Oberstdorf' ('The Coup in Oberstdorf'), 1 December 2000, issue 37.

25 Dabelstein to Mezger.

26 *Berliner Morgenpost*, 5 October 1944.

27 Dabelstein to Mezger.

28 Noichl.

29 *Unser Oberstdorf*, 'Oberstdorf vor 50 Jahren', 1 June 1998, issue 32.

30 Gehring to Schratt et al., 5 December 1945, Archiv Marktgemeinde Oberstdorf, Box 108/5.

31 Friedrich Prinz, *Die Integration der Flüchtlinge und Vertriebenen in Bayern* (*The Integration of Refugees and Displaced Persons in Bavaria*) (Augsburg: Haus d. Bayer. Gesch., 2000), p. 4.

32 Martin Broszat, Klaus Dietmar Henke and Hans Woller (eds), *Von Stalingrad zur Währungsreform: Zur Sozialgeschichte des Umbruchs in Deutschland* (*From Stalingrad to Monetary Reform: On the Social History of Change in Germany*) (Berlin: Walter de Gruyter, 1990), p. 384.

33 Carl Zuckmayer, *Deutschlandbericht für das Kriegsministerium der Vereinigten Staaten von Amerika* (*Germany Report for the War Department of the United States of America*), ed. Gunther Nickel, Johanna Schrön and Hans Wagener (Göttingen: Wallstein, Zuckmayer Publications, 2004), p. 111 f.

34 Victor Gollancz, *In Darkest Germany* (London: Gollancz, 1947), p. 28.

35 *Allgäuer Anzeigeblatt*, 21 December 1946.

36 *Allgäuer Anzeigeblatt*, 22 December 1948.

Chapter 23

1 Noack-Mosse to Zuckmayer, 19 July 1946, Carl Zuckmayer Collection, Deutsches Literaturarchiv (German Literature Archive), Marbach.

2 Ibid.

3 Christa Horn, *Die Internierungs- und Arbeitslager in Bayern 1945–1952* (*Internment and Labour Camps in Bavaria 1945–1952*) (Frankfurt am Main: Peter Lang, 1992), p. 22 f.

4 Zuckmayer, *Deutschlandbericht* (*Germany Report*) (Göttingen: Wallstein Verlag, 2004), p. 137.

5 Claudia Kalesse, 'Spruchkammerakten im Staatsarchiv Augsburg' ('Spruchkammer Files in the State Archive'), in Peter Fassl, *Das Kriegsende in Schwaben 1945* (*The End of the War in Swabia, 1945*) (n.p.: Satz und Grafik Partner, 2005), p. 249 f.

6 *Allgäuer Anzeigeblatt*, 29 October 1946.

7 Compiled by Elisabeth Luther-Heckel, 'The Oberstdorf Branch of the NSDAP', unpublished MS, Berlin 2009. Her list includes the one that was also compiled by the American occupying forces, Archiv Marktgemeinde Oberstdorf. Other names have been subsequently added.

8 Archiv Marktgemeinde Oberstdorf, *Spruchkammer* Box.

9 Ibid., certified copy of Schubert file, 16 April 1952.

10 Landesarchiv Baden-Württemberg Sigmaringen (Baden-Württemberg State Archives, Sigmaringen): Wü 13 T 2 654 – 010, Wü 13 T 2-2713 – 028, Wü 13 T 2-2839 – 004, Wü 13 T 2-2653/082.

11 Carl Zuckmayer, *A Part of Myself* (New York: Carroll & Graf, 1984), p. 397. See also Angelika Patel, 'Ein unbekannter Mensch in der Maske des Bösen' ('An Unknown Man Wearing the Mask of Evil'), *Unser Oberstdorf*, 1 June 2006, issue 48.

12   Bavarian State Archives, Munich, Section A, Box 410, certified copy, 19 April 1948.
13   Baden-Württemberg State Archives, Wü 13 T 2- 2653/082, Dr Fritz Kalhammer, p. 7.
14   Landesarchiv Sigmaringen, Wü 13 T 2 2839/004, 23 April 1950.
15   See *Allgäuer Anzeigeblatt*, 8 March 1946 in which a forty-one-point checklist appears for all those claiming non-complicity with the Nazis. The list, however, makes no mention of the murders of civilians, Jews, the disabled, Gypsies and homosexuals. See also Wolfgang Benz, *Auftrag Demokratie. Die Gründungsgeschichte der Bundesrepublik und die Entstehung der DDR 1945–1949* (*Mission Democracy: The Founding History of the Federal Republic and the Emergence of the GDR 1945–1949*) (Berlin: Metropol, 2009), p. 93 f.
16   Richard Evans, review in the *New Statesman*, 11 March 2011 of Frederick Taylor, *Exorcising Hitler: The Occupation and Denazification of Germany* (London: Bloomsbury, 2011).
17   Interview with Fink's daughter Ute Menzel, 29 October 2019.

Bibliography

Allaz, Camille, *The History of Air Cargo and Airmail from the 18th Century* (London: Christopher Foyle Publishing, 2005)

Allen, William Sheridan, *The Nazi Seizure of Power: The Experience of a Single German Town 1922–1945* (London: Penguin Books, 1989)

Angier, Carole, *Speak, Silence: In Search of W.G. Sebald* (London: Bloomsbury Circus, 2021)

Baird, Jay W., *The Mythical World of Nazi War Propaganda, 1939–1945* (Minneapolis: University of Minnesota Press, 1975)

Baranowski, Shelley, *Strength Through Joy: Consumerism and Mass Tourism in the Third Reich* (Cambridge: Cambridge University Press, 2004)

Bartov, Omer, *The Eastern Front 1941–1945: German Troops and the Barbarization of Warfare* (Palgrave Macmillan, 2001)

Bartov, Omer, *Hitler's Army: Soldiers, Nazis, and War in the Third Reich* (New York: Oxford University Press, revised edition, 1992)

Bauer, Josef Martin, *Unternehmen "Elbrus": Das Kaukasische Abenteuer 1942* (*Operation 'Elbrus': The Caucasian Adventure*), (Esslingen: Bechtle, 1950, revised edition 1976)

Beevor, Antony, *Stalingrad* (London: Penguin 2007)

Below, Nicolaus von, *Als Hitlers Adjutant 1937–1945* (Frankfurt am Main: Hase & Koehler, 1980)

Bergmeier, Horst J.P., and Lotz, Rainer E., *Hitler's Airwaves: The Inside Story of Nazi Radio Broadcasting and Propaganda Swing* (New Haven: Yale University Press, 1997)

Beyer, John C., Schneider, Stephen A., *Forced Labor under the Third Reich* (Washington DC: Nathan Associates, 1999)

Biddiscombe, Perry, *Werwolf! The History of the National Socialist Guerilla Movement 1944–1946* (Cardiff: University of Wales Press, 1998)

Brendon, Piers, *The Dark Valley: A Panorama of the 1930s* (London: Pimlico, 2001)

Broszat, Martin, *et al.* (eds.), *Bayern in der NS-Zeit* (Munich: 1977–83) 6 Vols

Broszat, Martin; Dietmar, Klaus; Woller, Henke Hans, (eds.), *Von Stalingrad zur Währungsreform, Zur Sozialgeschichte des Umbruchs in Deutschland*

(*From Stalingrad to Currency Reform: A Social History of the Structural Change in Germany*), (München: Oldenbourg Wissenschaftsverlag, 2009)

Brysac, Shareen Blair, (ed.) *Resisting Hitler: Mildred Harnack and the Red Orchestra* (New York: Oxford University Press, 2000)

Buller, Amy, *Darkness over Germany* (London: The Right Book Club, 1945)

Bullock, Alan, *Hitler: A Study in Tyranny* (London: Odhams Press Ltd., 1952)

Burleigh, Michael, *Death and Deliverance, 'Euthanasia' in Germany, c.1900–1945* (London: Pan Books, 2002)

Burleigh, Michael, *Moral Combat: A History of World War II* (HarperPress, 2010)

Burleigh, Michael, *The Third Reich: A New History* (London: Macmillan, 2000)

Cole, Michael, *Just Back From Germany* (London: Faber & Faber, 1938)

Cranach, Michael von (ed.), *Psychiatrie im Nationalsozialismus: Die Bayerischen Heil- und Pflegeanstalten zwischen 1933 und 1945* (*Psychiatry under National Socialism: the Bavarian sanatoria and nursing homes between 1933 and 1945*), (Munich: R. Oldenbourg, 1999)

Dietrich, Donald J., *Catholic Citizens in the Third Reich* (Transaction Publishers, 1988)

Dimbleby, Jonathan, *Barbarossa: How Hitler Lost the War* (Viking 2021)

Ebermayer, Erich, *Denn heute gehört uns Deutschland: Persönliches und politisches Tagebuch*, (*Because Germany Belongs To Us: Personal and Political Diary*), (Hamburg and Vienna: Paul Zsolnay, 1959)

Elon, Amos, *The Pity of It All: A Portrait of Jews in Germany 1743–1933* (London: Allen Lane, 2003)

Evans, Richard J., *The Coming of the Reich* (London: Allen Lane, 2003)

Evans, Richard J., *The Third Reich in Power* (London: Allen Lane, 2005)

Evans, Richard J., *The Third Reich at War* (London: Allen Lane, 2008)

Farquharson, John E., *The Plough and the Swastika: The NSDAP and Agriculture in Germany 1928–1945* (London: Sage Publications, 1976)

Fassl, Peter, *Das Kriegsende in Bayerisch-Schwaben 1945* (*The End of the War in Bavarian Swabia*), (Augsburg: Wißner, 2006)

Fergusson, Adam, *When Money Dies: The Nightmare of the Weimar Hyperinflation* (London: William Kimber & Co. Ltd., 1975)

Fest, Joachim, C., *The Face of the Third Reich* (New York: Pantheon, 1970)

Fitzherbert, Katrin, *True to Both My Selves* (London: Virago Press 1997)

Flex, Walter, *Für dich mein Vaterland* (*For You my Fatherland*), (C.H. Beck, 1939)

Franck, Harry A., *Vagabonding Through Changing Germany* (New York: Grosset & Dunlap, 1920)

François-Poncet, André, *The Fateful Years*, trans. Jacques LeClercq (London: Victor Gollancz, 1949)

François-Poncet, André, *Carnets d'un Captif* (Paris: Librairie Arthème Fayard, 1952)

François-Poncet, André, *Tagebuch eines Gefangenen: Erinnerungen eines Jahrundertzeugen* (*Diary of a Prisoner*), Dr Thomas Gayda (ed.), trans. Barbara Sommer, Geneviève Unger-Forray, Konstanze Hollweg, Sybille Sgovia (Berlin: Europa Verlag, 2015)

Freestone, Julie, and Raab, Rudi, *Stumbling Stone* (Richmond, California: Alvarado Press, 2015)

Friedländer, Saul, *Nazi Germany and the Jews 1933–45* (abridged edition), (New York: Harper Perennial, 2009)

Gellately, Robert, *Backing Hitler: Consent and Coercion in Nazi Germany* (Oxford: Oxford University Press, 2002, illustrated)

Gellately, Robert, *The Gestapo and German Society: Enforcing Racial Policy 1933–1945* (Oxford University Press, USA, 1992)

Goldhagen, Daniel Jonah, *Hitler's Willing Executioners: Ordinary Germans and the Holocaust* (London: Abacus, 1996)

Gollancz, Victor, *In Darkest Germany* (London: Gollancz, 1947)

Griech-Polelle, Beth A., *Bishop von Galen: German Catholicism and National Socialism* (New Haven: Yale University Press, 2003)

Gruchmann, Lothar, and Weber, Reinhard, with Gritschneder, Otto (eds.), *Der Hitler-Prozess 1924*: *Wortlaut der Hauptverhandlung vor dem Volksgericht München* (*The Hitler Trial 1924: Text of the main hearing before the People's Court, Munich I*), (München: 1997–99)

Gruner, Wolf, *Jewish Forced Labor Under the Nazis: Economic Needs and Racial Aims, 1938–1944* (Cambridge: CUP, 2006)

Haffner, Sebastian, *The Ailing Empire: Germany from Bismarck to Hitler* (A. Fromm International Publishing Corporation, 1989)

Harrer, Heinrich, *The White Spider: The Classic Account of the Ascent of the Eiger* (London: Rupert Hart-Davies, 1st ed. 1959)

Heckmair, Anderl, *My Life* (Seattle: Mountaineers Books, 2002)

Heer, Hannes; Manoschek, Walter; Pollak, Alexander; Wodack, Ruth, *The Discursive Construction of History: Remembering the Wehrmacht's War of Annihilation* (New York: Palgrave Macmillan, 2008)

Herbert, Ulrich, *Hitler's Foreign Workers: Enforced Foreign Labor in Germany under the Third Reich* (Cambridge: Cambridge University Press, 1997)

Hitchcock, William, *The Bitter Road to Freedom: A New History of the Liberation of Europe* (The Free Press, 2009)

Hitler, Adolf, *Hitler's Table Talk, 1941–1944*, trans. Norman Cameron, R.H. Stevens (London: Weidenfeld & Nicolson, 1953)

Hoffer, Eric, *The True Believer: Thoughts on the Nature of Mass Movements* (Harper & Row, 1951)

Höhne, Heinz and Barry, R., *The Order of the Death's Head: The Story of Hitler's SS* (London: Secker & Warburg, 1969)

Holmes, Richard, *Acts of War: The Behaviour of Men in Battle* (London: Weidenfeld & Nicolson, 2004)

Homze, Edward L., *Foreign Labor in Nazi Germany* (Princeton: Princeton University Press, 1967)

Horn, Christa, *Die Internierungs- und Arbeitslager in Bayern 1945–1952* (*Internment and Labour Camps in Bavaria 1945–1952*), (Frankfurt am Main: Peter Lang, 1992)

Hoyer, Katja, *Blood and Iron: The Rise and Fall of the German Empire 1871–1918* (Cheltenham: The History Press, 2021)

Hughes, Matthew, and Mann, Chris, *Inside Hitler's Germany: Life under the Third Reich* (Dulles, Va.: Brassey's Inc., 2000)

Jähner, Harald, *Aftermath: Life in the Fallout of the Third Reich 1945–55*, trans. Shaun Whiteside (London: W.H. Allen, 1921)

Jünger, Ernst, *In Stahlgewittern* (first published 1920, many subsequent editions)

Kaltenegger, Roland, *Major der Reserve Heinz Groth* (*Major of the Reserve Heinz Groth*), (Würzburg: Flechsig, 2016)

Kasparek, Fritz, *A Mountaineer* (Salzburg: Bergland Books, 1939)

Kater, Michael H., *Doctors under Hitler* (Chapel Hill: University of North Carolina Press, 1989)

Kater, Michael H., *Hitler Youth* (Harvard University Press, 2006)

Kent, Madeleine, *I Married a German* (New York: Harper & Brothers, 1939)

Kershaw, Ian, *Hitler 1889–1936: Hubris* (London: Allen Lane, 1998)

Kershaw, Ian, *Hitler 1936–45: Nemesis* (W.W. Norton & Co, 2001)

Kershaw, Ian, *The 'Hitler Myth': Image and Reality in the Third Reich* (Oxford: Clarendon Press, 1987)

Kershaw, Ian, *Popular Opinion and Political Dissent in the Third Reich: Bavaria 1933–1945* (Oxford: Clarendon Press, 1983)

Kessler, Charles (ed./trans.), *Berlin in Lights: The Diaries of Count Harry Kessler 1918–1937* (New York: Grove Press, 1999)

Klemperer, Victor, *I Shall Bear Witness: The Diaries of Victor Klemperer 1933–1941* (London: Weidenfeld & Nicolson, 1998)

Klemperer, Victor, *To the Bitter End: The Diaries of Victor Klemperer 1942–1945* (London: Weidenfeld & Nicolson, 1998)

Klemperer, Victor, *The Lesser Evil: The Diaries of Victor Klemperer 1945–1959* (London: Weidenfeld & Nicolson, 2003)

Larson, Erik, *In the Garden of Beasts* (New York: Crown Publishers, 2011)

Lifton, Robert Jay, *The Nazi Doctors* (Basic Books, 1986)

Longerich, Peter, *"Davon haben wir nichts gewusst!"*: *Die Deutschen und die Judenverfolgung 1933–1945* ('We knew nothing about it!': *The Germans and the Persecution of the Jews 1933–1945* (trans. Shaun Whiteside), (Pantheon, 2007)

Longerich, Peter, *Holocaust* (trans. Shaun Whiteside), (Oxford: Oxford University Press, 2010)

Lucas, James, *Hitler's Mountain Troops* (London: Cassell, 1992)

Luther, Craig W. H., *The First Day On The Eastern Front: Germany Invades the Soviet Union June 22, 1941* (Guildford, Conn: Stackpole Books, 2019)

Mann, Klaus, *The Turning Point: The Autobiography of Klaus Mann* (London: Otto Wolff, 1984 reprint)

Mayer, Milton, *They Thought They Were Free: The Germans 1933–45* (Chicago: University of Chicago Press, 1955 and 2017 with an afterword by Richard J. Evans)

Merriam, Ray, (ed.), *Gebirgsjäger: Germany's Mountain Troops* (Vermont: Merriam Press, 2015)

Meyer, Hermann Frank, *Blutiges Edelweiß* (Berlin: Ch. Links, 2008)

Mühlberger, Detlef, *Hitler's Voice: The Volkischer Beobachter, 1920–1933* (Peter Lang, 2004)

Naumann, Markus, *Spuren im Wald: Messerschmitt/Werkzeugbau Kottern und das KZ-Außlanger in Fischen* (Traces in the Forest: Messerschmitt/ Werkzeubau Kottern and the KZ Aussenlager in Fischen), (Friedberg: Likias, 2017)

Noack-Mosse, Eva, *Last Days of Theresienstadt* (Madison: University of Wisconsin Press, 2018)

Nübel, Otto, *Die Oberstdorfer Christuskirche im Dritten Reich* (Christ Church in Oberstdorf in the Third Reich), (Oberstdorf: Evangelische Kirchengemeinde, 2017)

The Nuremberg Trial against the Chief War Criminals from 14 November 1945 to 1 October 1946: Documents and other Evidence, Vol. XXVI, first published Nuremberg 1947, (Munich: Delphin, 1989)

Patel, Angelika, *Ein Dorf im Spiegel seiner Zeit: Oberstdorf 1918–1952*, (*A Village in the Mirror of its Time*), (Oberstdorf: Markt Oberstdorf, 2010)

Pitrof, Daniel Ritter von, *Gegen Spartakus in München und im Allgäu* (*Opposing Spartacus in Munich and the Allgäu*), (Bavaria: C. Gerber, 1937)

Prinz, Friedrich, *Die Integration der Flüchtlinge und Vertriebenen in Bayern* (*The Integration of Refugees and Displaced Persons in Bavaria*), (Augsburg: Haus d. Bayer. Gesch., 2000)

Rees, Laurence, *Hitler and Stalin: The Tyrants and the Second World War* (Viking, 2020)

Reuth, Ralf Georg (ed.), *Josef Goebbels: Tagebücher 1924–1945* (Munich, 1992, Vols. 1–5)

Riefenstahl, Leni, *Leni Riefenstahl: A Memoir* (USA: Picador, 1995)

Roth, Joseph, *What I Saw: Reports from Berlin 1920–33* (London: Granta Books, 2003)

Sands, Philippe, *East West Street* (London: Weidenfeld & Nicolson, 2017)

Sands, Philippe, *The Ratline: Love, Lies and Justice on the Trail of a Nazi Fugitive* (London: Weidenfeld & Nicolson, 2021)

Sheffer, Edith, *Asperger's Children* (New York: W.W. Norton, 2018)

Smith, Howard K., *Last Train from Berlin* (London, Cresset Press, 1942)

Solomon, Harvey, *Splendid Prison: Diplomatic Detainment in America During World War II* (Potomac Books, 2020)

Speer, Albert, *Inside the Third Reich: Memoirs* (New York: Macmillan Company, 1970)

Stackelberg, Roderick, and Winkle, Sally (eds.), *The Nazi German Sourcebook: An Anthology of Texts* (Routledge, 2002)

Statiev, Alexander, *At War's Summit: The Red Army and the Struggle for the Caucasus Mountains in World War II* (Cambridge: Cambridge University Press, 2018)

Stephenson, Jill, *Women in Nazi Society* (Routledge, 2001)

Stöckle, Thomas, *Grafeneck 1940: Die Euthanasie-Verbrechen in Südwestdeutschland* (*The Euthanasia Crimes in Southwest Germany*), (Tübingen: Silberburg, 2002)

Taylor, Frederick, *Exorcising Hitler: The Occupation and Denazification of Germany* (London: Bloomsbury, 2011)

Tobias, Fritz, *The Reichstag Fire: Legend and Truth*, trans. Arnold J. Pomerans (London: Secker & Warburg, 1963)

Tusa, Ann, and Tusa, John, *The Nuremberg Trial* (New York: Skyhorse Publishing, 2010)

Uhlman, Fred, *Reunion* (London: Vintage Books, 1971)

Waddy, Helena, *Oberammergau in the Nazi Era: The Fate of a Catholic Village in Hitler's Germany* (New York and Oxford: Oxford University Press, 2010)

Walther, Peter, *Darkness Falling: The Strange Death of the Weimar Republic, 1930–33* (Apollo, 2021)

Weissenberger, Ingrid, *Das Trettach Hotel* (Hamburg: Tredition GmbH, 2018)

Zayas, Alfred-Maurice de, *A Terrible Revenge: The Ethnic Cleansing of the East Germans 1945–1950* (New York: St Martin's Press, 1993)

Zuckmayer, Carl, *Als wär's ein Stück von mir: Horen der Freundschaft* (Fischer Taschenbuch Verlag, 1975)

Zuckmayer, Carl, *A Part of Myself*, trans. Winston, Richard and Clara (New York: Carroll & Graf, 1984)

Index